W9-AXZ-160

Corporate Bodies and Guilty Minds

CORPORATE BODIES AND GUILTY MINDS

The Failure of Corporate Criminal Liability

WILLIAM S. LAUFER

The University of Chicago Press   Chicago and London

WILLIAM S. LAUFER is the director of the Zicklin Center for Business Ethics Research and an associate professor of legal studies and business ethics, sociology, and criminology at the Wharton School, University of Pennsylvania.

The University of Chicago Press, Chicago 60637
The University of Chicago Press, Ltd., London
© 2006 by The University of Chicago
All rights reserved. Published 2006
Printed in the United States of America

15 14 13 12 11 10 09 08 07 06   1 2 3 4 5

ISBN: 0-226-47040-7   (cloth)

Library of Congress Cataloging-in-Publication Data

Laufer, William S.
    Corporate bodies and guilty minds : the failure of corporate criminal liability / William S. Laufer.
        p.   cm.
    Includes bibliographical references and index.
    ISBN 0-226-47040-7 (cloth : alk. paper)
    1. Criminal liability of juristic persons—United States.
    2. Corporation law—United States—Criminal provisions.
    3. Corporations—Corrupt practices—United States. I. Title.

KF9236.5.L38 2006
345.73'0268—dc22   2005030547

⊗ The paper used in this publication meets the minimum requirements of the American National Standard for Information Sciences—Permanence of Paper for Printed Library Materials, ANSI Z39.48-1992.

For Edith and Jack Laufer

Contents

Preface

Given the daily revelations of corporate misdeeds, one might expect *Corporate Bodies and Guilty Minds* to chronicle the inner workings of Adelphia, Arthur Andersen, Bristol-Myers Squibb, Computer Associates, Dynegy, Enron, Global Crossing, HealthSouth, Marsh & McLennan, MicroStrategy, Parmalat, PeopleSoft, PNC Financial Services, Qwest, Rite Aid, Tyco, Waste Management, WorldCom, Xerox and the malfeasance of those who joined the rogues' gallery of white-collar criminals. This book could have chronicled the activities of the fine accounting firms that audited these leading companies, including Arthur Andersen, Deloitte & Touche, Ernst & Young, KPMG, and PricewaterhouseCoopers. There now exists, however, a considerable library of exposés of the victims, gatekeepers, and victimizers involved in the recent wave of corporate scandals.

Instead, *Corporate Bodies and Guilty Minds* raises questions about the failure of corporate criminal law. This book is as much about Enron as it is about Lockheed, as much about Lockheed as it is about Standard Oil, and as much about Standard Oil as it is about New York Central and Hudson River Railroad. Corporate deviance is a historical fixture, and waves of scandals are as familiar as are periods of reform. Unfortunately, there is scant evidence that reforms necessarily bring about lasting change in corporate behavior in spite of convincing rhetoric to the contrary. This book offers some reasons why that is so, while arguing strongly for greater reliance on principles of criminal liability that recognize the complexity of organizational behavior, the difficulty of obtaining evidence of corporate wrongdoing, the privileges and responsibilities that come with ascribing personhood to corporations, and the law's ambivalence over ascribing blame to corporate entities. Arguments are made mindful of the dearth of systematic empirical research on corporate crime and punishment, research that is critically needed to fashion coherent policy, draft effective legislation, and leave lasting reform.

Corporate Bodies and Guilty Minds offers a critical account of corporations seeking to bolster perceptions of responsibility, law abidance, and citizenship by institutionalizing a brand of compliance-driven ethics. Those executives and employees who dare violate codes, regulations, or laws do so at their own peril. Corporate miscreants are nothing more than wayward agents who, in spite of compliance initiatives, walk up to and over the line—or so the script goes. In distancing the entity as a decision-making body from its agents, corporations through the actions of top management try to support the self-serving perception that the criminal law is a less-than-optimal form of social control or, better yet, that it serves a very limited regulatory purpose.

Extant law and supportive doctrine are often nothing more than an opportunity for clever corporate counsel to exploit as part of a larger, corporate-wide management of reputation. In recent years, corporate criminal law has become a blueprint of preventive law for organizational entities. Avoiding the strictures of corporate criminal law is too often a matter of gaming both prosecutors and regulators with a mix of cooperation, disclosures, and audits. Skills and strategies for this game are available for sale at a host of high-priced "ethics" conferences, from a new breed of reputation and integrity management firms, from tried-and-true consulting firms, and from a legion of prosecutors-turned-defense-counsel who, better than most, know when to bluff, raise the ante, or fold. Gaming is implicitly encouraged by prosecutors who, in their vast discretion, make offers and deals aimed at producing inculpatory evidence that is otherwise shrouded by the corporate form. Where compliance failures undermine their standing, corporate public relations offers a cure with glossy and elegant annual reports detailing social and environmental accomplishments. Corporations that want to be seen as ethical "stewards," but have much to hide, wash their reputations—"greenwash" environmental violations or "bluewash" by suggesting ethical leadership and affiliating with the United Nations or other strategic nongovernmental organizations or standards groups.

We should see beyond the often cosmetic veil of organizational compliance, corporate gamesmanship, and washed reputations by construing corporate fault in a way that allows for reasonable attributions of liability and culpability. Here I propose a constructive corporate liability, a liability rule that frees those who regulate and prosecute corporations of proving fault vicariously. Instead of a strict attribution of fault, the nexus between an individual agent's and a firm's fault is at issue. Reasonable attributions of blame replace vicarious liability. Constructive fault therefore invites prosecutions that, due to concerns over the harshness of vicarious fault or reasons of corporate gaming, are now unlikely or failed. Perhaps the logic and appeal of a constructive corporate fault will engender a constituency advocating the use of substantive corporate criminal law that will, ultimately, affect the law enforcement priority accorded corporate prosecutions.

Promoting such a constituency assumes that we should give greater priority to the enforcement of criminal laws against corporations when and where deserved. It assumes a value in proceeding against the corporation as an entity, in addition to any individual officers, directors, or agents who might be deserving of blame—no matter how senior or subordinate. It assumes that the criminal law can play an important role in making standards of corporate governance and governance reforms more than incidental, nonbinding conduct codes. It assumes that failures of corporate governance—failures of boards and their committees, for example, to monitor compliance and code enforcement on behalf of the shareholders—are seen also as failures of compliance. It assumes that the name of the game from the enforcement side is access to inculpatory evidence through cooperating witnesses and increased protections afforded to whistle-blowers. It also assumes the importance of a credible and predictable criminal law that considers the criminal offense over the corporation's postoffense behavior. And, finally, in considering the importance of a constituency supporting a substantive corporate criminal law, the historically powerful role of politics in fashioning corporate reforms must never be forgotten. Too little attention is given to the instrumental role of corporate lobbyists, corporate donations, and willing legislators.

These are far from extraordinary themes. Yet, remarkably, there is no constituency with a voice that genuinely and consistently favors resort to the corporate criminal law. Businesses seek to avoid it, fearful of reputational effects and the potential for liability in some industries to limit lines of business, as in the health-care field. Regulators and prosecutors generally shy away from prosecuting corporations for reasons having as much to do with resources as the perception that the real offenders—officers, managers, and subordinate employees—must be prosecuted for justice to be served. It would be a mockery of justice, most would say, to take principles of vicarious liability so seriously that Fortune 500 corporations are ultimately executed due to the acts of disloyal, miscreant agents. A significant value of the corporate criminal law, prosecutors admit, is its ability to close a deal. Threat of criminal indictment results in favorable civil settlements and workable plea agreements.

Legislatures lack the political will in the face of heavy corporate lobbying to meaningfully reform the substantive corporate criminal law. The failure of the Brown Commission is an obvious illustration. Less obvious, though equally on point, is the commanding and largely undeserved role enjoyed by the United States Sentencing Commission. So much law reform has come from this commission in recent years that it makes federal criminal law reform, including the tinkering of Sarbanes-Oxley, look feeble and the federal corporate criminal law appear wholly inadequate. Even worse but certainly not surprising, the effect of the commission's guidelines successfully moved the locus of discretion, and resulting concerns with disparity, from the chambers of federal judges to the many offices of the United States attorneys, where prosecutorial guidelines give no more than the pretense of uniformity. It is unclear where discretion will ultimately rest after the Supreme Court's decision to recast the mandatory nature of the guidelines.

In the absence of a constituency that advocates reliance on corporate criminal law, prosecutions are rare events in the criminal justice system. There are many reasons to shy away from proceeding directly against guilty corporations, and, unfortunately, they are all too often relied on. Without apology, I do not seek optimal enforcement or penalties or, for that matter, standards of culpability that maximize the deterrence function of the criminal law. I take the necessity and survival of the corporate criminal law for granted, simply as a matter of justice.

Of course, not all agree. Economists challenge the premise of anything more or less than an optimal enforcement and punishment regime. To their chagrin, the criminal law can and often does lack efficiency. Philosophers and legal scholars continue their diatribe on corporate personhood, the value of *integrity-based* corporate compliance, and different strategies or styles of self-regulation. Employees and shareholders are only further victimized by corporate crimes. And, finally, as prodemocracy advocates fight against thinly veiled neoliberal ideologies and the perceived evils of global corporate domination, they reject the notion of a corporate person, the requisite for corporate criminal liability.

The fire behind my account is the same that moved Justice Jackson in the seminal case of *New York Central & Hudson River Railroad v. United States*—with the benefit of an additional century of reflection on the artful and cunning nature of corporate stratagems. This decision by the United States Supreme Court, more than any before it, laid out a clear case that public policy requires extending the criminal law to corporations. At the turn of the twentieth century, corporate criminal liability foreshadowed the rise of the regulatory state as an indispensable weapon in the seemingly weak arsenal of social controls over the dramatic expansion and concentration of corporate power, an expansion and concentration marked by an increasing separation of ownership from control. Of course, those were different times. But with the rise of the regulatory state and the move away from command and control regulatory styles, the corporate criminal law was neglected if not all but forgotten. We are left with century-old liability rules that are resurrected for reasons of prosecutorial convenience or symbolic need. The only substantive reform came in piecemeal fashion or through the back door of sentencing and prosecutorial guidelines.

The rapid globalization of the corporate form and the dramatic rise of corporate power renew the call for principles of corporate criminal law that give strength, legitimacy, and integrity to regulatory and administrative law. Without a strong criminal law overseeing the regulation of corporate entities, there is far too little at stake in the game. Without a strong criminal law, regulation is perceived to be entirely voluntary, it is gamed, and regulators lose credibility. And, perhaps most important, without principles of liability that accommodate the law's ambivalence with ascribing blame to corporations, all will seek to avoid corporate liability in favor of other less-formal social controls.

It may be said with some confidence that little has changed over the past hundred years in the evolution of the corporate criminal law. Sadly, the legal questions raised by recent corporate scandals are remarkably similar to those in the early 1900s. These cases are all too familiar, and there is scant empirical evidence that corporate deviance has been affected—or is now affected—by recent reform efforts. What is needed is a sea change in how the criminal law is applied to corporations. Such a change requires the abandonment of vicarious liability in favor of a model of corporate liability that leverages objective judgments of fault that mix personal ascriptions of blame with the very characteristics, attributes, and actions of the entity that gives rise to liability. Reform to the substantive criminal law must follow so that it comports with the changes brought about by the Sentencing Guidelines for Organizations. Such reform entails a reconceptualization of corporate governance in relation to corporate compliance. It also requires according priority to corporate crime cases in federal law enforcement. Without these and other changes, without a constituency advocating the use of corporate criminal liability, a pessimist's and skeptic's account of corporate crime and corporate liability prevails.

The first three chapters set the stage for a critical look at the law's ambivalence with the corporate criminal law. Chapter 1 surveys the modest evolution of the corporate criminal law. Its history reflects many significant milestones, many notable cases, and many notorious companies. It also reveals scant progress toward a coherent body of legal principles. The reason offered for this modest progress is a central theme throughout this book—an ambivalence with applying the criminal law to corporations. Chapter 2 suggests one important reason why progress has been slow. Over the past century, the corporate criminal law has failed to resolve the seemingly intractable problem of personhood and, at the same time, to articulate a theory of liability that considers the organizational form—aspects of the corporate person—in relation to blame. Prosecutorial and sentencing guidelines count the actions and inactions of entities that the substantive law disregards. Chapter 3 proposes a constructive corporate liability doctrine as a preferred solution for at least some aspects of this intractable problem. Unlike principles of vicarious liability, constructive liability casts blame in relation to aspects and attributes of the organization. Reasonable attributions of fault facilitate the finding of organizational liability. Constructive corporate liability allows the substantive law to meaningfully join sentencing law, taking the law's ambivalence into consideration and accommodating the stratagems of firms.

The balance of *Corporate Bodies and Guilty Minds* details the risks of maintaining the law's status quo. Chapter 4 describes strategies employed by some corporations to avoid the strictures of criminal liability. Such strategies include gaming regulators who, in spite of much rhetoric to the contrary, are constrained by principles of vicarious liability and lack the necessary tools to evaluate the effectiveness of a company's compliance efforts, no less its governance practices. The rise of internal and external audits as evidence of compliance is noted and discussed. Chapter 5 considers the critical importance of corporate cooperation in defeating the attribution or imputation of blame to the entity; the desirability of trading prosecutorial favors for corporate cooperation is explored. Chapter 6 reviews the disconnect between corporate representations of integrity and ethicality. For some companies, business ethics is reputation management, where the ethical leaders, those leading the ethical charge, are often the worst corporate offenders. The problem of greenwashing is discussed in relation to the case of *Nike v. Kasky*, the first legal challenge of reputation washing as consumer fraud. Finally, Chapter 7 briefly details why the skeptic's and pessimist's account of recent reforms is, unfortunately, most plausible.

Books that wrestle with corporate crime face a number of predictable challenges. The problem of corporate deviance resists simple description, simplistic generalizations, and simpleminded theory. Crimes in the healthcare, financial services, and manufacturing sectors, for example, share important similarities and critical differences. The range of misbehaviors associated with corporate crime also varies widely, as does the status or statuses of offenders. And finally, the law does little to overcome or undo unrealistic and unfair stereotypes of corporations as large, decentralized, publicly traded entities. Knowing that these and other difficult challenges remain makes the study of corporate crime both fascinating and humbling.

My thanks to Gil Geis, Vic Khanna, Hans van Oosterhout, Ron Sarachan, Steve Solow, Djordjija Petkoski, Prakash Sethi, Andrew Hohns, Crystalyn Calderon, Ryan Burg, Marc Frenkel, Natalie Cotton, and a host of anonymous reviewers for their valuable comments. Portions of this book were written during my sabbatical as a visiting scholar at NYU School of Law. My appreciation to Jim Jacobs, Harry First, and other members at the criminal-law faculty of NYU for their critical take on the book's arguments. As always, Lauretta Tomasco, Selma Pastore, and the staff of the Carol and Lawrence Zicklin Center for Business Ethics Research provided strong support.

Research for *Corporate Bodies and Guilty Minds* developed through the preparation of a series of law review and journal articles on the corporate criminal law. In various places throughout this book, I draw generously from this work. My appreciation to the editors and reviewers of Social Accounting and the Corporate Greenwashing, 43 J. Bus. Ethics 253–61 (2003); Corporate Prosecution, Cooperation, and the Trading of Favors, 87 Iowa L. Rev. 123–50 (2002); Corporate Liability, Risk Shifting, and the Paradox of Compliance, 54 Vand. L. Rev. 1343 (1999); Due Diligence, Corporate Integrity, and the Limits of the Good Citizen Corporation, 34 Amer. Bus. L.J. 157–81 (1996); Corporate Bodies and Guilty Minds, 79 Emory L.J. 649–732 (1994).

Gerhard O. W. Mueller inspired my interest in the corporate criminal law during law school and while I attended graduate school. For this inspiration, and for his continued wise counsel, I am most grateful.

PART ONE

The Law's Ambivalence

CHAPTER ONE

The Evolution of Corporate Criminal Law

During the past year the American economy has faced several sudden challenges, and proven its great resiliency. Terrorists attacked the center and symbol of our prosperity. A recession cost many American workers their jobs. And now corporate corruption has struck at investor confidence, offending the conscience of our nation. Yet, in the aftermath of September the 11th, we refuse to allow fear to undermine our economy. And we will not allow fraud to undermine it either.

With well-timed tax cuts we fought our way out of recession and back to economic growth. And now with a tough new law we will act against those who have shaken confidence in our markets, using the full authority of government to expose corruption, punish wrongdoers and defend the rights and interests of American workers and investors.

My administration pressed for greater corporate integrity. A united Congress has written it into law. And today I sign the most far-reaching reforms of American business practices since the time of Franklin Delano Roosevelt. This new law sends very clear messages that all concerned must heed. This law says to every dishonest corporate leader: you will be exposed and punished; the era of low standards and false profits is over; no boardroom in America is above or beyond the law.

This law says to honest corporate leaders: your integrity will be recognized and rewarded, because the shadow of suspicion will be lifted from good companies that respect the rules.

This law says to corporate accountants: the high standards of your profession will be enforced without exception; the auditors will be audited; the accountants will be held to account.

This law says to shareholders that the financial information you receive from a company will be true and reliable, for those who deliberately sign their names to deception will be punished.

This law says to workers: we will not tolerate reckless practices that artificially drive up stock prices and eventually destroy the companies, and the pensions, and your jobs.

And this law says to every American: there will not be a different ethical standard for corporate America than the standard that applies to everyone else. The honesty you expect in your small business or in your workplaces, in your community or in your home, will be expected and enforced in every corporate suite in this country.

I commend the Congress for passing a strong set of reforms.[1]

*

With these comments, President George W. Bush signed Sarbanes-Oxley 2002 into law on July 30, 2002. This "groundbreaking" legislation and a host of regulatory reforms came on the heels of countless revelations of corporate fraud, multiple waves of accounting scandals, innumerable restatements of corporate earnings, evidence of "naked greed," and a very shaken market.[2] The result was predictable: Regulators and legislators carefully examined the gatekeeping and oversight role of all corporate stakeholders, including auditors, boards of directors, investment banks, credit rating agencies, and lawyers. Questions were raised about the effectiveness of existing laws, regulations, and regulatory bodies.[3] Reform bills were introduced in Congress. The New York Stock Exchange and Nasdaq announced governance reforms. So, too, did the Securities and Exchange Commission. Criminal investigations and prosecutions of corporate miscreants followed. The costs and burdens of regulating compliance for firms dramatically increased. And the conventional wisdom quickly emerged that what matters most is that investors are protected and our confidence in the integrity of corporations restored.[4]

These legislative and regulatory responses are more comforting and reassuring than meaningful. Reforms are proposed and unveiled by government functionaries with an uncomfortable share of righteousness and moral outrage. Prosecutions are orchestrated media events designed to convey a strong symbolic meaning about investor confidence, the strength of regulatory oversight, and the potency of corporate sanctions. The federal government declared war on corporate fraud. All of this encourages the unsuspecting to believe that solutions to corporate deviance for some of the most powerful multinational corporations may be found in narrowly drawn governance and accounting standards, that combating elite deviance through criminal prosecutions will remain a high priority of federal and state law enforcement, that politics has little to do with law enforcement or regulatory priorities, and that this is the first generation to watch our most powerful firms and financial icons fall precipitously from grace.[5]

We too willingly buy expensive, glossy images of good corporate citizenship; allegations that corporate crime is a simple function of the perverse incentives of stock options and the excesses of executive compensation; the deterrence afforded by symbolic prosecutions of once powerful and now "unknowing" corporate executives; renewed calls for director independence and reinvigorated audit committees; well-dressed rhetoric of good corporate governance; stories and anecdotes by corporate leaders of gut-wrenching trade-offs between tempting business opportunities and actions that require "doing the right thing." Naiveté, along with a shared desire to restore confidence and legitimacy in our markets, encourage all to blame Wall Street's many watchdogs while ignoring the persistence of corporate crime and a history of the corporate criminal law that inspires little change.

WEAK BODY OF LAW

The central thesis of this book is that we have failed to make sense of the corporate criminal law. Conceptions of corporate criminal liability and corporate blame are muddled. Existing liability rules, nearly a century old, are routinely disregarded by prosecutors and regulators. They are replaced by a brand of cooperative regulation that allows firms to opt out of the criminal justice system, strategically recast blame, and cleverly manage their reputation. In short, the corporate criminal law is decidedly weak and, as Kenneth Mann once noted, "deeply impoverished."[6] The concern with a poorly conceived corporate criminal law is not only that too few actors fear its effects. A more important concern is that the law's weakness undermines the potential for regulatory suasion and credibility, particularly with a decentralized and porous regulatory system.[7]

Where cooperative models of regulation and corporate criminal liability coexist, the criminal law is more than the prosecutor's last resort.[8] The threat of the criminal law is the ultimate lever that empowers less formal social controls, such as self-regulation, voluntary disclosure, and corporate cooperation.[9] "Without a strong state capable of credible deterrence and incapacitation," as John Braithwaite notes, "you cannot channel regulatory activity down to the base of the pyramid, where trust is nurtured."[10] There must be a formidable and credible weapon sitting in the background available for use when regulatory authority meets frustration or capture.[11]

The threat of the criminal law is the single most potent incentive for ensuring corporate cooperation, information disclosure, and evidence sharing —a necessary incentive given the extraordinary challenge of building cases against large, complex, and well-counseled multinational corporations.[12] In this chapter, some critically important developments distinguishing the seven historical phases of the law's evolution are discussed. Notwithstanding many notable legal and regulatory milestones, this history is remarkable in only one sense: so little has changed in well over a century of spectacular growth in commerce and business enterprises.

SO LITTLE CHANGES

In an address to the membership of the States Attorneys' Association of Illinois in 1899, Judge Cicero J. Lindley asked the audience to consider the potential for crimes by corporations as commercial life in the United States continued to mature. "From the very nature of the organization of a corporation it is apparent that nearly every crime known to the law can be committed by it," cautioned Lindley. Concentrated private wealth, large corporate conglomerates, and the prospect of intense commercial activity in interstate commerce pose a distinct challenge to law and law enforcement. "It sometimes occurs," he remarked, "that acts of corporations are so closely allied with illegal and criminal acts of individuals, acting in conjunction with corporations, that it becomes necessary on the ground of public necessity, and to preserve the general peace and welfare of the people, that an officer charged with the execution of the law has to reach both the corporation and the guilty individual."[13]

The development of the United States, argued Lindley, may be credited to combinations of individual wealth collected in large corporations. For this, the country owes a great debt to businesses. At the same time, as the nation continues to develop and wealth accumulates in a small number of successful entrepreneurs, there is an increased risk that the number and seriousness of corporate crimes will increase. The criminal law must stand ready. Lindley's admonition came at a distinct turning point in the history of corporations and the criminal law. By the end of the nineteenth century, William Vanderbilt, Andrew Carnegie, Henry Clay Frick, John D. Rockefeller Sr., J. Pierpont Morgan, and other captains of industry had formed industrial pools, associations, and combinations that seemed to defy the criminal law.[14] At the same time, courts were increasingly hearing cases of corporate nuisance, corporate misfeasance, and corporate malfeasance. Even with limited experience with for-profit corporations, judges no longer felt bound by a common law heritage that did not contemplate a corporate criminal law.[15] As business enterprises proliferated, the complex nature of both the corporate form and the metaphysics of corporate personhood were insufficient obstacles. Logic and the absence of biology gave way to the necessity of corporate criminal liability.[16]

In the early 1900s, however, the divergence between the literal requirements of corporate criminal liability and regulatory policy grew.[17] There are many reasons for this divergence, including the intermittent weakness of corporate criminal liability in practice and the glaring absence of substantive criminal law reform. The best reasons, I conclude, reflect a shared ambivalence with attributing criminal blame to corporations marked by a separation of ownership and control and, concomitantly, the strategic abilities of businesses to avoid the strictures of law while managing both regulators and their reputation.

AMBIVALENCE WITH LIABILITY

The history of substantive corporate criminal law reveals a profound ambivalence with the idea of a *criminal* corporation that is both elementary and seemingly intractable: (1) corporations are aggregates of innocent stakeholders who unfairly suffer from a criminal investigation, indictment, and conviction, but serious consequences must result from corporate deviance; (2) markets encourage corporate risk taking and innovation, but corporations—particularly in certain sectors and industries—require vigilant regulation and faithful compliance; (3) civil and administrative law remedies for organizational deviance already exact a huge toll on corporations, but few doubt the unique role of the criminal law to encourage law abidance or voluntary disclosure of wrongdoing; and (4) the government must support and maintain close ties to the business community, but such ties may inhibit regulation or make resort to the criminal law problematic.[18] Other sources of ambivalence, those discussed below and in subsequent chapters, are no less complex and subtle.

All point to themes, however, as simplistic, trite, and obvious as they are true. The history of corporate criminal liability and the development of a corporate criminal liability reflect the perennial tension between the regulatory power of government and corporate power. It is all about the social control of business and the turn-of-the-twentieth-century notion of individualism.[19] It is all about government regulation versus deference to the business community and its markets. It is all about balancing the power to regulate corporations and the specter of regulatory overreaching. And, finally, it is all about controlling business deviance through a combination of regulation and resort to criminal law.

Throughout American history, maintaining the legitimacy of the government's response to corporate deviance has mediated all of these tensions. Throughout American history, corporations and the corporate bar have sought relief from regulation and the strictures of the criminal law with dogged perseverance and costly stratagems—all designed to maintain a pristine corporate reputation while deflecting regulation and law enforcement. History reflects a poorly choreographed dance between the assertion of governmental power and the interests of the business community, between political administrations that promote corporate accountability and those that do not or see blame for corporate harm as decidedly personal.

HISTORY AS A GUIDE

Sadly, if history is any guide, not much changes after the dust of the scandals settles.[20] Regulators shy away once again from escalating the regulatory process. Prosecutors, who investigated and indicted high-profile white-collar criminals with a combination of vigilance and sense of righteousness, find that economic crimes have lost political currency and are no longer office or departmental priority.[21] Before and after the scandals, corporate prosecutions—particularly of large, publicly traded entities—remain an exception, rare in some jurisdictions and extraordinary in others. Actions against small, privately held companies predominate.[22] And most of the regulatory activity with companies of any scale turns on audit and disclosure policies that snag some corporations that commit crimes, prompt seemingly law-abiding companies to voluntarily disclose crimes, and—one must assume—deter others from crime commission. But the numbers of cases are still dreadfully small given even conservative estimates of the incidence of corporate crime.[23] Successful regulation likely results in plea agreements that entail carefully drafted cooperation, integrity, or deferred prosecution agreements requiring nothing less than a compliance reincarnation.

As the history of corporate criminal liability reveals, it may be best to discount the spectacle of Andersen, Enron, Rite Aid, Global Crossing, Tyco, Merrill Lynch, WorldCom, Adelphia, and other "governance failures" targeted by recent corporate crime reform. Corporate crime legislation most often arises during weak economies, as do pressures for regulatory changes, and aggressive, high-profile prosecutions that naturally follow are notable but illusory milestones of corporate reform.

After all, who remembers the dramatic and sordid details of the E. F. Hutton, the Equity Funding Corp. of America, Lockheed, A. H. Robbins, and Prudential-Bache Securities scandals?[24] In twenty years, it is likely that the same question will be asked of Enron, WorldCom, and Andersen, no less PNC Financial Services Group, Inc. (paid $90 million in restitution and $25 million in penalties as part of a deferred prosecution agreement on criminal charges of conspiracy to violate securities laws), or Qwest Communications International (incorrectly accounted for $1.6 billion in sales, among other accounting restatements).[25] And many of the best-known and most admired companies that may have crossed the line will likely emerge unscathed by the adverse publicity garnered by the first, second, and third waves of scandals. This group includes AIG, AOL Time Warner, Bristol-Myers Squibb, CMS Energy, Duke Energy, El Paso, Halliburton, Homestore, Kmart, Merck, Mirant, Nicor Energy LLC, Perigrine Systems, Reliant Energy, and Xerox.[26] We are more likely to remember the grimacing faces of Bernard Ebbers (WorldCom), Richard M. Scrushy (HealthSouth), Kenneth Lay (Enron), and L. Dennis Kozlowski (Tyco) as they marched to and from the federal courthouse.

PHASES OF CORPORATE CRIMINAL LIABILITY

The historical phases of the substantive corporate criminal law discussed below share the tension accompanying the social control of business enterprises, whether this tension appears as concerns with the metaphysics of personhood (phase one), the rise and obscure fall of vicarious liability (phase two), the routine risk-shifting between agents and principals (phase three), the successful and failed attempts at model state and federal codes (phase four), the reactions to a "new" regulatory state (phase five), the gaming of regulators by the "good citizen" corporation (phase six), or the reactive prosecution and regulation following a period of scandals marked by widespread accounting fraud and governance and compliance failures (phase seven). These seven phases overlap significantly and are far from discrete. They do, however, provide one account of some of the more important trends and milestones of the corporate criminal law.

Notably, all phases reflect the powerful influence of the public and segments of the business community in lobbying for or inhibiting legislative reform. These influences remain once legislation is passed, and they often dictate the extent to which laws are largely ignored or rigorously enforced. While not the subject of this book, different brands of "crony capitalism" mark the relations of corporate boards of directors, management, auditors, investment bankers, lawyers, and credit-rating agencies. The result is a distinguished history of special interests facilitating and inhibiting legislative and regulatory reform.

Phase One: Concerns with Personhood

Commentators were obsessed over the importance and meaning of corporate personhood from the mid-1800s to the turn of the twentieth century. The economy was at first almost entirely agrarian and mercantile, and private corporations in the colonies were at best a novelty and at worst the object of distrust and suspicion.[27] Settlers were still steeped in the tradition of mercantilism and worked on behalf of the interests of the British Crown. Colonial legislatures rarely chartered corporations.[28] When they did, there was a narrow grant of power with few privileges. Most businesses with corporate charters had a quasi-public character and pursued public purposes.[29] Industrial production came from small individual enterprises, single proprietorships, and partnerships.[30] Without a significant history of purely private corporations in England, few were sure how to treat deviance in business enterprises that grew rapidly with the rise of a vast agricultural economy. "We do not find many precedents for the regulation of corporations in the laws of the colonies or in the early legislation of the States," notes former Solicitor General Frederick W. Lehmann, "for there were not many corporations here to deal with, nor were they much in favor

1. Concerns with Corporate Personhood

Without a soul, corporations cannot have a "wicked" intent. Only human beings can be charged with perjury, treason, and violent crimes. Most crimes go beyond the purposes and powers of a corporation. Corporations, however, may be charged with nonfeasance and some affirmative acts. *State v. Morris & Essex Railroad* (1852); *Commonwealth v. Proprietors of New Bedford Bridge* (1854)

The emergence of large scale multidivisional organizations, the move from horizontal to vertical integration, the separation of corporate ownership and control, and the rising prominence of railroad conglomerates in interstate commerce led Congress and then federal courts to implement the power of the criminal law as a regulatory weapon.

Santa Clara County v. Southern Pacific Railroad (1886)

Interstate Commerce Act (1887)

Sherman Antitrust Act (1890)

2. The Rise and Fall of Vicarious Liability

The nonfeasance-misfeasance distinction is abandoned for reasons of practicality. Immunizing corporations from the criminal law would deprive the law of a powerful form of social control

Corporate criminal liability extended to crimes of intent

New York Central & Hudson River Railroad v. U.S. (1909)

3. Risk-Shifting Between Agents and Principals

Continued calls for voluntary or mandatory federal incorporation

Assertion of corporate constitutional rights

Emergence of due diligence defenses

Securities Act of 1933 and Securities Exchange Act of 1934

Market crash and a host of financial reforms

4. Model Codes

Rise of regulatory state, e.g., federal environmental regulation

National Commission on Reform of Federal Criminal Laws

Model Penal Code provisions on corporate criminal liability

Standard Oil Company of Texas v. U.S. (1962)

Heavy Electrical Equipment Antitrust Cases (1961)

5. New Regulatory State

"Golden Age" of white collar crime prosecution

Increased power given to OSHA, EPA, and other federal agencies with the passage of a host of regulatory statutes

Sentencing Guidelines for Organizations (1991)

Foreign Corrupt Practices Act (1977)

Defense Industry Initiative (1986)

A.H. Robbins (1985)

6. Birth of Good Corporate Citizenship

Post-Guidelines enforcement and prosecution determined by compliance with Guidelines and regulatory statements

Liability is inspired and constrained by the role of organizational cooperation

Holder Memo (1999)

In re Caremark Int'l Inc. (1996)

7. Failed Governance and Selective Prosecutions

NY State Attorney General Prosecutions

Federal Corporate Fraud Task Force Prosecutions

SEC Cases

Enron Andersen WorldCom Tyco Int'l

Sarbanes-Oxley (2002)

1850 1860 1870 1880 1890 1900 1910 1920 1930 1940 1950 1960 1970 1980 1990 2000 2005

Figure 1.1 The Development of the Corporate Criminal Law—United States, 1850–present

in England at that time or believed to be well-adapted to the conduct of business generally."[31]

The individualistic bias of common law crimes also made the attribution of liability to a *persona ficta* seem both strange and wrong. To some, the conception of personhood was bounded by a methodological individualism that limits the understanding of social and group phenomena—corporate action—to the acts of individuals or agents. The features of biological and corporate persons differ in critically important ways. Without a soul and a will, judges concluded that the idea of attributing a guilty state of mind or a corporate mens rea was too much of a fiction.[32] Corporations are a "mere abstraction of law."[33] Without a body, the act requirement of the criminal law also could not be realized. And without the power to commit crimes, any attribution of illegality was well outside the scope of their authority, or ultra vires.[34] The capacity of a corporation is simply no greater than the power conferred by its corporate seal or constitution.

How then may a corporation be indicted? Corporations, being incorporeal, cannot appear at the bar for trial. The state does not charter corporations to commit crimes. To punish both the corporation and the members of the body corporate seemed nothing less than double punishment. It was simply inconceivable that corporations could act in ways that contravene the justification for their creation.[35]

The law throughout the early 1800s was just as Chief Justice Marshall noted in *Dartmouth College v. Woodward* (1819). A corporation, according to Marshall, existed only by virtue of the concession granted by the sovereign. A corporation is "an artificial being, invisible, intangible, and existing only in contemplation of law."[36] As the Supreme Judicial Court of Maine ruled in 1841, "A corporation is created by law for certain beneficial purposes. It can neither commit a crime nor a misdemeanor by any positive or affirmative act, nor incite others to do so, as a corporation."[37]

The earliest cases of corporate criminal liability in the United States were against towns, municipalities, and businesses that worked on the construction of bridges, turnpikes, and canals. Most of the indictments were for the crime of nuisance and were limited to acts of nonfeasance. In the mid- to late 1800s, however, as many crimes by corporations reached state courts, judges noted exceptions to the general rule against entity liability from acts of nonfeasance to those of misfeasance.[38] The list of crimes initially increased to where only cases of malicious wrongs, wrongs involving specific intent, or wrongs of personal violence were excluded.[39] But, as the Court recognized the personhood of corporations with the 1886 case of *Santa Clara County v. Southern Pacific Railroad Co.*, the list was soon all-inclusive.[40]

Santa Clara County personified corporations at a time when states realized that permissive chartering laws could generate vast amounts of needed revenue. In transforming the conception of a corporation from a lifeless, artificial being to a legal person, by allowing businesses to incorporate freely, and with the divergence of municipal and business corporations, the criminal law became the state's response to all sorts of corporate wrongs, from the indictment of railroad companies for the killing of pedestrians by improperly designed and recklessly operated trolley cars to elaborate prosecutions of conglomerate companies for illegal combinations.[41]

Countless examples of early corporate prosecutions for substantive law violations are rarely noted. In late March 1885, for example, Mary Ann Medinger was struck and killed by a trolley car owned and operated by the Brooklyn Heights Railroad Co. She was one of many victims of speeding top-heavy trolleys with dangerous front fenders that in collisions with pedestrians killed them on impact. The mayor of Brooklyn, Charles Schieren, was outraged. "It is absolutely necessary," he argued, "to put an end to the recklessness with which the cars are run."[42] Two months later, a Kings County grand jury returned an indictment for second-degree manslaughter against the railroad company for the death of Medinger.[43] The grand jury concluded that the Brooklyn Heights Railroad Co. "did feloniously, and culpably, carelessly and negligently kill."[44]

The Brooklyn Heights Railroad case was followed by indictments for manslaughter filed against the New York Central Railroad in December 1901. A fire erupted in a railroad roundhouse in Herkimer, New York, that contained several hundred pounds of dynamite in violation of state law and village ordinances. The fire led to an explosion that killed six workers.[45] Indictments were later obtained against the New York, Susquehanna, and Western Railroad for deaths and injuries resulting from failures to protect grade crossings,[46] against the Brooklyn Heights Railroad for labor law violations,[47] and against the Adams Express Co. for violations of the internal revenue laws.[48] Three indictments for manslaughter against New York Central Railroad came from the tragic 1907 train wreck of the Brewster express due to "overspeeding" in Woodlawn, New York, which killed twenty-four passengers. The motorman and engineers were experienced with steam locomotives but had no experience and limited training with electric locomotives like the Brewster.[49]

These early cases reflected an increasing consensus that corporations have a responsibility that only the criminal law can discharge—especially in the absence of effective state and federal regulation. Criminal cases brought against corporations for injuries due to negligence or recklessness, however, were soon far overshadowed by allegations of antitrust violations. The focus was on unconstrained corporate power and authority without accountability.[50]

After an initial two-year period of prosecutorial inaction, the Department of Justice brought actions under the Sherman Antitrust Act of 1890. The first test case was with indictments of the directors of the Whiskey Trust.[51] Subsequently, prosecutors targeted corporate officials and offending corporations with criminal cases against the sugar trust, steel trust, meat trust, tobacco trust, and a host of other illegal combinations.[52] Efforts to dissolve trusts and bar companies from transacting business across jurisdictions were then initiated from New York to Tennessee and Texas.[53] Many of the trials were front-page news, with detailed coverage of dramatic courtroom testimony.[54] Rising concerns over new forms of market power, market integration, and the rapid transformation of partnerships to business corporations captured the public's attention and raised fears of unbridled corporate concentration, corruption, and fraud.[55]

This period culminated in the Progressive movement, a movement that marked a distinct shift from laissez-faire to government activism. The Progressive agenda called for an end to corruption and distinct limits on the power of trusts. The champion of this movement, Theodore Roosevelt, feared that the consolidation of corporate power and wealth in the hands of a few threatened the United States. Roosevelt sought to protect the nation from its own excesses by enforcing the criminal law against business organizations. "[T]he existing concentration of vast wealth under a corporate system, unguarded and uncontrolled by the nation, has placed in the hands of a few men enormous, secret, irresponsible power over the daily life of the citizen; a power insufferable in a free government and certain of abuse," argued Roosevelt. "This power has been abused, in monopoly of National resources, in stock watering, in unfair competition and unfair privileges, and, finally, in sinister influences on public agencies of State and Nation."[56]

Fears of corporate abuses were only exacerbated by a financial crisis in 1907, with associated bank failures, corporate bankruptcies, and a demoralized stock market.[57] Reports of corporate misgovernance, not to mention political corruption, were widespread and bear an eerie resemblance to the present day. In an all-too-familiar ritual, high-profile criminal cases were brought against brokers and their firms (e.g., Hulburd, Warren & Co.) for illegal practices, such as bucket shopping[58] and making fictitious sales.[59] Cases of other white-collar crimes were commonplace, including elaborate insurance fraud schemes, all of which raised questions about the locus of fault in cases of corporate misgovernance and the potential liability of directors.[60] The value of such liability, according to an editorial in the *New York Times,* "is that it will impress upon Directors of corporations the obligation of abiding by the requirements of the law as other citizens are compelled to do."[61]

The use and abuse of corporate power were primary concerns of legislatures as well.[62] Regulating the unconstrained and uncontrolled railroads topped the list.[63] Widespread discrimination against people and localities, bribing of legislators, stock manipulation, and formation of pools were engaged in with near impunity. General James A. Garfield reflected on the formation of the republic by concluding that "the effects of the states to regulate their railroads have amounted to little more than feeble annoyance. In many cases the corporations have treated such efforts as impertinent intermeddling."[64] The railroads left many with the impression that corporations were more powerful than the very states that regulated them.[65]

"The best of state laws," wrote one commentator, "will never do away with the present abuses. Congress alone can, with safety, provide a method by which reasonable combination may be permitted. The relative merits of a federal license or a national incorporation law are beyond question."[66] Popular opinion argued in favor of federal regulation of large corporations in "national" commerce in order to ensure the general welfare of the public. And, with few exceptions, the business community was as solicitous of public approval as it was frightened of public disapprobation.[67]

The transformation of the state's role in promoting economic development was nothing short of remarkable. In less than fifty years, states evolved from catalysts of economic growth to guardians of corporate integrity and governance. Yet many wondered whether the power of state government was sufficient to control the insatiable interests and entrepreneurial designs of corporations. "The influence of financial men has become so powerful and far reaching in self-interest," according to one commentator, "that doubt is expressed whether its iron grip on government and business can ever be destroyed. This mighty power has crippled or destroyed competition by placing a limitation in the field of production. . . . The spirit of competition seems to have almost vanished, being superseded by extortion." [68]

The notion that corporations are not "persons" but only artificial entities outside the scope of the criminal law was now nowhere to be found. If anything, some began to question the limits of personification. As corporations grew in size and sophistication, were courts and legislatures ascribing too many human characteristics to corporate entities? Should corporations have the full canopy of constitutional protections to stave off unwarranted regulation? Critics sat on the sidelines expressing concerns about overregulating the corporate person. A plea from attorney Walter Logan in 1900 for fairer treatment for corporations asked whether corporations were punished for the excessive fortunes of individual corporate elites, such as Cornelius Vanderbilt and John D. Rockefeller. "The law-making power of the State of New York," according to Logan, "has put on the same footing prostitutes, gamblers and corporations. It discourages in every possible way the existence of any one of them within this State. The only difference in the treatment of the three things is that the State enforces its laws for the discouragement of corporations with relentless severity, while its enforcement of the laws as applied to the other two is mild, unoppressive and sporadic. It is a great deal safer . . . to be a prostitute or a gambler than it is to be a corporation."[69] Six years later, another member of the bar wrote: "We appear to have gone 'reform mad,' and in our efforts to curb the power of capital and allied corporate interests, we have failed utterly, to realize that the trend of modern business makes the corporation an imperative necessity."[70]

Phase Two: The Rise and Fall of Vicarious Liability

That these critics of corporate regulation were in the minority became clear as courts finally acceded to the realities of rising monopolistic powers and rapid market integration by expanding the fiction of corporate criminal liability.[71] Criminal liability, as well as the emergence of regulatory law (e.g., the Interstate Commerce Act of 1887 and the Sherman Antitrust Act of 1890) and the birth of key administrative agencies (e.g., the Interstate Commerce Commission), provided some needed relief from the risks associated with the rise of the modern corporation.[72] Courts first extended the criminal law to corporations for crimes of nonfeasance, and then for crimes of misfeasance where proof of intent was not required.[73] Finally, with the antitrust action in *Standard Oil of Indiana* (1908) and the rate discrimination case of *New York Central & Hudson River Railroad Co.* (1909), the corporate criminal law was applied to all crimes, including those requiring proof of mens rea.[74]

The idea that criminal liability gained favor from the perceived inadequacies of regulatory law is supported by the United States Supreme Court in *Hudson*.[75] The United States sought criminal penalties against the New York Central & Hudson River Railroad Co. for the acts of an assistant traffic manager who illegally offered rebates to preferred customers. The briefs submitted to the Court by the government make clear the practical importance of a vicarious liability for corporations. "If punishment for such payments when prohibited by law can be administered only on proving authorization from the president or directors no railway corporation can ever be legally punished for such payments," prosecutors argued. "But, on the other hand, if a railroad corporation may be made criminally responsible for the acts of its officers or agents, to whom have been delegated power to control its corporate action *within the sphere represented by the transaction* then no case can more completely show ground for liability than the case at bar."[76] Agents are vested with corporate powers, and where and when they act on behalf of the principal within their authority, it is as though the corporation itself has acted.[77]

The court did not struggle with this agency argument or with the notion that corporations must share in the risks of conducting business by internalizing the costs for the wrongdoing of its agents.[78] Given the prominence of corporations in interstate commerce, their immense potential to do wrong, and the absence of other more effective regulatory mechanisms, a powerful deterrent would have been lost by restricting criminal liability to the acts of agents.[79] The court went so far as to say that "it would be a distinct step backward to hold that Congress cannot control those who are conducting this interstate commerce by holding them responsible for the intent and purpose of the agents to whom they have delegated the power to act in the premises."[80] Individuals and organizations, it was thought, have few incentives without the prospect of vicarious liability.[81] With joint and several liability, however, both the principal and its agents share a distinct risk of liability and, from it, a reciprocal incentive for law abidance.[82]

The ingenuous public policy that emerged in *New York Central & Hudson River Railroad* shared the allocation of risks to both principal and agent.[83] Corporate liability deters crime; it moves risk of loss away from risk-averse officers and directors toward the firm; it efficiently distributes liability risk between the firm and employees.[84] Without significant entity liability or even shared liability, some argued, incentives would be seen as too weak to ensure an organizational commitment to law abidance.[85] As one commentator concluded, "[c]orporate criminal responsibility tends to prevent crime not only by influencing the corporation's representatives of all degrees to abstain from conducting its business in unlawful ways, but also by influencing those of higher or more remote degrees to restrain subordinates."[86]

Vicarious liability should align organizational incentives (e.g., increases in payroll compensation, significant bonuses, and promotion to higher positions in the corporation) with corporate policies, codes, standards, and procedures that maximize law abidance. Top management is put on notice that the failure to align such incentives with implicit messages to deviate from the law risks entity liability. Successful managers must institutionalize an adequate control system to identify deviance, exercise great care in the delegation of significant corporate responsibility, and clearly communicate the importance and relevance of policies, code provisions, standards, and procedures, while defining those acts that are within the scope of an agent's authority.[87]

The premise of a shared risk between principals and agents seems to have been more apparent than real. The notion of risk sharing is often eroded by strong incentives to quietly discipline or terminate wayward employees so that a strict imputation of liability to the entity might be avoided.[88] Detecting employee misconduct subjects the corporation to incrimination and, thus, to a tax.[89] An awareness of this problem emerged immediately after *Hudson* as corporations considered the expenditure of their enforcement costs.[90] Predictably, some firms avoided the reach of vicarious liability by obscuring illegalities,[91] asking courts to consider good-faith efforts to prevent illegal activity,[92] exploiting the fact that liability is restricted to the illegal acts of more significant corporate actors[93] and shifting losses away from the firm.

Soon after *Hudson* was decided, corporations were asking courts to consider the complexity of the corporate form, the critical importance of clearly stated firm policies prohibiting unethical and illegal acts, and the efforts of firms to ensure compliance with the law.[94] Good-faith demonstrations of obedience to law, it was argued, should suffice.[95] Of course, not all courts responded by ruling that corporations are absolved of liability or are due less blame when their agents engage in criminal acts against express instructions. In fact, a number of courts went so far as to hold entities liable when not a single employee was to blame.[96] Others held steadfast to the value of imputed fault, particularly in antitrust actions.

Even so, in a series of cases that followed *Hudson*, the application of vicarious liability was limited where the rule would have been harsh—where the rule, as one court observed, "would carry corporate responsibility beyond . . . the boundary to which we think corporate criminal responsibility should be carried."[97] The realization that vicarious liability strictly binds corporations immediately posed a "sticky room" problem. Dan Kahan describes the inevitable failure of judges and legislatures to change norms with laws perceived to be harsh, severe, and thus unfair.[98] Hard shoves, in contrast to gentle nudges, do not work. Those responsible for carrying out hard shoves, in this case courts interpreting *Hudson*, were simply reluctant to do so. And many balked at the strict nature of vicarious liability.

Some courts expressed a particular sympathy with the tough realities of corporate life. For example, in *United States ex rel. Porter v. Kroger Grocery & Baking Co.*, Circuit Judge Major acknowledged that "[a]s the magnitude of a business increased, with its personal supervision further removed, we apprehend that the difficulties were correspondingly enhanced. Certainly 100% compliance could not be expected in any event; in fact, it would be impossible." [99] In the 1911 rebating case against the Philadelphia & Reading Railroad, Lehigh Valley Railroad, and Bethlehem Steel Co., the jury's verdict included the recommendation of mercy for all corporate defendants.[100] Authors of popular treatises in the early 1900s noted a particular sympathy to a corporation's diligence as well. In the business community there was a very real sense that corporations got the criminal law's message. "The reckless disregard by many corporation managers of statutory enactment and moral precept," according to one commentator, "is gradually being superseded by rules of conduct that recognize not only an observance of the laws of the land but also that competitors and the public have rights which should be respected."[101]

Claims of due diligence, mercy, and consideration reflect the post-*Hudson* conflicts and shifts in opinion about how to best regulate corporate behavior. There was the strong rhetoric of Attorney General Wickersham, whose fight against the trusts was legendary and whose tolerance for corporate criminals was limited. "The only way the great corporations can avoid prosecution," according to the attorney general, "is by strictly complying with the law, and they are fools if they do not see that."[102] Yet Wickersham's threats neglected the more significant though subtle ambivalence over how these new laws, the necessity of which went unquestioned, might inhibit business growth. There was, to borrow words from editorialists, a duel between law and industrial progress.[103] This ambivalence joined with cases reflecting claims of good faith and diligence, along with some old concerns that corporate entities were the wrong recipients of blame.

No less than one year after *Hudson*, Woodrow Wilson, then candidate for New Jersey governor, argued against the administration's harsh stance on criminalizing corporate entities in a campaign based on the premise that "guilt is personal"—quite a difference from Roosevelt's Progressive "anticorporate" reign. In his first gubernatorial campaign address in Essex County, New Jersey, Wilson challenged the idea of corporate criminal liability. "The trouble with all legislation in regard to corporations is that in respect of our punishments we treat them as person, like individuals, and they are not persons, they are not individuals. Don't you know that it is true that everything any corporation does was originated by some person in particular, or some body of persons, some Board of Directors, or some officer or some employee of a corporation? Do you suppose that there is any corporation whose business is so badly handled that the officers of the corporation could not tell you who originated any particular act of the corporation?"[104]

Add to this the fact that the corporate criminal law was said to be applied unevenly. In bemoaning the Supreme Court's ruling in *Standard Oil* and the tobacco cases, many begged for clarification. Wilson stated, "The federal courts have been, are, and will be overrun with cases requiring the interpretation of those tribunals to determine what the meaning of the law is. It cannot be construed literally, as it reads. If it were, widespread havoc would follow."[105] Other commentators demanded clarity, writing that the uncertainty of regulatory law "paralyzes businesses."[106] John Seymour, lead partner in the New York law firm of Seymour, Megrath & Billings, asked President Wilson in 1914 for a blanket business amnesty for all Sherman Antitrust Act violations: "Men and corporations have been advised wrong; some things are crimes now which a few years back were thought to be moneywise shrewdness."[107]

The business community was more than adept in recognizing the costs associated with criminal liability and leveraging the apparent ambivalence with corporate liability. Corporations quickly conceived strategies to avoid the attribution of blame, including the assertion of their constitutional rights earned from the status of personhood, for example, Fourteenth Amendment rights against state regulation.[108] This trend was recognized in *Connecticut General Life Insurance Co. v. Johnson*, when Justice Black wrote that "of the cases in this Court in which the 14th Amendment was applied during the first fifty years after its adoption, less than one-half of one percent invoked it in protection of the negro race, and more than 50 percent asked that its benefits be extended to corporations."[109] As the next phase of corporate criminal law reveals, comparable strategies are captured by a period of active risk-shifting within the firm as well.

Phase Three: Routine Risk-Shifting between Agents and Principals
The corporate criminal law did not change much through the Great Depression and the New Deal, in spite of a renewed and then sustained interest in corporate law reform.[110] Neither did many of the same concerns and issues surrounding corporate criminal liability. Certainly the tension between and among the business community, regulators, and government remained. Calls for voluntary or mandatory federal incorporation and licensing of corporations continued in the 1920s and 1930s.[111] Not surprisingly, such business associations as the National Association of Manufacturers denounced these proposals as granting excessive power to the federal government.[112] They are, to quote the vice president of the New York University Men in Finance Club, "one of the most remarkable monstrosities presented in Washington in recent years."[113]

As a result of consolidations, mergers, and acquisitions, a large number of companies were once again in dominant positions, for example, General Mills, Armour & Co., Continental Baking, National Biscuit, and Borden Co. The Federal Trade Commission led the call for more vigorous enforcement of the Clayton Antitrust Act and the Patman Act. A series of price-fixing actions were initiated against rubber concerns.[114] The first rulings under the Robinson-Patman Anti-Price Act also were obtained against one of the world's largest brokerage and market information firms, the Biddle Purchasing Co.[115] Not surprisingly, many business owners questioned the politics and purpose of the antitrust campaign. Some argued that monopolies were strengthened by policies proposed or supported by the White House, all to the detriment of small-business owners. Others failed to see that monopolies in any way posed "a menace to the continuances of the government."[116]

Stock market manipulation and deception became a focal point for regulators during this period. The Securities and Exchange Commission (SEC) initiated investigations of a host of companies after its chairman, W. O. Douglas, complained that the New York Stock Exchange (NYSE) "too closely resembles a private club."[117] The SEC proposed new proxy rules, greater alignment with state regulatory bodies, new controls over the activities of protective committees in reorganizations, and new regulations governing investment trusts.[118] The SEC also brought high-profile cases enjoining, for example, the Fidelity Investment Association from operating due to evidence that it misled investors, concealed its indebtedness, failed to maintain sufficient deposits against liabilities, and materially misrepresented the value of investments.[119] Much of this increased regulation met with predictable concerns from business interests. Orval W. Adams, president of the American Bankers Association, laid his cards on the table—government must stop harassing businesses. "Stop throwing monkey-wrenches into the machinery and watch the pump work," Adams suggested. "Continue to threaten, harass and intimidate industry and no amount of financial 'pump priming' will ever bring recovery."[120]

The source of Adams's gripe was the realization that, as John M. Clark astutely noted, private business was no longer private—certainly not the way it once was. There was a sense among leaders in the business community that their autonomous decision-making authority was stripped away, that they no longer had authority to manage their businesses. Railroads and utilities were now publicly regulated. Businesses with transactions across state lines were governed by federal law. There was something unstoppable about the move toward regulation, according to Clark. "The trust movement and antitrust laws, conservation, the Federal Reserve system, vast developments in labor legislation, social insurance, minimum-wage laws and the compulsory arbitration of industrial disputes, pure-food laws and the growing control of public health, prohibition, control over markets and marketing, enlarged control over immigration and international trade, city planning and zoning, and municipal control of municipal growth in general, all have come about within this period."[121]

Corporations responded to economic regulations with a series of challenges under the due process clause of the Fourteenth Amendment.[122] As one commentator noted, the real effect of the due process clause for corporations "was to impose between the state legislatures and the industries of this country the judgment of the Supreme Court and to insure to individual businessmen complete freedom from state regulation other than that which the Supreme Court held to be a proper exercise of governmental power." [123] They also responded with strategic internal initiatives of firms to manage their exposure to criminal liability.[124]

In the third phase of the corporate criminal law, strategic posturing of corporations increasingly immunized firms from the risk and costs of criminal liability.[125] This posturing is certainly evident in large corporations where the separation between ownership and control, captured by A. A. Berle and

G. C. Means, was perfected.[126] It is also evident in tracking the history of corporate criminal law after *New York Central & Hudson River Railroad*. Corporations became indictable persons in the criminal law over the past century as their power and influence began to affect interstate commerce in ways that overwhelmed state and federal regulatory efforts (shifting liability toward the firm); shared liability with their agents as railroad companies and large industrials grew to dominate interstate commerce (sharing liability with agents); protected against losses caused by the criminal acts of employees through the purchase of fidelity insurance (shifting losses away from the firm); sought to recoup losses from director mismanagement and fraud through derivative actions (shifting loss to agents); actively shifted liability to agents as the diligent "good faith" efforts of firms were first recognized as a defense in both federal and state law (shifting liability toward agents); inherited liability from the indemnification of directors and high managerial agents (shifting liability toward the firm); and shifted losses directly to directors, officers, and high managerial agents through innovative derivative actions (shifting liability toward agents).

Empirical research examining this post–*New York Central Railroad* period supports both the concerns of courts in applying the criminal law and the somewhat less-than-successful management of liability risks by firms. Sutherland's groundbreaking exploration of the "crimes" of the seventy largest U.S. industrial corporations in the first half of the twentieth century, for example, revealed a rate of corporate offending that was truly surprising—but only if one groups violations of criminal, civil, and administrative law.[127] "This tabulation of crimes of the seventy largest corporations in the United States," Sutherland reported, "gives a total of 980 adverse decisions. Every one of the seventy corporations has a decision against it, and the average number of decisions is 14.0. . . . These decisions have been concentrated in the period since 1932. Approximately 60 per cent of them were made in the ten-year period subsequent to 1932, and only 40 percent in the forty-year period prior to 1932."[128]

Ninety-seven percent of Sutherland's sample of corporations were recidivists, committing antitrust violations, unfair labor practices, fraud, and other regulatory offenses. Notably, however, only 16 percent of the adverse decisions came from criminal courts. Sutherland concluded that the prevalence of corporate offending far exceeded the number of prosecutions. "[O]nly a fraction of the violations of law by a particular corporation result in prosecution," Sutherland reasoned, "and only a fraction of the corporations which violate the law are prosecuted."[129]

Financial crimes, now called "white collar" crimes by Sutherland, seem to have flourished during post–*New York Central & Hudson River Railroad* periods. Between 1920 and 1925, indictments were obtained for frauds in the sale of surplus war materials; seven corporations and six individuals were indicted on charges of using the mails to defraud investors; the Anchor Warehouse Inc., along with eight employees, were indicted for conspiracy and fraud related to the payment of duty charges; P. W. French & Co., a well-known interior decorating firm and art dealer, was indicted for bank fraud; the New York attorney general joined with prosecutors' offices around the state to combat bucket shops, fake investment firms, and illegal stock promotions; senior executives, including the former lieutenant governor of Montana and the former state treasurer of Massachusetts, were charged with conspiracy to commit fraud against the shareholders of the Boston & Montana Corp.; the Great State Petroleum Co. and ten of its executives were indicted on charges of using the mails to defraud investors; indictments against railroad officials for fraud stemmed from a three-year investigation; indictments against executives and injunctions against corporations all suspected of stock jobbing were obtained in a campaign by attorney general Carl Sherman; the D. G. Dery Corp. was placed in receivership after its president was indicted for forgery related to the company's inventory; and sixteen individuals and fourteen corporations, all members of the New York Cut Stine Contractors' Association, pled guilty to antimonopoly violations.[130]

Throughout the 1920s there were bank frauds by a host of well-known corporations and stock frauds by top-tier investment firms; even some fraud examiners were accused of fraud. The list of swindles and schemes reveals thousands of individuals and hundreds of corporations. By 1925, the annual loss due to stock fraud, insurance fraud, credit fraud, and embezzlement in the United States was estimated at $3 billion.[131] Losses due to embezzlement alone increased fivefold between 1910 and 1923.[132] Payments to firms by fidelity and insurance companies covered only a small fraction of losses due to frauds as corporations increasingly assumed the risks of criminal liability.

The 1930s and 1940s continued with high-profile investigations, prosecutions, and convictions. Richard Whitney, a five-term president of the New York Stock Exchange, was convicted of fraud and served three years and four months of a five-to-ten-year sentence in Sing Sing prison. News of Whitney's fraud prompted reforms in the New York Stock Exchange and other markets.[133] Notable, unreported cases were brought against the Missouri-Kansas Pipe Line Co. for mail fraud; the Fiscal Bond and Share Corp. of Baltimore for fraud; the president of the American Bond & Mortgage Co. in a $58 million fraud; the Bankers' Capital Corp., the Eastern Bankers' Corp., and the American Fiduciary Corp. for mail fraud and conspiracy; the president and vice president of Independent Bancontrol Corp. for mail fraud and conspiracy; and Carnegie-Illinois Steel Corp. on forty-seven counts of falsely certifying test reports to the government. Convictions were obtained in cases against Samuel Dunkel & Co. Inc., along with Sondra Egg Products Corp., for fraud in selling dried egg powder; and against Bankers Industrial Service Inc. and Hiltz & Co. Inc. for stock and mail fraud.[134]

Phase Four: Successful and Failed Model Codes

The well-known, reported cases from the 1920s to the 1950s that populate casebooks on corporate crime show the evolution of hornbook law. They do not, however, reveal the extent and diversity of corporate fraud during this period.[135] Leading up to the codification of the Model Penal Code (MPC) by the American Law Institute in 1962, there was a consistent stream of corporate fraud cases across virtually all industries in both federal and state courts, from stock fraud action against brokerage houses (e.g., Reynolds & Co. and Kimball Securities) and fraud by meatpacking concerns (e.g., American Meatpacking Corp.) in federal courts to criminal actions in state courts combating consumer fraud by companies (e.g., National Household Equipment Co.) and illegal rebanding of television tubes (e.g., Radio Corp. of America). It is little wonder that law reform efforts were designed to usher in a new era in uniform liability for corporate criminal law violations.[136]

Deliberations over the MPC were designed to bring order to the corporate criminal law. The MPC, aimed at state criminal law violations, identifies three distinct forms of liability: regulatory offenses, failures to discharge duties imposed by law, and penal law violations. First, corporations are liable for minor, regulatory offenses where a clear legislative purpose to impose liability is present, and the agent's actions were on behalf of the corporation and within the scope of his authority.[137] The basis of liability is vicarious, found in the doctrine of respondeat superior. Notably, the use of a due diligence or "good faith" defense limits the reach of this liability rule by allowing a corporation to escape conviction if it can establish that a responsible supervisory officer used due diligence to prevent the offense. Second, a corporation is liable where the offense is based on a failure to discharge a specific duty of performance imposed by law.[138] Finally, corporations are liable for all penal law violations, with few exceptions, where the "offense was authorized, requested, commanded, performed or recklessly tolerated by the board of directors or by a high managerial agent acting in behalf of the corporation within the scope of his office or employment."[139] This final category, which was the subject of much deliberation and debate, does not adopt the broad respondeat superior approach that section 207(1)(a) uses for regulatory offenses. Instead, it confines liability to a narrow class of criminal acts—those concerning high managerial agents whose acts reflect the policy of the corporate body.[140] Some states' legislatures found section 207(1)(c) too restrictive and thus proceeded cautiously in adopting this section. Most states, however, use section 207(1)(c) as a rough guide for drafting less-restrictive provisions.

Prior to the MPC, state legislatures had little guidance in crafting uniform criminal statutes that consistently defined mental states. In fact, an assortment of mental states with varied meanings could be found in state codes, including fault provisions that are quite difficult to interpret, for example, "unlawfully," "maliciously," "fraudulently," and "designedly."[141] Courts, for example, were forced to decipher the meaning of "heedlessly," "wickedly," "wantonly," and "wrongfully."[142] With the MPC, four culpable mental states were selected that represent a continuum or hierarchy of culpability, ranging from conduct that is *purposeful*, or consciously designed to bring about a certain result, to *negligent* conduct, where the actor should have known of a substantial risk of injury.

Drafters of the MPC did not believe that good-faith compliance efforts might compromise the incentives derived from vicarious liability.[143] They concluded that if sanctions were designed to encourage the reasonable supervision of employees, then failing to reward genuinely diligent compliance efforts would be a distinct disincentive, undermining the deterrent value of any fine or period of probation.[144] In a host of states, corporate exculpation follows the showing, by a preponderance of evidence, of due diligence by the supervisor of the wayward agent.[145] Thus, the compliance efforts of the corporation shifted the focus of the blame onto "wayward" employees. In cases that once met the standards of vicarious liability, courts following the MPC upheld the convictions of culpable agents with the caveat that "[t]o impose criminal liability on the corporation . . . would amount to a strict criminal liability in the absence of proof of fault."[146]

In cases where prosecutors and courts are hard-pressed to determine the effectiveness or authenticity of compliance efforts, a good-faith defense would tend to absolve the entity, perhaps without justification.[147] Further, a due diligence defense arguably corrodes the principles of delegation and authority that are at the foundation of a consensual agency relationship.[148] Organizations delegate authority to agents who act on their behalf as their representatives. The failure of an agent to perform as instructed is incidental to an organization's diligent efforts to prevent such failures.[149] Surely, some rational corporations will find less of an incentive to fashion effective compliance programs as their liability will be excused regardless of the success of compliance efforts.[150]

Although most prosecutors consider the diligent efforts of corporations in deciding whether to investigate, charge, and pursue an aggressive prosecution, those who do not raise reasonable concerns. The concern in crediting failed programs is that doing so may significantly diminish the incentives to make programs effective. Who would quibble that "[t]he ultimate goal, after all, is a compliance program that prevents crimes, not one that excuses the corporation in the event that one occurs"?[151] For some state and federal prosecutors, no evidence of diligence on the part of a company can shield the principal from the acts of the wayward agent. Here liability is absolute; the miscreant agent simply acts and speaks for the principal in the commission of a crime.[152]

Recognition of organizational due diligence as a defense allows organizations with ineffective, skeletal compliance initiatives to strategically shift blame to their agents and unjustifiably escape a strict imputation of fault.[153] John Coffee acknowledges this concern in cases where corporations are most interested in the cosmetic appearance of compliance.[154] This concern also extends to organizations that are indifferent to an effective compliance program and culture.[155] Survey research, described in some detail in chapter 4, suggests that in some (if not many) corporations, the role of compliance has more to do with maintaining the appearance of a compliant reputation than that of a meaningful culture of ethical awareness and law abidance.[156] Codes of conduct are often disregarded as "legalistic and one-sided."[157] Compliance also may be seen as a concession to regulators for some deference to the entity with a prospective or pending investigation, charging decision, or plea bargain.[158] In short, the strategic utility of compliance standards may be of far greater interest than any sort of organizational integrity.[159]

MPC drafters further shifted the risk of liability for nonregulatory crimes away from the entity by limiting corporate liability to actions taken by high managerial agents.[160] The objective was to restrict entity liability to those situations in which members of the board of directors, corporate officers, or agents sufficiently high in the corporate hierarchy engaged in criminal acts. Such acts were seen as reflective of the character of the corporate body. The drafters acknowledged that this rule was a partial rejection of the liability rule adopted by federal courts, preserving it for situations in which shareholders are well positioned to indirectly prevent corporate crime.[161] Prevailing federal law, in its application of fault throughout the corporate hierarchy, suggests that liability does not arise out of any particular relation between the entity and the agent, but rather that it is found in the organization's duty toward the public.[162] Corporations stand or fall with their choice of agents.[163]

The effect of this partial rejection by the MPC, however, did more than just renounce the harshness of vicarious liability. By limiting liability in cases where owners, officers, directors, and those responsible for the construction of corporate policies had no knowledge of the illegality, these new liability rules afforded organizations protection from criminal liability for acts of deliberate indifference by high managerial agents.[164] Of far greater concern, the MPC rules offered a marginal incentive to high managerial agents to delegate tasks and responsibilities to their subordinates in an indifferent, negligent, even reckless manner. As one commentator noted, senior management "can protect themselves from knowledge—and the corporation from liability—simply by delegating to subordinates full responsibility for those activities which might result in criminal violations."[165]

Serious reform was first discussed at length by the National Commission on Reform of Federal Criminal Laws (the Brown Commission) in the 1960s.[166] The Brown Commission recommended corporate liability for any offense committed by an agent whose action was authorized, commanded, or requested by (1) the board of directors, (2) an executive officer, (3) a person who controls the organization or is responsible for policy formation, or (4) a person otherwise considered responsible under a statute.[167] Members of the Brown Commission were hopeful that codification of liability rules would reduce uncertainty as to the extent of corporate liability for acts committed by agents.

The Brown Commission examined a number of draft proposals for a revised Federal Criminal Code during the late 1970s and early 1980s.[168] In the last version, found in the Criminal Code Reform Act of 1981, organizations would be liable for acts of any agent that (1) occur in the performance of their duties, (2) are within the scope of their authority, (3) are intended to benefit the organization, and (4) are ratified or adopted by the organization. Alternatively, liability may be found where there is a failure on the part of the organization to discharge a specific duty imposed by law. None of these proposals met with success. "The steam went out of the effort to adopt a comprehensive criminal code revision," contended Norman Abrams, "and Congress began again to consider crime bills that treat substantive criminal law piecemeal."[169] Criminologists looking at the lengthy work of the Brown Commission concluded that reform of the federal criminal law fell prey to pressures from interest groups.[170] Sadly, it has not yet been resurrected.

Phase Five: The Appearance of a New Regulatory State
Compliance with administrative and regulatory law overshadowed the threat of criminal liability at a time when the locus of enforcement was found in sweeping legislation, codified in a host of federal and state regulatory statutes. Landmark pollution control legislation in the late 1960s and early 1970s included environmental protection (the Clean Air Act, the Clean Water Act, the Federal Water Pollution Control Act, the National Environmental Policy Act, and the Endangered Species Act), workplace safety (the Occupational Health and Safety Act), and consumer protection (the Magnuson-Moss Warranty and the FTC Improvements Act or the Automobile Safety Act). By the end of this period and the beginning of a subsequent phase of deregulation, literally hundreds of thousands of criminal provisions were found in a wide range of federal statutory laws.[171]

Add to this legislation an aggressive nationwide program of civil injunctive enforcement actions by the Securities and Exchange Commission that began early in the 1960s. These cases, aimed at corporate governance failings, resulted in the Texas Gulf Sulphur litigation and actions against VTR, Agronomics, Coastal States Gas Corp., and Mattel. And, not to be outdone, add to this litigation a resurgence of antitrust prosecutions spurred by the Heavy Electrical Equipment Antitrust Cases of 1961 targeting, among others, General Electric and Westinghouse Electric corporations.[172]

Congress and state legislatures turned their attention to "social costs of a successful industrial economy" during what is often called the New Regulatory State, the Public Interest Era, or the Environmental-Consumerist Period by legal scholars.[173] As Robert Rabin observed, beginning around 1970 "a remarkable resurgence of regulatory reform activity occurred that is not so easily traced to a particular source—and which, nonetheless, reshaped the federal regulatory system."[174] Peter Yeager attributes the rise to "severe political pressure to *privatize* selected 'externalities' of production by mandating that industry contribute heavily to their alleviation."[175]

No matter what the cause, social activists and politicians alike noted what appeared to be a corporate crime wave filled with bribes, kickbacks, and political corruption.[176] This was the time of Robert Vesco's $2 billion con, the Equity Funding Corp. of America hoax, Hooker Chemical's dumping at Love Canal, and the Levy Caper. This was the time of the infamous Lockheed scandal and of the Watergate special prosecutor who, remarkably, led the way in obtaining convictions against nineteen companies for illegal political contributions to Nixon's 1972 reelection campaign.[177] The SEC tracked revelations of overseas "slush funds" used by companies to make illegal campaign contributions and corrupt payments to foreign officials. The most respected and largest corporations were also convicted of making political contributions to win overseas contracts. The list included American Airlines, Gulf Oil, 3M, Goodyear Tire and Rubber, and Northrop. This was also a time when corporations were known to put profits ahead of consumer safety. The most glaring example was with the death of three teenage girls in a Ford Pinto, resulting in the prosecution of Ford for reckless homicide.[178]

Consumer advocate Ralph Nader joined Senator Lee Metcalf and Congressmen Benjamin S. Rosenthal, Anthony J. Moffett, and Thomas J. Downey in warning Attorney General Edward H. Levi, "Only in the area of corporate law enforcement can so many law violators blend into their institutions and escape punishment."[179] Their solution: establish a Division on Corporate Crime in the Department of Justice; create a special group to evaluate existing law and its effectiveness; pass legislation to prohibit illegal payments to domestic or foreign officials for commercial purposes; and empower the Federal Trade

Commission to investigate cases where corporations seek foreign contracts through bribery.[180] Renewed calls for federal corporate charters,[181] jailing the company president or CEO,[182] increased fines for white-collar offenders,[183] and longer prison sentences followed.[184]

There was a sense of urgency for reform that may be explained simply as frustration with regular reports of corporate abuses without accountability. Judges were hesitant to convict and impose prison sentences on corporate executives for white-collar offenses, the enforcement powers of the SEC were perceived to be weak, regulators were slow to act, enforcement agencies and prosecutors' offices failed to give corporate crime priority, criminal violations of antitrust law were seemingly commonplace, and criminal penalties for white-collar offenses were lenient.[185] The stark difference between criminal justice for white-collar offenders and that for street offenders did not go unnoticed. In testimony before the House Judiciary Committee on Crime, former attorney general Ramsey Clark made the remarkable observation that "[w]e glorify the acquisition of wealth and property by the middle-class and the rich, but we punish the poor for stealing."[186] White-collar and corporate crimes were simply not considered criminal. Assistant Attorney General Donald I. Baker captured this sentiment in discussing the need to vigorously prosecute antitrust offenses: "Price fixing is a crime, not just an economic faux pas."[187] Moreover, as one top Justice Department official observed, "It's just a lot easier for us to pick on the small guy."[188]

Ralph Nader wrote of a double standard for corporation and individual miscreants. Large corporations "deliberately kept secret or falsified results for drugs, deliberately refused to notify owners of defective vehicles, deliberately bilked the government of millions in inflated cost submissions under government contracts, negligently wasted millions of public funds in wasteful or promotional endeavors. These acts often do not even result in sanctions and almost never in criminal penalties on the culpable officers."[189] Nader and his colleagues offered numerous proposals for reform, addressing failures in corporate disclosures, product safety, corporate citizenship, corporate governance, and corporate sanctions.[190]

Fueling the frustration with the failure to combat corporate crime was a strong suspicion that "crime in the suites" was commonplace.[191] Judge Howard R. Tyler Jr. noted, "The Justice Department doesn't even know the magnitude of what it's missing in terms of corporate crime."[192] Marshall Clinard and his colleagues did their best to assess the magnitude of what was missing in their much-heralded work *Illegal Corporate Behavior*.[193] In 1975, following the tradition of Sutherland's work, Clinard and his colleagues studied the nature and extent of corporate illegalities in 582 of the largest publicly owned U.S. corporations (with an average annual revenue of $1.7 billion). Data were compiled on all enforcement actions initiated or imposed by twenty-four federal agencies over a two-year period. More than 60 percent of the corporations in the sample had violated the law with at least one completed enforcement action. Those corporations with one or more averaged 4.2 actions. The most frequent sanction was an administrative warning, followed by monetary penalties. Penalties were generally small, with 80 percent of them less than $5,000. More than 85 percent of the sample received administrative sanctions. The vast majority of violations were not criminal. Clinard concluded, as Sutherland did some years before, that corporate crime is controlled by federal regulatory agencies, all of which have congressional authority to regulate and police.[194]

Critics of the New Regulatory State were outspoken in their opposition to regulation as a costly drag on the economy, an ineffective and flawed means of corporate crime control.[195] The politics of regulation distorted regulatory policy and practice, resulting in unbearable costs. Nancy Frank and Michael Lombness concluded that the regulatory justice system had outgrown itself. "Corporations spend literally billions of dollars annually complying with regulations, and still we constantly hear of scandals and tragedies, with a corporation at the center of the plot. If regulatory agencies were designed to control corporate behavior, they do not seem to be doing very well."[196]

Ralph Nader led the charge with proposals for corporate democracy and a fiery rhetoric, reminiscent of the voices for corporate reform in the early 1900s that kept the debate over corporate deviance and corporate responsibility in the public eye. The existing system of "shareholder democracy, and the state chartering of corporations that are, in some ways far larger than their host states," Nader and his colleague Mark Green wrote, "have as much chance of keeping our giant corporations virtuous as wigs on judges have of making them wise, and the wrist slaps called criminal law have deterred corporate crimes as effectively as a fishing net slows an elephant."[197]

Corporate accountability must be reconceptualized so that directors are truly independent, public disclosures of environmental and social impacts are made, plant relocation decisions are fairly decided, whistle-blowing statutes are passed, and sanctions for corporate and white-collar offenses are enhanced. The Project on Corporate Responsibility urged mutual funds to consider corporate policies in investment decisions.[198] Another group of lawyers, this time from the Center for Law and Social Policy, joined in pushing for social investing: "Our concern is for breaking open the closed circuit of decision-making in the corporations. It is important for the good guys to cut into that process any way they can. Corporate boards should have to listen to somebody besides the narrow corporate elite."[199] The social screening of investments by mutual funds was a less-than-popular idea, but by 1973, many Fortune 500 companies mentioned a commitment to social responsibility in their annual reports. Some went so far as to propose and discuss principles of social accounting.[200]

Nader had been pushing an agenda of corporate reform for many years. In 1970, for example, he organized a National Campaign to Make General Motors Responsible, including proposals for a shareholders' committee on corporate responsibility and board members representing the public interest.[201] General Motors went on a counterattack, expressing its commitment to the environment, safety, and urban society.[202] Moreover, James M. Roche, the chairman of the board of General Motors, engaged in unusual transparency in writing, "Corporate responsibility is a catchword of the adversary culture that is so evident today. If something is wrong with American society, blame business. Business did not create discrimination in America, but business is expected to eliminate it. Business did not bring about the deterioration of our cities, but business is expected to rebuild them. The dull cloud of pessimism and distrust which some have cast over free enterprise is impairing the ability of business to meet its basic economic responsibilities—not to mention its capacity to take on new ones."[203]

The reaction of many in the business community to calls for corporate responsibility, corporate democracy, increased regulation, and enhanced sanctions was once again consistent. Trade associations and industry groups complained vociferously. Small firms argued that laws were not applied evenly and consistently. The business lobby maintained pressure on legislative bodies and law reform commissions to continue to avoid the strictures of the criminal law. Corporations also thwarted governmental control by continuing the invocation of their rights under the Constitution. The First Amendment conferred protections on commercial and political speech. The Fourth Amendment, for example, was used to protect companies from surprise inspections and regulatory inspections without a warrant.[204] Corporations raised Fifth Amendment protections against double jeopardy. As one commentator noted, "Taken together, these Bill of Rights assertions represent a bold new challenge to government regulation. Denied the power of the fourteenth amendment when the era of substantive due process ended, corporations have taken refuge in the Bill of Rights."[205]

Yeager's study of environmental regulation powerfully illustrates the all-too-obvious point that businesses, to varying degrees of success, seek not only to comply with regulators and regulations but also to influence them. Strong opposition by a regulated constituency to new laws often prompts a cautious and conservative regulatory response so as to avoid litigation and legislative challenge. In short, legislation and regulatory policy evolve in a complex political and social environment. The implications are significant. Rates of business crimes or violations, as Yeager observed, are "the joint production of both business and regulatory behavior."[206] The extent of offending is a function of the relative burden placed on business by both regulatory requirements and the prevailing substantive criminal law. Nowhere was this more evident than with the deliberations over possible sentencing guidelines for organization in phase six, the late 1980s and early 1990s.

Phase Six: The Birth of Good Corporate Citizenship

This phase of the corporate criminal law began with some milestones in the history of the corporate criminal law. First, in 1977, Congress enacted the Foreign Corrupt Practices Act, which criminalized illicit payments to foreign public officials by U.S. businesses and individuals.[207] Businesses cried foul, not surprisingly, claiming that this pathbreaking piece of extraterritorial legislation made it difficult to compete successfully for overseas corporate contracts. Second, in the late 1970s, a series of legislative proposals for corporate governance reforms was introduced in Congress, and hearings were held examining possible legislative reform.[208] This process was followed by the first tentative draft of the American Law Institute's "Principles of Corporate Governance and Structure: Analysis and Recommendations," released in 1982. The business community was horrified by the idea that a bunch of law professors articulated legal standards for board oversight over management. "We don't require four law professors to tell us how to run our business," said Walter B. Wriston, chairman and chief executive officer of Citicorp.[209] And third, there was a series of high-profile criminal prosecutions, including a guilty plea to 2,000 felony counts of wire and mail fraud from the nation's fifth-largest brokerage firm. In the early 1980s, E. F. Hutton moved billions of dollars in its many accounts and banks so that it could use more than $250 million a day of bank funds without interest charges. The firm earned an extra $8 million income over a period of twenty months. The Justice Department took great pride in the $2 million criminal fine and $8 million payment of restitution. Attorney General Edwin Meese III said, "This action is part of the Justice Department's ongoing effort against economic crime and makes it clear to the business world that so-called white collar crime will not be tolerated."[210] But few, it seemed, believed that the effort to combat economic crime was genuine.

Ralph Nader once again spoke of a corporate crime wave and a double standard of justice—one standard for crime in the streets and another one for crime in the suites. His pitch changed, however, to include proposals for more diverse and effective corporate sanctions.[211] Calls for sentencing reform joined together with an increasing recognition that corporate crime was evidence of moral decay.[212] As one commentator noted, "Not since the mid-1970s, when a series of foreign corporate bribes and illegal political contributions shocked the body politic, have there been so many deep gashes in corporate America's moral armor."[213] And the gashes were deeper than regulators and the public knew. Financial fraud was rampant in the savings and loan industry throughout the 1980s. With a price tag of between $325 billion and $500 billion to be paid by the next generation of taxpayers, the thrift industry was rife with looting and what Henry Pontell and Kitty Calavita call "collective embezzlement."[214] The crimes of Charles Keating, Michael Milliken, and Ivan Boesky looked tame in comparison, as do the securities fraud, insurance frauds, junk bond manipulations, insider trading scandals, and leasing frauds of this time.[215]

Anger at the immorality of corporate America reached a high with the bankruptcy of A. H. Robbins Co. in 1985. A. H. Robbins had marketed the Dalkon Shield as a modern and safe intrauterine device when it was anything but that. More than 100,000 women became pregnant, with more than half suffering miscarriages. Other women died from septic abortions and pelvic inflammatory disease. Still others gave birth to deformed children, and thousands became infertile. Company officials destroyed documents, denied responsibility, misled investigators and regulators, and fired employees who raised concerns about the Shield's safety.[216] Calls for strengthening corporate self-governance with corporate credos, corporate codes of ethics, and compliance initiatives followed.[217]

The most tangible evidence of these calls was found far from the pharmaceutical industry. In response to findings of defense contractor fraud by Grumman Aerospace Corp., General Electric, General Dynamics, and Hughes Aircraft, the Blue Ribbon Commission on Defense Management (the Packard Commission) organized behind the Defense Industry Initiative (DII). The Packard Commission, in its 1986 final report, called for a renewed corporate self-governance, commitment to industry-specific codes of conduct, and development of internal controls so as to ensure public confidence in the defense industry.[218] The DII sought to increase the awareness of and commitment to business ethics "from the board room to the mail room" throughout the defense industry. All signatories to the DII are required "to adopt a written code of ethics and conduct, to provide employees orientation and training with respect to the code, to provide employees with a mechanism (such as a hotline or helpline) to surface concerns about corporate compliance with procurement laws and regulations, to adopt procedures for voluntary disclosure of violations of federal procurement laws, to participate in best practices forums, and to make public information which shows the commitment to do all of these things."[219]

The DII did not change principles of corporate criminal liability. They remained underutilized and without reform. But, its emphasis on corporate self-governance, the creation of codes, internal disciplinary mechanisms, and internal controls surely influenced the next phase of the corporate criminal law. The United States Sentencing Commission took its mandate from Congress in 1985 to create guidelines for organizational sanctions. The Sentencing Commission, established by the Sentencing Reform Act of 1984, introduced guidelines for organizational crimes at time when the only standards of corporate compliance were found in the DII and when, as Nader suggested, corporate sentences lacked uniformity, creativity, and clout. The standards of organizational due diligence, first articulated in the DII and later refined in the guidelines, became a litmus test for "good corporate citizenship." The guidelines also finally provided some consistency in sentencing, if nothing else.[220]

The road to the commission's concept of organizational due diligence was not smooth. Though the Sentencing Commission's mandate called for an integration of "just punishment, deterrence, public protection and rehabilitation," the first two proposals before the commission in the late 1980s were derived from optimal penalty theory, that is, devising a scheme in which punishment would be fashioned according to the harm done divided by the probability of detection.[221] Critics argued that both proposals ignored the relationship between penal theory and the larger aims of the substantive criminal law. Little attention was paid by the Sentencing Commission to the moral connotations represented in the intent requirements found in the criminal law. That blame, in general, can be imposed only when the actor is "responsible" for its actions, and that the extent of culpability must affect the degree to which an actor may be held blameworthy went largely unaddressed.

Even so, trade associations were vehemently opposed because "[n]either proposal takes into account [the situation where] a corporation has done all it can to comply with the law and just has some aberrant, low-level employee, or people who simply don't understand all the complicated new laws being thrown at corporations today." A persistent lobby publicly attacked the proposed fine levels; asked for the incorporation of a wide range of mitigating circumstances; argued implicitly in favor of proportionately higher fines for small businesses; and sought to maintain the status quo in sentencing law so that judges, rather than prosecutors, would retain full discretion to fashion corporate sanctions.

The third attempt captured the moral sphere of culpability, accommodating some of the concerns of the business lobby. In these guidelines, the Sentencing Commission required judges to consider four mitigating factors that reflect culpability. Evidence of such factors, in the form of a mitigation score, would reduce the multiplier.[222] Courts would consider the following questions:

1. Did the offense occur without the knowledge of any person who exercised control over the organization?

2. Did the offense occur despite a meaningful compliance program?
3. Did the organization voluntarily and promptly report the offense?
4. After discovering the offense, did the organization take reasonable steps to remedy the harm, discipline those responsible, and prevent a reoccurrence?

In addition to these mitigating circumstances, courts would be required to consider, among other things, the "nature and circumstances of the offense and history and characteristics of the defendants."[223]

This carrot-and-stick proposal was also widely criticized. Michael Block and Jon Lott argued that the penalties were dramatically increased and reflected neither the seriousness of the offense nor the risk associated with apprehension. "In its rush," they asserted, "the Commission has created complicated and arbitrary guidelines that will produce bizarre and unintended results."[224] Amitai Etzioni was equally critical but for different reasons. The commission bent to heavy business lobbying, according to Etzioni.[225] The commission guidelines require the imposition of more significant fines, but there is a hitch. At the same time, the guidelines "allow judges to greatly reduce penalties if companies add internal compliance programs to insure observation of the law. This is hardly deterrence."[226]

Much of the criticism of the guidelines was grounded in concerns over the mitigation score. Would large publicly held corporations fare better than small privately held firms? Would reduced penalties for compliance programs or monitoring lead to cosmetic programs and lax regulatory oversight? Significant criticism resulted in the final proposal, which took some additional steps.[227] The Sentencing Commission agreed that fines should reflect the seriousness of an offense as well as the culpability of the offending corporation. The former would be determined by the pretax gain to the corporation, amount of loss caused by the corporation, and a predefined ranking of offense seriousness. The latter would be approximated by a culpability score calculated on the basis of an organization's (1) involvement in or tolerance of criminal activity (scaled according to the size of the organization and highest level of corporate knowledge), (2) prior history, (3) record of violations of orders, (4) attempts to obstruct justice, (5) maintenance of an effective compliance program, and (6) willingness to self-report, cooperate, and accept responsibility.[228]

The Sentencing Commission decided that organizations are more culpable when a "high-level" employee "participated in, condoned, or was wilfully ignorant of the offense."[229] Here "condone" means knowledge of and a failure to prevent or terminate an offense. Willful ignorance approximates the mental state of recklessness insofar as it concerns a conscious disregard of a substantial and unjustifiable risk. Alternatively, organizations are more culpable where "tolerance of the offense by substantial authority personnel was pervasive throughout the organization."[230] In this provision, tolerance appears as a reasonable proxy for negligence, that is, a high managerial agent should have known of a substantial and unjustifiable risk.

Thus, in these two provisions, the Sentencing Commission provided judges with a culpability assessment that hierarchically grades blameworthiness by proxies for knowledge, recklessness, and negligence.[231] The commission also provides five postconviction culpability measures, ranging from an assessment of prior history, which considers the number of previous adjudications, to the maintenance of an effective compliance program. The guidelines cover an organization's action prior to the offense, during the offense, and after the offense. This is notable as it is a rare but certainly welcomed acknowledgement of differences in individual versus organizational culpability.[232]

As corporations allocated vast resources over the past decade to be "in compliance with the Guidelines," the notion of corporate integrity assumed new meaning.[233] The concept of organizational due diligence became a proxy for corporate ethics.[234] Due diligence is an organizing principle of behavior that imposes both ethical and legal obligations on corporations and their agents.[235] It requires the articulation of ethical standards of conduct.[236] Due diligence satisfies intentionality requirements by demanding action in accordance with these self-selected and self-imposed values.[237] It compels the acceptance of responsibility and the affirmative obligation to disclose practices that violate the law.[238] Diligent action hinges on responsible proactive and reactive corporate behavior consistent with prescribed standards of conduct.[239]

Those who distinguish strategies of ethics institutionalization think of corporate compliance efforts as different from integrity-based approaches.[240] Integrity approaches, it is argued, are "based on the concept of self-governance in accordance with a set of guiding principles."[241] Ethical values drive the entity and shape the organizational structures, processes, and decision making.[242] The commitment of top management is decisive.[243] The brand of organizational due diligence outlined in the commentary of the sentencing guidelines, however, has a legal and intellectual history that both embraces and reflects organizational responsibility and integrity.[244] Its legal roots are grounded in the rich tradition of agency theory and the law surrounding corporate governance.[245] Its intellectual roots are found in more than a decade of active scholarly debate over corporate self-regulation.[246] The concept of organizational due diligence encompasses far more than minimal "legal compliance."[247] Indeed, a good case can be made that the ideal of due diligence, as an organizing principle for firm behavior, approximates the notion of corporate integrity.[248]

In the years following the passage of the guidelines, United States attorneys began considering evidence of due diligence in the early stages of
their investigation of cases.[249] A short time later, it was clear that evidence
of organizational due diligence implicitly or explicitly affected charging
decisions.[250] Plea agreements followed evidence of due diligence, promises
of future diligent efforts, and, more frequently, elaborate integrity agreements.[251] Policy statements discussing the effect of organizational due diligence on liability followed from branches of the Department of Justice and
other regulatory agencies.

The importance of the guidelines' prescriptions was tested in the more
general context of corporate governance. Should boards of directors be held
liable for failing to ensure the presence of effective compliance programs
and procedures? In *Caremark International, Inc.*, shareholders sought recovery from directors of fines paid following the criminal conviction of their
company for employee violations of laws regulating health-care providers.[252]
Caremark International pled guilty to mail fraud and paid significant civil
and criminal fines.[253] In a creative marriage of the business judgment rule,
the American Law Institute's Principles of Corporate Governance, and the
Sentencing Guidelines for Organizations, the fiduciary duties of corporate
directors were extended to matters of organizational compliance.[254]

The Delaware Chancery Court ruled that the duty of a director includes
the assurance of compliance procedures and reporting systems reasonably
capable of preventing law violations.[255] Accordingly, "a failure to do so under
some circumstances may, in theory at least, render a director liable for losses
caused by noncompliance with applicable legal standards."[256] In the aftermath of the decision, corporate counsel preach the new "post-*Caremark*"
gospel by advising boards to assume a proactive role in ensuring that sufficient resources have been allocated to ensure the active monitoring of agents
throughout the corporate hierarchy.[257]

The wisdom of this gospel was tested in a settlement of Securities and
Exchange Commission (SEC) charges against senior officers and directors of
W. R. Grace & Co. for their failure to make required disclosures to shareholders.[258] Following an investigation by the staff of the Division of Enforcement
in 1996, the SEC charged the chairman of the board, the chief executive
officer, and various directors and officers with a failure to disclose details
of a retirement package as well as certain negotiations to sell a subsidiary
to the ex-chairman's son. The SEC concluded that the absence of disclosures
violated securities laws, and the likely culprit was top management's acceptance of the corporate culture at W. R. Grace. While SEC chairman Arthur
Levitt had urged corporate counsel not to interpret the W. R. Grace & Co.
case as an extension of the board's responsibility, commentators viewed the
investigation and subsequent SEC ruling as a complement to the decision

in *Caremark*; further evidence that the duty of corporate directors to protect shareholder interests includes an obligation to use effective compliance systems to monitor management and subordinate employees.[259]

In the first set of federal prosecutorial guidelines, Federal Prosecution of Corporations (1999) (hereinafter referred to as Holder Memo, after Eric H. Holder, the deputy attorney general who issued the Federal Prosecution of Corporations guidelines), there is an explicit renunciation of vicarious liability by the U.S. Department of Justice.[260] In acknowledging the vast discretion of prosecutors, eight factors are identified as critical in charging decisions.[261] These include a wide range of variables, from efforts of organizations in responding to the discovery of illegalities to concerns about the collateral consequences of criminal charges to innocent agents (see chapter 2).[262] Reflecting the efforts of a Corporate Fraud Task Force, created in the wake of the Enron scandal, a revised set of Principles of Federal Prosecution of Business Organizations (hereinafter referred to as the Thompson Memo, after Larry D. Thompson, the deputy attorney general who issued the revised Principles of Federal Prosecution of Business Organizations) was issued on January 20, 2003. The Thompson Memo addressed some concerns with crediting less-than-complete corporate cooperation and the cosmetic nature of some corporate compliance programs.

The compliance industry today deftly markets the story that evidence of organizational due diligence likely forestalls a criminal investigation, minimizes the likelihood of a criminal indictment, and regularly leads to creative plea agreements, grants of governmental leniency, or even amnesty. Prosecutors craft elaborate corporate integrity agreements that, in cases of health care fraud, for example, mandate monitoring by independent review organizations (IROs); for example, an IRO performs billing, systems, and compliance reviews. In such cases, prosecutions end where corporations demonstrate a commitment to compliance and actively cooperate with authorities. Declinations reward firms for their proactive, reactive, and cooperative efforts, reserving resources for the most abusive firms. The focus, it seems, is almost entirely on postoffense behavior.

Policy statements issued by the largest regulatory agencies reinforce the move away from command and control strategies to a brand of negotiated compliance, coerced cooperation, and regulatory persuasion. Most offer generous leniency and amnesty programs for corporate cooperators. Organizational cooperation and acceptance of responsibility are exchanged by corporations for mitigation, exculpation, or absolution. In fact, corporations have little choice but to trade favors with authorities with the threat of significant sentencing guidelines—prescribed fines.

Over time, the good corporate citizenship movement produced a new enforcement landscape, one of corporate cooperation, CIAs, IROs, substantial assistance, mitigation credits, and voluntary disclosure.[263] In theory, the substantive corporate criminal law is unchanged since *New York Central & Hudson River Railroad*. In practice, negotiated plea agreements followed by compliance prescriptions all but replace prosecutions under substantive law. Forthright corporate cooperation that facilitates the flow of evidence to authorities is the critical feature of this strategy.[264]

Phase Seven: Failed Governance and Selective Prosecutions
There was a time when the motivation for earnings manipulation was to attract external financing at more competitive rates.[265] Research on restatements between 1971 and 2000 from a large sample of corporations suggests that capital market pressures moved companies to adopt aggressive accounting policies.[266] Enron's failure and WorldCom's collapse set in motion an avalanche of earnings restatements reflecting something far more nefarious—widespread if not systemic fraud in some of the most reputable and once high-flying companies that devastates debtholders and stockholders. Market capitalization losses due to earnings restatements exceeded $100 billion between January 1997 and June 2002.[267] These restatements reflect firms that are playing the numbers game, according to Arthur Levitt, "a gamesmanship that says it's okay to bend the rules, to tweak the numbers and let obvious and important discrepancies slide, a gamesmanship where companies bend to the desires and pressures of Wall Street analysts rather than the reality of the numbers."[268]

Enron is also a classic demonstration of gatekeeper failure, John Coffee writes, deference to clients by auditors, securities analysts, and debt rating agencies.[269] This deference, Coffee explains, comes from undeterred gatekeepers. The risk of auditor liability declined in the decade preceding Enron and WorldCom, at the same time that the benefits of auditor acquiescence dramatically increased. Add this acquiescence to some obvious conflicts of interest, such as cross-selling consulting services, and there is one solid explanation. An alternative explanation offered by Coffee is the euphoria that subsumed the equities markets in the late 1990s, making gatekeepers all but irrelevant. "Indeed, in an atmosphere of euphoria in which stock prices ascend endlessly and exponentially," Coffee argues, "gatekeepers are largely a nuisance to management, which does not need them to attract investors. Gatekeepers are necessary only when investors are cautious and skeptical, and in a market bubble, caution and skepticism are largely abandoned."[270]

One can find a host of other explanations offered, including the incentives from stock options to maximize equity valuations and the absence of competition in the Big Five accounting firms.[271] All point to a single-minded ethos of profit maximization combined with systemic failures of corporate governance. A new enforcement landscape emerged with the much-heralded

Sarbanes-Oxley 2002 legislation (the statutory title of which is the Public Company Accounting Reform and Investor Protection Act of 2002) and the new rules from the SEC, NYSE, and Nasdaq. These postscandal reforms, addressing vulnerabilities in internal financial control systems and problems of board independence, reflect the nature and characteristics of the offenses committed by Enron, Arthur Andersen, and WorldCom. All involved "corporate looting by insiders," as Richard Posner concludes.[272] The fact that these corporate offenses involved the enrichment of officers with benefits that were concealed or inadequately disclosed made legislation much easier to conceive, draft, and pass. Requiring increased independence of auditors, directors, and analysts; increased disclosure in annual reports; and changed accounting rules are obvious solutions. So, too, is placing the firm's audit committee as an intermediary between the firm and its auditors, shifting the burden of monitoring internal accounting controls.

The focus of Sarbanes-Oxley 2002 accounts for the trend over the past several years to make management more accountable (e.g., CEO certifications); increase financial disclosures (e.g., off–balance sheet disclosures); strengthen the role, authority, and responsibilities of advisers, and gatekeepers (e.g., requiring independent audit committees); limit or remove conflicts of interest of management and auditors (e.g., prohibiting insider loans and further limiting nonaudit services); establish a required government-sponsored regulatory oversight body (Public Company Accounting Oversight Board); and enhance the power of the SEC. Sarbanes-Oxley 2002 simply attempts to bolster the power of compliance by expanding the role of the board in monitoring and overseeing it, and the authority of gatekeepers and advisers. Thus, the problem is not that strong compliance efforts may still produce failures—as we see with some of the more noteworthy offenders of late—but that companies with strong compliance programs were insufficiently monitored, overseen, and audited.

The two critical mechanisms needed to protect against future gatekeeper-related offenses, however, may not be fully in place. As George Benston and his colleagues at the AEI Brookings Joint Center for Regulatory Studies noted, there must be "improved monitoring or oversight of the auditors themselves; and better (and more finely calibrated) incentives for those who conduct audits to carry them out properly."[273] These changes will surely become the critical features of any successful compliance or governance reform, as subsequent chapters will suggest. The challenge remains: Who should monitor the monitors? Who should audit the auditors? And what incentives are needed to ensure that all do their job?

A critic might add other challenges. First, in a report by the American Assembly on the Future of the Accounting Profession, Rod Hills and Russell Palmer argue that recent reforms to financial reporting systems require good judgment as much as good rules and procedures. They conclude that rules-based (GAAP) and principles-based (IASB) accounting methods must be wholly integrated. Second, never underestimate the perseverance of corporations to avoid the burden of regulations—this includes developing a new set of strategies in complying with certification requirements, including going private and for foreign firms delisting from major exchanges.[274] And finally, focusing on board and audit issues, as current governance reforms do, may simply take attention away from the unsettling idea that strong compliance programs and even effective enforcement strategies may have little to do with law abidance in certain firms.

If there is a defining feature of this most recent phase of corporate criminal law, it is the selective vigilance of federal law enforcement. This selectivity is most apparent when the scorecards of the SEC and other federal regulators are compared with that of state and local authorities. The aggressive use of the criminal law by the New York state attorney general and the district attorney of New York, in the immediate aftermath of Sarbanes-Oxley 2002, made most of their federal counterparts look like lapdogs, to once again borrow words from John Coffee. New York County District Attorney Robert Morgenthau and New York Attorney General Eliot Spitzer's battle against corporate deviance has many fronts: complex money-laundering schemes, complex economic crimes, conflicts in Wall Street research, mutual-fund abuses, excessive executive compensation, predatory lending by commercial banks, labor abuses in a number of retail industries, and marketing methods of health-care companies. Crossing many industries and types of crime, Spitzer looks for regulatory gaps that only the criminal law—or the threat of the criminal law—can fill. After targeting the insurance-brokerage unit of Marsh & McLennan, Spitzer observed, "It is clear that the federal government's hands-off policy with regard to insurance, combined with uneven state regulation, has not entirely worked."[275]

To its credit, the SEC under the leadership of William Donaldson and then Christopher Cox approved governance rules requiring, for example, mutual-fund companies to have independent chairpersons and that 75 percent of fund boards consist of independent directors. The SEC also distinguished itself with a series of high-profile transnational investigations and proceedings against Royal Dutch/Shell Group, Parmalat SpA, Ahold NV, Vivendi Universal, and Nortel.[276] And the SEC initiated an extraordinary number of Securities and Exchange Act and securities fraud cases against, among others, Walt Disney, American International Group (AIG), Raymond James Financial Services, Computer Associates International, Janus Capital Management, Bristol-Myers Squibb Co., Halliburton, Banc One Investment Advisors, Pilgrim Baxter & Associates, i2 Technologies Inc., Symbol Technologies, Strong Capital Management, Lucent, PIMCO Equity Funds' Mutual Fund Advisers,

CMS Energy Corp., Columbia Management Advisors Inc. and Columbia Funds Distributor Inc., Bank of America, Massachusetts Financial Services Corp., Grant Thornton LLP, Doeren Mayhew & Co. P.C., Northshore Asset Management, Banc of America Capital Management, BACAP Distributors, Banc of America Securities, Southwest Securities, TV Azteca SA de CV, and Azteca Holdings SA de CV.[277]

Also, the Corporate Fraud Task Force, formed in July 2002, initiated hundreds of new corporate fraud cases, and the Department of Justice continues to aggressively file cases. This aggressive posture is most evident as the Department of Justice and SEC increasingly collaborate. It is also apparent with the rise in the numbers of health care fraud criminal investigations, charges, and convictions.[278] But these numbers, as impressive as they seem, are still small. Most target individual white collar offenders rather than corporations. Moreover, the sustainability of law enforcement vigilance remains to be seen, particularly in light of the overturned conviction of Arthur Andersen, the now voluntary nature of the sentencing guidelines, and the premium placed on counter-terrorism and homeland security by federal law enforcement.[279]

If there is optimism for meaningful legislative and regulatory reform in the post-Enron era, it must be tempered by the reception given to the corporate criminal law over the course of history by courts, legislatures, and the business community. The failure to resolve questions of corporate personhood and blame, the duel between the aims of the regulatory state and the progress of business, and the inevitable gaming of regulations and regulators by corporations reflect a fundamental ambivalence over the use of the criminal law as a means of corporate social control. This is one of the best and yet least-offered explanations for the failure of the criminal law to effectively curb corporate deviance during alternating periods of corporate scandals, regulatory reform, and permissiveness. It is one of the best and yet least-offered explanations for why so little has changed from the turn of one century to the next. Those who credit current revelations of corporate fraud to the separation of ownership from control, failures of disclosure, gatekeeping, and enforcement may be right but, at the same time, mistaking pieces of the puzzle for the puzzle itself. The problem of corporate crime is more profound than improper revenue and expense recognition, improper asset valuation, and use of merger reserves.

CONCLUSION

For more than one hundred years, courts struggled with the very same basic issues of regulation in relation to matters of personhood, liability, blame, and punishment. All the while, legislatures sought solutions that often did little more than placate. Businesses managed reputations and regulators, not to mention their appearance of integrity. Investors, employees, consumers, and civil society activists cried foul again and again. The evolution of corporate criminal law was and is predictably disappointing.

One may look at present-day reforms and the business community's reaction or look back a full century. The strongly worded speeches of President Theodore Roosevelt in 1903 pushed for corporate accountability with an agenda that included a far greater federal role in the control and oversight of corporations, along with the possibility of a constitutional amendment granting such power. "When, as is now the case, many of the great corporations consistently strain the last resources of legal technicality to avoid obedience to a law for the reasonable regulation of business," Roosevelt said, "the only way effectively to meet this attitude on their part is to give the Executive Department of the Government a more direct, and therefore more efficient, supervision and control of their management."[280] Trust-busting meant taking on the largest of all corporations, focusing on the entity as an entity.

The response from Charles Dawes, president of the Central Trust Co. of Illinois:

> We do not want these general laws which cannot be enforced, and which malefactors laugh at, and honest businessmen fear as they fear any law which interferes with those acts on their part, which may not be harmful, which may be right, but are still placed under its ban. For, say what you will, the average American business man is a law-abiding citizen. . . . And these unworthy laws hinder him in his efforts to build up his community through his business. It is a blight today upon the proper progress of this whole country.[281]

Knowing the history of corporate criminal law, it seems likely that popular writers who tell the "inside" story of Wall Street's near boundless greed and den of thieves are far too generous in their prognoses for reform. It is difficult to ignore the constraints and failures of regulation and substantive law, not to mention the near boundless resources of businesses to shape regulatory policy and reform.[282] From generation to generation we hear of reputable business leaders committing crimes, watch spectacular courtroom dramas, and sense relief from stiff sentences that send a clear message to employees, managers, directors, bankers, accountants, and lawyers—violate state or federal law at your own peril. Modern-day robber barons, born-again corporate raiders, and aging white-collar icons are expected to learn important lessons about the government's intolerance for the perception that our markets are compromised by corporate fraud.[283]

Social scientists and legal scholars appeared similarly convinced when celebrating a new period of harsh corporate sanctions born from the Sentencing Guidelines for Organizations in 1991. In the era of postguidelines cases that followed, corporations are encouraged to implement expensive compliance systems that will, at once, promote business ethics and law abidance. Those organizations that resist the prescription of good corporate citizenship and fail to heed the lessons of the guidelines will face draconian sanctions, or so the cautionary tale goes. Once again, a strong message has been sent. And one cannot imagine a clearer message than the criminal indictment, conviction, and subsequent downfall of Arthur Andersen LLP. Joseph Berardino, former CEO of Arthur Andersen, reportedly told Michael Chertoff, then chief of the Criminal Division of the Department of Justice, "If you want to kill us, go kill us."[284] And they did.

With a certain sense of regulatory bravado, names of some of the most respected companies on Wall Street are now held out as deviant and deserving of criminal sanctions. If history is any guide, though, this period of active regulation will see a change, a regulatory shift that accommodates economic prosperity brought about by new forms of business innovation and risk taking. One day, perhaps not so long from now, the inevitability of regulatory laxity will bring about waves of seemingly unprecedented scandals that will surprise and shock us all, again.

CHAPTER TWO

Recognizing Personhood

Charlotte Williams worked tirelessly for Arthur Andersen for more than twenty years of the firm's eighty-nine-year history. In March 2002, she and hundreds of other devoted employees protested the criminal indictment of their beloved firm in front of the federal courthouse in Houston, Texas. "I was not involved in Enron," said Williams, "and I bet you couldn't find six people here who were."[1]

Senior managers at Andersen admitted shredding truckloads of Enron documents at the Houston office. But they said that none of the document destruction was authorized by the directors and officers from the firm's headquarters. These deeds were done without their knowledge and complicity. With tens of thousands of accounts, eighty-five thousand employees, and $9.3 billion in annual revenues worldwide, the odds were in their favor. The United States Attorney General's Office thought otherwise. "The indictment charges that destruction of evidence extended far beyond Andersen's Houston-based Enron engagement team. This is the indictment of a firm, of a partnership."[2]

The indictment was aimed directly at the partnership:

> On or about and between October 10, 2001, and November 9, 2001, within the Southern District of Texas and elsewhere, including Chicago, Illinois, Portland, Oregon, and London, England, ANDERSEN, through its partners and others, did knowingly, intentionally and corruptly persuade and attempt to persuade other persons, to wit: ANDERSEN employees, with intent to cause and induce such persons to (a) withhold records, documents and other objects from official proceedings, namely: regulatory and criminal proceedings and investigations, and (b) alter, destroy, mutilate and conceal objects with intent to impair the objects, integrity and availability for use in such official proceedings."[3]

All of this was done, according to prosecutors, after senior Enron officials made the Andersen audit team aware of the SEC inquiry into Enron's "special purpose entities" and the possible complicity of Enron's chief financial officer. Andersen was seen as attempting to undermine the government's investigation by destroying crucial evidence. "[W]hen determining whether to charge an entity with criminal conduct," Deputy Attorney General Larry Thompson noted, "we consider many factors, including the seriousness of the alleged offense, the firm's history of wrongdoing, the pervasiveness of the wrongdoing, and the need to deter others from similar activity. Under these standards, we felt compelled to seek the indictment of the Arthur Andersen partnership."[4]

When Andersen went to court facing federal criminal charges, Williams and other Andersen employees in Chicago, Philadelphia, and Washington, D.C., protested, wearing "I am Arthur Andersen" T-shirts and chanting "Drop the indictment! Save Andersen!" The image of Williams and thousands of employees staking a claim in *the firm* was designed to dispel any doubt that Andersen is more than a lifeless entity. Before the merger of Coopers & Lybrand and PriceWaterhouse in 1997, Andersen was the largest, most profitable, and arguably most prestigious of the top six accounting firms. Talent from the best business schools and very well-heeled clients were drawn to "the Andersen Way." The firm was consistently rated by *Fortune* magazine as one of the top one hundred U.S. companies to work for. Clients also gave it extremely high ratings.[5] Andersen maintained an entrepreneurial meritocracy with high standards and expectations throughout the organization. A criminal conviction would take a devastating institutional and human toll.

Andersen had weathered storms earlier. In 1997, it was a defendant in more than thirty lawsuits regarding advice it had given investors who lost hundreds of millions of dollars in the wake of the collapse of Colonial Realty of West Hartford, Connecticut. Andersen paid out more than $90 million to settle the case. In 2001 Andersen and its client Waste Management agreed to pay $229 million to settle a class-action suit about its questionable accounting practices. Andersen also faced a $7 million civil fine and an injunction forbidding the firm from future wrongdoing from the SEC, which accused it of "knowingly or recklessly" issuing false and misleading audit reports for Waste Management. Andersen, it was alleged, inflated Waste Management's earnings by $1.4 billion over the course of four years. In the end, the auditing firm was forced to pay Waste Management $20 million to settle malpractice charges. "Arthur Andersen and its partners failed to stand up to company management," Richard Walker, the SEC's director of enforcement, said, "and thereby betrayed their ultimate allegiance to Waste Management's shareholders and the investing public."[6] And there were other allegations of accounting fraud or irregularities in Andersen's past, from its work with the Sunbeam Corp. and audits of Mutual of Omaha and the Baptist Foundation of Arizona.

No plea or last-minute settlement could make the Enron matter go away. Andersen was convicted, given a $500,000 fine, and put on five years of probation. The conviction barred Andersen from auditing public clients. According to insiders, the indictment of the firm months earlier was nothing less than a corporate death sentence. Andersen came to an inglorious end in the spring of 2002, its remaining assets destined for bankruptcy court. The United States Supreme Court ultimately overturned the conviction for reasons having to do with the trial judge's jury instructions, but this decision was, at best, a hollow, symbolic victory for this once great firm.

The bright orange and black T-shirts of the protestors proclaiming "I am Arthur Andersen" conveyed considerable symbolic meaning. They signified that the firm was so much more than the few corporate officials who appeared in court to fight its last legal battle. It was more than its reputation on Wall Street or its market capitalization. Andersen was Charlotte Williams and her many coworkers. Andersen was its maintenance workers, executive assistants, auditors, accountants, managers, partners, and a host of other employees. Andersen was a human collective, a person in its own right consisting of tens of thousands of human beings. This collective reflected a distinct corporate culture, personality, and ethos grounded in a long-standing and grand tradition.

In a message to his firm in 1988, Duane R. Kullberg, Andersen's former managing partner and chief executive officer, captured the essence of this heritage. "Times change, traditions don't. Nor do such fundamental values as our commitment to clients, to innovation and to productive change . . . our commitment to the most stringent standards of professional and business ethics . . . our commitment to integrity and candor as embodied in Arthur Andersen's exhortation to 'think straight, talk straight.'"[7] Integrity, objectivity, and independence of thought and actions form the cornerstone of Andersen's value system.[8]

How could a firm of this scale, reputation, and rich corporate history die such a sudden and ugly death? How could the law-abiding work of so many be associated with the illegal acts of so few? One Andersen employee from Singapore echoed the views of many: "I could not say what was right and what was wrong, but one point I want to get across is that there were a lot of good people working at Andersen. And a lot of people lost their jobs for, I would say, no reason at all. To us, it just wasn't fair. And I am talking about people all over the world. Who would have thought? We were so far away from all that was happening in the States."[9] Others, including some staff credited with the foresight to leave Andersen before its demise, thought that the firm had lost its moral compass.

A deceptively simple answer to many of the questions surrounding Andersen's fate is that organizations can themselves be criminally liable. Andersen was indicted, prosecuted, convicted, and essentially executed because corporations, partnerships, and other business organizations are criminally liable and blameworthy as "corporate" persons, much as if they were "human" persons.[10] Implicit in this dual system of liability is the notion that there are times that, for reasons beyond regulatory convenience, corporate prosecutions are preferable if not important to satisfy penal objectives. That Andersen's prosecution was designed to send a strong message of intolerance for corporate malfeasance; that the indictment and zealous prosecution of Andersen was a clear exception to prevailing prosecutorial practice; that it took a special task force of the best federal prosecutors from around the United States; and that Andersen was a convenient brunt of the government's ire make for a far more complete answer.

To indict, prosecute, and convict firms like Andersen, corporations and partnerships are granted the status of a legal person separate and apart from their many employees and employers scattered in regional headquarters and field offices around the world. Corporate personhood is a metaphor with great descriptive power.[11] Personhood not only provides the fiction for attributing criminal liability, it also reflects a legal status that grants constitutional rights and privileges.[12] It transforms the concept of property, limits liability, and determines who has citizenship and who may be sued.[13] The recognition of personhood also reveals much about the function and purpose of the firm.[14] How personhood is conceived shapes and reshapes what is considered human and how corporations are ultimately defined.[15] And, for those who see law more generally as regulation, the grant of personhood is a perennial prerequisite.[16]

This chapter reviews the place of corporate personhood in the criminal law. The rhetoric of personhood and its evils are discussed. The challenges of making personhood relevant are also considered, first, in terms of existing regulatory law and practice and, second, as a foundation of substantive criminal law. There is a wide range of reactions to the ascription of human characteristics to corporate entities, from a vocal minority who attribute the evils of globalization to corporate personhood to a majority who do not know what to make of it; reject it as anthropomorphic, irrelevant; think it inefficient; or are simply ambivalent.[17] Reactions turn on the meaning and consequences of accepting or rejecting attributions of personhood. Most people seem to agree that if the law receives it as a fiction, legislatures and courts must wrestle with just how relevant it is and how it should be recognized. I conclude that corporate personhood is relevant, that the metaphor of personhood is integral to the notion of corporate criminal liability, and that the abolition of personhood will only further undermine the social control of corporations.

PERSONS AT THE LAW'S CONVENIENCE

Notwithstanding some important work on the personhood of organizations by Peter French, Thomas Donaldson, Joel Feinberg, Philip Pettit, and other moral philosophers, the rhetoric of corporate personhood has been far less profound than convenient. Courts and legislatures are far from shy in using the notion of personhood to expand a firm's rights and privileges. Judges, for example, do not wrestle with the subtle metaphysics of a corporation's existence when conceiving its rights under the equal protection clause of the Fourteenth Amendment to the United States Constitution. Questions of moral agency and the ontology of social collectives are nowhere to be found.[18] Confidence in these metaphysics is lost, however, and the legal fiction is somehow stretched too far when thinking of personhood together with principles of corporate criminal liability and blame. As we shall see, the prosecution of Andersen is very much an exception to a well-founded convention of individualism—a natural gravitation by regulators, legislatures, judges, and jurors to see corporate criminal liability as a singular product and function of human action.[19]

That corporations are persons at the law's convenience is accepted uncritically. Legislators and courts that seem to struggle with extending the idea of personhood to matters of liability and blame nevertheless watch as it is incorporated without reflection in both prosecutorial and sentencing guidelines. This dichotomy makes the substantive criminal law look both strange and weak: strange because prosecutors and judges sidestep the substantive law, still grounded in principles of vicarious liability, in favor of ad hoc standards of corporate citizenship, corporate due diligence, and good corporate governance—much of it cast in terms of postoffense behavior; weak because the substantive law, in the context of sentencing law, is seemingly unable to conceive of an organization in organizational terms.

One can argue that a broad conception of corporate culpability is the luxury of prosecutorial discretion and, moreover, a cornerstone of the calculus of blame in fashioning a corporate punishment. This line of argument is certainly fair. Prosecutorial discretion is a fixture of the criminal process. Fashioning a sentence necessitates an expansive conceptualization of blame. This argument, however, fails to consider that prosecutorial and sentencing guidelines are set in place to limit and constrain discretion. Moreover, this argument fails to accommodate the substitution of guideline-generated standards of corporate behavior for clearly articulated liability rules necessary for the fair and consistent processing of cases. This discretion and substitution tend to emasculate the substantive corporate criminal law.

The proper place of corporate personhood is at the foundation of a coherent substantive law. This conclusion, discussed below and in the next chapter, requires that courts see past acts of individual corporate agents to the features, characteristics, and decisions of firms that properly conceived of corporate crime as reflecting an organization. In doing so, the construct of personhood balances the rights and privileges that it engenders with the responsibilities and sense of accountability that should naturally attend. In considering the old and new metaphors of personhood, striking this balance is perhaps the single most important challenge.

REJECTING OLD METAPHORS

Debates over personhood of associations and groups date back to both ancient Rome and medieval times. Otto von Gierke speaks of the juristic structure of medieval corporations, matters of corporate governance, and corporate rights, responsibilities, and personalities. Twelfth-century glossators document the delictual liability of illegal associations and organizations.[20] Towns, village communities, and church congregations were objects of collective blame.[21] Attributions of culpability to hospitals, universities, and then joint-stock companies followed.[22] Clearly delineated property rights of corporations may be traced to the reign of England's King Edward III in the 1300s and aspects of corporate personhood to Edward IV in the late 1400s.[23] The controversy then was much the same as it is today: With collective action, who is to blame? How should culpability be parsed when the acts of individuals and groups meld? What does it mean to ascribe blame to groups? Medieval conceptions of personhood, personality, and agency shape our modern understanding of corporate personhood.[24]

In the United States at the turn of the twentieth century, as noted in chapter 1, courts employing personhood as a threshold requirement for liability realized the costs of viewing corporations as nothing more than artificial beings, invisible, intangible, and existing only in contemplation of law.[25] Enforcement concerns heightened as the nation witnessed the emergence of interstate commerce without effective legislative restraint.[26] "The fiction theory of corporate action," wrote Mark Hager, "was seen as a failed attempt by the law to deal with corporate facts without departing from individualistic premises."[27] The object of the criminal law, according to the court in *Commonwealth v. Pulaski County Agriculture & Mechanics Association* (1891) was to "reach and punish the real power in the matter, and thus prevent a repetition of the offense."[28]

In time, distinctions between natural and artificial persons seemed increasingly irrelevant for reasons far more practical and political than philosophical. States freely granted incorporation with general statutes, revealing their dependence on business enterprises for economic growth. It is no coincidence that as corporations increased in scale, power, and reach, theories of personhood changed. Both natural and artificial persons are real, if compelling policy requires as much. Simeon Baldwin concluded that with the remnants of fiction theory, the law was brought into harmony with society.[29] No additional explanation or justification is needed. "The corporation was to be deemed a citizen of the State to which it owed its existence," wrote Baldwin, "not because it was an artificial person of its creation, having no right to exercise its franchise elsewhere; not because its managing officers were exercising its franchises there; not because all its shareholders were in fact citizens of the State; but because the court had concluded to make the false assumption that they were, and to hear no proof to the contrary."[30]

A business enterprise exists apart from its owners and has rights and obligations. It acquires a common will and has a continual life. It is more than merely the sum of its members. The independence of the entity from its members rendered the exact membership of the entity immaterial; allowed for ownership of property and the assumption of debts; limited liability for owners; and permitted the delegation of responsibilities down the corporate ladder.

Charles Little suggested another important reason for discarding the fiction theory. "The sooner the idea of the corporate personality as a pure legal fiction is abandoned," he noted, "the sooner will some logical theory of corporate responsibility both civil and criminal be evolved."[31] As long as courts ruled against corporations as distinct entities, as they did though the early 1900s, the logic and theory of corporate responsibility remained illusive and regularly disputed.[32] In 1910, W. J. Lampton, a noted satirist, captured one side of this perennial debate in a poem entitled *The Offender*.

It is the person, not the thing
  That does the wrong, and he
Who is behind that which offends
  Must pay the penalty.
The fire that burns the house is not
  Called into court to stand
And answer for the crime, but he
  Who wields the firing brand.
The gun that shoots the man to death
  Goes free what it has done.
But he must take the punishment
  Who held the deadly gun.

The man behind the corporate crime
  Must of himself make good;
The corporation merely does
  What he directs it should.
It is the person, not the thing,
  Who right from wrong must know,
And he must suffer for the wrong
  When Justice strikes the blow.[33]

In a classic exchange that reveals the defining differences between individualists and collectivists at the turn of the twentieth century, Donald Cressey, John Braithwaite, Brent Fisse, and Gilbert Geis argued the merits of personhood, battling over whether corporations are like real persons, whether corporations act, whether they have legal and ethical responsibilities, whether they can commit crime and suffer punishment, and whether the same interpretative theory should be applied to individual and corporate criminals.[34]

The exchange by Cressey and his collegial jousters illustrates how four of the more important figures in the criminology of corporate crime can be wrong at once—or at least not completely right. What each would agree to, I suppose, is that the metaphysics of corporate personhood is of much more intellectual interest than actual relevance to substantive corporate criminal law.[35] Considerations of corporate ontology are often no more than metaphors, symbols, and expressions used by courts and legislatures to justify an extension or restriction of the role of the criminal law in regulating commerce. The notable cases of *Santa Clara, Standard Oil, New York Central & Hudson River Railroad* along with their progeny are best cast as judicial exercises of public and economic policy without any genuine consideration of personhood and its implications.

With the abandonment of the fiction theory of corporate personality, corporations were regularly awarded rights and privileges without any justification and, often, without explanation.[36] The progression of the corporate criminal law over the past century has been almost entirely atheoretical—or with unarticulated theory—in spite of a spirited debate held on the sidelines by lawyers, judges, legal intellectuals, and philosophers. At most, this debate merely created a body of philosophical and legal scholarship that never made its way into the substantive law. The suspicion that some logical theory of civil and criminal corporate responsibility would follow the abandonment of fiction theory proved wrong.

None of this is to say that questions about the moral agency and responsibility of corporations, groups, and associations are unimportant. Few moral quandaries are more difficult to resolve than this one. Few questions have greater theoretical consequences. Few questions are more deserving of systematic normative and empirical study. But the issue is incidental or, as Steven Walt suggests, generally irrelevant in the corporate criminal law. As noted in chapter 1, the substantive corporate criminal law proceeded without reform and, thus, without any recognition of personhood. Of course, corporations are criminally indicted because the threshold requirement of personhood allowed for such an accusation. Liability rules and theories of culpability, though, never matured to the point where aspects of the corporate person, the very essence of personhood, are considered as evidence at trial. With vicarious liability, there is no basis for courts to allow exploration of the characteristics and features of the organization (e.g., size, specialization, and delegation) that caused or contributed to the alleged crime. The diffusion or abdication of responsibility that comes from a firm's hierarchical structure, for example, is legally irrelevant.[37]

No one, it seems, seeks to bring the notion of personhood into the substantive criminal law. Prosecutors prefer to proceed against human rather than corporate persons. Jurors do not understand corporate personhood. And corporations with the necessary resources endeavor to undermine it where there is perceived risk.

THE NEW RHETORIC OF PERSONHOOD

In recent years, the rhetoric of personhood has moved from questioning its relevance to calling for its abolition. Civil society activists are increasingly vocal about how corporate personhood represents the evils associated with wealth concentration, corporate domination, globalization, and neoliberal disingenuity. Their efforts to abolish the notion of corporate personhood reflect a mix of individualism, fierce distrust of multinational corporate power, worries over grants of governmental immunities to corporate interests, and concerns over the corrupting influence of large corporations on government.[38] A grant of personhood, it is claimed, gives corporations of scale undeserved rights and privileges, disproportional powers, and boardroom privacy in debates that should be public. Ascribing personhood tips the balance of power and rights in favor of corporate over individual interests. We have become, to borrow words from Ralph Nader, a corporate economy, a corporate society, and a corporate state.[39] And the time has come, it is argued, to end the equivalence of human and corporate persons by abolishing corporate personhood.

This grassroots abolitionist movement meets with few legal victories. At most there are now a handful of local ordinances that abolish personhood or otherwise limit aspects of the corporate person. On April 25, 2000, the City Council of Point Arena, California, passed a resolution that explicitly rejects the concept of corporate personhood.[40] Porter Township, in Clarion

County, Pennsylvania, is one of the first localities to eliminate corporate claims to civil and constitutional privileges.[41] In December 2002, the township declared that corporations cannot assert their legal privileges to defeat laws protecting residents from toxic sewage sludge. Finally, in 1978, Wayne Township, Pennsylvania, passed an environmental protection ordinance barring corporations from engaging in business or planning to do business if they have a history of "consistent violations of law."[42]

The abolitionist's call for explicit limitations on corporate power and concentration resonates with symbolic significance.[43] It is an expression of concern with the arguably limitless power and limited responsibility of a "corporate society." At times the language seems extreme, but the worries are far from unfounded. The critical question is how to best ensure accountability and responsibility in ways that thwart these very real asymmetrical threats.

The voices of prodemocracy, consumer, environmental, civil rights, and social activists reveal additional fears that personhood status, coupled with an unlimited life span and limited liability, creates a breed of corporate persons, superhumans, corporate Frankensteins, and business supremacies that can defy law. The evils associated with corporate decisions make for a lengthy list, from leaking nuclear power plants to pig genes in fish.[44]

With personhood, corporations attain an aristocratic privilege in relation to taxes, control over the legislative process, and the right to self-regulation.[45] They can disappear at will through strategic bankruptcies. They can and often do avoid the full force of the law in regard to industrial accidents. The penetration of corporate America pervades "government, politics, law, taxation, environment, education, communications, foundations, athletics and even institutions formerly believed to be outside their influence, such as family or organized religion."[46]

Personhood also gives corporations the means to weaken governmental restraints on both their behavior and their growth. The idea of corporate personhood, therefore, is tied to the growing gap between rich and poor, corporate and environmental interests, and the controversy over globalization. Trade and investment liberalization fuel a dangerous brand of global corporate power. "History," according to one critic, "demonstrates that commercialism knows few boundaries that are not externally imposed."[47]

The sheer size of the corporate person is evidence. As Marshall Clinard and Peter Yeager noted in their treatise on corporate crime, giant multinationals produce a large share of all manufactured products, significantly influence consumer choice, affect technological advances, and move economic, industrial, and social development throughout the world.[48] Big businesses comprise aggregates of wealth that, in many ways, may be compared with those of small and medium-size countries.

Consider the influence and potential influence of corporate power re-vealed in rankings of the annual gross domestic product (GDP) and annual sales of the world's largest corporations.[49] As table 2.1 shows, of the one hundred largest economic entities in the world, fifty-one are corporations and forty-nine are countries. The two hundred largest corporations in the world account for over a quarter of economic activity and yet employ less than 1 percent of the world's workforce. These corporations have sales that together exceed the combined economies of all countries except the ten largest. The combined sales of the top two hundred corporations are nearly twenty times the combined annual income of the 1.2 billion people who live in "severe" poverty.[50] And, not surprisingly, casting corporate power in terms of foreign direct investment, private flow of capital, or percentage of market share is no less humbling, with an all-too-familiar set of multinational corporations casting a long shadow. Even when you define corporate power informally as, for example, the degree of influence on legislation and rule making or degree of access to governmental officials, corporate power is nothing short of immense.[51]

Power, privilege, and rights come with money and scale. Corporations are in "an almost impregnable constitutional position."[52] For the purpose of federal diversity jurisdiction, they are citizens of the state in which they are incorporated.[53] They have equal protection and due process rights, as persons, under the Fourteenth and Fifth Amendments.[54] With such rights as free speech, double jeopardy protection, and the right to trial by jury in civil cases, corporations have been personified.[55] And these rights are used defensively as a shield against necessary governmental regulation. They are used offensively, in corrupt and capricious ways, to maximize profit at the expense of workers' rights and the environment. In many ways, the rights of corporations trump those of human beings. Consider that their exercise of free speech, for example, is joined by an ownership and control of the very media that transmit the speech.[56]

Personhood allows corporate wealth to overly influence governmental policy. It places the government in an intermediary position between the will of the people and the will of the corporate body. A perversion of democracy is achieved by giving corporate values and objectives exclusive priority over "lesser" stakeholders. In spite of advances made in recent years to consider the voice and collective conscience of stakeholders other than sharehold-ers, the perversion of democracy includes the compromise of the political machine, a familiar casualty of personhood. Corporate campaign financing blurs the line between public and private organizations, leaving an appearance that the private sector controls the public sector. Campaigns turn into auctions.[57] Corporations have a disproportionate voice in elections due to a wealth privilege.[58] Corporate political contributions influence outcomes in

Table 2.1. Top 100 Economies by Country/Corporation (GDP/sales in $ million)

#	Country/Corporation	GDP/sales	#	Country/Corporation	GDP/sales
1	United States	11,667,510.00	51	Pakistan	96,114.84
2	Japan	4,623,398.00	52	Citigroup	94,713.00
3	Germany	2,714,418.00	53	Chile	94,104.94
4	United Kingdom	2,140,898.00	54	IBM	89,131.00
5	France	2,002,582.00	55	Philippines	86,428.60
6	Italy	1,672,302.00	56	Algeria	84,649.01
7	China	1,649,329.00	57	American Intl. Group	81,300.00
8	Spain	991,441.60	58	Egypt, Arab Rep.	75,147.83
9	Canada	979,764.20	59	Romania	73,166.83
10	India	691,876.30	60	Hewlett-Packard	73,061.00
11	Korea, Rep.	679,674.30	61	Nigeria	72,105.84
12	Mexico	676,497.30	62	Peru	68,394.96
13	Australia	631,255.80	63	Verizon Communications	67,752.00
14	Brazil	604,855.10	64	Ukraine	65,149.34
15	Russian Federation	582,395.00	65	Home Depot	64,816.00
16	Netherlands	577,259.60	66	Berkshire Hathaway	63,859.00
17	Switzerland	359,465.30	67	Altria Group	60,704.00
18	Belgium	349,829.80	68	McKesson	57,129.20
19	Sweden	346,404.10	69	Bangladesh	56,844.49
20	Turkey	301,949.80	70	Cardinal Health	56,829.50
21	Austria	290,109.50	71	State Farm Insurance Cos	56,064.60
22	Wal-Mart Stores	258,681.00	72	Kroger	53,790.80
23	Indonesia	257,641.50	73	Fannie Mae	53,766.90
24	Saudi Arabia	250,557.30	74	Boeing	50,485.00
25	Norway	250,168.00	75	Morocco	50,054.92
26	Denmark	243,043.30	76	AmerisourceBergen	49,657.30
27	Poland	241,832.50	77	Target	48,163.00
28	Exxon Mobil	213,199.00	78	Bank of America Corp.	48,065.00
29	South Africa	212,777.30	79	Pfizer	45,950.00
30	Greece	203,401.00	80	Vietnam	45,210.45
31	General Motors	195,645.20	81	J.P. Morgan Chase & Co.	44,363.00
32	Finland	186,597.00	82	Time Warner	43,877.00
33	Ireland	183,559.60	83	Procter & Gamble	43,377.00
34	Portugal	168,281.40	84	Costco Wholesale	42,545.60
35	Ford Motor	164,496.00	85	Johnson & Johnson	41,862.00
36	Thailand	163,491.50	86	Dell	41,444.00
37	Hong Kong, China	163,004.70	87	Sears Roebuck	41,124.00
38	Iran, Islamic Rep.	162,709.30	88	Slovak Republic	41,091.85
39	Argentina	151,501.20	89	SBC Communications	40,843.00
40	General Electric	134,187.00	90	Kazakhstan	40,743.19
41	Malaysia	117,775.80	91	Valero Energy	37,968.60
42	Israel	117,548.40	92	Marathon Oil	37,137.00
43	ChevronTexaco	112,937.00	93	MetLife	36,261.00
44	Venezuela, RB	109,321.90	94	Safeway	35,552.70
45	Czech Republic	107,046.80	95	Albertson's	35,436.00
46	Singapore	106,818.30	96	Morgan Stanley	34,933.00
47	Hungary	99,712.02	97	AT&T	34,529.00
48	New Zealand	99,686.83	98	Medco Health Solutions	34,264.50
49	ConocoPhillips	99,468.00	99	Croatia	34,199.98
50	Colombia	97,383.93	100	United Parcel Service	33,485.00

Source: Ranking based on corporate revenue data from *Fortune,* October 1, 2005, and GDP data from *World Bank World Development Indicators (WDI) Report* (Washington, DC: World Bank, 2005).

ways that no private citizen can—to the point where elections are often determined by corporate interests. Even worse, many convicted corporations are the most generous donors. During the 2002 election cycle, for example, $7.2 million in corporate funds went to Republicans and $2.1 million to Democrats, including $1.7 million from Archer Daniels Midland, $1.1 million from Pfizer, $875,400 from Chevron, and $741,250 from Northrop Grumman.[59]

Personhood limits regulation by fostering an aggressive lobby that corrupts the political process. Unparalleled access to government is the birthright of corporate personhood. Corporate money—in fact, shareholder money, some claim—corrodes political Washington, D.C. "[M]oney from the Enrons and others," according to the director of Public Citizen, "bought loopholes, exemptions, lax law enforcement, underfunded regulatory agencies, and the presumption that corporate officials could buy anything they wanted with the shareholders' money."[60]

In the end, prodemocracy activists seek the repeal of corporate personhood by a decision of the United States Supreme Court, by an amendment to the United States Constitution, by amendments to state constitutions, or by local ordinances that repeal the right to personhood. Another proposed constitutional amendment would establish a presumption favoring the granting of constitutional rights to individuals over corporations. It also would make corporations nonpersons with rights afforded only through state legislation or by popular referenda.[61] Activists also ask for a reconceptualization of corporate citizenship and the notion of socially responsible corporations. To give credence to voluntary codes of conduct and other self-regulatory mechanisms vastly overestimates corporate commitments to ethics.

The weakness in the activist call for abolition of personhood is simple: to defeat personhood means that the fight against corporate crime will be forever directed against individual miscreants. Strip away personhood and even the pretense of a corporate liability goes. If much of the reform agenda turns on ensuring corporate accountability and corporate responsibility, and if this Samson and Goliath play over corporate power has even a remote chance of success, personhood as a function of liability and blame must be embraced, not abolished. It is a distinct advantage to once again think of corporate persons as culprits fully deserving of the strictures of criminal law in ways entirely comparable to their human counterparts.

REJECTING THE LAW'S STATUS QUO:
GENUINE CORPORATE FAULT

Corporations should be treated as corporate persons—persons who satisfy the conditions of criminal liability with distinctive attributes and features. Yet no court has successfully married the attributes and features of organizations with theories of liability and culpability. Appeals to the notion of a corporate will, as evidence of corporate intentionality, reflected the emerging alter ego theory or theory of corporate organs found in English law. But this doctrine never took hold, at least in the United States. In the 1950s, Gerhard O. W. Mueller was right in seeing the notion of corporate fault as a weed in the field of jurisprudence allotted to the criminal law. It is nothing more than a hybrid of vicarious liability and absolute liability, sprinkled with the degenerated seeds of mens rea. *Herba responsibilitas corporationis M.* just seemed to grow without care and cultivation.[62]

Its growth was unremarkable, made more so by the fact that few people, if any, challenged the idea that corporate fault may be something more than vicarious—that it may reflect the very nature of what makes an organization a person capable of satisfying the conditions of criminal liability.[63] Two exceptions are noteworthy. First, as discussed earlier, guidelines for prosecution and sentencing of organizations extend well beyond the notion of vicarious fault. And second, models of corporate fault proposed by legal scholars recognize the guidelines' basic theoretical precepts, for example, the failure of a corporation to act proactively to prevent a crime or to respond reasonably in light of the discovery of an illegality. These models, even with distinct limitations, start a very important discussion about how to conceive of a genuine corporate fault.

MODELING CORPORATE FAULT

Models of corporate culpability cast the intentionality of corporations as genuine corporate fault. A genuine corporate fault rejects vicarious liability and instead explores culpability in relation to features, aspects, and attributes of the corporate form. Where a corporation's practices and procedures are inadequate to prevent the commission of a crime, for example, there is proactive corporate fault (PCF).[64] Corporations are liable for failures to make reasonable efforts to implement policies and practices that prevent crime. Evidence of reasonable efforts to prevent crime commission come from (1) the development and implementation of safeguards to prevent crime commission and (2) the delivery of clear and convincing prohibitions of criminal behavior in the form of business conduct codes, ethics codes, and compliance training programs. In order to avoid a finding of proactive fault, senior executives and top management should implement effective compliance programs, institutionalize systematic compliance reporting, and engage in or supervise periodic internal assessments.[65] This effort, in its entirety, is overseen by the board of directors or other governing body. The litmus test for PCF is a variant of the due diligence defense found in many other areas of corporate law.[66]

Proactive corporate fault was at the foundation of the recent criminal prosecution of Banco Popular de Puerto Rico for failure to report suspicious financial activity. In not filing "suspicious activity reports" accurately or on a timely basis, as required by the Bank Secrecy Act, Banco Popular compromised the ability of federal law enforcement officials to investigate possible money-laundering efforts. "Banks are our first line of defense against money launderers, drug dealers and even terrorists who would attempt to abuse our financial institutions," according to Assistant Attorney General Chertoff. "Banks that disregard their duty to conduct adequate due diligence and report suspicious financial activities allow themselves to be exploited for criminal purposes."[67]

A second model of genuine corporate fault, building on the notion of due diligence in PCF, shifts the focus of liability from fault prior to the time of the actus reus to fault in reaction to the actus reus. The reasonableness of a firm's reaction following the commission of a crime becomes the basis of finding both liability and culpability. Failure to undertake corrective measures in reaction to the discovery of an offense is the reactive corporate fault (RCF). At first, RCF was suggested only for less-serious offenses. Later scholars extended it to all criminal offenses.[68]

Consider the recent history of Koppers Industries Inc., the world's largest distiller of coal tar. Koppers is a leading producer of chemicals, carbon compounds, and treated wood products. Its corporate headquarters are located in Pittsburgh. In August 2002, Koppers pleaded guilty to two felony violations of the Clean Water Act and one felony violation of the Clean Air Act for hazardous environmental discharges causing air and water pollution. Restitution of $900,000 was paid to a trust, and the company was placed on probation for three years. No more than five months later, Koppers reached a settlement with the United States, agreeing to pay $2.9 million to resolve thousands of Clean Water Act violations. The settlement, comparable to others before it, required a commitment on the part of the corporate defendant to implement a risk-management program—an Environmental Protection Agency (EPA)-approved environmental management system—that will ensure compliance with federal and state environmental laws. This requirement will be bolstered by independent third-party audits of the company's compliance with all relevant environmental laws. The objective is simply to force Koppers to respond reasonably after the discovery of any future violations, rather than continuing a pattern of reactive fault.

Theories of corporate ethos (CE) differ from PCF and RCF in attributing fault to an organizational culture or personality that encourages corporate agents to engage in unethical and criminal acts.[69] Such an ethos is revealed in the corporate hierarchy, corporate goals and policies, efforts to ensure compliance with ethics codes and legal regulations, and the indemnification of employees.[70] Questions relating to the oversight role of the board of directors and how the corporation has reacted to past violations, if any, will supplement the inquiry. CE and corporate character theory are nearly indistinguishable. Corporate character theory finds culpability where there is (1) an illegal policy and an agent who carries out the policy; (2) an illegal act that is committed, authorized, ordered, or endorsed by a high managerial agent; and (3) the implicit ratification or endorsement of the violation by the corporation.

Corporate actions reflect a melding of individual decisions set within an organizational structure and embedded in an organizational culture.[71] Decisions and choices are communicated through corporate policy (CP). According to Peter French, the components of the corporation's internal decision structure (CID structure), consisting of the corporation's flowchart and procedural and recognition rules, make up the elements that define corporate intentionality. Whether the action is legal or illegal, the corporation establishes certain goals and objectives for the purpose of carrying forth the action or intention. Corporate intention may be found in the express corporate policy when an illegal act is accompanied by any one of the following three criteria: (1) a corporate practice or policy violates the law; (2) it was reasonably foreseeable that a corporate practice or policy would result in a corporate agent's violation of the law; or (3) a corporation adopts or ratifies a corporate agent's violation of the law.

Efforts to move beyond elementary imputations of intention and action are a positive step in the development of a conceptually sound body of law. These models, however, have distinct limitations.[72] Proposals for genuine corporate culpability, for example, were drafted with little concern for the basic requirements of criminal law. PCF, RCF, and CE models all but abandon the requirement for finding a mens rea, or a mental state associated with corporate acts.[73] Corporate culpability, like individual culpability, requires proof of scienter or a culpable mental state that corresponds to each objective element in an offense. Culpability must be considered in relation to the conduct of an agent or entity, the circumstances in which the conduct occurs, and the results that stem from the conduct.[74]

Under most state penal laws, proof of one of four mental states—purpose, knowledge, recklessness, or negligence—for each objective element satisfies the mens rea requirement.[75] The federal law is far less straightforward, with a hodgepodge of more than one hundred culpable mental state terms and combinations of those terms in the federal criminal code alone. Notwithstanding their number and form, these mental state requirements limit the reach of the criminal law to those individuals and organizations that demonstrate a certain willfulness, recklessness, intention, purpose, or knowledge in committing a prohibited act. In the recent case of *Arthur Andersen v. United States* (2005), for example, establishing a knowing act or consciousness of wrongdoing by Andersen is key in proving guilt beyond a reasonable doubt.[76]

Without some significant reconceptualization, models of genuine corporate culpability cannot be incorporated wholesale into the thousands of federal statutory provisions that allow for corporate criminal liability. Short of a recodification of the federal criminal code, a move to the adoption of a general scienter standard, or additional theoretical development, these models fail for reasons of implementation. For further theoretical development to be successful, commentators would have to address the fact that models such as PCF and RCF reflect only one level, or at the most two levels, of culpability. Legal theorists would have to account for an entire range of mental states, from purposeful to negligent corporate acts. That said, proactive and reactive fault may be used to guide prosecutors in charging decisions and with judges in fashioning sentences. They also serve as mitigating and aggravating evidence at the time of sentencing.

Moreover, both RCF and CE should be reserved to assessing post-trial culpability. Neither RCF nor CF accomplishes the narrow inquiry required by current preconviction culpability assessment. Architects of ethos- or culture-based models acknowledge this anomaly. Jennifer Moore agrees that "the corporate character theory is more suitable for use at sentencing than at trial."[77] Short of abandoning existing liability rules, any reliance on the conditions that predate or postdate the commission of a crime, as PCF and RCF prescribe, may also result in two kinds of decision-making errors. First, there is the risk of false positives, where a court in a preconviction assessment of culpability may find sufficient evidence of blame, which may result in a conviction, when there is insufficient evidence of culpability in relation to liability. And second, there is a risk of false negatives, where there is insufficient evidence of blame prior to conviction, which may result in an acquittal, when there is more than sufficient evidence of culpability in relation to liability.

RCF also fails to capture a genuine corporate culpability to the extent that a reactive program of a corporation reflects an entity's response to the discovery of an illegal act rather than the commission of the act itself. CE models explain little in the way of organizational culpability. They are models of organizational liability rather than culpability, which is made apparent by a summary of circumstances in which corporate fault may be found.

These limitations suggest the need for a conceptualization that allows for the definition and identification of organizational intentionality and action that are tied to the corporate person. This new conceptualization should make use of existing standards or grades of culpability and must be capable of implementation without a recodification of the federal criminal law or significant alteration of state law. A constructive model of corporate fault, described in chapter 3, accommodates these requirements.

INSPIRATION FOR A NEW THEORY OF CORPORATE LIABILITY

Following passage of the United States Sentencing Commission Guidelines, federal prosecutors developed their own guidelines and strategies that allow for the diversion from the criminal process corporations undeserving of criminal prosecution. United States attorneys were first guided by the spirit of informal and somewhat vague Department of Justice policy statements. These statements credited active cooperation by target companies; considered the proposed changes to firms that are designed to address organizational deficiencies; examined the willingness of a particular firm to enter into consent civil judgments; and acknowledged the payment of significant civil and administrative fines.[78]

As noted in chapter 1, the Holder Memo is an explicit renunciation of vicarious liability.[79] Eight factors identified in the Holder Memo guide prosecutorial discretion (see table 2.2). These factors include a wide range of variables, from efforts of organizations in responding to the discovery of illegalities to concerns about the collateral consequences of criminal charges to innocent agents. It is notable that the Holder Memo asks prosecutors to consider organizational factors that reveal organizational fault. In the absence of law reform, these factors are elevated in status to the default liability rules under federal law.

Throughout the Holder Memo, prosecutors are cautioned about resorting to vicarious liability where it would be unfairly strict to the "corporate person," that is, where it would be unfair. In considering whether to charge an organization, for example, prosecutors are asked to reflect on the pervasiveness of wrongdoing in the firm because "it may not be appropriate to impose liability upon a corporation, particularly one with a compliance program in place, under a strict *respondeat superior* theory for the single isolated act of a rogue employee."[80] The Holder Memo asks prosecutors to accept the fact that "[a] corporation, like a natural person, is expected to learn from its mistakes. A history of similar conduct may be probative of a corporate culture that encouraged, or at least condoned, such conduct, regardless of any compliance program."[81]

The Holder Memo also supports the previously informal policy of "flipping" culpable employees in exchange for prosecutorial leniency,[82] the consideration of a corporation's willingness to make restitution,[83] whether the corporation adequately disciplined wayward employees,[84] whether charging the corporation criminally is appropriate given the seriousness of the harm done,[85] and the extent to which innocent officers, directors, employees, and shareholders may suffer from a criminal indictment.[86]

The Thompson Memo, issued on January 20, 2003, by deputy attorney general Larry D. Thompson, makes some notable changes. First, another factor is added to the list of eight: the adequacy of the prosecution of individuals

Table 2.2. Holder Memo: Federal Prosecution of Corporations (1999)

Factors to be considered in charging corporations	Organizational factors to be considered in determining whether to seek an indictment
1. Nature and seriousness of offense	A. The corporation's preindictment conduct B. Whether a corporation has made a full disclosure
2. Pervasiveness of wrongdoing	A. The presence of a compliance program when a rogue employee has committed a single criminal act
3. The corporation's history of similar conduct	A. Evidence of a corporate culture that encourages or condones illegalities B. A pattern of similar charges suggesting that the corporation has not "learned from its mistakes"
4. The corporation's timely and voluntary disclosure of wrongdoing and willingness to cooperate	A. The corporation's willingness to identify the culprits within the organization B. The corporation's willingness to waive attorney-client privilege
5. The existence and adequacy of compliance programs	A. Whether the compliance program is well designed B. Whether the compliance program works
6. The corporation's remedial actions	A. The corporation's discipline of culpable employees B. The corporation's willingness to pay full restitution
7. Collateral consequences	A. The extent to which innocent employees are being harmed by the indictment B. The fairness of punishing innocent shareholders
8. The adequacy of noncriminal remedies	A. The fact that a corporation has been subjected to noncriminal sanctions without proper mediation

responsible for the corporation's malfeasance. Further, the Thompson Memo asks that prosecutors consider whether the corporation, while purporting to cooperate, engaged in conduct that impeded the government's investigation (see chapter 5), such as overly broad assertions of corporate representations of employees or former employees, inappropriate directives to employees or their counsel, incomplete production or delay in production of records, or failure to promptly disclose knowledge of illegalities. Most significant, the new guidelines direct prosecutorial attention to evidence of the authenticity and apparent efficacy of corporate compliance programs (see chapter 4).

Even a casual reading of the Holder and Thompson Memos leads to the conclusion that prosecutors used their vast discretion to craft a new set of liability rules, without legislative assistance, that largely abandon principles of vicarious liability and attempt to replace the substantive law with recognition of corporate personhood. But both sets of guidelines are no substitutes for the substantive law. While purporting to be part of a rigorous program of corporate prosecution, the guidelines reveal an equivocation that is remarkable. On the one hand, they admonish prosecutors that "[c]orporations should not be treated leniently because of their artificial nature nor should they be subjected to harsher treatment. Vigorous enforcement of the criminal laws against corporate wrongdoers, where appropriate, results in great benefits for law enforcement and the public, particularly in the area of white collar crime."[87] Yet on the other hand, the guidelines caution that "[p]rosecution of a corporation is not a substitute for the prosecution of criminally culpable individuals within or without the corporation. Because a corporation can act only through individuals, imposition of individual criminal liability may provide the strongest deterrent against future corporate wrongdoing. Only rarely should provable individual culpability not be pursued, even in the face of offers of corporate guilty pleas."[88]

Prosecutors are not alone with guidelines that extend well beyond the substantive law and yet fail as an adequate substitute. For example, judges have discretion at the time of sentencing to acknowledge organizational action and intention in mitigation or aggravation. One of the most remarkable things about the Sentencing Guidelines for Organizational Defendants, aside from the immense impact that they have had on the business community, is their extensive references to attributes of the organization that reflect blame and determine culpability (see table 2.3). The sentencing guidelines treat corporate fault as genuine, not attributed, imputed, or strict. According to the introductory commentary, culpability is uniquely organizational, "determined by the steps taken by the organization prior to the offense to prevent and detect criminal conduct, the level and extent of involvement in or tolerance of the offense by certain personnel, and the organization's actions."[89]

Of course, the assessment of blame following conviction is, by design, far broader than determining blame in relation to liability. But, the sentencing guidelines, like the Holder and Thompson Memos, look entirely out of place in relation to liability rules that clearly disregard aspects and characteristics of the organization. The sentencing guidelines tie the grading of culpability to the size of the organization, the prior criminal history, the firm's

Table 2.3. United States Sentencing Guidelines for Organizational Defendants (1991)

Factors to be considered in sentencing organizations	Organizational factors to be considered in sentencing
1. The organization must have established compliance standards and procedures to be followed by its employees and other agents that are reasonably capable of reducing the prospect of criminal conduct.	1. The size of the organization increases its culpability.
2. Specific individual(s) within high-level personnel of the organization must have been assigned overall responsibility to oversee compliance with such standards and procedures.	2. If the nature of business means it is more likely that deviance will occur, the organization is more culpable if it failed to put in place and enforce policies to prevent such deviance from occurring.
3. The organization must have used due care not to delegate substantial discretionary authority to individuals whom the organization knew, or should have known through the exercise of due diligence, had a propensity to engage in illegal activities.	3. Prior criminal history of the organization will increase its culpability.
4. The organization must have taken steps to communicate effectively its standards and procedures to all employees and other agents.	4. Corporate compliance programs that are perceived to be effective decrease culpability.
5. The organization must have taken reasonable steps to achieve compliance with its standards, e.g., by utilizing monitoring and auditing systems reasonably.	5. Organizational obstruction or impedance of justice increase culpability.
6. The standards must have been consistently enforced through appropriate disciplinary mechanisms, including, as appropriate, discipline of individuals responsible for the failure to detect an offense.	6. Organizational cooperation, admission of guilt, and acceptance of responsibility all reduce culpability.
7. After an offense has been detected, the organization must have taken all reasonable steps to respond appropriately to the offense and to prevent further similar offenses—including any necessary modifications to its program to prevent and detect violations of law.	7. Closely held organizations may be alter egos of management.

acceptance of responsibility, the presence of strong compliance initiatives, and so on.[90] Vicarious liability is mentioned only once in the introductory commentary, while organizational attributes of the "good citizen" corporation are noted in virtually every provision.

Amendments to the sentencing guidelines approved by Congress in 2004 are designed to give further guidance to organizations, regulators, prosecutors, and courts about the criteria for an effective compliance program, and they significantly extend the personhood analogy. Among a variety of other changes, these amendments recognize (1) the importance of corporations promoting an "organizational culture that encourages a commitment to compliance with law"; (2) that evidence of an organization's due diligence requires that a firm's governing authority, for example, its board of directors and "leadership[,] shall be knowledgeable about the content and operation of the program to prevent and detect violations of law"; and (3) that organizations "use reasonable efforts and due diligence not to include within the substantial authority personnel any individual whom the organization knows, or should have known, has a history of engaging in violations of law or other conduct inconsistent with an effective program."[91]

An argument may be made, perhaps a good one, that these guidelines amount to little more than a legal prop. The prosecutorial guidelines suggest an order and logic to the receipt, referral, and processing of cases that is simply not there. A matter becomes criminal or stays civil depending on which agency or department first receives or refers the case. With the sentencing guidelines, the issue is not one of random or arbitrary assignment. It is one of diversion. A relatively small percentage of all federal cases against corporations resolve with a conviction under which chapter 8 of the guidelines apply.

No matter how random the assignment or infrequent the use, however, the disconnect between these guidelines, the substantive law relied on in the guidelines, and the general part of the corporate criminal law remains a critical problem of law reform—a problem made more significant by the now voluntary nature of the guidelines. This disconnect calls for the adoption of liability rules that reflect the actions and intentions of an organization, rules that reflect corporate personhood.[92] Such adoption should be accomplished by maintaining an allegiance to the general part of the substantive criminal law that requires a finding of fault in relation to the person, the corporate person.[93]

CONCLUSION

Failure to specify the features and attributes of an organization that satisfy the conditions and requirements of the criminal law runs a number of risks. First, there is a risk that the factors resulting in the attribution of liability

and blame will remain mired in a strange brew of law enforcement, prosecutorial, and judicial discretion. In defending the reasoning behind the
decision not to indict KPMG for selling abusive tax shelters, former United
States attorney David Kelly concluded, "Really you have to think about what
is most effective, what serves the American people best."[94] And what serves
the public best? What is fairly deemed individual versus corporate liability?
The impact that a criminal investigation, indictment, and conviction might
have on a firm? The impact on an industry? The fact that criminal liability
is distinctly personal, that it requires human action? Of course, but as one
of the nation's leading prosecutors acknowledges, the decision is not really
reducible to a specified set of principles, factors, variables, or judgments. "It
is not fair to try to get into an analysis of our discussions within the department about the best approach to take in this case," Kelly argues. "What is
most important is that the product came out at the end of the day. You look
and try to analyse how a hot dog is made: what is important is how it tastes
when it comes out, and I think the taste we have is pretty good."[95]

Second, there is a risk that those charged with authority to make this
hot dog, to make and mix this brew, will not know which ingredients to use.
Consider the factual questions that jurors grappled with at the end of the
Andersen trial. Was the scramble by the firm to shred Enron-related documents a calculated effort to prepare for lawsuits and criminal probes? Did
Andersen act with a consciousness of wrongdoing? In closing arguments,
Assistant U.S. Attorney Sam Buell told jurors that Andersen was "girding for
the Enron wars." Rusty Hardin, Andersen's lead lawyer, countered by claiming that prosecutors failed to introduce evidence that anybody destroyed
documents, or otherwise obstructed justice, with an improper purpose. It
was merely "routine compliance with a policy designed to protect client
confidentiality."[96]

After some time deliberating, jurors were deadlocked. They sent a series
of notes to U.S. District Judge Melinda Harmon, the most important of which
read: "If each of us believes that one Andersen agent acted knowingly and
with corrupt intent, is it for all of us to believe it was the same agent? Can one
believe it was Agent A, another believe it was Agent B, and another believe
it was Agent C?"[97]

"I'm kind of in a position of a case of first impression, which is terrifying
for a district judge," Judge Harmon said from the bench. "If someone knows
of a case that's directly on point, I would really urge you to give me a cite
right now so I don't make a mistake and rule incorrectly."[98] Her ruling that
jurors do not have to agree on who committed the crime so long as each
juror believes that somebody at Andersen did translated common sense and
gut intuition into law. But, in the most important trial of one of the most important global accounting firms in the world, is it conceivable that liability

rules are so unsettled as to be unclear to the presiding judge? The answer, regrettably, is yes. With all of the efforts to fix blame on Andersen, KPMG, and a host of other firms, and with all of the regulatory and prosecutorial resources the federal government has, the only thing that everyone forgot was a substantive criminal law that applies to organizations.[99]

CHAPTER THREE

Constructing Fault

WorldCom's chief executive officer, Bernard J. Ebbers, adopted an elementary business strategy at the helm of the telecommunications giant: growth through acquisition using company stock. The success of his strategy hinged on market timing and relationships. Most of all, he needed WorldCom's stock price to continue its meteoric rise while carefully managing Wall Street's often unreasonable expectations for quarterly numbers. This challenge proved too much for Ebbers, whose demands for vigorous top-line growth in a declining marketplace could not be met legitimately. While deftly building a personal fortune, Ebbers effortlessly deceived the board of directors, WorldCom employees, and the investor community into believing revenue and profit numbers that were next to pure fantasy. As the disconnect between what Ebbers said and the company's performance grew, Scott Sullivan, chief financial officer, and David Myers, WorldCom's controller, sought to cover the difference by inflating reported revenue, by playing with the capitalization of line costs, and by making other accounting entries that violated generally accepted accounting principles. Ebbers, later convicted of fraud and making false filings, apparently knew of these fraudulent practices, and so did employees in the general accounting group at corporate headquarters, as well as the staff in other financial and accounting groups that were complicit in the scheme. When the dust settled, there was more than eleven billion dollars in false or unsupported accounting entries made from 1999 until 2002 in the financial systems of WorldCom. This is the largest accounting fraud in history. The civil penalty paid by WorldCom was certainly one of the largest—$2.25 billion.

The investigation of WorldCom focused on the corporate culture set by Ebbers. It was a culture that considered revenue and profit targets above all else; inhibited dissent from Ebbers's dictates; limited the flow of financial information to those who needed to know; and delegated responsibility to senior managers known to having acted unethically—if not illegally. In one of two board-sponsored reports on WorldCom submitted to the Securities and Exchange Commission, Ebbers was described as the centrist figure responsible for the pressures and inept leadership that resulted in this massive fraud. According to the report, Ebbers "demanded the results he had promised, and he appeared to scorn the procedures (and people) that should have been a check on misreporting. When efforts were made to establish a corporate Code of Conduct, Ebbers reportedly described it as a 'colossal waste of time.' He showed little respect for the role lawyers played with respect to corporate governance matters within the Company. While we have heard numerous accounts of Ebbers's demands for results—on occasion emotional, insulting, and with express reference to the personal financial harm he faced if the stock price declined—we have heard none in which he demanded or rewarded ethical business practices."[1]

The scale of fraud may have been remarkable, truly remarkable, but the story is an old one. From the days of robber barons to the near downfall of Salomon Brothers, each generation lays claim to its own incomparable scandal. Never before have markets been so affected. Never before has there been a collapse of this scale. Never before have we reached such a low point in corporate governance. Never before have so many of the "bad guys" escaped indictment.

In 1903, the downturn on Wall Street was attributed to the overreaching of those whose sins and excesses were outdone only by their greed for conquest, power, and money. President Theodore Roosevelt decried the malefactors of great wealth and the crooked ways of the Street in pushing the government's role in combating corporate deviance.[2]

Unethical and illegal practices cut across a wide range of industries. Beyond those who exploited lax enforcement of state laws lay a vast combination of companies and subsidiaries.[3] Officers and directors of legendary companies were indicted, along with their parent and subsidiary corporations, in an unparalleled battle against trusts and a concentration of individual wealth.

High-profile prosecutions of demonized corporations were front-page news in the early 1900s, as much as, if not more so than, today. One of the first companies to achieve such notoriety was Standard Oil Co. of Indiana, convicted of 1,462 counts of rate discrimination in 1907. The presiding federal district court judge, Kenesaw M. Landis, became somewhat of a folk hero after imposing his sentence of a $29,400,000 fine. Thereafter, Judge Landis was known as the Tamer of the Standard Oil Octopus. The message to Wall Street was unmistakably clear: corporations with cultures that allow for a knowing and reckless violation of laws will face fines and, where fines are insufficient, dissolution.[4]

Accounts of corrosive corporate cultures; cultures of swashbuckling bravado; risk taking without accountability; profit taking without disclosure; conflicts without safeguards; excessive arrogance and corrupted institutions with no accountability; rewards for those who set no limits on legality; leadership that encourages managers to mislead with "financial engineering"; and slavery to the Wall Street numbers game are as timely today as they were a hundred years ago. And one need not go back that far in time. *Liar's Poker, Barbarians at the Gate, The Great Wall Street Scandal, Serpents at the Rock, In Good Faith,* and *Den of Thieves* seemed grand and insidious not so long ago. Of course, no more so than today's *Company of Fools, Power Failure, Anatomy of Greed, The Number, Take on the Street, Final Accounting, The Corporation, Conspiracy of Fools,* and *Smartest Guys in the Room.* Each portrays good guys and bad guys and reveals much grey. Each captures misdeeds by the wealthy elite that are traceable to an errant corporate culture, perverse incentives, failed leadership, intense pressure to perform, and lax oversight from boards, regulators, and auditors. All end in an unimaginable but nevertheless predictable fall from grace, leaving difficult and sometimes intractable questions about responsibility and blame.

A CONSTRUCTIVE CORPORATE FAULT

While the scripts of these crimes are all too familiar, there are no theories of corporate criminal liability, beyond those described in chapter 2, capturing the essence of what makes a corporate crime an organizational crime rather than a crime committed in an organization by an agent. After a long history of corporate crimes, we still do not know how to answer some of the most basic legal questions: In which cases should liability and blame for criminal acts of corporate agents be attributed to corporate entities? How should liability and blame be conceived and then attributed to a company? In what ways does the conception of corporate liability and blame affect possible punishment?

These three deceptively simple questions are answered below in offering a model of constructive corporate fault that extends well beyond existing law by considering aspects of the corporate person and thus attempts an accommodation between the collectivists and the individualists, the Roosevelts and the Wilsons. Constructive fault assumes that corporations may be distinguished from individual agents or aggregations of agents on the basis of their structure, decision making, size, formality, functionality, and complexity.[5] It also assumes that corporate criminal liability should be reserved for crimes committed by agents whose actions and intentions are related in ways that reflect features and attributes of the organization, and agents whose relationship to the organization is such that their actions are in the name of the firm and thus those of the organization.[6] Evidence of corporate criminal liability under a model of constructive fault may be found in distinct aspects of the organization, such as policies, goals, and practices that reveal more than the individual or collective nature of agents' intentions and actions.[7]

These assumptions explicitly reject principles of vicarious liability, instead shifting the focus of inquiry to the identification of a principal's or entity's acts and intentionality, rather than an agent's or employee's. There are countless examples of the problems with vicarious attributions of fault in corporate crime cases. Most turn on the disconnect between actions of a wayward agent and corporate policies and processes; a disconnect that at times approaches strict liability.[8] An extreme but telling example is found in *United States v. Hilton Hotels*, where a purchasing agent violated corporate policy and the express instructions of management in threatening a supplier with the loss of business over an illegal payment of an association fee. In a very strict interpretation of vicarious fault, the United States Court of Appeals for the Ninth Circuit ruled that a corporation is liable under the Sherman Act for the act of an agent even when such acts disregard general corporate policy and the express instructions given to the agent.[9]

Finding corporate fault should require much more. Courts should rely on evidence of organizational action and intention that is constructive, that is, constructive in the sense of construing facts, circumstances, conduct, and intentionality of an organization, prompting a fair or reasonable attribution of liability. Constructive corporate liability exists where there is proof of an illegal corporate act and a concurrent corporate criminal state of mind. The former requirement may be satisfied by sufficient evidence of an act that is owned or authored by the corporation. The terms *ownership* and *authorship* reflect the connectedness between an agent's acts or intents and that of the organization. The latter captures an action or intention that is not attributable to any single agent or group but comes from the organization. Such actions and intentions will almost always be derivative of individual or group action.

Beyond laying the groundwork for a substantive corporate criminal law—one on par with that crafted by the Sentencing Guidelines for Organizations, constructive fault serves other important objectives. As shall become apparent in subsequent chapters, corporations are deft at gaming both regulators and prosecutors with strategies that use the complexity of the corporate form. These strategies include avoiding the application of law, exploiting lack of law enforcement, and shifting blame away from the entity. Each plays on the ambivalence over corporate criminal liability and the consensus that existing law, grounded in theories of vicarious liability, does not fairly approximate or attribute fault. Liability rules must look past the actions of individual agents and instead examine the actions of the organization as an "organizational" actor.

Constructive fault permits fact finders to move beyond the strictures of subjective evidence of culpability in order to find corporate states of mind that may be more reasonably deduced or inferred—with or without the assistance of subjective evidence of the defendant. The search is for the best possible estimation of a corporate mental state through actual knowledge, as well as through reasonable inferences. Did the actions of the corporation, given the circumstances, objectively manifest intention or purpose, awareness or knowledge, indifference or recklessness? Did the corporation, given its size, structure, and complexity, know of the risks of injury? Notwithstanding any evidence of actual knowledge, these are the central questions of constructive fault.

CORPORATE ACTION

Culpable organizational action may be identified through an objective test where it is determined that *given the size, complexity, formality, functionality, decision-making process, and structure of the corporate organization, it is reasonable to conclude that the agents' acts are those of the corporation.* This reasonableness test is a threshold assessment that separates cases in which corporate acts have occurred from individual noncorporate acts or secondary acts. It replaces vicarious liability with a constructive test of primary corporate action.

If ever there were a case to be made for objective criteria in a determination of culpability, it is in the context of corporate criminal liability. This is not to say that a new objective standard of corporate liability is warranted or desirable. There is a critical distinction between objectivity as a nonsubjective method of determining culpability and objectivity as an external standard of behavior. This distinction is made with great clarity by Hall, who contrasts the "reasonable man method" of determining culpability with "objective liability." The reasonable man method, recognizing its limited gender reference, is an appraisal of available evidence by reference to a reasonable person or, for our purposes, an organization of like size, complexity, and so on. Such an appraisal is the objective feature of constructive culpability. The objective liability method, on the other hand, is a standard, not a method of appraising evidence. It erects an objective standard of what a person or corporation should have done, based on what a reasonable person (corporation) would have done in like circumstances. This distinction is essential, because constructive action and fault do not represent a new standard of corporate liability. Constructive action and intention simply facilitate the determination and attribution of blame to an entity.

Liability rules found in the Model Penal Code (MPC) approximate a constructive test as a means of determining organizational action.[10] In determining whether it is reasonable to conclude that agents' acts are those of their corporations, courts and juries will no doubt develop a calculus, considering evidence relating to delegation, authorization, and reckless toleration, as well as the status of the agent who has acted, and the scope of his or her authority.[11] Even though such evidence is critical and often dispositive, it may not always be sufficient. Notably, some courts have dispensed with the requirement, found in most state statutes, that the prosecution prove that the conduct in question was performed, authorized, ratified, adopted, or recklessly tolerated by directors, officers, or high managerial agents. Consider, for example, the case of *Commonwealth v. Beneficial Finance Co.*, where a Massachusetts court upheld a trial court's instruction that the definitive test of corporate liability is the existence of a relationship between the offending individuals and the corporation, such that "the acts and the intent of the individuals were the acts and intent of the corporation."[12] It is this very relationship that lies at the heart of the reasonableness test. The stronger the agent-entity relationship, the more reasonable it is to consider an agent's action to be a construction of the corporation's.[13]

As the agent-entity relationship increases, choices that form actions become more impersonal. Agents who have been given the authority through delegation to carry out their duties, with a certain power and responsibility, act for the organization, on behalf of the organization, and with a consideration of organizational goals and objectives. Ladd labeled these choices social decisions, or actions "performed by an official as actor but owned by the organization as author."[14] The reasonableness test looks to the relationship of the agent to the entity and determines who, constructively, is the author. The strength of authorship determines the reasonableness of the construction.

Searching for authorship of action under a constructive test will likely lead to many of the same dispositions in cases where the entity-agent relationship is strong. Strength of the entity-agent relationship may be assessed in a number of ways. As a preliminary matter, fact finders will no doubt focus on the status of the agent in the corporate hierarchy. Were the defendants the officers, directors, or senior managers of the firm? Members who constitute the "alter ego" or "inner circle," as Mueller has so aptly described, are clothed with corporate authority and considered to be extensions of the corporate entity.[15] In other cases, however, where the entity-agent relationship is unclear or remote, the determination of constructive corporate action will be far less mechanical than it would be for standards of vicarious liability.

Corporate Action in Practice

Theories of corporate liability translate poorly in practice. This point is worth noting because liability rules may be elegant, conceptually clear, and generally ignored. Consider that following the President's Executive Order on July 9, 2002, creating a Corporate Fraud Task Force, an order that marshaled the resources of a host of federal agencies to combat corporate crime, there have been criminal and civil enforcement actions against innumerable firms, including Adaptec, Adelphia, Allfirst, Alliance, Anicom, AremisSoft, Biocontrol, Capital City Bank, Capital Consultants, Cendant, Commercial Financial, Countrymark, Critical Path, eConnect, HealthSouth, HPL Technologies, Homestore, ImClone, Indus, Informix, Leslie Fay, Manhattan Bagel, McKesson, Mercury Finance, Motorcar Parts, NewCom, Peregrine Systems, PinnFund, Quintus, Rite Aid, Robles/Svoboda, Sirena Apparel, Smith Technologies, Targus Group, Unify, WorldCom, and Zurich Payroll.

If extant law were taken literally, most of these firms would have been prosecuted as firms. All indictments, however, were against individual corporate officers and employees. Organizational defendants were difficult if not impossible to find. This is far from surprising given the definition of corporate fraud adopted by the Department of Justice. Corporate fraud includes (1) falsification of corporate financial information, (2) self-dealing by corporate insiders, and (3) obstruction of justice, perjury, witness tampering, or other obstructive behavior relating to any of the aforementioned categories. But it is remarkable given the prevailing law of vicarious liability.

In addition to an individualist frame of reference for "corporate" fraud, there is a sense that fraud is less a function of an organization than its agents. Corporate crime generally is not conceived of as a pervasive failure of organizations; it is a function of failed governance or failed leadership by officers and directors in a select few companies. "Our financial markets had been shaken by a series of episodes of significant criminal conduct at the highest levels of some American corporations," notes Larry D. Thompson, the chairman of the Corporate Fraud Task Force, "I emphasize *some* corporations. This aberrant business and corporate behavior has occurred in, I believe, a small minority of American businesses."[16]

Interestingly, in the first annual report of the task force to the president, criminal prosecutions of organizations as "corporate fraud defendants" were clearly the exception—and the exception discussed is Andersen. Of course, the United States Sentencing Commission reports between two hundred and three hundred convictions of corporations under chapter 8 of the guidelines each year. A rather extensive list of criminal indictments and plea agreements of corporations is also promoted by the Department of Justice and other federal agencies. But the numbers, even including reported state prosecutions of corporations, are still small and arguably insignificant given the number and seriousness of individual prosecutions. Also, as we shall see in subsequent chapters, the same may not be said of civil and regulatory enforcement, especially given the growth of citizen-initiated false claim act cases called qui tam suits.

The recent scandal at Rite Aid, a large, publicly traded retail drugstore chain, is a fine illustration of a limited conception of corporate action, in addition to a common trend to spare firms from vicarious criminal liability no matter how systematic and pervasive the fraud is and no matter how senior the perpetrators are. In a case that resulted in the largest single restatement of corporate earnings in our nation's history, allegations of fraud, witness tampering, fabrication and destruction of evidence, and false reporting of financials totaling more than $1.6 billion led to a thirty-seven-count indictment of the former Rite Aid chief executive officer, chief financial officer, chief operating officer, counsel and vice chairman of the board, and senior vice president—the highest-ranking corporate managers. Charges included conspiracy, securities fraud, false statements, mail fraud, wire fraud, obstruction of justice, perjury, and misprision of a felony.

At the heart of the complaint were allegations that Martin Grass, former chief executive officer, Frank Bergonzi, former chief financial officer, and Franklin Brown, former vice chairman, conducted a wide-ranging accounting fraud scheme that significantly overstated Rite Aid's income in each quarter from May 1997 to May 1999. The overstatements were consistent and dramatic, resulting in a restatement of the company's pretax income by $2.3 billion and net income by $1.6 billion. The SEC chronicled additional illegalities, including the systematic inflation of deductions taken against vendors for damaged and outdated products; the failure of Rite Aid to record an accrued expense for stock appreciation rights it had granted to employees; the reversal of actual expenses incurred and already paid; the making of improper adjusting entries to reduce cost of goods sold and accounts payable to manipulate Rite Aid's reported earnings; the overstatement of net income by overcharging vendors for undisclosed markdowns; and the false recording of entries to reduce accounts payable and cost of goods sold reflecting rebates purportedly due from two vendors.

Wayne M. Carlin, SEC regional director of the commission's Northeast Regional Office, offered these somber words about Rite Aid on behalf of the SEC: "The charges announced today reveal a disturbing picture of dishonesty and misconduct at the highest level of a major corporation. Rite Aid's former senior management employed an extensive bag of tricks to manipulate the company's reported earnings and defraud its investors. At the same time, former CEO Martin Grass concealed his use of company assets to line his own pockets. When the house of cards teetered on the edge of collapse, Grass fabricated corporate records in a vain effort to forestall the inevitable. The Commission's enforcement action, and the related criminal prosecutions announced today, demonstrate that there will be no refuge for corporate executives who commit this kind of wrongdoing."

After a host of guilty pleas, fines, and short terms of imprisonment, the old Rite Aid is a distant memory. Rite Aid now has a new management team.

"This is a new Rite Aid," corporate spokesperson Karen Rugen notes. "We've overhauled the way Rite Aid does business, established a new corporate culture, put in strict financial controls, and significantly improved our operations, financial performance, and balance sheet." Most interesting, most telling, and most prescient, their corporate logo is adorned by the words With Us, It's Personal. After all, the conception of Rite Aid's liability was personal—affixed to its agents—and not the corporate person.

It is only fair to ask how representative is the case of Rite Aid. There is, however, no ready answer to this question. Examining countless cases that meet the test of constructive corporate action reveals few discernible patterns of prosecution. Consider, for example, the case against HealthSouth, the nation's largest outpatient surgery, diagnostic imaging, and rehabilitation health-care services firm, with nearly seventeen hundred locations. In an investigation launched in March 2003, the FBI, IRS, and other federal and state law enforcement agencies uncovered an elaborate accounting fraud stretching back to 1996, when senior officers determined that they were producing sufficient earnings to meet Wall Street's expectations. The CFO from 1984 to 1997, along with a group of corporate officers, inflated earnings and falsified reports of HealthSouth's financial condition, resulting in misstatements of net income, receivables, EPS, assets, and liabilities in required financial statements. The accounting fraud also resulted in false financial statements to HealthSouth lenders. In the ongoing criminal investigation of the company's finances, fifteen former officers and senior corporate officials have been charged with fraud. Recently the CEO was indicted on eighty-five counts of fraud and other federal offenses, the first prosecution under Sarbanes-Oxley, alleging that earnings at HealthSouth were fraudulently inflated by $2.7 billion at his request. In spite of evidence of action and complicity at the highest levels of the company, the CEO was acquitted and, as of this writing, HealthSouth has not been criminally indicted.

Just For Feet Inc. (JFF) joins Rite Aid and HealthSouth as candidates deserving of constructive corporate fault. In 1999, JFF was the second-largest shoe seller in the United States, with sales of $775 million and stores in thirty states. Later that year, the company lay in ruins seeking bankruptcy protection. The company's downfall was attributable to fraudulent accounting practices involving JFF's president, an executive vice president, and executives from some of JFF's key vendors, Fila USA, Adidas America, and Logo Athletic. Senior management engaged in a conspiracy with these vendors to convince outside auditors of additional receivables in order to assist JFF in fraudulently overstating its earnings. All were convicted of conspiracy and fraud offenses, including JFF's president.

Those who peek into the black box of prosecutorial discretion identify a host of factors that influence charging decisions, including the party or source initiating or referring the investigation; the quality of defense counsel's preindictment advocacy; the defendant's postoffense behavior; and the collateral consequences of indictment and conviction. None of this is to suggest, however, that the single most significant factor is the strength and availability of inculpatory evidence. But, surprisingly, this evidence is not measured against a consistent and clear liability rule. Vicarious liability, in large part because of its strict attribution, is generally ignored. The standard of constructive corporate action is proposed in its place in order to facilitate fair and reasonable attributions.

CORPORATE MENTAL STATES

A constructive corporate act must be joined with a corresponding and concurrent corporate mental state. Under current federal and state law, mental states of agents are imputed to the entity and immediately become an attribute or ingredient of the corporation.[17] Inferences made from the agent's behavior form the basis for the attribution of intention.[18] Unfortunately, the attribution may be far from satisfactory.[19] Again, the same criticisms raised in examining the attribution of criminal acts to corporations are prominent. An organization, no matter how large or small, centralized or decentralized, is given a state of mind from a single agent or, on rare occasions, a collective of employees. This attribution may be acceptable when the organizational agent is an owner or officer but unacceptable when it is from an actor who, despite attempts to benefit the corporation, does not bear a meaningful relationship to the organization. To overcome this problem, constructive tests identifying corporate acts are joined with a comparable method of approximating corporate culpability, a constructive assessment of culpability that is met by both objective and subjective evidence.

Constructive culpability considers a wide range of states of mind derived from organizational attributes, features, processes, and structures in relation to the actions of corporate agents. In contrast to other models of corporate fault, constructive culpability considers corporate intention, knowledge, recklessness, and negligence. Constructive fault, therefore, is quite different from corporate ethos (CE), proactive corporate fault (PCF), reactive corporate fault (RCF), and models of vicarious negligence, which are proxies for single mental states. It is unlike the English Crimes Act, which relies exclusively on evidence of corporate policies, or reactive and proactive fault. The same may be said of the Australian Model Criminal Code, which turns on certain kinds of corporate cultures or the tacit approval of the board of directors or a high managerial agent.

In 1970, the National Commission on Reform of Federal Criminal Law acknowledged the "confused and inconsistent ad hoc approach" of federal courts to mens rea.[20] This observation was repeated in 1990 by the Federal

Courts Study Committee, which again called for a recodification of the federal criminal law.[21] With over one hundred different mental states and mental state combinations in Title 18 alone, it is not unreasonable to reexamine the integrity of the United States Code.[22] Yet while the federal law contains a very extensive and odd collection of culpable mental states, it does not defy classification. The drafters of the Model Penal Code provided a hierarchy of culpable mental states for state law that captures many of the mental state distinctions found in the federal criminal law as well.[23] Corporate mental states are discussed below in relation to the MPC classification.

Purposeful Corporate Acts

The notion of intention, or the definite expectation that certain consequences will follow a given act or volition, is traditionally tied to three elements: purpose, foresight, and desire.[24] Purpose reflects motives, aims, and objectives that accompany intention. A purpose is a reason for doing something or an explanation of one's action or intention. The corporation did X to accomplish this purpose, or the purpose of the corporation's action was to accomplish Y. But there is also a very different use of the term *purpose.* The drafters of the MPC preferred the term *purpose* rather than *intention* to convey action that is engaged in with desire and foresight.[25] Action is purposive, and most culpable, when it is one's conscious object (desire) to engage in an act or cause a particular result.[26] Implicit in this conscious desire is the assumption that the result was foreseeable, that is, the result was a natural and probable consequence of the act.[27] In short, the corporation has acted purposely where it engaged in acts with a desire to bring about a certain, foreseeable result. Where the material elements of the offense entail external circumstances, as they often do, the accused must at minimum know or believe that these requisite circumstances exist.[28]

Following the determination that there was a constructive corporate act, courts and juries would examine any evidence of a purposeful state of mind, or a desire to engage in certain behavior (which is illegal), coupled with the foresight that harm would result from this behavior. Such evidence would appear in the form of (1) policies and practices that explicitly, implicitly, or through operation promote and encourage illegality, (2) efforts to ratify or endorse the violation of law, and (3) express or tacit authorization, approval, consent, or support of the illegality. Constructive corporate culpability considers this evidence by asking whether the average corporation of like size, complexity, functionality, and structure, given the circumstances presented, purposely engaged in the illegal act.

Perhaps the most obvious example of a purposeful corporate act is the participation in a conspiracy to fix prices and allocate market shares in violation of antitrust laws. In recent years the antitrust offenses of F. Hoffman—La

Roche, Ltd. (vitamin conspiracy), BASF Aktiengesellschaft (vitamin conspiracy), SGL Carbon Aktiengesellschaft (graphite electrode conspiracy), UCAR International Inc. (graphite electrode conspiracy), Archer Daniels Midland (lysine and citric acid conspiracy), Haarman & Reimer Corp. (citric acid conspiracy), and Hoechst AG (sorbate conspiracy) evince purposeful acts. There are also large-scale frauds, like those of Daiwa Bank (covering securities losses), Sears Bankruptcy Recovery Management Services (bankruptcy fraud), and Damon Clinical Laboratories Inc. (false claims to Medicare). Add to them food and drug offenses by Copley Pharmaceutical Inc. (fraudulently changing FDA-approved manufacturing methods), C. R. Bard Inc. (marketing an FDA-unapproved heart catheter), and Genentech Inc. (marketing an FDA-unapproved prescription drug, Protropin). And, there are devastating environmental offenses, like those committed by Louisiana-Pacific Corp. (numerous Clean Air Act and False Statement Act violations) and Royal Caribbean Cruise Ltd. (dumping wastewater and hazardous chemicals).

Most corporate crime cases that fall into this category, it seems reasonable to speculate, are small firms existing solely for the purpose of committing fraud. A. R. Baron & Co., a New York brokerage and investment bank, is a good example. In 1998, Baron was indicted as a criminal enterprise for defrauding more than forty-five investors of more than $75 million during a five-year period. In a 174-count criminal indictment, the New York County district attorney charged Baron and thirteen of its most senior executives and stockbrokers of lying to investors, inducing investors to buy certain securities, manipulating aftermarkets, ignoring customer complaints, forging documents, and making unauthorized trades. According to Manhattan district attorney Robert Morgenthau, "A. R. Baron was created and existed for no other reason than to line the pockets of its executives and employees at the expense of unsuspecting members of the investing public. Today's indictment depicts an investment firm totally out of control." Convictions were obtained across the entire corporate hierarchy, from the president and chief financial officer to the chief compliance officer and many of its brokers.[29]

Another example is the 2004 case against Mutual Benefits Corp., a South Florida investment company that offered viaticals, or interests in the life insurance policies of the terminally ill or elderly. In an effort to perfect an elaborate fraud, Mutual Benefits promised 12 percent to 72 percent on these viaticals, raising more than $1 billion from more than 29,000 investors. According to the SEC, Mutual Benefits fraudulently determined the life expectancies for 65 percent of their policies. The result is that assigned life expectancies are wrong in more than 90 percent of the policies, significantly affecting the rate of return on the investment. The SEC seized the assets of Mutual Benefits and targeted the two principals, Joel and Leslie Steinger, both of whom have a history of fraudulently misleading investors with the sale of viaticals.[30]

Knowing Corporate Acts

What evidence is there that the corporation had a knowing state of mind with respect to conduct, circumstances, or a result of its actions? Did the organization permit or tolerate the illegality? Was there evidence that the corporation was willing to allow the illegality? Given any evidence of actual awareness, permission, toleration, or willingness, would an average corporation of like size and structure have been aware of the nature of its conduct? These are the central questions for the second-highest degree of culpability—knowledge. The mental state of *knowing* may be traced to the epithet in Roman law *de delictis*. In the fourteenth, fifteenth, and sixteenth centuries, however, the expressions of "wittingly" and "willingly" appeared, gradually replacing statutory references to "knowing" action. The term *knowingly* reappeared in a significant number of statutes during the late nineteenth and early twentieth centuries in both England and the United States as a proxy for the accused's awareness that the conduct was of a certain nature and would likely lead to the prohibited result. Courts have considered willful ignorance, or deliberately abstaining from knowledge, as actual or positive knowledge. In England, willful ignorance, known more generally as *connivance,* is considered by some courts to be knowledge of the second degree. However, in the United States, the degree of culpability is the same.

The distinction between purposeful and knowing action is simply a matter of desire. Purposeful acts, as noted above, are desired and have as their objective a certain result. Knowing behavior requires only awareness, not a desire that conduct will lead to a result. To modify ever so slightly the words of a consultant for the Brown Commission, it seems reasonable that the law should distinguish between a corporation that wills a particular act or result and one that is merely willing that it should take place.[31]

A significant share of corporate crime cases fall into this category, especially cases where the most senior of management knows, condones, or tacitly approves of illegal acts.[32] Here, too, even a fair representation of crimes involves too many to list. Examples range from financial crimes, such as that committed by Bankers Trust (making false entries in bankbooks and records), through a wide range of environmental offenses and large-scale cases of Medicare and Medicaid fraud, to the most significant prosecutions of our day, such as the document destruction in the case against Arthur Andersen.[33] Notably, some cases fall somewhere between purposeful and knowing states of mind, where the criminal act is known and it is unclear whether it was desired. Others fall between knowing and reckless, where senior managers strongly suspected but consciously disregarded the illegal acts of subordinates, for example, and thus may or may not have directly known of the harm committed.

Circuit Judge Easterbrook recognized corporate knowledge in *United States v. Ladish Malting Co.*[34] Easterbrook reversed a district court's conviction of the Ladish Malting Co. for an Occupational Safety and Health Administration (OSHA) violation stemming from the collapse of a fire escape that killed a worker. The statute required a willful violation from an employer, which, the court held, was synonymous with a knowing state, not standards amounting to that found with criminal negligence. "Corporations 'know' what their employees who are responsible for an aspect of the business know," Judge Easterbrook ruled. "If 'authorized agents' with reporting duties acquire actual knowledge, it is entirely sensible to say that the corporation has acquired knowledge."[35]

Reckless Corporate Acts

Unlike purposeful or knowing corporate acts, reckless corporate action entails a disregard of substantial and unjustifiable risk of harm. Drafters of the MPC left courts and juries with a simple test for assessing the substantiality and unjustifiability of such risks. Did the accused's disregard of risks involve "a gross deviation from the standard of conduct that a law-abiding person in the actor's situation would observe"? This question may be translated, more generally, into the simple inquiry: Considering the circumstances known, and the nature of the conduct committed, was the entity's disregard of risks substantial and unjustifiable? Fact finders must critically examine the entity's disregard of risks.

The MPC takes a decidedly subjective view of recklessness, focusing on risks that the accused took rather than an objective recklessness that is concerned with the reasonableness of the risks taken.[36] At the core of a subjective vision of recklessness is the accused's awareness of risk and the extent to which the risks appeared reasonable to him or her. In determining constructive recklessness, reference is made to the risks that an average, comparable corporation would have known or been aware of in like circumstances. Once again, the use of objective criteria in concert with relevant subjective evidence facilitates the discovery of a constructive mental state.

Attributing a reckless mental state to corporate behavior assumes unreasonably risk-laden behavior without actual, positive knowledge of the illegality.[37] Consider, for example, that Emery Worldwide Airlines, an air cargo carrier that ceased operations in 2001, pled guilty to twelve violations of the Hazardous Materials Transportation Act in 2003 and agreed to a $6 million fine, along with the promise of new compliance procedures. Emery admitted that its employees placed potentially hazardous materials, such as flammable liquid and explosive and radioactive material, aboard its aircraft in 1998 and 1999 without properly notifying its pilots. There was insufficient evidence of positive knowledge of by senior Emery executives, but there were credible allegations that management must have been aware of the problems with hazmat shipments and, at the very least, disregarded positive knowledge.

Recklessness is alleged, implicitly or explicitly, in allegations against some of the most notable corporate officers who during their reign failed to engage in the kind of diligent actions expected of a person in the position of a chief executive. In the absence of positive knowledge, or at least its denial, a conscious disregard may be reasonably assumed. Bernard Ebbers, John Rigas, Dennis Kozlowski, Richard Scrushy, Jeffrey Skilling, and Kenneth Lay are but a few icons whose defense combated claims of a deliberate indifference to illegalities that, arguably, were simply too apparent if not blatant to go unnoticed. The conviction of Ebbers, for example, followed a trial with scant direct evidence connecting the defendant to the crime. Jurors constructed fault, much as they would do for reckless corporate acts, by considering how Ebbers's actions and inactions disregarded substantial risks to WorldCom.

The notion of corporate recklessness, however, is an old one. Clinard and Yeager provided a detailed account of the deliberate indifference of corporate officers in *Corporate Crime* (1980). So, too, did Richard Barnet and Ronald Muller in *Global Reach: The Power of the Multinational Corporation* (1974) and Christopher Stone in *Where the Law Ends: The Social Control of Corporate Behavior* (1975). Stone wrote, "Directors and high-up officers of corporations could not know of everything their organization was doing even if they tried—and often, preferring not to know, they arrange patterns of reporting so they cannot find out (or, at least, if they do find out, they find out only in such a way that it can never be proved)."[38]

Negligent Corporate Acts

Corporate negligence is found in cases where an entity inadvertently creates a substantial and unjustifiable risk of which it ought to have been aware. Unlike cases requiring other mental states, there is no need to prove a positive state of awareness with negligence.[39] Once again, the substantiality and unjustifiability of risks play a central role. Liability hinges on a determination that the corporation's failure to perceive the risk involved a gross deviation from the standard of care expected from an average corporation in its situation.

Cases of corporate negligence span a wide range of behaviors, including crimes where the subordinate and midlevel employees engage in fraud, for example, where senior management is unaware but should have known. In 2003, AstraZeneca Pharmaceuticals LP agreed to pay $355 million to resolve charges that its employees gave away thousands of free samples of the prostate cancer drug Zoladex to urologists, knowing that Medicare and Medicaid would be billed for the samples. This action, along with other inducements from its aggressive marketing plan, resulted in one of the most significant health insurance frauds in history. AstraZeneca acknowledged the fraud, accepted responsibility, but said it was unknown to upper management. Prosecutors did not single out specific culpable employees, and no indictments of current or former employees were contemplated. This case came on the heels of a comparable fraud perpetuated by TAP Pharmaceutical Products Inc., which paid $875 million in 2001 to settle criminal charges that it also induced physicians in the mid-1990s to bill federal health programs for free samples of Lupron, a prostate cancer drug.

Hierarchical standards of constructive culpability, corporate mental states, relevant organizational variables, and required evidence appear in Table 3.1. It should be noted that the range of culpable mental states, from purpose to negligence, is inclusive of the numerous mental state requirements found in various federal statutes. For example, willfulness is captured by the range of purposeful to reckless action; acting intentionally is equivalent to acting purposely; and acting with a conscious risk is the same as acting recklessly.

It should also be noted that the determination of corporate mental states turns on explicit reference to, and consideration of, organizational variables. Thus, purposeful corporate action is determined with evidence of desire or foresight found in organizational features such as policies, goals, and evidence of ratification, as well as in the behavior of agents. Constructive fault hinges on the notion that the intentionality of complex social systems, such as corporations, can be determined only by examining the nature of the corporate form in relation to human action (see Table 3.1).

The structural and contextual variables referred to in Table 3.1 shape and define organizational intentionality. From management's determination of goals and strategies to the effectiveness of an organization's authority structure and the way in which power and influence are exerted, structural and contextual variables derive primary intention. Many of these variables are significantly interrelated, for example, size and strategy, culture and hierarchy of authority, formalization and specialization, centralization and complexity.[40] All are designed to accommodate those on both sides of the personhood debate by maintaining the personal nature of fault within the context of an organization.

JUSTIFYING SUBJECTIVE, OBJECTIVE, AND HYBRID FAULT

At the heart of the problem with any conception of corporate fault is how to make a subjective inquiry of blame with an incorporate person. How

Table 3.1 Constructive Corporate Fault

Constructive culpability	Corporate mental states	Organizational variables	Examples of evidence required
Purpose: A corporation acts purposely if its object or goal is to engage in conduct or cause a result and, if the offense involves attendant circumstances, there is an awareness of such circumstances or a belief that they exist.	Desire and foresight (conduct/result); awareness or belief (circumstances)	*Size,* e.g., the number of employees *Goals,* e.g., statements and evidence of long-term corporate objectives *Strategies,* e.g., plan of action with a consideration of resource allocation	Desire to commit an illegality, coupled with foresight that action will result in harm; policy or practice that encourages illegality; the ratification or endorsement of the violation by the corporation; express or tacit authorization of illegality
Knowledge: A corporation acts knowingly when there is an awareness that conduct exists of a certain nature, or there is an awareness that it is practically certain that its conduct will cause a result.	Awareness of conduct; awareness that it is practically certain that conduct will cause result; awareness of circumstances	*Culture,* e.g., central or key values, norms, and beliefs shared by organization *Specialization,* e.g., extent to which tasks are divided into job assignments	Tolerated the illegality; permitted the illegality; consented to or indulged the activity; willing to have crime occur
Recklessness: A corporation acts recklessly when there is a knowing disregard of a substantial and unjustifiable risk that a material element of the offense exists or will result. The risk must be such that its	Knowing disregard; willful disregard of risks	*Formalization,* e.g., extent to which there is written documentation of organizational behavior and activities	Deliberate inattention to substantial risks of harm; willful neglect; knowing indifference

(continued)

Table 3.1 (*continued*)

Constructive culpability	Corporate mental states	Organizational variables	Examples of evidence required
disregard involves a gross deviation from the standard of conduct expected of a corporation in its situation.			
Negligence: A corporation acts negligently when it should be aware of a substantial and unjustifiable risk that the material element of the offense exists or will result. The risk must be such that the failure to perceive it involves a gross deviation from the standard of care exercised by the average corporation in its situation.	Inadvertent creation of a substantial and unjustifiable risk	*Hierarchy of authority*, e.g., level of employee responsibility in relation to span of control *Centralization*, e.g., extent to which authority is maintained at the highest levels of the hierarchy of authority or delegated to lower levels *Complexity*, e.g., the number of levels within the hierarchy; the number of corporate locations; and the number of jobs across an organization	Inadequate management, control, or supervision of employees; management should have known of a substantial risk of harm given employees' activities; failure to make reasonable efforts or take reasonable precautions to prevent crime commission; proactive due diligence; unreasonableness of corporate practices and procedures; harm was foreseeable but did not prompt corporate response

should one capture the corporate equivalent of the "sense of doing something which one ought not"? Architects of corporate fault models, discussed earlier in chapter 2, chose to define this "sense" in terms of organizational attributes. It is the failure of the organization to react, respond, prevent, report, or engage in due diligence; or the fault lies in corporate policies and organizational decision making. These failures and faults are conceptualized as both normative and subjective. They require an inquiry into those aspects of an organization that may be said to reflect fault or intention, and they stress the determination of blame and corporate wrongdoing. There is little doubt that these models are an improvement over the mechanical imputation of an agent's mental state to an entity found in vicarious liability. However, the same architects have done little to bring those models of fault back into the criminal law. These normative and subjective conceptualizations of corporate fault need some descriptive analysis in order to join existing state and federal criminal law. Thus, how do models such as corporate ethos and corporate character reflect a range of mental states of the corporation? When it is claimed that the personality of the organization has encouraged corporate agents to commit a criminal act, does that reflect organizational intention, knowledge, recklessness, or negligence?

Subjective Fault
Failure to show how these models relate to existing mental state conceptions is a challenge in definition. The next and perhaps more difficult problem is with identification of a subjective corporate mental state. The challenge of identification is met by providing proof of a mental state. As noted, the identification of an agent's mental state requires fact finders to make inferences of such states from overt behavior. Once defined, how will prosecutors go about proving a subjective mental state of a corporation? Is it possible to accomplish such a task short of retreating to models of vicarious liability where the mens rea of one agent is imposed on the entire entity? It is difficult to imagine courts capturing a subjective corporate mens rea guided by one of the corporate fault models without reference to the behavior and intentions of its organizational agents. And once there are such references, the difference between the subjective model and a vicarious liability model of corporate fault may be more apparent than real.

Unfortunately, the facts gathered to support a case of subjective corporate fault versus a case of imputative culpability would likely be indistinguishable. This is so given the difficulties of first defining and then identifying a subjective corporate fault. Perhaps the best analogy is with the well-developed alter ego doctrine in English law. British courts consider the corporation to be an abstraction but at the same time ascribe a personality and ego to the entity. Courts look for evidence of agents who may be considered the corporation's "active and directing will," acting through delegation of authority as representatives of the corporation's personality. Evidence of a corporation's will is thus indistinguishable from evidence of the intention and actions of agents.[41]

Because of problems of definition and identification, theorists have not chosen more orthodox, descriptive ways of assessing culpability, through the theoretical construction of mental states in relation to standards of corporate fault. If the task seems intuitively easy, consider the MPC hierarchy of mental states.[42] How should models of corporate fault be defined given this hierarchy? And, if this task can be accomplished, how will standards of proof be satisfied? In attempting to answer these questions, it will soon become clear that little may be gained by selecting a subjective vision of corporate mens rea over reliance on existing models of imputation.

Objective Fault

If there is one primary rationale for resorting to reasonableness judgments in determining culpability, it is the difficulty, and sometimes impossibility, of establishing subjective mental processes by direct evidence. As a result, some courts have allowed fact finders to consider objective criteria. Other courts have allowed juries to find mental states on the basis of reasonable inferences from conduct of the parties, their representations, and their relative positions. Where actual knowledge is difficult if not impossible to ascertain, courts generally permit inferences of knowledge on the basis of circumstantial evidence.[43]

Purely objective standards of culpability, where the focus shifts away from the accused's state of mind, may not be compared with reasonableness judgments as objective criteria. Purely objective standards are difficult to justify and have been ignored in relation to corporate culpability for at least two reasons. First, there is a good argument to be made that the criminal law is weakened by moving away from requiring proof of a culpable state of mind. An exclusive reliance on external standards of fault rather than culpable states of mind would strip the law of its moral meaning and render it indistinguishable from the civil law. Universal and time-honored principles of law hold that "an injury can amount to a crime only when inflicted with intention."[44] Acting with intention implies an awareness of one's behavior, knowing the consequences of one's behavior, and freely choosing to engage in certain behavior. And second, there is the misdirected argument that anything short of requiring proof of a subjective mental state must result in strict liability. Of course, there is a vast difference between dispensing with the requirement of proving mens rea, which is the case in strict liability offenses, and allowing for reasonable inferences of corporate scienter that underwrite constructive corporate fault. This difference should become clear with the hybrid models of fault that are considered next.

Hybrid Fault

When the word *objective* is used in the context of fault in the criminal law, it immediately brings to mind the notion of negligence. Criminal negligence, suggesting that the accused should have known of a substantial and unjustifiable risk of harm, has an objective meaning.[45] The inquiry centers on both the "substantiality of the risk" as well as the "elements of justification." Was the risk so substantial and unjustifiable that the actor deserved condemnation for its failure to perceive it? In answering this question, courts focus on what the accused "reasonably should have known" rather than on what the accused actually knew. Negligence, as Glanville Williams once wrote, "signifies a failure to reach the objective standard of the reasonable man, and does not involve any enquiry into the mentality of the defendant."[46]

Objectivism, however, has reached much further into the criminal law. In the late 1800s, Oliver Wendell Holmes was at the forefront of a short-lived movement to expand the role of objectivism in criminal law. Borrowing from the scholarship of British utilitarian jurisprudence, Holmes espoused the wisdom of adopting "general" and "external" standards of liability that are independent of evil motive and intent.[47] Culpability must be determined and judged by the standards that meet societal expectations. The utilitarian rationale given for such a shift comes from the overriding purpose of the criminal law to induce external conformity to law regardless of the accused's motive or apparent intent.[48]

Holmes was not denying that blameworthiness forms the foundation of criminal liability. Rather, in Holmes's own words, "it is only intended to point out that, when we are dealing with that part of the law which aims more directly than any other at establishing standards of conduct, we should expect there more than elsewhere to find the tests of liability are external, and independent of the degree of evil in the particular person's motives and intentions."[49] Holmes justified this position by arguing that the criminal law establishes clear standards for behavior that is prohibited. The criminal law presumes freedom of choice, rational action, and behavior at one's own peril. "A man must find out at his peril," according to Holmes, "things which a reasonable and prudent man would have inferred from the things actually known."[50] Thus, failure to meet reasonable standards, given these presumptions, results in liability regardless of one's tender sensibilities or incapacities—short of a few selected defenses.

The appropriate standard of culpability, according to Holmes, would be tied to the ideal conception of the ordinary person of reasonable prudence.[51] Consideration would not be paid to the subjective intentions and motives of the agent. In fact, the familiar epithets that accompany attributions of intention, such as *willfulness, malice,* and *wrongfulness,* should be considered objective states of mind. Courts would assume that a reasonable person engaging in action X, given circumstances Y, would have the state of mind Z.[52] Applying this simple formula to corporations, courts would ask: Would an average corporation, of like size, complexity, functionality, and structure, engaging in an illegal activity X, given circumstances Y, have the state of mind Z?

There are clear boundaries to Holmes's objectivism, however, that make his position far more attractive than critics suggest. He believed that while the general test of mens rea should be objective, any circumstances in which the accused actually had knowledge must be considered in estimating fault. Actual knowledge, which may be inferred from the conduct of an agent, reveals much about what an average person of reasonable prudence should have foreseen. Actual knowledge also reveals much about what a reasonable person should have known about the circumstances of his or her act.[53] There is nothing surprising about taking an objective standard of culpability and yet allowing for proof of a subjective knowledge or awareness. As Packer wrote, "There simply isn't a definite line between imputations of a subjective awareness and those of objective fault: they are points on a continuum."[54]

If there is one theorist who has wandered along that continuum, it is George Fletcher. In parting with Holmes's strict allegiance to a calculus of utility, Fletcher proposed a mixed objective/subjective model of liability.[55] As noted earlier, the primary concern of the objective dimension is the act, while the subjective dimension focuses on the accountability of the actor for the wrongdoing. The latter requires reference to and analysis of the actor's particular situation. But, unlike other subjective approaches, Fletcher's vision of subjectivity was explicitly normative: "Could the actor have fairly expected to avoid the act of wrongdoing? Did he or she have fair opportunity to perceive the risk, to avoid the mistake, to resist the external pressure, or to counteract the effects of mental illness?"[56] No longer should the criminal law focus on a literal reading of the actor's state of mind—this is a factual, descriptive matter. Culpability, blame, and fault are normative matters to be determined by asking whether or not an actor engaged in wrongful behavior while believing that he was doing wrong.[57]

A normative theory of corporate liability is attractive for many reasons, including its resolution of problems of definition. Adopting a normative view of corporate culpability would free us of the hairsplitting distinctions that descriptive theorists have imposed on the state-of-mind requirements of the criminal law. The difference between and among purposeful, knowing, reckless, and negligent wrongdoing is incidental to a normative assessment. Differences in the descriptive hierarchy of mental states are important only if they reflect important normative differences. As Fletcher wrote: "If mens rea refers not to a specific subjective state but to the actor's moral culpability in acting as it does, then there might logically be a way to establish personal culpability without referring to a state of mind."[58]

Unfortunately, what makes normative theory most attractive is also its greatest weakness. With the normative model's focus on a subjective judgment of attribution, it dispenses with an essential requirement of the criminal law: proof of a state of mind.[59] In other words, normative theory allows for proof of moral culpability without reference to mental states. It is this feature of normative theory that makes any application to corporate culpability less than desirable. Mental states have been considered "indispensable to ascriptions of moral and legal responsibility because they are the touchstones of moral agency."[60] From the turn of the twentieth century, when corporations first encountered criminal liability, this touchstone of moral agency has been woefully lacking. While the prospects of forgoing the difficult process of developing proxies for corporate mental states would make the task of law reform easy, it is this very exercise that is necessary for the construction of standards of culpability that are consistent with liability rules and capable of implementation in existing law. It is this very exercise that will allow the law to progress beyond the obscurity of fictional imputations of mental states.

The lesson of normative theory in relation to corporate culpability is that the law must still require culpable mental states but that those mental states need not be proven by an entirely subjective standard. This point was made nicely by Greenawalt, who wrote that "in expanding what one has intended, the law may adopt a kind of intermediate position between a completely subjective approach and an objective one."[61] Greenawalt, Fletcher, and other commentators have successfully argued that a completely subjective inquiry into mental states is not a necessary condition for criminal culpability. Thus, in its place, a model of constructive culpability evaluates facts and circumstances with reference to nonsubjective standards and subjective evidence.

Constructive corporate culpability, derived with some support from Holmes's theory of liability, evaluates corporate purpose, knowledge, recklessness, or negligence, with the assistance of reasonableness judgments. Following the general tenets of Holmes's theory, any evidence of actual knowledge on the part of the accused also may be considered. Thus, constructive culpability is not strictly objective. Unlike a model of culpability that evaluates behavior with exclusive reference to that of an ordinary or reasonable corporation, constructive culpability accommodates evidence of actual circumstances, characteristics, and states of mind. This is not to say that constructive culpability erects a notional corporation that is invested with all the characteristics and attributes of the accused. The difference between a subjective and a constructive standard would then all but disappear. Rather, constructive culpability takes an intermediate position between orthodox subjectivity and orthodox objectivism.

The constructive assessment does not ask corporations to conform to an external standard. Thus, the legal question is not: Did the organization, under the circumstances, act reasonably given its size, complexity, and structure? Requiring conformance to an external standard extirpates the inquiry into the accused's state of mind and would degrade the corporate criminal law. The constructive test also does not simply modify the standard of proof required in existing corporate prosecutions. Courts will not require that evidence "reasonably" establish a corporation's state of mind. Rather, constructive corporate culpability facilitates proof of the presence of a corporate mental state. Hall made this critical distinction in discussing operative facts, evidence, and reasonableness. There is a fundamental difference between defining the quality and quantity of evidence necessary to establish a mental state (articulating the standard of culpability) and determining whether sufficient evidence is present to sustain a conviction (providing proof of the mental state's presence).

Four threshold criteria should be considered in making decisions about the selection of objective and subjective criteria in the criminal law. First, in deciding on an objective conceptualization such as constructive corporate culpability, there must be significant evidence of its relevance. Are the corporate states of mind sufficiently connected to constructive culpability? Next, constructive corporate fault should cohere with the reality of corporate existence, structure, and organization. Third, constructive culpability should allow for the reasonable discovery of evidence. Finally, and perhaps most important, constructive culpability should maintain the moral stature of the criminal law.

Relevance of Standards

If the use of a nonsubjective standard of culpability has any place in criminal law, it is in the arena of corporate criminal liability. This is so because while it may be said that existing standards of fault work well in assessing an agent's mens rea, they often have no more precision than strict liability for the corporate entity. After all, there is no serious inquiry now into the mens of the corporate person or any organizational attributes relevant to corporate fault. At present there are no standards of corporate fault that ensure that the agent's state of mind is a true proxy for the corporation's. Thus, to the extent that an inquiry into objective fault considers the corporate state of mind that appears most reasonable in light of the external elements of the offense and the corporation's size, complexity, and structure, there is a far greater likelihood that it, rather than imputed intent, more accurately reflects the intentionality of the entity.

As noted earlier, there are in fact relatively few successful federal corporate prosecutions. Those that are successful tend to result in convictions of small, privately held firms where an owner or officer had—or should have had—direct knowledge of the illegality. The current allegiance to models of vicarious and imputative fault may well explain both of these facts. The utility of vicarious fault may be measured in relation to an organization's size. With a focus squarely on the delegation of duties and responsibilities between the agent and the organization, vicarious liability proves to be less appropriate with large corporations. As will be discussed in chapter 4, large, decentralized entities often distance themselves from the decision making of management through delegation of responsibilities and employee empowerment.[62] Prosecutors, as a result, tend to use their resources to establish a meaningful connection between the agent and the entity in small, centralized companies where the delegation of authority and responsibility is most apparent.[63]

If empirical research revealed that corporate criminal activity flourished only in small corporations, then a standard of culpability with an exclusive focus on the agent-entity relationship would be acceptable. But there is more than enough evidence that criminal activity and organizational deviance exist in large, publicly held corporations as well as small, privately held corporations.[64] Thus, a standard of culpability must be selected that is multidimensional—one that considers the agent-entity relation but is not limited to it. This standard must consider delegation but also direct evidence of primary intention.

Coherence with Reality of Corporate Existence

Vicarious and imputative fault do not consider variables that are critical to the explanation of organizational functioning and existence.[65] Unfortunately, some of the proposed models of corporate fault in chapter 2 also fail to capture a full range of explanatory features of complex organizations. For example, the agency principles that underlie imputative fault do little to reflect facts about employee role requirements, organizational leadership, group relations, and corporate systems and structures.[66] How does the display of authority frame employee role perceptions? What effect do organizational demands have on the toleration or tacit authorization of illegal behavior? What are the goals and standards of corporate leadership? How strong is their base of power? How cohesive are group relations? What are the goals and objectives of various departments or teams? What kinds of control and reward systems are in operation? How is power distributed throughout the organization, and what is its structure?

Questions like these are simply not relevant to models of imputative fault. The corporation as an entity, while the object of blame and sanction, is entirely overlooked by existing standards of imputative fault.[67] Of course, the point is not that courts overlook those factors that are responsible for making the corporation profitable or unprofitable, effective or ineffective.[68] Rather, the point is that the very nature of corporate intentionality or knowledge may not be reducible to the state of mind of one agent. Agents exist within complex organizational environments that have distinct structures, identities, cultures, countercultures, and subcultures.[69] Culpability is often inextricably intertwined with the control and reward systems, the objectives and goals set by leadership, and the group relations of the organization. Constructive corporate fault allows for a consideration of these factors in ascribing a corporate state of mind.

Allowance for Reasonable Discovery of Evidence

The shift from a focus on proving human mental states to corporate mental states facilitates the determination of culpability for at least three reasons. First, it appears as if prosecutions of corporations have been limited under standards of vicarious fault in cases where criminal activity persisted and yet no culpable agent could be identified. The identification of human agency would no longer be a prerequisite to finding fault. Second, shifting away from determining human fault to corporate fault allows for a consideration of the complex nature of the corporate form in relation to judgments of culpability. This consideration prevents efforts to obscure or neutralize vicarious illegalities through the decentralization of corporate decision making and minimizes the effects of an ever-increasing trend toward corporate diversification.[70] And third, the evidence that supports a determination of constructive fault is easier to gather than the circumstantial and direct evidence submitted in cases of vicarious fault. Of course, both standards of liability require evidence of inferences made from overt behavior—whether human or corporate. But evidence of corporate fault will likely be available from far more sources than evidence of a single agent's intentions with vicarious fault.[71]

If nothing else, with the transition to standards of constructive fault, one should expect an increase in the number of prosecutions and convictions of medium-size and large corporations. Insofar as convictions are a measure of success, the federal criminal law is used most successfully with small, privately held corporations where the owner had direct knowledge of the illegality.[72] This success rate is likely an artifact of prosecutorial resources and expertise.[73] On the other hand, given the relative difficulties of gathering evidence of an agent's fault in large and medium-size corporations, a move to constructive fault may allow for indictments and convictions of organizations previously shielded from prosecution due to the complexity of the corporate form.

Maintenance of Moral Stature of the Criminal Law

There is little doubt that by proposing a constructive culpability for corporations, critics will first argue that, if enacted, the law will dispense with an essential condition of criminal liability: the subjective inquiry into the accused's state of mind. In its place, as H. L. A. Hart eloquently argued, will be a morally neutral, value-free standard that allows for punishment of those who could not help what they were doing.[74] A constructive standard would therefore undermine the notion that mens rea hinges on an individual's or entity's capacity for effectual and responsible decision.[75] Remove the subjective element of intention and the law will run the definite risk of punishing corporations for involuntary, unpreventable criminal acts. Remove the subjective element of intention and the law will have dispensed with the "only morally blameworthy element in the definition of the crime."[76]

These concerns are entirely unfounded. First, such concerns would be appropriate and perhaps even justified if constructive culpability affected the external standard of care by which corporations are judged. Thus, if constructive culpability were an entirely objective standard of liability, rather than a method by which the mental states of entities are proven, critics would have a justifiable argument. Fashioning a method of fact-finding for incorporated persons, however, should not be confused with the creation of a standard by which contested facts are judged. Constructive culpability simply devises corporate states of mind so that evidence of primary intention may be introduced and explored.

Second, the moral relevance of a constructive standard of culpability must be measured against existing standards of culpability. Thus, it is necessary and appropriate to ask how constructive fault compares with vicarious fault. The answer is simple. The risk of casting moral blame on an entity for involuntary, unpreventable acts is greater with vicarious fault. Vicarious fault and agency principles do not consider the corporation's capacity for rational, voluntary action. Moreover, vicarious fault obscures and then deserts the time-honored requirement of finding culpability by examining the mental state of the accused. In place of the accused organization, standards of vicarious fault consider an agent's state of mind. Through a fictional attribution, the law assumes that the entity thought the same, knew the same, and intended the same as the agent. Finally, by not requiring a finding of genuine fault, vicarious liability obscures the distinction between the civil and criminal law.[77] As Judge Learned Hand noted in 1918, "Now, there is no distinction in essence between the civil and criminal liability of corporations, based upon the element of intent or wrongful purpose. Each is merely an imputation to the corporation of the mental condition of its agents."[78]

If it is true that the moral requisite of the criminal law requires an inquiry into the "inner facts" of an entity, then why would a constructive assessment of those facts be any less moral than its vicarious fictionalization? The answer is that any objective consideration of fault raises the specter of blame for entities for whom blame is not justified. Objective considerations raise the possibility that aggregate judgments of reasonableness will miss the mark and impose unrealistic standards as well as undeserved punishment on well-intentioned organizations. At the core of this argument is the concern that corporations lacking in culpability will be sanctioned. This concern is greatest with vicarious fault. But the weakness of this argument is that the risk of misplaced blame and unfair standards is far greater when juries and judges examine the conduct of one agent in relation to the facts and circumstances surrounding organizational illegality. At least constructive fault examines primary corporate action in determining intention. At least constructive fault is determined in relation to organizational variables that reveal intention.[79] After all, mens rea is reducible to factual inferences of intention. This point was made by the drafters of the MPC in their commentary on objectivity in standards of culpability. Even in the absence of specific statutory language, "it will generally be true that the actual mental state of the actor in most cases will be inferred from the circumstances as they objectively appear to the jury."[80] As the Supreme Court noted some years ago, "The state of a man's mind is as much a fact as the state of his digestion. It is true that it is very difficult to prove . . . , but if it can be ascertained it is as much a fact as anything else."[81]

Finally, what has been touted as the critical distinction between the assessment of corporate versus incorporate mens rea—the method by which mental states of corporations are determined—appears less critical with further inspection. After all, the very nature of attributing states of mind to human action requires reasonableness judgments. Factual inferences of intention are really nothing more than reasonableness judgments. Attributing a knowing state of mind to human behavior, for example, may be made only through what reasonably appears to be knowing conduct. If X acts in such a way as to suggest knowing action, knowledge is attributed because it is reasonable that X would have had knowledge given its actions. This assumption is at the heart of judgments based on circumstantial evidence.

Hall argued that there is a certain convergence between subjective and objective standards if the actors are, in fact, reasonable.[82] Thus, according to Hall, objective standards are both accurate and just in cases of simple means-end situations, and they may fail only in other "complex" situations. Such complex situations, where the accused acts in a less-than-reasonable way, are well considered by constructive fault. As noted, evidence of actual knowledge or awareness informs the determination of constructive fault. The allowance of actual knowledge supplements the objective inquiry in such a way that the convergence of subjective and objective fault is all but complete.[83]

CONCLUSION

In a letter dated March 19, 2003, sent to the commissioner of the Securities and Exchange Commission, former attorney general William P. Barr asked how WorldCom, responsible for perpetrating the largest corporate fraud in the history of the United States, was left to profit from the fruits of its illegal activities. "WorldCom engaged in a concerted program of manipulation over three years by which it fraudulently manufactured $9 billion in income," Barr writes, "making victims of investors, pension funds, and every honest company struggling to survive the telecom meltdown. Investors lost roughly $175 billion—more than three times the losses at Enron. And WorldCom's brazen scheme dramatically deepened the crisis of confidence in corporate America, imposing incalculable costs across the country. While the SEC and the Justice Department have focused on pursuing the *individuals* who perpetuated this crime, the government seems poised to allow WorldCom *as a company* to escape with the fruits of its unlawful conduct."[84]

Barr's point was simply that by allowing WorldCom to reorganize under bankruptcy laws, it would escape with the fruits of its unlawful conduct—an injustice as gross as the underlying fraud itself. His conclusion about the liability of WorldCom is blunt and forceful: "WorldCom apologists also claim that the company deserves leniency for cooperating with the government's investigation. But cooperation cannot trump the numerous other factors that dictate action again the corporation in this case, including the crime's unprecedented scale, its brazen nature, its catastrophic impacts, the involvement of senior officials, and the unscrupulous corporate culture that bred these offenses."[85]

Barr's frustrations that WorldCom played or gamed regulators are likely to remain in the absence of liability rules and standards of culpability that hold corporations accountable as entities. One central challenge of constructive fault, therefore, is to accommodate the games that corporations play.

PART TWO

The Law's Status Quo

CHAPTER FOUR

Playing Games

By 2001, it was the Most Innovative Company in America, according to *Fortune* magazine, for a whopping sixth consecutive year; one of the 100 Best Companies to Work for in America for the third consecutive year; ranked number 25 on the All Star List of Global Most Admired Companies; and ranked number 29 among the 100 Fastest-Growing Companies. With a net income exceeding $1.3 billion, recurring EPS up 25 percent, and an impressive 89 percent total return to shareholders, insiders said it was on the verge of being the "world's leading company."

None of this apparent success, of course, happened by accident. This company leveraged intellectual capital, created and opened new markets, maximized efficiencies, and demonstrated a leading-edge commitment to corporate ethics and social responsibility. In October 2000, it established a corporate responsibility task force staffed with senior managers and business unit representatives to consider and reconsider the company's social and environmental record. It added oversight of issues of corporate responsibility to the Nominating and Corporate Governance Committee of its board of directors; integrated ethics and responsibility materials into the hiring process and new hire orientation; hosted an e-conference for all employees on the value of corporate responsibility; launched an intranet site on corporate responsibility so that employees would have access to the latest corporate information on best practices; communicated to senior and midlevel managers the meaning of corporate responsibility; established a significant home page Internet presence on the company's commitment; and worked closely with nongovernmental organizations on the continued development of its corporate responsibility presence.

The company's ethics code reflected well-conceived core values—shared and distilled widely throughout the organization:

Respect: We treat others as we would like to be treated ourselves. We do not tolerate abusive or disrespectful treatment. Ruthlessness, callousness and arrogance don't belong here.

Integrity: We work with customers and prospects openly, honestly and sincerely. When we say we will do something, we will do it; when we say we cannot or will not do something, then we won't do it.

Communication: We have an obligation to communicate. Here, we take the time to talk with one another . . . and to listen. We believe that information is meant to move and that information moves people.

Excellence: We are satisfied with nothing less than the very best in everything we do. We will continue to raise the bar for everyone. The great fun here will be for all of us to discover just how good we can really be.[1]

This company did more than merely produce an ethics code and distribute it among employees. It did more than devise ethics training programs, produce glossy ethics material, and give impressive multimedia presentations. It led many Fortune 500 companies with a wide variety of social and environmental initiatives around the world. In doing so, its stock was chosen for inclusion in the best socially screened mutual funds. *Chief Executive* lauded its board of directors as one of the top five for governance structure and guidelines.[2] *CFO Magazine* recognized its chief financial officer for innovations in "capital structure management" with an excellence award.[3] This exemplary corporate citizen was Enron.

Enron, and many other companies with cutting-edge programs and initiatives in corporate ethics, institutionalized "organizational due diligence," "corporate compliance," and a brand of "proactive" and "reactive" ethics during the height of the good corporate citizenship movement.[4] As noted in chapter 1, this movement—inspired by the "Ill Wind" defense procurement scandals of the 1980s—first emerged in the early to mid-1990s as organizations looked to the prescriptive commentary of the 1991 U.S. Sentencing Guidelines for Organizations.[5] Corporate compliance for large, decentralized multinationals became a valuable commodity, sold as a cost-effective form of risk management and insurance. Compliance codes and programs were available for purchase in a marketplace of experts from "business integrity" consulting boutiques to diversified insurance and accounting firms, including an unusually talented group at Arthur Andersen's Ethics and Responsible Business Practices.[6] Ethicists and ethics consultancies took great pride in citing the adoption rates of ethics codes among Fortune 500 companies and the flourishing number of ethics and compliance officers. Companies, including many of those now on the Corporate Crime Reporter's list of the 100 Greatest Corporate Criminals of the Decade (1990–2000), also took great pride in touting their commitment to compliance, corporate ethics, corporate social responsibility, and environmental stewardship.

Throughout the 1990s, corporate counsel heard that evidence of organizational due diligence would likely forestall criminal investigations, minimize the chance of a criminal indictment, and lead to a possible grant of governmental amnesty. And, for the most part, they heard right. Lawyers from white-shoe law firms advised corporate clients about the peril of not being in compliance with the sentencing guidelines. And former prosecutors in private practice were far from shy about strategy: "[A] corporation that fully cooperates and provides the government with information, access to witnesses and perhaps even access to otherwise privileged information, has a far better chance of avoiding indictment than one that does not. So, too, the corporation that disciplines or even terminates the wrongdoer employee, and installs management systems designed to detect and prevent such violations from recurring before charges are filed, can avoid indictment."[7]

In some jurisdictions, prosecutors were more likely to decline cases where organizations modeled compliance programs after the guidelines' prescriptive steps. This likelihood of declination was especially true in complex white-collar and corporate crime cases (e.g., antitrust and securities fraud) requiring significant investigative and prosecutorial resources.[8] Declinations rewarded firms for their proactive and reactive efforts; focused scarce resources on the most abusive firms; and targeted organizations that would not benefit from the guidelines' mitigation credit. A litany of plea agreements followed, including deferred and non-prosecution agreements.[9]

To argue that the purchase of ethics codes and programs to be "in compliance" with guidelines became a game may seem overly reductionistic and wrong. After all, many if not most firms purchased compliance programs in order to comply with the law. Some well-conceived ethics programs fairly and genuinely reflected the commitment of corporate leadership and the motivation of the firm to maintain a culture of integrity.[10] And some compliance schemes in certain industries appeared to be working.[11] At the same time, it is certainly fair to say that corporate compliance and the strategies used by firms to be compliant became commonly held strategic chips in a deceptively simple regulatory game between and among firms, employees, prosecutors, and regulators.[12] The object of the game from the firm's perspective: Purchase sufficient compliance programs so that the company may conduct business with minimal regulatory scrutiny, free of liability. If compliance expenditures buy less scrutiny and liability, there is a fair return on investment. Not surprisingly, for companies with less-than-moral tendencies, or those which consciously disregarded the possibility that acting on advice from accountants or auditors would result in a crime, the object of the game included walking up to the line and sometimes crossing it. Between captured accounting firms and a poorly articulated and loosely enforced corporate criminal law, compliance chips proved far more valuable than expected in influencing the likelihood and intensity of regulatory scrutiny, no less the mix of regulatory persuasion and possible punishment.

The purchase of compliance changed the shape, hierarchy, and perceived legitimacy of the regulatory pyramid, a theoretical pyramid fashioned with cooperative regulatory strategies at the base and progressively more punitive (command and control) responses as the pyramid narrowed. At times, compliance expenditures undermined the progression of increasingly formal social controls, allowing firms to simply opt out of the criminal law. Of course, there are always weaknesses and failures in regulatory strategies involving cooperative compliance or "responsive" regulation, as John Braithwaite and his colleagues have written.[13] A weak or failed regulatory strategy, though, must be offset or accommodated by the strength of other progressively formal or informal strategies—something conspicuously missing in the 1990s. Ultimately, an impressive line of research suggests that successful corporate compliance in self-regulatory systems is inextricably linked to both compliance evaluations and the strong enforcement of laws. "Effective, permeable self-regulation only occurs," argues Christine Parker, "when government and non-government regulators (including stakeholders) actively evaluate and hold accountable corporate management of responsibility."[14]

Reliance on corporate self regulation without necessary metrics and strong enforcement of laws is costly, fails to achieve its law enforcement objectives, and undercuts perceptions of regulatory legitimacy and the force of other civil and administrative regulations. As the report of the Organisation for Economic Cooperation and Development (OECD) in 2000 on the challenges of regulatory compliance noted, "Systemic failures of compliance (that is, widespread and durable non-compliance) are failures of public governance that devalue regulatory instruments and ultimately break down the credibility of government and governance under the rule of law. Businesses and the public expect governments and regulators to be able to demonstrate that regulatory systems are designed to be effective."[15] This report and others underscore the need for more than additional piecemeal legislative and regulatory reforms.

This chapter and the two that follow reveal the effects of an abandoned substantive corporate criminal law, where prosecutorial discretion trumps liability rules; where there is a whim and arbitrariness to corporate liability.[16] This chapter considers how compliance games are played, their distinct objectives, rationales, and rules. It reviews how the game of compliance as business ethics seems to have magically changed in the postscandals era. Finally, I conclude that there is a paradox to compliance that may offer a valuable lesson for the corporate governance movement. Without liability rules that fairly and justifiably construct blame, regulation will, at times, prompt some corporations to dissimulate in artful, gamelike ways.

COMPLIANCE GAMES

There are multiple compliance games across a wide variety of industries and regulatory settings, virtually all with similar law abidance prescriptions. In recent years, these games reflect a move by regulators and prosecutors away from strict command and control approaches to strategies that encourage strong law and rule abidance, also called good corporate citizenship. From the perspective of regulators and prosecutors, compliance games are designed, at least theoretically, to reward effective firm compliance with tempting incentives and to punish failed, weak, or nonexistent self-regulation with the imposition of increasingly formal social controls, up to and including the use or threatened use of the criminal law. From the firm's perspective, the game revolves around the purchase of sufficient compliance to stave off regulatory scrutiny and, by doing so, minimize liability risks.

William B. Lytton and Win Swenson, both largely responsible for the inspiration behind the last iteration of the Sentencing Guidelines for Organizations, offer compelling reasons for the carrot-and-stick approach.[17] There are distinct limits on what courts and the law enforcement community alone can do to inhibit and fight corporate crime, argue Lytton and Swenson. Given the closed nature of corporations, the complexity of the corporate form, and limited prosecutorial resources, firms must join law enforcement as partners in ensuring good corporate citizenship. The private sector must join the public sector. Further, the law of vicarious criminal liability is overly broad. It unjustifiably snares corporations with good intentions that, in spite of management's best citizenship efforts, are undermined by acts of wayward, rogue agents. Finally, scaling punishment by a corporation's commitment to compliance creates powerful incentives to adopt compliance programs and, in doing so, engage in self-regulation.

Lytton and Swenson's rationale for the carrot-and-stick approach coincides with a growing realization—an all-too-familiar one—that courts were inadequately crediting corporations for their efforts to comply with laws. The government must not only consider how corporations may be regulated and punish corporate misconduct, argued advocates for business interests. The government must also design incentives so that companies will understand why it is in their interests to fashion strong and effective compliance mechanisms.[18]

Old Games

In the most commonly seen postguidelines compliance game (Game 1), firms invest in response to specific regulatory incentives. Being "in compliance"

with the prescribed standards of corporate behavior (for example, those derived from both prosecutorial and sentencing guidelines) is risk management for the firm. This is so largely because compliance is sold aggressively
as insurance against liability, no matter how limited regulatory resources are
to monitor individual firm compliance and no matter how remote the risk
of detection, investigation, indictment, conviction, and a criminal sentence.
"Learn how to protect your company from liability" became the compliance
catchphrase in the 1990s, and with some variations, it continues to be today.
Compliance is a hedge against liability, the business community is told, no
matter how arbitrary or happenstance the decision is as to whether allegations of harm are investigated as possible criminal, civil, or administrative
violations.

   Putting aside the overestimation of liability risks, limited regulatory resources, and the arbitrary nature of case referrals, what makes Game 1 so
remarkable is the absence of rigorous and commonly accepted metrics used
by key stakeholders (from firms to prosecutors) to evaluate the effectiveness
of firm-initiated compliance. This observation is not meant to suggest that
all self-regulatory measures put in place after the sentencing guidelines are
without measurement and assessment. Notably, the Environmental Protection Agency (EPA) has instituted industry-specific compliance programs with
elaborate audit protocols tailored to legislative and regulatory requirements.
These programs eliminate gravity-based penalties for firms that disclose and
correct violations of federal environmental law. Corporations sign corporate
audit agreements with specific disclosure and compliance requirements. In
addition, the Office of Inspector General (OIG) in the U.S. Department of
Health and Human Services (HHS) developed elaborate self-disclosure protocols with compliance program guidelines that are also industry-specific.[19]
Unlike many other agencies, the OIG requires audits from independent review organizations (IROs) under stringent standards for auditor independence.

   That these are exceptions, however, is made clear by the absence of systematic compliance assessment and measurement in the vast majority of
prosecutions under guidelines with nonspecific compliance metrics. Prosecutorial and sentencing guidelines are heavy on prescription and extremely
light on helpful metrics. The Thompson Memo, for example, acknowledges
that the Department of Justice "has no formal guidelines for corporate compliance programs." In place of these guidelines, prosecutors are asked to
consider: "Is the corporation's compliance program well designed?" and
"Does the corporation's compliance program work?" To be fair, it is suggested that prosecutors attempt to determine if a corporation's compliance
program is merely a "paper program," but the means to determine this are
left very much to their discretion. Prosecutors are told to consult federal and

state agencies that have expertise to evaluate the adequacy of a program's design and implementation.

In recent years, compliance assessment by the EPA has been guided by two axioms: (1) "what gets measured, gets done" and (2) "be careful what you ask for, you might get it."[20] The first axiom is unmistakable: successful compliance initiatives require careful measurement. The second reflects a concern that poorly defined metrics (such as measures of success) will, at best, prompt inefficiencies. These axioms reflect the state of corporate compliance. With an all-too-insignificant number of exceptions, assessment of corporate compliance across all industries is either absent or poorly defined. Work on compliance with the Australian Competition and Consumer Commission (ACCC) is both representative and exemplary of the experience in the United States. Models of self-regulation require stringent evaluation, according to research on the ACCC. But the motivation to evaluate is diminished by the conventional wisdom that regulators and other stakeholders lack the capabilities to assess a firm's progress toward compliance. Methods for the evaluation of corporate compliance are critically underdeveloped.[21]

If winning is defined by firms as conducting business with minimal regulatory scrutiny and free of liability, the game may be a lock for those who have invested in compliance, regardless of whether the investment is made in programs that are effective. Corporations, for example, may "win" Game 1 with compliance expenditures generally seen by regulators or prosecutors as evidence of the firm's due diligence in the absence of measures of effectiveness. Much like insurance, where carriers or underwriters monitor an insured for the purposes of determining the costs of premiums, compliance costs are fixed until or unless violations require additional expenditures. And, with little doubt, the comfort that comes from this insurance adds to the odds of winning the game, particularly as firms adopt prescriptive strategies from guideline and agency policies.

These strategies, many of which have redefined how we conceive of compliance, are now legend throughout all industries and in the compliance community: self-policing prior to any discovery of misconduct; remediation, including termination of or disciplinary action against wrongdoers; the drafting and incorporation of corporate codes of conduct; ensuring adequate delegation of oversight responsibility for compliance; the provision of training for employees; mechanisms for reporting violations; creating a culture of compliance; self-reporting of violations to authorities; wholesale cooperation with authorities; the waiver of attorney-client and work product privileges; crafting an integrity or comparable agreement so as to avoid an indictment; and the making of sufficient disclosures to earn a substantial assistance reduction in the very, very unlikely and surely unfortunate event of a criminal investigation, indictment, and conviction. As noted in earlier chapters, most federal and many state agencies have additional compliance requirements, including HHS, the Securities and Exchange Commission (SEC), and the EPA.

The transparency and widespread adoption of Game 1 strategies in no way minimizes their complexity and resulting challenges for firms, regulators, and prosecutors. In considering whether to self-report, for example, firms must decide whether the government would likely discover the illegality but for the disclosure; whether the firm is in an industry that is highly regulated, with a zero-tolerance policy where self-reporting is expected; whether by self-reporting the firm's liability might be spared in return for culpable employees of lesser rank; whether self-reporting would lead to a disruption of business that the company could ill afford; whether self-reporting would place the company at risk for additional, unrelated investigations of criminal violations; and whether a failure to self-report might be seen as concealing or attempting to conceal criminal wrongdoing. Other strategies, such as corporate cooperation (which will be discussed in chapter 5), entail even greater assiduousness.

Add to these challenges the fact that the compliance game is complex and, as Donald C. Langevoort notes, fraught with biases and errors in the over- and underestimation of compliance effectiveness and costs.[22] For regulators and prosecutors there is also the challenge of relative comparisons. Guidelines require discretionary judgments in the absence of objectivity, carrying weighty consequences: How serious is the offense? Was the corporation's disclosure timely enough? Was cooperation sufficient? Were compliance programs adequate? Were the company's remedial actions sufficient? How significant are the collateral consequences of a particular case? Are there adequate noncriminal remedies? Answers to these Herculean questions are given within complex political organizations, constrained by limited resources, with varying priorities attached to corporate crime.

The sentencing guidelines' embedded standards in Game 1 come with a prescriptive hitch. Satisfying the standards, a priori, diminishes the rationale and incentive to investigate, prosecute, and convict an offending firm. Satisfying the standards reduces the potential fine level and therefore the justification for pursuing corporate liability in the first place. This is a good outcome if the vast majority of firms—both large and small—are law-abiding and blameworthy only to the extent that wayward agents disregard compliance policies. Yet there is no evidence, empirical or anecdotal, that such is the case. Estimates of the billions of dollars spent on corporate compliance reveal a marked increase attributable to a combination of guidelines-inspired expenditures and compliance costs from increased regulation.[23] Too few ask, however, whether these expenditures actually reduce deviance. There is little systematic evidence that the good corporate citizenship movement and corporate compliance expenditures actually decreased organizational deviance. In fact, research demonstrates no positive effects from compliance programs modeled after the guidelines.[24]

Obtaining empirical evidence of any effect is made more difficult by the fact that firms playing this compliance game rarely receive significant regulatory attention. Examples, no doubt countless, are hardly public knowledge. And, even if one assumes a deterrent effect from at least some level of compliance expenditure, and that such expenditures make wrongdoing more difficult, for reasons of transparency and reporting, how much should be spent? How should regulators, prosecutors, and courts determine optimal compliance expenditures?

A sense of how the game is played and how deviance is hidden under the veil of apparently diligent compliance efforts, though, comes from False Claim Act cases, also known as qui tam suits.[25] Qui tam provisions allow citizens who defraud the government to sue corporations, as "private attorneys general." Those who sue, qui tam relators, are typically inside corporate whistle-blowers, suing on behalf of the government. The incentives are dramatic. Where the government joins the litigation, the relator's share of the judgment is between 15 and 25 percent. Otherwise it is between 25 and 30 percent.

Since the passage of key amendments to the False Claims Act in 1986, the government has recovered more than $12 billion in False Claims Act cases. Of the top one hundred false claims settlements, fifty-six involved corporations in the health-care sector and twenty five came from defense contractors. The top twenty cases (by settlement) contain some very healthy corporations with very distinguished brands and elaborate compliance and governance programs, including United Technologies ($150 million), Blue Cross Blue Shield of Illinois ($140 million), Northrop Grumman ($111 million), Shell Oil Co. ($110 million), Abbott Laboratories ($400 million), SmithKline Beecham Clinical Laboratories ($325 million), AstraZeneca ($266 million), and Bayer Corp. ($257 million). The judgment against Bayer Corp. illustrates the pretense of ethics and how difficult it is for firms to lose the compliance game in the absence of a well-placed whistle-blower.

"Everyone is expected to obey the law—not only the letter of the law, but the spirit of the law as well. You will never be alone to adhere to the high standards of the law. Should you feel prodded, speak with a lawyer, or call me. I'm serious about that."[26] These words, from a video address by the head of Bayer's $9.3 billion operation in the United States, started the mandatory corporate ethics training session for employees on February 9, 1999. In attendance was George Couto, a Bayer marketing executive who watched his peers burst into laughter. Couto had a reason to laugh as well. In spite of Bayer's very detailed Program for Legal Compliance and Corporate Responsibility, compliance officers, compliance committees, a two-tier governance structure with a *board of management* that has executive functions and a *supervisory board* with monitoring powers, and extensive ethics training, Couto knew that his company had overcharged and defrauded Medicaid out of $100 million by failing to offer the government its best available prices on a number of prescription drugs, including Cipro, an antibiotic, and Adalat CC, an antihypertensive. In this "lick and stick" scheme, Bayer deeply discounted prices and altered its labels on pills destined for Kaiser Permanente Medical Care Program, one of its largest customers, to avoid paying some of the required quarterly Medicaid rebates.

Reporting unethical and illegal acts to a compliance committee is required under Bayer's code. Couto reported this matter, but to no avail. In 2000, Couto filed a qui tam suit that led to a civil settlement of $251 million between Bayer and the government—the single largest Medicaid fraud recovery in United States history. Bayer also pled guilty to violating the federal drug laws and paid a $5.5 million fine. According to Bayer, its value is based on values. *"Lawful and ethical conduct," according to Bayer's code, "is fundamental to Expertise with Responsibility, which is the key driver of Bayer's success."* The code continues by stating that among all of the factors that Bayer singles out as the key to its success "is our employees' sense of responsibility."[27]

New Games

Much of the support for this admittedly cynical view of corporate compliance comes after the fall of Enron, WorldCom, and Andersen. Surprisingly, the attention paid to good corporate citizenship in the period after these icons were in ruins seemed to change in an instant, and so too did the appearance of the much-touted guidelines-inspired compliance game. Citizenship concerns, regrettably reduced to matters of compliance in many companies, are overshadowed in Game 2 by calls for corporate governance reforms in which the issue is how the company's compliance with law is overseen—not only by corporate insiders but by the fulcrum between those who own and those who control, the "independent" boards of directors.[28] The state of corporate governance is now at issue; the responsibilities, composition, liability, and operation of boards of directors; the responsibilities of audit, compensation, and nominating committees; the legal oversight over corporate governance; their compliance with SEC, NYSE, and NASDAQ standards and the requirements of Sarbanes-Oxley.

After more than a decade of debate over how to build in compliance with the wholesale adoption of "ethics" codes and programs, compliance failures are regularly recast as misgovernance traceable to the abject failure of professional gatekeepers, blatant conflicts of interest, and failed internal financial controls. The focus on ensuring programs to prevent and reasonably respond to illegalities is replaced by crafting checks and balances between the board, management, investors, and those intermediaries who provide necessary verification and certification. This is a distinction with discernable differences. The best and most thoughtful explanations of Enron's deviance, for example, turn on such matters as the limited incentives of shareholders to monitor officers, gatekeeper risk, and herding/persistence biases.[29]

Concerns over corporate responsibility, corporate accountability, and corporate liability, billed as corporate compliance with laws, are hard to find. It is as if a decade of business ethics institutionalization with billions of dollars of compliance expenditures never took place.[30] Remarkably, in 2001, the United States Sentencing Commission noted with some pride that the "guidelines have had a tremendous impact on the implementation of compliance and business ethics programs over the past ten years. [They] prompted a serious reconsideration within the American business community of methods and rationale for improved corporate governance."[31]

Perhaps most notable, the overnight transformation from compliance to governance raises significant empirical questions about the extent of deviance outside those industries that are most heavily and closely regulated. As Russell Mokhiber and Robert Weissman astutely observe, "Here is one of the most remarkable aspects of the still-unfolding financial scandals swirling around WorldCom, Xerox, Global Crossing, Enron, Arthur Andersen, Tyco and a growing number of other companies: The fraud occurred in the most heavily regulated and monitored area of corporate activity."[32] Beyond the constraints of corporate compliance, it is worth considering how the disclosure requirements of these publicly traded corporations somehow failed to raise serious questions; how independent research by investment firms also missed the mark.

To be fair, there are a handful of notable efforts to connect compliance and governance. For instance, the amended sentencing guidelines attempt an accommodation between the compliance standards of Game 1 and this newfound vision of corporate governance. To be "in compliance" now, no matter how voluntary or mandatory the guidelines are, corporations must have corporate directors who are knowledgeable about the firm's compliance programs, must have top-level managers ensure that the firm has effective compliance procedures, and must give those with day-to-day operational responsibility for the compliance function direct access to the board of directors or appropriate board committees. Corporations must also periodically assess the risk of criminal conduct (assessing compliance risks), have an organizational culture that promotes ethical conduct, and incorporate incentives to comply with compliance programs.

Joe Murphy, a long-standing champion of compliance, anticipated the amendments in examining the governance lessons learned by the demise of Enron. With regard to a corporation's standards and procedures, he reframed the sentencing guidelines in the context of governance by asking: Are corporate codes of conduct more than "high-sounding words"? Must gatekeepers (professional advisers) follow the code? Is there a match between the company's code and the culture of the firm? Have risk assessments underscored vulnerable compliance programs? Will compliance procedures check the misuse of corporate power? In terms of the compliance infrastructure, Murphy questioned: Does the corporation's compliance officer have the authority to thwart and then address the wrongdoing of superiors? Is the Audit Committee sufficiently independent and empowered to accomplish compliance oversight? Murphy's questions, nearly seventy in all, make unique and important connections between the governance lapses in Enron and traditional compliance failures. Deloitte & Touche followed with an impressive guide to the integration of corporate compliance and governance, geared in large part to sections of Sarbanes-Oxley.

These are exceptions, and the question remains: why is it that explanations of failed compliance and corporate misgovernance rarely converge? One possible answer is that theories of corporate liability sidestep the traditional governance concerns found in Game 2. Vicarious liability, for instance, imputes the blame of agents to the entity. Theories of liability, if genuine, reflect the decision, processes, and structures of a blameworthy entity. In contrast, theories of corporate governance turn on the actions or inactions of decision makers and strategists largely outside and independent of management. This is far from a satisfactory answer—one that neglects obvious unanswered questions. For example, where are all of the business ethicists and compliance experts who lauded the sea change in organizational behavior brought about by guidelines-inspired compliance? Are they hard to find because one would not expect, and should not expect, such significant compliance failure or governance failure, for that matter, at the height of such a successful compliance movement?

Much of the shift in game focus, admittedly, is attributable to the idiosyncrasies of accounting irregularities, the offenses underlying the recent corporate scandals.[33] As noted at the end of chapter 1, all of the highest-profile corporate fraud cases of late involve exploitation by and enrichment of corporate officers. In part the shift also reflects a realization that corporate accountability requires internal and external controls left largely untouched by the sentencing guidelines, specifically, and the good citizenship movement, more generally. This shift also reflects a realization that boards of directors are not yet active enough in ensuring the presence and overseeing the operation of firmwide ethics initiatives. Boards were simply absentee stakeholders in the good corporate citizenship movement. There is much evidence of this, including a survey of more than eighty ethics, human resources, and legal officers taking part in the Conference Board's 2003 Ethics Conference in New York. Results showed that 73 percent of the participants never held a single ethics or compliance training session for their directors. More than 55 percent reported that their boards were "not engaged enough" in major ethical issues. Fewer than 10 percent reported directly to the board of directors, and 15 percent never even met with the board.[34] As the Conference Board noted, "Even where ethics officers are able to institute ethics/compliance training and programs, little is being done to enforce them. . . . Bottom line concerns seem to be overriding ethical ones, and in fact, 54 percent of these companies don't even have ethics or compliance measurements in their performance appraisals."[35]

A significant reason for the current fixation on corporate governance also comes from the recognition that some companies known to be good corporate citizens—recognized for their ethics and compliance initiatives—are now known better as corporate criminals or icons of corporate misgovernance. David Vogel calls this development the "split personality" of corporate America, a problem with roots in failed incentives for law abidance. Corporations learned to be good corporate citizens, he argues, while also adopting the creative accounting methods of weak gatekeepers. Leading and lagging in ethics are not necessarily inconsistent. "Before its well-known transgressions came to light," writes Vogel, "Enron was long regarded as an exemplary corporate citizen. The firm and its senior executives were generous supporters of community institutions in Houston, and it captured international attention by building a power plant in India without resorting to bribing government officials."[36]

Vogel's observation about the apparent consistency between good citizenship and creative deviance is better supported by the disconnect between what corporate leaders say about their good corporate citizenship and the reality of their company's commitment (which will be discussed at length in chapter 6). One variation of this disconnect extends Lynn Paine's early and very thoughtful work on the distinction between compliance and values-based programs. From it one might conclude, as the fellows of the Ethics Resource Center did, that many corporate leaders

- define their organization's focus as ethics- or values-oriented but develop and implement corporate programs in a manner essentially limited to compliance;
- communicate their organization's focus as ethics-oriented, thus creating expectations among staff and other critical stakeholders that may be unfulfilled;

- implement compliance-oriented methodologies, systems, and structures that inhibit promoting values as a basis for individual and organizational decision making;
- fail to recognize that ethics-based programs and compliance programs require different definitions of success.[37]

After considering this disconnect, it is only reasonable to ask whether the governance reforms that brought about Game 2 are susceptible to the same compliance vulnerabilities found in the old game of business ethics.[38] A strong argument can be made that assuring good corporate governance raises comparable and analogous concerns tied to problems of information disclosure, the dominance of reactive rather than proactive board cultures, the pressures to maintain conformity without dissent, and, most important, the difficulties associated with internal and external validation of ethical corporate cultures and good governance practices. Certainly, the 2004 amendments to the Sentencing Guidelines for Organizations raise a host of interesting and difficult empirical questions, not the least of which is defining what constitutes an ethical corporate culture. Rudimentary, scripted "cultural assessments" marketed by firms providing business ethics consultation may easily miss the mark.

Gaming the New Game

In this post-Enron period, corporate governance reforms from Congress, the SEC, the New York Stock Exchange (NYSE), and Nasdaq have shifted the locus of concern from corporate-wide compliance initiatives to a host of board-focused initiatives and safeguards falling neatly into three categories: (1) corporate governance practices, (2) audit practices, and (3) the domain of disclosure, compliance, and ethics. All of these reforms reflect a shift in authority, responsibility, and power from the exclusive domain of managers to boards of directors and management.

An independent, effective, and diligent board of directors is responsible for providing direction to and oversight of the corporation. Board members exercise strategic monitoring and oversight of internal controls, as active fiduciaries, tracking the company's progress toward an agreed-upon set of goals. The board's actions should follow an approved set of corporate governance guidelines, and, if desired, leadership in these matters may come from the appointment of a chief governance officer. Board members also must ensure that the company's internal controls include an effective risk-management system and a rigorously enforced code of business conduct. Consideration must be given to the structure of the board, including the benefits of separating the chairperson and chief executive officer (CEO) positions. Companies should have independent nominating and corporate governance, audit, and compensation committees.

While many boards have well served their purpose, an impressive number of boards and individual directors justifiably earn ridicule if not liability for their incidental and dilettantish oversight of corporate affairs, for not "rocking the boat," for avoiding dissent, and for blind reliance on the representations of the chief executive officer. The conventional wisdom, according to Robert A. G. Monks and Nell Minow, is that despite repeated reforms and much rhetoric to the contrary, "boards have seldom succeeded in effectively overseeing management. Rather, the CEO/chairman wields the power in the boardroom, and directors mostly serve at his pleasure. . . . [B]oards are mostly reactive, not proactive."[39] This wisdom may be somewhat dated, given recent trends, but until the early 1990s, boards often deserved the accolade of "window dressing," "ornaments on a corporate Christmas tree," or "parsley on fish."[40]

The failure of boards to exercise their duty of care—passive directors who go by the numbers or by the book—is the second all-important element in many cases of corporate misgovernance. And the history of such misgovernance is long-standing: from the "decoy" directors of Home Insurance Co. of New Haven in 1871[41] to the poor judgment, corruption, and frivolous behavior of Penn Central's board in the early 1970s;[42] from the incompetence of directors in the United States Foundry Co. in 1903[43] to the sleeping directors of Empire Blue Cross and Blue Shield in 1993.[44] More recently, there have been shocking revelations about how the Royal Dutch/Shell Group's management shielded its board members from the company's oil and natural gas reserves accounting methods. With memoranda that the company's ousted chairman, Sir Philip Watts, was aware of the reserves for at least two years before they were publicly disclosed, prosecutors from the United States Attorney's Office in New York, along with regulators from the SEC, are on the trail. A complete list of offending boards that neglected to address the failures of management would be book length.

Whether current governance reforms will contribute in a meaningful way to the evolution of proactive boards turns on the rigors of regulatory enforcement, the costs and perceived costs of compliance, the difficulties of detection, the integration of new governance requirements into firmwide compliance initiatives, the strength of sanctions for noncompliance, and importantly, the direction of the sanctions. It also depends on further closing the gap, discussed some years ago by Arthur J. Goldberg, between the role of the director conceived by law and the reality of management control. In 1972, Goldberg noted that boards do not control large corporations. They simply are not well equipped to do so. Directors provide an advisory and legitimizing function, one that stands in contrast to "the role of policy maker and guardian of shareholder and public interest contemplated by the law of corporations."[45]

Goldberg's words seem out of touch with the transformation in board structure and function over the past decade, including changes in director compensation (aligning their interests with those of the shareholders), judicial decisions that demand effective board processes and oversight if board decisions are to receive deference under the business judgment rule, and an active market for shareholder control.[46] As Stephen Bainbridge observed, "modern boards of directors typically are smaller than their antecedents, meet more often, are more independent from management, own more stock, and have better access to information."[47]

Three years before Wall Street was rocked by Enron and WorldCom, Ira Millstein and Paul W. MacAvoy also noted important changes from the management-dominated corporations of the 1970s and 1980s. Boards quite simply are no longer the same, they wrote. No longer are a majority of directors selected from management. Independent directors are chosen by independent board committees. And, most important, "board participation in agenda-setting and in determining information flow is more active, and executive sessions of independent directors, separate from management, rather than being considered to be high treason, have been used to evaluate management."[48]

There still appears to be a "Goldberg gap" even with all of these positive changes. Closing it seems unlikely with voluntary, self-regulatory, governance initiatives or, for that matter, best practices from the leading business and law organizations: the Business Roundtable, the National Association of Corporate Directors, the Conference Board, the American Law Institute, and the Business Law Section of the American Bar Association. Survey research reveals a reticence on the part of firms in the United Kingdom, for example, to adopt governance reforms in the absence of strict legal requirements and incentives to do so. "Overall 64% of the FTSE 350 failed to comply fully with the recommendations of the Code. Five years after the Code was published," researchers observed, "many of the UK's top companies have still not wholly bought into the concept of corporate governance."[49]

The experience in the United States with nonbinding prescriptive requirements for good corporate governance is not much better. The fate of the Caremark decision, for example, appears distressingly similar. As discussed briefly in chapter 1, *Caremark* considers the duty of directors to include the assurance of compliance procedures and reporting systems reasonably capable of preventing law violations. Boards, according to Chancellor Allen, must be active monitors of corporate compliance. They are duty-bound to assure that information and reporting systems exist *and* that both are adequate to assure that the board will be provided with compliance information in a timely manner. A failure to discharge this duty may leave directors liable for losses caused by noncompliance.[50]

Corporate counsel and the white-collar defense bar carefully packaged *Caremark* as evidence of a new gospel of corporate governance immediately after the 1996 decision, one that requires boards to take a more proactive role in monitoring and oversight activities throughout the corporate hierarchy.[51] Unfortunately, in spite of a new generation of practitioner conferences that educated legions of corporate counsel on the *Caremark* era, few jurisdictions explicitly endorsed the notion of director liability for compliance oversight failures. With only a handful of cases recognizing *Caremark* principles, most notably *In re Abbott Laboratories Derivative Shareholders Litigation*,[52] *Dellastatious v. Williams*,[53] and *McCall v. Scott*,[54] its potential for promoting the centrality of the board in corporate governance far outstrips any precedential value in law.

The failure of *Caremark* as a catalyst of corporate governance reform suggests that the transformation called for by the Conference Board—the move from reactive boards that rubber-stamp management's agenda and compliance initiatives to boards of active and proactive fiduciaries—will require more.[55] If history and survey research on compliance are any guide, well-intentioned, prescriptive yet nonbinding guidance will be insufficient. Even prescriptive and legally binding requirements such as that found in the 2004 amendments to the sentencing guidelines may be not enough if (1) the conventional wisdom emerges that objective assessments of board action and inaction fail to truly capture effective oversight, (2) there is a growing "accountability deficit" (a decrease in regulatory accountability where regulators rely heavily on managerial self-evaluations and self-controls), (3) assessments and audits calling for governance and/or compliance reforms fail to produce actual change, and (4) director and officer insurance (D&O insurance) covers real and perceived liability risks. In regard to director liability and D&O insurance, recent shareholder settlements between former WorldCom directors and former Enron directors requiring personal reimbursement not covered by insurance is likely to remain an exception rather than a new rule.

Then there is the issue of costs. Already, costs associated with reforms—particularly compliance with Sarbanes-Oxley—are raising concerns about the diversion of important staff resources not directly benefiting the shareholders. "The real cost isn't the incremental dollars, it is having people that should be focused on the business focused instead on complying with the details of the rules," explains the chief accounting officer of General Motors Corp.[56] Surveys of corporations with revenues exceeding $5 billion will spend on average $4.7 million each for Rule 404 compliance, along with another

$1.5 million for auditors to assess controls. One estimate places the total cost of Sarbanes-Oxley rule-making events at $1.4 trillion.[57] And, not surprisingly, the cost of compliance as a function of revenues places that much more of a burden on smaller firms. This burden is made more difficult by dramatically higher auditing fees.

As one chief financial officer concluded, "It is a lot of cost to the system without a lot of benefit."[58] It is unclear at present how many senior managers suspect that the costs of compliance possibly outweigh prevailing regulatory risks. Certainly there is talk about the Sarbanes-Oxley effect on competitiveness and risk aversion. With an increasing perception that disclosure requirements of public companies are overly burdensome, going private and private equity have never been more attractive.

Then there are those firms that, in a climate of fear over heightened regulatory oversight, simply terminate those agents who raise even the slightest doubts about its ethicality or good governance. In 2005, for example, Wal-Mart, AIG, Boeing, and Bank of America fired employees to forestall questions of impropriety. As discussed in the next chapter, gaming regulators by this form of reverse whistle-blowing has significant value if the motivation behind the corporate housecleaning is perceived as something less than an attempt to obstruct justice or prevent the flow of incriminating evidence to relevant third parties.

Then there are worries about the inherent limitations of third-party auditors, in particular their reliance on risk-based audit methods. A variation of this risk-based method—where auditors rely primarily on their individual business knowledge of the client firm to identify key risk areas—was used, for example, in HealthSouth Corp.'s 2002 audit by Ernst & Young. The planning papers for this engagement later revealed an embarrassing naiveté, a uncritical reliance on the misrepresentations of HealthSouth officials that led this top accounting firm to conclude that its executives were ethical, that the financial systems were reliable, and that the "management had designed an environment for success."[59] After more than fifteen indictments of Health-South senior executives, it seems as if nothing could be further from the truth. The scandals at WorldCom, Andersen, Tyco, and Parmalat involved failed risk analyses as well. To no one's surprise, the leading accountancies maintain this practice today, from KPMG to PricewaterhouseCoopers.

The most significant challenge is all too familiar to those tracking the progress of corporate compliance. How should "good" corporate governance be assessed? To avoid the pitfalls associated with corporate compliance, the governance-compliance connection must insure against the substitution of corporate reputation for substantive change in governance practices.[60] Reform must therefore anticipate the need for transparency, so that gatekeeper audits and verification of corporate governance representations are routine,

effective, and verifiable. The critical issue remains disclosure and information flow in boards with a proactive culture.[61] Management will always have
an information advantage over directors as to the issues and problems facing the day-to-day operation of the business. The board, therefore, is wholly
dependent on receiving accurate and timely information.

Even with frequent and timely disclosures, though, boards and other out-
siders are hard-pressed to make definitive judgments about their veracity.
Consider that even with the most astute and experienced judges of board
competence—for example, Robert W. Lear and Boris Yavitz—Enron's board
was rated one of the top five in the country by *Chief Executive* magazine in
2000. "While somewhat concerned with large board size (18), and the presence of a very active executive committee (10 meetings)," Lear and Yavitz
noted, "we are heartened by the overall corporate governance structure and
by its governance guidelines, which call for a regular evaluation of director and executive performance."[62] Assessing the efficacy of corporate governance simply shares many of the same challenges associated with judging
the effectiveness of compliance.

So, how did Enron's board make it to the top? Enron won this coveted
recognition by watching its outsider-insider ratio, minimizing potential
conflicts of interests, limiting investors representing special interests, maintaining a diverse board, encouraging stock ownership by directors, defining
committee roles and structures, and forming a corporate governance committee. In October 2000, at a time when signs of misgovernance and systemic
conflicts should have been apparent, the most reasoned judgment was that
"[o]n the whole, the state of American corporate governance health [is] much
improved."[63]

Finally, consider the experience of Robert C. Nakasone, former CEO of
Toys "R" Us, who joined Tenet Healthcare's board in a major overhaul of
its corporate governance practices in 2003. Over the course of nine months,
at least on the surface, Tenet did all the right things, from promoting an
independent board to creating an ethical corporate culture. But according
to Nakasone, who resigned in April 2004, these "changes" and associated
governance reforms were more apparent than real. "After nine months on
the board, I am personally frustrated by the lack of progress on all fronts,"
Nakasone reportedly wrote.[64] His experience and that of other directors who
have resigned or were discharged illustrate the difficulty of determining the
extent to which governance reforms have taken hold.

The most obvious solution to this problem of transparency and verification is to conceive of new and creative means of integrating governance and
compliance initiatives in ways that extend beyond the prescriptions of the
amendments to the sentencing guidelines. The OIG and the American Health
Lawyers Association (AHLA) attempted one such integration, with specific

attention paid to the challenges of health-care organization directors. The OIG and AHLA asked boards to consider eighteen structural and operational questions, including: How is the board structured to oversee compliance issues? How does the organization's compliance reporting system work? How frequently does the board receive reports about compliance issues? What are the inherent limitations in the compliance program? Does the compliance program address the significant risks of the organization? How were those risks determined, and how are new compliance risks identified and incorporated into the program? How has management determined the adequacy of the resources dedicated to implementing and sustaining the compliance program?

These questions and the explanatory commentary of the OIG and AHLA are helpful. They accomplish what most reforms neglect: connecting compliance objectives with governance practices. But these and other guidelines may be less than meaningful without force of law. An explicit legal connection must be made between failures of corporate governance and the failure of corporate compliance. None of the legislative reforms or agency and exchange rules proposed of late make this connection explicit or legally binding. Describing Enron, Andersen, and WorldCom as corporate governance failures without noting the dramatic failures of compliance reveals how much work must be done.

For some, the obvious candidate for law reform is the sentencing guidelines. At the behest of Congress, Sarbanes-Oxley 2002 (Section 805(a)(5)) required that the U.S. Sentencing Commission's Advisory Group of Organizational Guidelines discuss and debate the merits of amending the guidelines to specifically consider governance issues. From this discussion came the amendments described earlier. Testimony from industry associations and government regulators and prosecutors fell into predictable camps.[65] The former generally rebelled against expansion of the guidelines. "It is not the function of the Sentencing Commission to create new corporate governance rules," argued James W. Conrad Jr. of the American Chemistry Council. "That is properly the province of Congress and the numerous regulatory bodies that have been delegated the authority to promulgate and enforce regulations on this topic."[66] Naturally, prosecutors took the opposite track, even after *Booker and Fanfan.*

The governance-related revisions of the guidelines by the Sentencing Commission raise at least three distinct concerns. The first relates to whether new standards of governance should be attributed to the entity (rather than individual directors) and, if so, whether they should be criminalized.[67] As boards are asked to assume increasing oversight responsibility once reserved at least in large part for management, it is only reasonable to ask whether their failures should be attributed or imputed to the entity. Thus, instead of thinking about corporate misgovernance as an aggravating circumstance to be raised at time of sentencing, board failures may be evidence of corporate fault, something more than individual civil liability. Consider that the acts of agents throughout the hierarchy of a firm bind the entity, but the acts of boards cannot.

A second concern, well-articulated by representatives of industry associations, is whether the commission, rather than legislative bodies such as Congress, should be the catalyst driving good corporate governance practices in the private sector. To this concern there is a definitive answer. The commission has been asked, once again, to cover for failures of substantive law reform with guidelines and commentary that are no substitute. The amendments simply widen the gap between substantive corporate criminal law and the law of sentencing. The more difficult question raised once again is the effect of substituting elaborate guideline prescriptions for our neglected criminal liability rules.

Perhaps the single most pressing concern is the previously noted conundrum of assessment. Cases reported to the commission following the passage of the guidelines point to the power of compliance programs—no matter how effective or ineffective—as preventive law.[68] Only two of the corporations convicted in federal courts from 1996 through 2004 had what was determined by a court to be an "effective" compliance program.[69] Annual commission data also reveal that mitigation credit for having a compliance program—effective or not—is rarely offered to the few corporations that go to trial and are convicted.[70]

The absence of effective compliance programs and the failure of corporations to obtain even nontrivial mitigation credit may be interpreted in several ways. First, reasonably constructed compliance initiatives effectively shift prosecutorial attention to alternate civil remedies, consent decrees, and plea agreements, as well as the criminal investigation of individual agents. As one former prosecutor put it, "[y]ou must recognize the role of prosecutorial discretion in the bringing of charges. This is the other fundamental reason why a compliance program is essential. . . . Having an effective compliance program to pull out of your portfolio and lay on the prosecutor's desk is a key weapon. . . . You cannot get to first base with a prosecutor without having a compliance program, and having one may land you a home run."[71] A more interesting and important question, however, is whether ineffective compliance initiatives also inhibit the criminal process. As the deputy assistant attorney general in the Criminal Division of the Department of Justice once observed, prosecutors often require corporations to contractually promise to establish a compliance program or strengthen an existing ineffective initiative as part of an agreement not to prosecute. "In other words, even if you don't have a compliance program at the time you come into the prosecutor's office, you ought to think about setting up an effective one and offering this up as part of a plea bargain or an agreement not to prosecute the corporation."[72]

This concession, that firms may strengthen an ineffective program, or even create one if none is present, is made because of the difficulty both prosecutors and courts have had in determining what "effective" compliance means, particularly in large and complex corporate bureaucracies. What combination of ombudsmen, review boards, hotlines, disciplinary mechanisms, internal audits, training programs, and code complexity must be present to make such a determination? How should prosecutors assess the commitment of top management? Prosecutors admit comfort with identifying the easy cases where there is a "nice compliance program with a little gold seal at the bottom and a frame around it, and the company's officers and employees go out and violate the law anyway because the program is not an effective one."[73] These easy cases may still exist within small, privately held firms that are poorly counseled in preventive law. The real challenge, if the corporate criminal law still has meaning, is the comfort level of prosecutors and courts in evaluating compliance effectiveness with those corporations that rarely if ever go to trial—the large, diversified, publicly held corporations. Here, there simply does not exist an accepted metric used to assess program design, operation, and outcome. And, as Langevoort carefully demonstrates, judicial and administrative intuitions about compliance effectiveness and monitoring capabilities are fraught with errors and biases.[74]

Some commentators point to a growing consensus of what constitutes an "effective" compliance program. For some, consensus is reflected in the conditions and requirements of the court-imposed criminal plea agreements and civil consent decrees against such firms as National Medical Enterprises, Conrail, Con Edison, Caremark, Inc., Northrop Grumman Corp., and Prudential Securities.[75] Trying to distill a set of objectives, no less subjective metrics, from these cases requires more creativity than is currently available. Moreover, these are a very select few of the hundreds, if not thousands, of federal investigations of organizations each year that never result in a criminal indictment, no less a trial. One must question whether the importance of their treatment by prosecutors stems from significant name recognition or the generalizability of regulatory treatment and oversight. For others, survey research reveals the relative superiority of values-based ethics programs over those whose focus is compliance oriented. The former, for example, result in an increased awareness of ethical issues at work; a willingness to seek ethical advice; greater commitment to organization; beliefs that it is acceptable to deliver bad news to superiors; and less unethical behavior.[76]

Substituting intuitive determinations of compliance effectiveness from regulators or courts in plea agreements risks the kind of error that results in a case such as Enron. Field research that examines compliance orientations in relation to ethical behavior is helpful but has not yet considered organizational crime as a dependent variable across a wide range of industries. Thus, without an internally consistent set of objective criteria—and short of a company whose failure brings about post hoc scrutiny—courts are as stymied as business ethicists and compliance experts in providing anything but limited anecdotal and empirical evidence of compliance effectiveness.

The difficulty with obtaining objective indicia of compliance effectiveness haunts business ethics research on compliance where the bulk of the work consists of employee surveys.[77] Evidence of increased reliance on compliance procedures, such as a rise in the number of calls to an ethics office or an ethics hotline, may indicate effectiveness (i.e., the existence of procedures reasonably capable of preventing law violations), ineffectiveness (i.e., an increase in the extent of deviance within the firm), or both. Courts are capable of assessing adherence to the prescriptive steps in the guidelines, but establishing adherence is quite different from assessing effectiveness. According to the National Center for Preventive Law, "[w]hile some rudimentary tests are contained in the Sentencing Guidelines and other legal standards, these tests provide little concrete direction on how to create effective programs."[78]

Prosecutorial discretion is neither guided nor constrained by reasonable proxies of effectiveness. This would be less of a problem but for the fact that the reach of the criminal and civil law is now determined by the subjective discretion of prosecutors who, shielded by the legitimacy of the Thompson Memo, balance matters of compliance effectiveness with concerns over the harm caused, the difficulties of obtaining evidence, the deterrence value of making an example of a corporate defendant, the politics of prosecution, and the available resources of their office. Governance reforms invite many of the same measurement concerns.

GAMING AND ITS HAZARDS

Our exaltation of compliance and governance as the pillars of corporate due diligence, combined with the haunting problem of assessment and verification, lead to another, more serious problem. With some corporations—Enron and Andersen may be good examples—once compliance and governance expenditures are made, care levels may be expected to decrease if the consensus view emerges in the firm that those expenditures wholly protect against liability. Corporations are freed from the inhibitions that accompany rigorous regulatory oversight. In the absence of external audits of compliance and governance effectiveness or metrics that allow for such evaluations, corporations with less-than-legal tendencies or those that face extraordinary situational pressures have essentially free rein. After all, who is watching? Mounting compliance expenditures build a nearly impenetrable wall against the prying eyes of regulators and prosecutors. Cutting-edge governance structures and practices have the same effect. Even though this hypothesis certainly does not apply to all of the corporate crimes in recent times, it remains very appealing, especially given the weaknesses in corporate criminal law discussed in earlier chapters and in light of the recent spate of scandals by companies whose reputations were made with seemingly credible citizenship efforts.[79]

Compliance as Insurance and Self-Insurance

Traditional insurance products are made available to organizations for a host of compliance-related risks, from losses caused by the fraudulent acts of rogue traders to the costs of violating environmental statutes.[80] The range of fidelity policies available to firms, with coverage for a host of crimes and torts, is remarkable.[81] With each policy or coverage, the insured (organization) pays a price that effectively transfers the risk of loss associated with law violations to a third-party insurer (insurance company). To the extent that organizations spend considerable resources in the name of risk management to internalize the costs of compliance failures, how similar is this to the risk-retention and risk-funding rationale that has driven many large corporations to self-insure?[82] How similar are the reasons for traditional insurance with the rationale of firms that purchase compliance in order to shift liability away from the entity?

The short answer to both of these questions is that there are a surprising number of similarities even though the purchase of compliance fails to meet most, if not all, of the legal requirements and nonlegal assumptions of insurance and other risk-financing alternatives. Instead of maintaining a fund to pay claims for covered employees, as is the case in traditional forms of self-insurance, firms purchase compliance to insure against the inevitability of compliance failures. This "fidelity" insurance is as much self-insurance (not to mention self-protection) as the purchase of a fire extinguisher by a concerned homeowner.[83]

The primary justification for the purchase of compliance, however, is to insure that employee infidelity will be viewed as an individual rather than a corporate act. Compliance, like insurance, is a method of greatly reducing a known risk. Consistent with the view that organizations are utility maximizers, and with the pretext of good corporate citizenship, organizations presumably select compliance purchases at the minimum level of expenditure necessary to shift liability to the agent.[84] Any expenditure beyond this level may be seen as inefficient. The costs to the firm are highest where there is little to no compliance (costs rise due to significant employee deviance that is imputed to the firm) or overcompliance (employee deviance is not imputed to the entity, but costs rise due to compliance expenditures). Firms maintain a level of compliance within an operating range that minimizes costs while at the same time shifting liability.

Even with these similarities, no one would suggest that the purchase of compliance satisfies many of the nonlegal and the legal requirements of insurance or, for that matter, self-insurance. Courts have carefully drawn definitions challenging the deductibility of premiums as business expenses, requiring for proof of insurance a clear showing of risk shifting and risk distribution.[85] Risk shifting is narrowly defined by courts as the transfer of risk of loss from one entity to another. Risk distribution requires a showing that losses will be spread across entities. Self-insurance, on the contrary, requires some risk retention in addition to funding and encompasses a wide range of risk-financing alternatives to traditional insurance.[86]

Notwithstanding these critical differences and generous violations of assumptions, the underlying rationales for underwriting compliance (shifting risk of loss to agents and minimizing costs due to compliance failures) are remarkably similar to those that support a broader interpretation of insurance and self-insurance.[87] Consider the central role of risk transference and risk control in the purchase of both insurance and compliance. Consider, in addition, that self-insurance may be conceptualized broadly as "any plan of risk retention in which a program or procedure has been established to meet the adverse results of a financial loss."[88] Such an interpretation supports risk-retention and risk-funding plans that fail the legal requirements of pooling and inviolate reserves but are nevertheless conceived of as self-insurance in many businesses.[89]

If it is true that firms purchase compliance as risk management to the point of insurance and generally minimize costs by spending only that amount necessary to effectively shift liability, it is critically important to consider how this practice might affect incentives and disincentives to institutionalize law abidance in firms. Such a consideration must address the adverse consequences of firms purchasing compliance in a manner similar to the purchase of insurance.[90]

Compliance and Moral Hazards

For many years, the problem of moral hazards and their accompanying inefficiencies was discussed in relation to insurance contracts.[91] Scholars debated the detrimental effect that insurance has on an insured's incentives to avoid losses associated with a host of avoidable and unavoidable events, for example, an automobile accident or a house fire. Insurers concluded that a combination of the character of the insured and the incentives (or disincentives) from the purchase of insurance prompted a distinct risk of loss. Where an insured is of poor moral character, the purchase of insurance results in a temptation to engage in risk-bearing behaviors.[92] Short of taking optimal precautions, which is uncharacteristic of the morally weak, empirical research supported the experience and intuitions of a growing insurance industry. An insurance contract may compromise incentives, affecting an individual's care and activity levels, as well as the likelihood of loss.[93] In short, "insurance inevitably increases the occurrence, magnitude, or cost of that which is insured against."[94]

Kenneth Arrow first discussed the economics of moral hazard in the context of health insurance in 1963.[95] Over the next three decades, the notion of moral hazard was extended to all forms of insurance. Scholars stretched its impact past traditional insurance to any situation in which one party's action may affect the risk of loss assumed by another.[96] Neoclassical economists found moral hazard problems in strict product liability regimes, cases of contributory negligence, workers' compensation benefits, and virtually all agency relations.[97]

In recent years, the notion of moral hazard has been used to explain the perverse consequences of such well-intentioned and socially minded initiatives as welfare programs for the poor, product liability coverage for the injured, and health insurance for the sick. As some commentators have observed, albeit with much suspicion, the lesson of neoclassical moral hazard theory is that the more one tries to safeguard against the consequences of poverty, accidents, and uncompensated illness, the greater the likelihood of poverty, injuries, and illness.[98] Attempts to minimize the consequences of certain risk-bearing behaviors through compensation (which approximates insurance) will do nothing more than encourage additional risk taking and loss.

The problem of moral hazard would be inapplicable to corporate compliance if such initiatives aligned principal and agent incentives; if compliance programs prompted meaningful ethical change in organizations; if compliance was more than a guise for strategic risk management; and if the rationale for purchasing compliance did not resemble the objectives of insurance and self-insurance. It is more than likely that ex ante moral hazards pose a problem, however, given that expenditures for compliance are bounded by risk-shifting and risk-management rationales. The likelihood increases significantly when one adds the inability of prosecutors and courts to objectively judge the effectiveness of compliance efforts, with research revealing that organizations resist meaningful cultural change. The prospects of moral hazards are as much as confirmed after viewing the evidence that corporate deviance is often tolerated, if not tacitly encouraged, by an implicit agenda of top management—where compliance initiatives originate.[99]

Corporate Deviance and "Winking" of Top Management

Of all internal factors accounting for corporate crime, not one comes close in importance to the role of top management in tolerating if not shaping a corporate culture that allows for deviance.[100] In some firms, senior management is well known for sending conflicting signals to middle management about short-term expectations and mandatory objectives as well as contingent incentives and reward systems. This signaling risks encouraging deviant norms while promoting a coercive organizational culture.[101] The consensus view emerging among corporate crime scholars is that "corporate wrongdoing is more often the result of actions or inactions, deliberate or inadvertent, by the top managers of the organization."[102]

The line distinguishing the advertence or inadvertence of managerial actions, however, is often difficult to draw, as recent prosecutions of chief executive officers and chief financial officers reveal. For example, it has been argued that it is not uncommon for top management to lose control and direct supervision over subunits as well as subordinate employees once an organization reaches a certain size, level of complexity, and specialization.[103] Jeffrey Skilling and Kenneth Lay took great pride is saying that "the quality of ideas is proportional to the distance from the 50th floor."[104] This loss of supervisory control by top management, or authority leakage, allows for corporate deviance by lower-level employees, often without any evidence of the knowledge or approval of top management.[105] Despite evidence of knowledge, tacit approval, or at least deliberate indifference, as appears to be the case in WorldCom, top management can be quite successful in demonstrating its ignorance of middle management or subordinate employee deviance.[106] Typical are the remarks of Senator Estes Kefauver, who, after extensive hearings on the Electrical Equipment Antitrust cases in the early 1960s, concluded that "it has been found many times that top executives 'wink' at criminal antitrust violations going on right under their noses. Rather than assure that the antitrust laws were being obeyed by their subordinates, such executives take great pains to make certain that they have no 'knowledge' of any illegal activities."[107]

The subtleties of the top management perspective were captured as early as 1955 by drafters of the Model Penal Code, who commented that organizational crime may be "produced by pressures on subordinates created by corporate managerial officials even though the latter may not have intended or desired the criminal behavior and even though the pressures can only be sensed rather than demonstrated."[108] Given the role of top management in charting the course of legal and ethical compliance in corporations, it is difficult to underestimate the importance of subtle pressures to walk the fine line between law abidance and law deviation. Few underestimate the less-than-subtle pressures to maximize profits, reduce costs, and meet sales goals or quotas.[109]

The range of pressures felt by middle managers and subordinate employees must be considered in light of the perception by employees that top managers are often aware of legal and ethical violations—that they are winking.[110] The phenomenon of winking is further complicated by the tendency of subordinate employees and middle management not to question the policies, judgments, and decisions of senior management;[111] to foist blame on unwary agents when a line is crossed.[112] Much of this behavior is facilitated by the ease with which violations of both the corporate policy and the law may be hidden in the complexity of the corporate form.[113] As one commentator noted, "Big business implicitly encourages scapegoating by their complete lack of any tracking system to trace responsibility."[114]

Empirical research in the banking industry, for example, suggests that top management's winking is linked to features of the corporate form.[115] There is a segmentation of moral views by rank, status, or hierarchy within the organization. As one commentator noted, "Corporations implicitly house a division of moral labour according to which managers at different ranks are inclined to perceive dilemmas from differing moral angles."[116] The importance of this segmentation is evident when top management expresses an allegiance to corporate values and policies while implicitly supporting if not encouraging unethical or illegal actions.[117] In such situations, there is often an untenable conflict between top management's perception of a business need, the primacy of business goals, and what appears to be a restrictive corporate policy.[118]

The critical role of top management, along with the perception of its winking, has led courts to caution that "to conceal the nefarious acts of their underlings by using the shield of corporate armor to deflect corporate responsibility, and to separate the subordinate from the executive, would be to permit 'endocratic' corporations to inflict widespread public harm without hope of redress."[119] This caution, however, is without meaning for firms in certain industries and markets where pressures are, at times, too much for middle managers, supervisory personnel, and subordinates to bear.[120]

The Paradox of Compliance and Its Resolution
Much has been made of the paradox of moral hazard—less loss from loss means more loss.[121] The paradox of cosmetic compliance as a form of risk management reflects the same basic economics and logic. The purchase of compliance sufficient to shift the risk of liability and loss, in certain firms, has the effect of decreasing levels of care. Decreased levels of care with a top management that winks foster an environment of tacit acceptance of illegalities. This acceptance, coupled with the constant pressure on middle

management to produce results, leads to increased deviance throughout the corporate hierarchy.[122] It is so in spite of any increase in offense rates that would be expected with greater monitoring activity. Of course, increased enforcement activity naturally results in higher rates of offending. The purchase of compliance for purposes of liability shifting and cost internalization results in a redefinition of this deviance. Acts that were once held to be those of the firm now remain those of individual employees. The evisceration of vicarious liability, along with unbridled prosecutorial discretion in the intuitive evaluation of compliance effectiveness, may be used to explain the steady increase in white-collar prosecution. Moral hazard theory reveals that certain compliance orientations have the counterintuitive effect of increasing white-collar deviance or, at the very least, allowing for such increase.

The paradox of compliance may be addressed by limiting the incentives that lead firms to purchase only those programs and initiatives that successfully shift liability and loss. In theory, a resolution might be accomplished in two ways. The first requires substantial changes in discretionary prosecutorial policies: Prosecutors would have to resist undermining principles of vicarious liability by rewarding due diligence. Resisting an award of due diligence becomes increasingly important given the absence of consensus on the meaning of effective compliance. The consideration of corporate compliance in relation to corporate liability is a task appropriately reserved in law for sentencing judges. Judicial determinations of compliance effectiveness, along with verifiable measurements of the same, will undercut incentives to diminish care and reduce monitoring levels.[123] Alternatively, regulators and prosecutors might agree on specific criteria for effectiveness. It seems too much to ask organizations to move beyond the rhetoric of "effective" compliance before prosecutors have been able to meaningfully assess the difference.[124] The absence of a metric is more than unfortunate because organizational integrity, corporate ethics, and good corporate citizenship, after all, are said to impair moral hazards.

CHANGES IN DISCRETIONARY POLICIES

The debate over the proper role and efficiency of prosecutorial and regulatory agencies continues.[125] At the center of this debate is a body of scholarship that considers the ideal relation between regulators and corporations.[126] Braithwaite's Enforced Self-Regulation Model and Fisse and Braithwaite's Accountability Model, for example, suggest the importance of corporate standards of conduct and disciplinary mechanisms as a form of reciprocal constraint.[127] Organizations self-regulate to the deference of regulators. Practical considerations such as the grant of prosecutorial amnesty or the receipt of mitigation credit from the guidelines lend support to the importance of these idealized models. The extent of a corporation's self-regulation will determine active criminal investigation versus prosecutorial declination; enforcement or nonenforcement; formal versus informal measures; monetary or nonmonetary sanctions; and civil proceedings or criminal indictment.

Left all but unattended in both theory and practice, however, is the capacity of regulators, prosecutors, and courts to evaluate the effectiveness or authenticity of corporate self-regulation. Pretend for a moment that there is no history of risk shifting by corporations, that there is no evidence of internal or external initiatives on the part of organizations to minimize entity liability by pushing blame down the organizational hierarchy. Disregard the fairness of allowing prosecutors to craft new liability rules for corporate crimes, all in the name of discretion. Put aside concerns that this absence of metrics undercuts the full force of vicarious liability and results in diminished levels of care and incentives to police due to moral hazards. Forget that businesses with significant resources will be advantaged and small, privately held businesses, often without access to legal counsel, will remain the disadvantaged target of criminal prosecution. Even if one pretends, disregards, and forgets, it remains that there is little wisdom in the birth of new standards of corporate self-regulation without an agreed-upon method of assessing compliance with those standards.

That no such method exists is made far worse by the fact that corporations are all too aware of this fact. It is worth asking how organizations assess the value of their compliance and governance expenditures, no less the effectiveness of internal standards and procedures.[128] It is critically important to ask how the inability of regulators, prosecutors, and courts to assess effectiveness influences corporate compliance expenditures and programs. Even conservative answers to these two questions favor limited prosecutorial consideration of corporate compliance programs. If one should add to them the problem of incentives and moral hazards, then the case for restructuring prosecutorial discretion becomes compelling.

SUBSTANTIVE LAW AND LASTING CHANGE

Adopting constructive fault may offer a lasting solution to the moral hazards of compliance, the redefinition of deviance, and, in particular, efforts to unfairly shift liability risks. The objective reasonableness test that lies at the heart of constructive fault accounts for those organizational features or attributes—such as complexity, formality, decision-making processes, and structure—that, at once, allow for gaming and yet reveal culpability. In the absence of liability rules derived from substantive law, firms game guidelines or agency policy statements, and liability turns on their apparent diligence, rather than actions or inactions reflecting corporate fault. Lost are the connections made between the illegal acts of top management, for example, and the firm as an entity. A standard of genuine corporate fault, such as constructive corporate liability, offers few opportunities for gaming regulators through compliance expenditures or with paper programs.

CONCLUSION

The idea that compliance and principles of corporate governance must be effective is deceptively simple. It is overly simplistic, for example, to say that compliance consultants preach a strict adherence to the seven prescriptive steps found in the sentencing guidelines and that ethics consultants see the integrity approach as the integration of ethical values into corporate culture. Vastly different compliance initiatives will share the same outcome criterion, such as effectiveness, but will define it quite differently. Governance principles face comparable challenges. Maintaining a recommended board structure with independent directors and state-of-the-art governance guidelines may earn recognition, win awards, and yet lead to a colossal failure of governance.

The lessons learned from corporate compliance should inform efforts to ensure good corporate governance. Organizations invest in compliance for a host of reasons, including satisfying the perceived legal requirements, shifting liability down the corporate hierarchy, reducing unethical or illegal behavior, increasing the reporting of unethical or illegal behavior, promoting an ethical culture, and effecting corporate strategy.[129] Determinations of effectiveness also vary by compliance orientation, whether law-based, ethics- or integrity-based, or a hybrid.[130] Assessments of effectiveness will vary, depending on the formality of the compliance orientation and the rationale supporting its implementation. So, too, do the budgeted expenditures for compliance, the degree of regulatory risk in a given industry or market, and the methods used to assess effectiveness. To move beyond the rhetoric of "effective" compliance, therefore, there must be consistency between organizational assessments and those of regulators, prosecutors, and courts. The same may be said of corporate governance. To move beyond gaming, there must be a substantive law that constructs fault on the basis of harm committed in the name of the organization, as the organization.

The alternative, the status quo, is all too familiar. Jeffrey Sonnenfeld bemoans the efforts by many companies to blindly embrace governance reforms offered by reincarnated ethics consultancies. "Some of what is being sold by the close to 100 governance training programs offered by consulting firms and universities," according to Sonnenfeld, "is truly disturbing because it is often anchored more in clichés and myths than in careful research."[131] A laundry list of governance reforms, similar to the list of compliance initiatives in the 1990s, has set the stage for the purchase of corporate governance as a product—and the next round of gaming.

CHAPTER FIVE

Shifting Blame

A few months after McKesson Corp. acquired the HBO & Co. (HBOC) in January 1999, it announced that auditors had discovered accounting irregularities. Wall Street's reaction was harsh. McKesson's stock fell nearly 50 percent, reducing its market value more than $9 billion. Nearly ninety shareholder suits followed in both state and federal courts. McKesson's reaction was also swift and decisive. It ordered its audit committee to immediately provide a review; retained the law firm of Skadden, Arps, Slate, Meagher & Flom to conduct a thorough internal investigation; entered into confidentiality agreements with both the Securities and Exchange Commission (SEC) and the U.S. Department of Justice (DOJ); and agreed to waive all attorney-client and work product privileges. Seven months after McKesson's discovery of the accounting irregularities, the company turned over its audit committee's final report to the SEC and DOJ, along with volumes of documents, including interviews of thirty-seven present and former employees.

With this report and supportive memoranda, prosecutors brought securities fraud, mail fraud, and wire fraud indictments against two former copresidents of HBOC. Separate SEC fraud charges were also filed against the former general counsel, senior vice president of finance, chief financial officer, and senior vice president of sales of HBOC. Specifically it was alleged that these six former top officers and other employees of HBOC booked revenue on incomplete deals, backdated contracts, falsified the company's financial records, and lied to the outside auditors to conceal the fraud. In light of McKesson's willingness to cooperate, no civil or criminal charges were filed against the company.[1]

In exchange for unwavering cooperation, Seaboard Inc. was also spared entity liability. From 1995 through the first quarter of 2000, the controller of Chestnut Hills Farms, a subsidiary of Seaboard Inc., caused both the subsidiary's and the parent company's books and records to overstate deferred cost assets by more than $7 million. She also understated related expenses and violated the books and records and reporting provisions of the Exchange Act. Within a week of finding out about the controller's misconduct, Seaboard's internal auditors began a preliminary review and advised management as well as the board's audit committee. The full board was soon advised, authorizing the hiring of outside counsel to conduct an internal investigation. Seaboard immediately fired the controller and informed both the SEC and the investing public that its financial statements would be restated. Next, Seaboard worked collaboratively with the SEC, providing details of its internal investigation, and waived any attorney-client or work product privileges. The company added significant controls in Chestnut Hill's financial reporting systems.[2]

The SEC holds out the Seaboard case as the best example of corporate cooperation. "Our willingness to credit such behavior in deciding whether and how to take enforcement action benefits investors as well as our enforcement program," according to the SEC Statement on the Relationship of Cooperation to Agency Enforcement Decisions.[3] The rationale for crediting cooperation, like that by McKesson and Seaboard, is simple: "When businesses seek out, self-report and rectify illegal conduct, and otherwise cooperate with Commission staff, large expenditures of government and shareholder resources can be avoided and investors can benefit more promptly."[4]

McKesson and Seaboard are but two recent examples of a long-standing practice of sparing a corporation criminal liability for its active cooperation with regulators and prosecutors. Some of the most prominent firms are still with us today by the grace of cooperation agreements with the government. For example, Prudential Securities was charged with making false statements about both the risks and the returns of more than seven hundred limited energy partnerships sold in the late 1980s. The fraud against nearly 340,000 investors cost the company more than $9 billion in losses. Prudential Securities was able to negotiate a cooperation agreement with the United States Attorney's Office, Southern District of New York, and escape certain death by acknowledging the wrongdoing, dramatically rehabilitating its compliance practices after the discovery of illegalities, and aggressively satisfying the informational needs of investigators.

Before the federal prosecutors filed their complaint, attorneys for Prudential asked that they consider how the firm had learned its lesson, how it had changed. "The firm is under new management and it has instituted extensive new compliance procedures," lawyers from Davis Polk wrote. "It has apologized to the past and current clients and has spent over $1 billion to fund and administer the legitimate claims of partnership investors. It has actively worked with all levels of the government to resolve its past problems and get on with the business of serving its clients of today."[5]

So, what does it get you if your firm increases its compliance staff from twenty-six to ninety-five full-time employees; raises its compliance budget from $1.1 million to $10.4 million; adds new, state-of-the-art business controls; completely revamps its training department; enhances the programs in its audit department; and forms an internal risk management group, marketing review department, new product analysis group, and business review committee? The answer: freedom from prosecution.

But the price that Prudential Securities paid included more than compliance and compliance-related expenditures. The cooperation agreement was just that—an agreement that conditioned deferred prosecution on the truthful disclosure of information and evidence that ordinarily would have been impossible for prosecutors to obtain. Such information included, according to terms of the cooperation agreement, "all information with respect to the activities of Prudential Securities, and its respective officers and employees concerning all matters about which the government authorities inquire of them. . . . This obligation of truthful disclosure includes an obligation upon Prudential Securities to provide to the governmental authorities, upon request, any document, record or other tangible evidence relating to matters about which the governmental authorities inquire of them. This obligation of truthful disclosure further includes an obligation to provide to the governmental authorities unlimited access to Prudential Securities' facilities, documents, and employees."[6]

A quick read of Kurt Eichenwald's *Serpent on the Rock* or Kathleen Sharp's *In Good Faith* suggests just how important Prudential Securities' postoffense cooperation and compliance efforts must have been.[7] Indeed, cooperation—and all of the evidence that it affords prosecutors—is another strategic chip in the old compliance game, a chip characterized by the trading of favors between corporate officials and the government.[8] It is a sophisticated exchange of firm- and employee-related evidence for prosecutorial leniency or exculpation. In regulatory periods that prize a corporate-government partnership, this practice is the glue that holds it together. And the value of postoffense cooperation extends to civil or administrative cases where the threat of a criminal indictment looms, even if remote.

In approving a settlement between WorldCom and the SEC, for example, Judge Jed Rakoff noted with approval that under the watchful eye of a court-appointed corporate monitor, WorldCom promised "not just to clean house but to put the company on a new and positive footing—not just to enjoin future violations but to create models of corporate governance and internal compliance for this and other companies to follow—not just to impose penalties but to help stabilize and reorganize the company and thereby help preserve more than 50,000 jobs and obtain some modest, if inadequate, recompense for those shareholder victims who would otherwise recover nothing whatever from the company itself."[9]

WorldCom strategically placed the court-appointed monitor in a watchdog position, overseeing new internal controls and governance reforms. WorldCom also replaced its entire board of directors; hired a new chief executive officer; recruited other senior managers from outside; fired or accepted resignations from every employee implicated in the fraud; fired or accepted resignations from every employee who was "insufficiently attentive" in preventing the fraud; agreed to a complete overhaul of WorldCom's governance principles and practices; provided employees with specialized training in accounting, public reporting, and ethics; and obtained sworn ethics pledges from the chief executive officer and senior management. Judge Rakoff's conclusion: "The Court is aware of no large company accused of fraud that has so rapidly and so completely divorced itself from the misdeeds of the immediate past and undertaken such extraordinary steps to prevent such misdeeds in the future."[10] Following the conviction of the former chief executive officer and the chief financial officer, not to mention a host of adjudicated civil and administrative and shareholder claims, WorldCom is MCI. And, remarkably, MCI is not only a corporation whose integrity is now beyond repute but also an attractive takeover target in the telecom market.[11]

In this chapter, the connection between corporate cooperation and corporate liability is questioned. This discussion is preceded by considering the fairness of trading corporate cooperation for government-granted favors when this cooperation implicates and scapegoats subordinate employees. Ever-increasing levels of corporate cooperation have become general proxies for organizational due diligence, in part because of the shift in regulatory orientation away from command and control strategies and, to be fair, in the absence of adhered-to liability rules. This proxy is unlike other aspects of compliance in that it is observable, easily quantified, easy to demand and barter for, and critically helpful to prosecutors in gaining leverage in investigations and negotiations with complex, multitiered firms where decision making is diffuse and evidence is otherwise difficult or impossible to obtain.[12] Cooperation is also critical outside of the labyrinth of a large decentralized bureaucracy. In fact, it is that much more important in firms where corporate units and subsidiaries are wholly centralized, allowing what Mary Zey described as "fraud networks" to thrive.[13] In the push for inculpatory evidence, it is difficult to avoid the conclusion that on occasion, and perhaps more frequently, corporate cooperation unfairly shifts and deflects the burden of blame.

COOPERATION AND THE PARTNERSHIP

As noted in earlier chapters, drafters of the U. S. Sentencing Guidelines for Organizational Defendants wanted corporations to face the threat of significant punishment and, at the same time, the possibility of mitigation, leniency, and amnesty.[14] In the ideal, the objective was to construct regulatory strategy at once both provocative and forgiving.[15] The Holder and Thompson Memos extend a comparable strategy to charging decisions and plea negotiations. This strategy drives guidelines that prompt reciprocal promises—organizational cooperation and acceptance of responsibility in exchange for mitigation, exculpation, or absolution.[16] With an arsenal of sanctions in the regulatory background, a bargained-for exchange or trading of favors is a decision template for prosecutors and judges in cases of corporate crime.[17]

Corporations face little choice but to trade favors with authorities, given the threat of significant guideline-prescribed fines, debarments, suspensions, and other intermediate sanctions.[18] And the importance of and need for these reciprocal promises is rarely challenged.[19] Given extremely limited resources, the complex nature of the corporate form, and the accompanying evidentiary challenges facing prosecutors, it is little wonder that the government often exchanges leniency for conciliatory postoffense behavior. Strict enforcement, sanctioning, or deterrent styles of regulation focusing on criminalization and prosecution have long been recognized as significantly inhibiting corporate cooperation by keeping control of information and incriminating evidence in the hands of the regulated rather than the regulator.[20] If anything, this kind of regulation promotes a different kind of gaming by organizations and, according to some commentators, encourages law evasion and deviance.[21]

To free the hand of regulators and prosecutors and minimize the costs of compliance, reciprocity and negotiated forbearance are now preferred strategies.[22] Substantial assistance departures and mitigation credits, as well as voluntary disclosure, leniency, and amnesty programs, populate the enforcement and regulatory landscape.[23] In theory, the substantive corporate criminal law is ruled by principles of vicarious liability.[24] In practice, cases of corporate crime are adjudicated by a brand of negotiated compliance. Corporate cooperation, through the forward and reverse assignment of blame, facilitates the flow of evidence to authorities and is the critical feature of this regulatory strategy.[25]

FORWARD WHISTLE-BLOWING

Corporate cooperation is susceptible to gaming, much like corporate compliance generally. Corporate games turn on who is the ultimate target of the prosecution, for example, a senior corporate officer, a subordinate employee, or the corporate entity itself.[26] Since the early 2000s, law enforcement's counteroffensive against corporate fraud has focused on avenging the actions and inactions of senior corporate officers rather than targeting corporate entities. The criminal investigations of Enron, WorldCom, Andersen, and other icons as corporate entities soon took a backseat to the identification of its most culpable senior officials. This strategy was first made clear in 2002, when the Executive Branch proposed, among other reforms, to

- double the maximum prison term for mail fraud and wire fraud to ten years, and increase the prison time served for fraud committed by corporate leaders.
- create a new Corporate Fraud Task Force to increase DOJ's ability to oversee and coordinate the investigation and prosecution of fraud and related criminal activity.
- empower the SEC to freeze improper payments to corporate executives while a company is under investigation.
- end the practice of allowing corporate officers to receive loans from their companies.
- prevent CEOs or other officers from profiting from erroneous financial statements.
- ensure that CEOs or other officers who clearly abuse their power lose their right to serve in any corporate leadership positions.
- require corporate leaders to tell the public promptly whenever they buy or sell company stock for personal gain.
- strengthen laws that criminalize document shredding and other forms of obstruction of justice.
- challenge CEOs in America to fully comply with the spirit of existing SEC rules by explaining prominently and in clear English why their compensation packages are in the best interests of their companies.
- strengthen the SEC by seeking an additional $100 million in FY 2003 for the SEC to help hire more enforcement agents and improve other prosecutorial activities.[27]

The strategy behind targeting high-level corporate officials became that much clearer in 2003 when deputy attorney general Larry Thompson cautioned prosecutors: "Because a corporation can act only through individuals, imposition of individual criminal liability may provide the strongest deterrent against future corporate wrongdoing. Only rarely should provable individual culpability not be pursued, even in the face of offers of corporate guilty pleas."[28]

To obtain incriminating evidence on a CEO or CFO, for example, prosecutors sought the cooperation of employees with increasing seniority, working up the corporate hierarchy to eventual targets. This forward assignment of blame, which may be called forward whistle-blowing (FWB), often entails a gift of prosecutorial leniency or amnesty to subordinates, midlevel managers, and even senior managers, in exchange for their cooperation in blowing the whistle on the crimes of their superiors. Snitching on one's superiors is now as familiar as the progression from the middle of Enron to the top:[29] from Kopper, Fastow, and Skilling to Lay; from Sullivan to Ebbers; and from Owens to Scrushy. Most recently, New York attorney general Eliot Spitzer did the same, masterfully working indictments of low-level Marsh & McLennan insurance executives for bid rigging and steering as he targeted senior management.

In its first two years, the newly created Corporate Fraud Task Force produced a literal graveyard of CEOs and CFOs by relying in large part on FWB. With the priority of securing senior white-collar indictments, prosecutors traded up the corporate ladder. Consider, for example, that the CEO, senior vice president of business development, and director of finance of L90 Inc. pled guilty to securities fraud; the former CEO, CFO, vice president, and outside member of the board of NewCom Inc. were charged with securities fraud, money laundering, and embezzlement; the former chairman of Manhattan Bagel Inc. joined the president of its largest subsidiary in pleading guilty to conspiring to falsify revenues; the former CEO, president, and chairman of Informix Corp. was charged with criminal securities and wire fraud; the former CFO and controller of Network Associates pled guilty to securities fraud; the former chairman and vice chairman of Cendant Corp. were charged with securities fraud, mail fraud, and wire fraud; guilty pleas were obtained against the former chief accounting officer and former vice president of Symbol Technologies for a series of accounting fraud offenses; the former CEO and CFO of American Tissue Inc. were indicted on charges of securities fraud, bank fraud, and obstruction of justice in a scheme that defrauded investors of more than $300 million; the former CEO, CFO, and chief operating officer (COO) of Sharp International Corp. pled guilty to defrauding its lenders of more than $50 million; and, among countless other cases, the former chairman and CEO, CFO, executive vice president (EVP) of operations, vice president of finance, and vice president of treasury of Adelphia Communications Corp. were charged with conspiracy, securities fraud, wire fraud, and bank fraud.[30]

The practice of FWB is the preferred prosecutorial strategy during heightened periods of regulatory scrutiny and, in particular, periods of corporate scandals that shake public perceptions of corporate ethics and the very legitimacy of our markets. The political pressure to swiftly identify and prosecute senior corporate officials can be overwhelming. Before the creation of the Corporate Fraud Task Force, criminal investigations of corporate fraud would take three to four years, according to Deputy Attorney General Thompson. "What we have asked our prosecutors and investigators to do," Thompson now reports, "is to work in a different way. And we have actually undertaken these investigations in a way that we have brought to justice in a much quicker manner many of the corrupt executives that were involved in these matters. I would submit that that kind of action has helped—not fully participated in it—but helped restore Americans' confidence in their financial markets."[31] Many corporate leaders play into the prosecutor's hand by pleading or feigning ignorance—the "aw, shucks" defense. Nothing galvanizes public support for swift and harsh justice more than incredible claims of innocence by self-aggrandized executives.

REVERSE WHISTLE-BLOWING

Toward the end of a heightened period of regulatory enforcement and during periods of lax enforcement where the premium is not on symbolically showcasing the prosecution of senior executives, a very different kind prosecutorial strategy is frequently adopted. Prosecutors secure the cooperation of senior corporate officials who—after an internal investigation offered to regulators, a criminal investigation by prosecutors, or in response to a threat of a criminal investigation or indictment—offer evidence against culpable subordinate employees in a trade for promises of corporate leniency or possible corporate amnesty.[32] This practice, known as reverse whistle-blowing (RWB) is quite different from FWB and the more familiar practice of employee whistle-blowing (EWB).[33] Instead of subordinate employees implicating senior officials or employees identifying and providing evidence of "corporate" deviance, organizations through senior management engage in RWB by scapegoating deviant employees. There is something quite unique about the kind of scapegoating in RWB. That said, given the extent of retaliation against EWBs—typically intensified after covering up the alleged illegality—there is also some common ground. This commonality is especially true in terms of the extent to which both RWBs and EWBs are victimized, for example, lost jobs, negative job evaluations, and blacklisting from employment in the field. Survey evidence reveals rates of victimization often exceeding 60 percent.[34]

In otherwise compliant organizations, RWB is part of an effective compliance strategy to root out expendable wayward employees. Unfortunately, some firms that are themselves complicit and criminally culpable use RWB to displace rather than fairly direct blame. In both cases, RWB plays off of the predisposition of prosecutors to see corporate crime as necessitating individual action, a predilection to assign blame personally, and a desire to leverage the authority and information advantage of senior managers to quickly assign blame.[35]

Three variants of RWB may be undetectable to regulators or prosecutors. In the consensual form, described as consensual scapegoating some time ago by Fisse and Braithwaite,[36] a corporate agent—typically a more senior manager or an executive—is paid to assume responsibility for a corporate wrong.[37] In the nonconsensual form, the concern of much of this chapter, culpable though not entirely deserving agents receive an unjustifiable share of blame and, depending on the perceived demands of the regulatory environment, are fired. "All too often legal and social responsibility and blame is attributed to individuals," according to one commentator, "often relatively junior individuals, who may have been the immediate cause of a corporate misdemeanor, rather than attention and responsibility being attributed to the structural and systemic problems which may have given rise to or allowed the problem to emerge."[38] With all variants, RWB is rationalized in many ways, including as an acceptable and necessary compromise to maintain the viability and health of the entity.[39]

When employees are singled out for blame that the organization deserves, as with nonconsensual RWB, there is a definite need for constraints on the value accorded to postoffense cooperation by prosecutors and judges. To a certain extent, this need is recognized in the Holder Memo. "A corporation should not be able to escape liability merely by offering up its directors, officers, employees, or agents in lieu of its own prosecution," according to these guidelines. "Thus, a corporation's willingness to cooperate is merely one relevant factor; one that needs to be considered in conjunction with the other factors, particularly those relating to the corporation's past history and the role of management in the wrongdoing."[40]

Unfortunately, this admonition is more strongly worded than regularly enforced. As one defense counsel observed, "federal prosecutors are telling major companies they have to turn over the results of privileged investigations, rat on their employees and cut them off from the flow of information."[41] In the immediate wake of a long series of notable corporate crimes, RWB once again has made newspaper headlines. KPMG's tax partner, Jeffrey Eischeid, is one of the latest casualties. When the government started to scrutinize some of KPMG's tax shelters that Eischeid had championed, the firm placed him on leave, then asked him to resign, and threatened not to cover his legal expenses unless he cooperated fully with investigators and, in doing so, risked self-incrimination. Notably, the tax shelters were fully approved and backed by the firm. In fact, KPMG sent Eischeid to testify about the merits of these very shelters before Congress. As the threat of criminal liability for KPMG became real, the firm issued the following apology: "KPMG takes full responsibility for the unlawful conduct by former KPMG partners during that period, and we deeply regret that it occurred. . . ."[42] For its cooperation, contrition, and promise of reforms, KPMG paid a $456 million fine and accepted a deferred prosecution agreement. Eischeid was criminally indicted along with seven other KPMG partners.

Similar high-profile midlevel investigations and prosecutions were seen at Dynegy Inc., Computer Associates Inc., and Qwest Communications International, where questions linger about senior managers being sacrificed by firms to protect higher-ups. Jamie Olis, a midlevel tax manager at Dynegy was sentenced to more than twenty-four years in prison, without the chance of parole, after refusing to cooperate by shifting blame up the corporate ladder. A lawyer representing a midlevel exeuctive at Qwest spoke openly about the prosecutor's desire to scapegoat his client to maintain the appearance of a committed fight against corporate crime. Ultimately he asks, "Who was driving the bus?"[43]

DEFLECTING BLAME DOWNWARD: THE DARK SIDE OF GUIDELINES-INSPIRED INCENTIVES

For many scholars and practitioners, the sentencing guidelines and prosecutorial guidelines are a regulatory blessing.[44] Sentencing disparity in federal courts is squarely addressed. Prosecutorial and judicial discretion are constrained with sufficient room to account for unique cases. Clearly articulated standards of corporate behavior replace an absence of stated expectations. Corporations are relieved of liability or sentences are mitigated if, after the discovery of an offense, management works cooperatively with prosecutors and regulators. Organizational due diligence and cooperation are an inspired prescription for compliance.

Those who express concern over this new age of corporate-government cooperation reflect on the changing direction of management allegiances in an organization where the loyalties of corporate counsel, outside counsel, and prosecutors continue to converge.[45] A central and long-standing concern of the criminal defense bar is the evisceration of certain time-honored privileges for employees during an internal corporate criminal investigation or audit.[46] Freedom from self-incrimination and rights of confidentiality are being increasingly sacrificed in the name of efficient law enforcement. In making disclosures, must employees waive attorney-client and work product privileges? Should evidence of employee wrongdoing be offered freely to government investigators and regulators in crafting a deal? Should internal communications be privileged? These very legitimate defense concerns, still largely unresolved, prompt commentators to wonder about the boundaries of self-policing and whether, in the words of two former prosecutors, the "government is deputizing 'Corporate America' as an arm of law enforcement at the expense of principles that lie at the core of our adversarial system of justice."[47]

The continuing debate over compromised privileges, however, masks a more troublesome artifact of a regulatory trend that, as noted earlier, peaks during periods of lax enforcement. A number of notable cases both prior to and during the tail end of the recent spate of corporate scandals reveal that organizations facing the specter of a criminal investigation or indictment are doing more than simply trying to appease prosecutors by waiving attorney-client, work product, and self-evaluative privileges.[48] In an effort to meet and exceed prosecutorial expectations, firms often collaborate with government investigators and regulators in ways that few would have predicted before the sentencing guidelines. As corporate counsel often admit, an internal investigation is a search for the truth and, all too often, a capitulation to the authorities. "Federal prosecutors are no longer content to build criminal cases by relying on the powerful tools of grants of immunity and grand jury subpoenas for non-privileged evidence," according to two former United States attorneys. "Instead, they now often insist, even at the outset of an investigation, that corporations turn over privileged communications, attorney work product, and incriminating statements from corporate employees as a condition of favorable treatment in the exercise of the prosecutor's considerable discretion."[49]

Not so long ago, corporations would routinely embrace, counsel, and indemnify employees suspected of wrongdoing—especially those who offered significant value to the firm.[50] Far fewer do so today. Who would have guessed that the government and targeted companies would jointly sponsor criminal probes and inquiries, engage in covert operations extending to key customers or deep into the supply chain, and conduct surprise work site and employee home investigations?[51] Corporate and retained counsel have a distinct incentive to align themselves with prosecutors by opening internal investigative files and, at times, turning or "flipping" culpable employees over to the government in deals orchestrated to win favor.[52]

The extent to which organizations, through corporate or retained counsel, cater to prosecutorial demands has led the defense bar to voice many concerns. The attribution of blame to subordinate employees may often be a matter of shielding senior managers and the entity from criminal liability. The harsh and often unjustified discipline of employees by employers may be practiced solely to satisfy external perceptions of guidelines compliance. The focus on securing evidence of wrongdoing runs the risk of compromising the rights of employees, including the right against self-incrimination. Prosecutors may coerce employers to isolate and pressure suspected employees. Concerns over waivers of attorney-client privilege chill internal investigations. The mad dash to the prosecutor's office by organizations to self-report can, in certain cases, compromise the quality of inculpatory information tendered. There is also a concern about simultaneous representation and the extent to which corporate counsel may be conflicted in representing the interests of the firm at the same time as its officers, directors, or employees.[53]

As a result of these trends, there has been a discernable shift in the role of corporate counsel from employee advocate to government agent or informant, in spite of countless proposals for the protection of privileges and corporate whistle-blowers. As Richard Gruner observes, "Amnesty effectively aligns the interests of companies in these areas with those of law enforcement officials, creating a 'practical partnership' regarding the prevention and punishment of illegal activities within corporate environments."[54] Finally, there is now so much fear over being a casualty of regulatory zeal that firms are firing agents who pose even the slightest threat to their reputation for good governance.

The strong rhetoric of the white-collar criminal defense bar has some empirical support. Survey research reveals that employees generally believe that illegal behavior in organizations is caused, in large part, by pressures to meet schedules and unrealistic earnings goals. In a KPMG survey of organizational integrity, researchers cautioned, for example, that "[c]ompanies are sending the wrong message to employees on how to meet business goals. These percentages of employees believe misconduct is caused by: Pressure to meet schedules 70%; Pressure to hit unrealistic earnings goals 65%; Desire to succeed or advance careers 56%; Inadequate training 50%; Desire to steal from or hurt the company 22%."[55]

Employees report that it is easier to comply with corporate standards if companies set more realistic earnings and growth projections.[56] Compliance is also facilitated when employees do not feel as if they need to cut corners to meet schedules, deadlines, or expectations.[57] Finally, most employees report that compliance is often a function of the extent to which a company's culture is consistent with its values or principles, the level of commitment from top management, the support offered by management when compliance issues are raised, and the organizational incentives—or lack of incentives—for upholding ethical standards.[58] Most employees who feel pressure to compromise ethical standards—or say they do—attribute the source either to a supervisor or to top management. Not surprisingly, employees generally feel uncomfortable reporting an observed violation to senior management, a chief executive officer, or the firm's legal department. According to a survey by the Ethics Resources Center, "The fact that more than one in three employees who feel pressure attributes it to their supervisor and/or top management suggests a continuing internal challenge for organizations. Those with the most power are perceived to exert the greatest pressure on others to compromise organizational ethics standards."[59]

To some of those better known in the white-collar defense bar, these sentiments reflect the dark side of the incentives fueling both prosecutorial and sentencing guidelines.[60] That there is a dark side should not surprise those who track the evolution of corporate criminal liability. Every year following passage of the sentencing guidelines and with every new regulatory or prosecutorial guideline, there has been a noticeable escalation in the government's expectation of organizational cooperation.[61] This escalation reflects the realization of a new regulatory era exemplified by the highly publicized criminal investigations of, for example, Prudential Securities. In this new era, "it is almost fatal for a company to try to resist or defend against criminal investigations," one attorney familiar with this case said. "The government has made it clear, anyone who decides to stand and fight is almost guaranteed indictment. The only way to avoid indictment is to cooperate."[62]

In these and many other cases, crimes were ultimately recast as something less than criminal—or actions of wayward employees, rather than those of the organization—after the targeted corporation satisfied ever-stringent demands for cooperation.[63] In sharp contrast to the fate of E. F. Hutton, Bankers Trust, or Drexel Burnham Lambert Inc., firms that denied liability and failed to cooperate with prosecutors, the defense bar watched with glee as giants of Wall Street escaped criminal indictment, much less conviction, by embracing rather than rejecting prosecutorial overtures. As famed white-collar defense lawyer (and now U.S. District Court judge) Jed S. Rakoff wrote, "prosecutors are reluctant to bring the criminal law to bear against organizations that appear more rueful than recalcitrant. Simply put, prosecutors tend to view themselves as avenging angels in simple morality plays where evil is banished and social order restored."[64] The takeaway from Prudential Securities and its progeny is simple—in the unlikely event that criminal activity is identified in an organization, joining with prosecutors in offering boundless cooperation may very well avert even a near-death experience. But at whose expense?

If the trading of cooperation affected only the targeted company and agents of the government, fairness and desert concerns would be very similar to those found with the granting of leniency for cooperation in individual prosecutions.[65] The discussion would turn on the need of prosecutors to gain leverage and the corresponding potential of the bargain to compromise the perceived legitimacy of the law enforcement role. Commentators addressing corporate cooperation would discuss the characteristic uncertainty of the cooperation bargain.[66] This discussion would focus on the sequelae of snitching: fear of economic or physical retaliation and the shame of betrayal.[67] Concerns would be expressed that such trading could, on occasion, result in "inverted sentencing" where prosecutors trade down rather than up, for example, cooperation of a high-ranking member of an organized crime family results in conviction of low-level drug dealers.[68]

Similarly, if cooperation took place only in criminal investigations where corporations bear the blame that is independently due to management's actions or inaction, that too would be different. This deflection of blame upward, according to Vic Khanna, receives some anecdotal and empirical support.[69] No doubt it accounts for at least some of the variance in corporate criminal activity. However, the pairing of corporate or retained counsel and government regulators has not prompted these questions in these particular instances. Instead, the conventional wisdom of the white-collar defense bar raises a very different concern—that the very incentives responsible for the good corporate citizenship movement can produce a disassociation between management and employees, a divergence of interests that inevitably leads to actions that appear far less than fair, such as the scapegoating of subordinate employees for the acts or policies of the company, its senior management, or its senior officers.

The fear is that in some organizations, subordinate employees who succumbed to the pressure of superiors will be seen as expendable when serious "cooperative" negotiations over criminal liability begin. Brent Fisse raised this concern back in 1984: "By offering a splendid sacrifice the hope is that prosecutors will feel sufficiently satisfied with their efforts and refrain from pressing charges against the corporation or members of its protected managerial elite."[70] Prosecutors, after all, wield vast discretion in determining the type and extent of liability. Moreover, a substantial body of research in social psychology reveals that causal explanations about who is to blame and who should be held accountable covary.[71] The assessment of blame and the assignment of responsibility, therefore, are likely to be influenced by one's position in the corporate hierarchy. Ann McGill offered a telling example of how responsibility judgments and attributions are affected by rank and perceptions of rank: "For example, managers of the company whose train derailed might identify the action of the engineer who sped around the bend as the cause of the accident. Management response to the accident might therefore be to fire the engineer and to send memos to all employees reminding them to be very careful, not to speed, to follow safety regulations, and to stay alert. . . . It is unlikely that management would assume any responsibility for the accident or make changes to existing systems and policies, arguing that most of their trains do not derail and that the train in question was running along fine until the engineer exceeded speed limits."[72]

According to corporate counsel at General Electric, to avoid corporate criminal liability, "[y]ou want to convince the government that this is aberrant behavior by a very small number of people and that the company doesn't tolerate this type of behavior."[73] "If you want any credit," according to another commentator, "your company must roll over and flip the culprits to the prosecutors." Dean Starkman noted this trend in a high-profile article that appeared in the *Wall Street Journal*. "Corporations under government investigation," he concluded, "are increasingly turning on their employees to win leniency for themselves."[74]

In generally law-abiding and compliant organizations, where individual deviance is clearly distinguishable from any culpable corporate action, this kind of RWB appears to be both wise and fair.[75] Cooperation is certainly fairly offered and received when blame is justifiably deflected upward. In fact, the nonmonetary incentives supporting the flipping of culpable employees are, in cases of compliant organizations, very similar to incentives underlying EWB by concerned or disgruntled workers, such as the desire to expose and curtail corporate wrongdoing. An emerging body of research, however, suggests that corporate deviance is more than widespread. This brand of deviance is most often related to the actions of top management and more generally to organizational processes, decisions, structures, hierarchy, and culture.[76] Crime that occurs in a complex organization often reflects more than an individual or group act—it is, as discussed in chapter 3, an organizational act. As Marshall Clinard and his colleagues so eloquently stated: "Illegal corporate behavior is a form of collective rule-breaking in order to achieve the organizational goals."[77] In some cases, therefore, an organization's identification of employee culprits—RWB—may unfairly attribute and displace blame. Blame is deflected downward. This is especially the case where an employee violates the law by acting within the scope of his or her authority, for the benefit of the corporation, and with the express or implied authority of management. Of course, beyond issues of fairness, RWB seriously interferes with a thorough investigation and the appropriate attribution of blame.

SCAPEGOATING AND THE LIMITS OF POSTOFFENSE BEHAVIOR
If there is a prototypical case of RWB, it is with an organization in which senior management winks at the illegal behavior of subordinate employees when under significant pressure to meet revenue or profit objectives. Long before the sentencing guidelines, John Coffee Jr. captured a phenomenon associated with deviance in large corporations. Large companies may view midlevel managers as "a fungible commodity that can be sacrificed as convenient scapegoats and easily replaced. Senior managers can piously express appropriate shock at their subordinates' actions while still demanding strict 'accountability' on the part of such managers for short-term operating results."[78]

The likelihood of this phenomenon increases in a number of settings. Management may delegate responsibility down the corporate hierarchy and at least appear to rely more on subordinate decision making. There may be significant performance pressure placed on middle management and subordinates, and middle management may fail to question policies, judgments, and decisions of senior management. With such pressure, it may be difficult to prove that a policy, directive, command, or authorization originated with top management. Finally, top management may display deliberate indifference to or ignorance of employee deviance, strategically shielding itself from positive knowledge of illegal acts.[79]

Winking promptly changes to condemnation, however, when regulators and prosecutors seek evidence of wrongdoing. As Brent Fisse and John Braithwaite noted, "Corporations, if left to their own devices, will try to deflect responsibility to a select group of sacrificial personnel, often at a lower level than the actual source of skullduggery."[80] As evidence emerges, senior managers are known to distance themselves from the decisions and actions of "wayward" employees, assuming a defensive posture to protect the entity from blame.[81] Corporate scapegoating is a defensive act that channels, displaces, and disposes of blame to protect the organization and maintain legitimacy. Blame and liability are directed away from the firm and toward vulnerable targets.[82] Deception, self-deception, denial of responsibility, and lack of repentance all reflect the cleansing aspect of scapegoating.

The concept of scapegoating that underlies both consensual and nonconsensual RWB allows a corporation, as an entity, to achieve absolution. Organizations minimize or escape punishment free of any guilt. An agent is selected to stand in for the corporation. After all, "[s]omeone has to take the blame to allow the rest of us to continue our normal functions, nominally at least, free of guilt or responsibility for events past."[83] Scapegoating acts as more than a mere ritual transfer of evil—the objective is to displace blame and cleanse the organization by blaming those both unclean and disposable.

At least five variables determine the risk that RWB will raise fundamental questions of fairness. First, the extent of the connection between the criminal act and the actions, policies, or culture of the entity is, in part, determinative. The greatest risk lies where a significant connection exists between the acts of an employee and the actions (or inaction) of the entity. For example, risk of unfairness is great where top management is complicit or where middle management, in spite of a comprehensive compliance program, tacitly encourages subordinate employees to engage in illegalities.

Of course, organizations are more than aware that the risks of attributed liability increase when its structure is tightly coupled. Corporations gravitate toward decentralized, loosely coupled structures as they mature in size and specialization. This evolution, some claim, "allows the corporation to take advantage of opportunities as they arise and react quickly to threats, in and from the task environment. It also allows the organization to distance itself from illegal actions, illegal actors, and undesirable attention."[84] Determining a significant connection between the actus reus of the corporation and the individual's act, therefore, is often extremely difficult.[85] Loosely coupled organizations are well designed to scapegoat employees successfully without detection.

Second, fairness concerns are also related to the extent to which officers, senior executives, and senior managers condoned the commission of the offense or knew or consciously disregarded knowledge of the illegality. Where senior managers directed others to commit the offense, were aware of the illegalities, or consciously disregarded the commission of the offense, the risk is greatest. This state-of-mind variable, like the action variable discussed above, is related to firm size and decentralization. Evidence of corporate knowledge or action is much more difficult to obtain in organizations where decision making is tied to an informal culture of "nudges and winks, of rules which are not really meant to be obeyed."[86]

A third variable of significance is the status or relationship of offending employees to those cooperating with the government. The risk of unfairness is greatest where the status of the employee being investigated or charged is far subordinate to those cooperating with the government. The notion of scapegoating requires more than mere substitution; scapegoats must be disposable and worthy of being disposed.[87] Ideally, from the perspective of the corporation, a scapegoat should be weak and unable to retaliate.

Fourth, the character and quality of compliance initiatives are critical. Nonconsensual RWB appears that much more likely, and thus unfair, in cases where firms purchase compliance to the minimum requirements of prevailing laws—purchases that go to satisfy the impressions of regulators.[88] Finally, corporate culture will be partly determinative. The existence of a corporate culture embraced by leadership and committed to organizational integrity minimizes fairness concerns.[89]

Consider the contribution of each of these variables in the criminal investigation and prosecution of Darling International Inc., a meat and meat-processing company located in Minnesota, for violations of the Clean Water Act.[90] *United States v. Darling* is often held out as representing a trend of management exchanging or trading culpable employees for leniency.[91]

Darling 1

In 1989, Darling International bought a rendering plant in Blue Earth, Minnesota. Under significant pressure to increase production to meet sales objectives, the company's wastewater system soon became overloaded.[92] Beginning in 1991, employees sought to remedy this situation by illegally dumping millions of gallons of ammonia- and blood-contaminated water into the Blue Earth River, causing significant environmental damage. Soon thereafter, on orders of the plant manager and with the knowledge of the vice president of environmental affairs, employees attempted to hide the illegal dumping by diluting and tampering with at least nine wastewater samples sent to state pollution control authorities. The government had evidence that employees also fabricated and submitted discharge-monitoring reports and related documents that were later sent to state regulators.[93]

The federal government's investigation into these environmental crimes stalled until Darling's board required retained counsel to cooperate with authorities and provide evidence of any criminal acts by its employees.[94] With newly offered evidence, prosecutors obtained criminal convictions of four employees, all of whom had been fired by Darling after fully cooperating with counsel retained by the company and with federal prosecutors.[95] Darling entered into a plea agreement, and prosecutors recognized the company's cooperation by recommending a significantly mitigated fine—one-quarter of the originally recommended fine.[96] The company promptly implemented an environmental compliance program, adopted a code of business conduct, and created a corporate ombudsman position to "encourage employees to report suspected problems even when they are reluctant to go directly to their supervisors, legal counsel, or someone else in management."[97]

Darling is notable for several reasons: the complicity and knowledge of management, the distance between the employees held responsible and those cooperating with authorities, the absence of compliance initiatives or programs, and a culture that permits RWB and the deception that can and often does accompany it. The way in which *Darling* was adjudicated also supports many of the defense bar's concerns. Darling was rewarded for relying on the assistance of employees who were fired and prosecuted. These employees faced very real dilemmas. As in many cases, the power of organizational obfuscation complicated the ascription of blame. The strong desire by prosecutors to secure a guilty plea encouraged nonconsensual RWB. Further, knowledge of illegalities was shared across hierarchical levels in the corporation, and the pressure to meet key revenue objectives contributed to deviance. Ultimately, subordinate employees were easy sacrifices in an organization that perceived little choice but self-perseverance. This strategy succeeded as *Darling* was rewarded for postoffense behavior even after unfairly attributing blame by RWB.[98]

One additional lesson of *Darling*, however, is that evidence that senior management has knowledge of the illegalities, the status of corporate cooperators, the extent of compliance programs in place, and the quality of the corporate culture dramatically changes the perceived fairness attributions of liability, not to mention the practice of RWB. For example, conclusions regarding liability and culpability change when evidence of management's complicity or knowledge is absent. Consider the following two variations of *Darling*. In each, changes in the variables associated with risk to fairness reveal the extent to which *Darling* is a prototypical case.

Darling 2

In 1989, Darling International Co. Inc. bought an animal feed grinding plant in Blue Earth, Minnesota. Under significant pressure to increase production to meet sales objectives, the company's wastewater system soon became overloaded. Beginning in fall 1991, without the knowledge or consent of midlevel management, several subordinate employees sought to remedy this situation by illegally dumping millions of gallons of blood-contaminated water into the Blue Earth River, causing significant environmental damage. To conceal the illegal dumping, four employees diluted wastewater samples required by state pollution control authorities. All managers and employees received extensive compliance training and regularly heard from top management and officers of the company about the commitment of Darling to environmental ethics and compliance. One of these employees, seeking to obtain leniency, approached prosecutors with evidence of the illegal dumping and subsequent cover-up.

Darling 3

In 1989, Darling International Co. Inc. bought an animal feed grinding plant in Blue Earth, Minnesota. Under significant pressure to increase production to meet sales objectives, the company's wastewater system soon became overloaded. Beginning in fall 1991, employees sought to remedy this situation by illegally dumping millions of gallons of blood-contaminated water into the Blue Earth River, causing significant environmental damage. Soon thereafter, under orders of the plant manager and with the knowledge of the chief executive officer as well as senior managers, employees diluted wastewater samples required by state pollution control authorities in order to hide the illegal dumping. Darling retained a top-tier consulting firm that established an integrity management program that all employees attended. The government investigation into these environmental crimes stalled until Darling's board required corporate counsel to cooperate with authorities and provide evidence of crimes by employees. Prosecutors obtained criminal convictions of four employees, all of whom had been fired by Darling. Darling entered into a plea agreement, and prosecutors recognized their cooperation and compliance initiatives by recommending a significantly mitigated fine at sentencing—one-quarter of the originally recommended fine.

In Darling 2, should prosecutors offer leniency in exchange for an upward deflection of blame? What role should Darling's compliance program and corporate culture play in any trade for cooperation? What about the knowledge of midlevel management? In Darling 3, what weight should prosecutors give the orders and knowledge of the chief executive officer? Does it matter, for the purposes of any trade, that Darling's compliance program was designed and implemented by a top-tier consulting firm?

TRADING COOPERATION FOR LIABILITY AND BLAME

The Holder Memo instructs prosecutors that evidentiary obstacles are fixtures of corporate criminal investigations. How should prosecutors determine who did what and when? Lines of authority, channels of responsibility, and decision making are difficult to decipher from the outside looking in. All of this is made more complex by criminal conduct that is sustained over time. Employees are regularly promoted, transferred, or fired, or they may have quit or retired. Cooperation, according to the Holder Memo, may be the only way to secure evidence and identify any culprits.

Prosecutorial guidelines allow credit to be given where there is willingness to (1) identify the culprits within the corporation, including senior executives; (2) make witnesses available; (3) waive attorney-client and work product protection; and (4) encourage corporations, as part of their larger compliance efforts, to conduct internal investigations and disclose findings to the appropriate authorities. Prosecutors consider the timing and quality of a corporation's disclosure in judging management's commitment to compliance. Does the corporation appear as if it is protecting its culpable employees? Is the corporation engaging in conduct that impedes the investigation while giving the impression of cooperating? Is the corporation attempting to avoid liability by offering its employees and agents in lieu of its own prosecution?

These questions mirror those asked by the SEC when evaluating any possible trades for cooperation (see table 5.1).

It is a less-than-useful exercise to challenge the value of corporate cooperation or to suggest that trades for leniency or absolution be restricted or further limited. The value that the government places on cooperation is simply far too great. That said, it is helpful and perhaps important to consider how the idea of corporate cooperation fits into a larger conception of corporate personhood and corporate criminal liability.

Remarkably, there is little to no discussion about the idea of the corporate person when crafting incentives for companies to work "collaboratively" with prosecutors. No one seems to be asking: Who is the corporation? Is it fair to credit a corporate entity for its willingness to, for example, disclose the contents of interviews between employees and corporate counsel? The debate over personhood, it seems, makes sense only when courts consider expanding or limiting a corporation's constitutional rights or when there are attributions of criminal liability against an entity, with all of the associated externalities. This is further evidence that concerns over corporate

Table 5.1. SEC Guidelines

1. What is the nature of the misconduct involved? Did it result from inadvertence, honest mistake, simple negligence, reckless or deliberate indifference to indicia of wrongful conduct, willful misconduct or unadorned venality? Were the company's auditors misled?

2. How did the misconduct arise? Is it the result of pressure placed on employees to achieve specific results, or a tone of lawlessness set by those in control of the company? What compliance procedures were in place to prevent the misconduct now uncovered? Why did those procedures fail to stop or inhibit the wrongful conduct?

3. Where in the organization did the misconduct occur? How high up in the chain of command was knowledge of, or participation in, the misconduct? Did senior personnel participate in, or turn a blind eye toward, obvious indicia of misconduct? How systemic was the behavior? Is it symptomatic of the way the entity does business, or was it isolated?

4. How long did the misconduct last? Was it a one-quarter or one-time event, or did it last several years? In the case of a public company, did the misconduct occur before the company went public? Did it facilitate the company's ability to go public?

5. How much harm has the misconduct inflicted upon investors and other corporate constituencies? Did the share price of the company's stock drop significantly upon its discovery and disclosure?

6. How was the misconduct detected, and who uncovered it?

7. How long after discovery of the misconduct did it take to implement an effective response?

8. What steps did the company take upon learning of the misconduct? Did the company immediately stop the misconduct? Are persons responsible for any misconduct still with the company? If so, are they still in the same positions? Did the company promptly, completely, and effectively disclose the existence of the misconduct to the public, to regulators, and to self-regulators? Did the company cooperate completely with appropriate regulatory and law enforcement bodies? Did the company identify what additional related misconduct is likely to have occurred? Did the company take steps to identify the extent of damage to investors and other corporate constituencies? Did the company appropriately recompense those adversely affected by the conduct?

9. What processes did the company follow to resolve many of these issues and ferret out necessary information? Were the Audit Committee and the Board of Directors fully informed? If so, when?

(continued)

Table 5.1. (*continued*)

10. Did the company commit to learn the truth, fully and expeditiously? Did it do a thorough review of the nature, extent, origins, and consequences of the conduct and related behavior? Did management, the board, or committees consisting solely of outside directors oversee the review? Did company employees or outside persons perform the review? If outside persons, had they done other work for the company? Where the review was conducted by outside counsel, had management previously engaged such counsel? Were scope limitations placed on the review? If so, what were they?

11. Did the company promptly make available to our staff the results of its review and provide sufficient documentation reflecting its response to the situation? Did the company identify possible violative conduct and evidence with sufficient precision to facilitate prompt enforcement actions against those who violated the law? Did the company produce a thorough and probing written report detailing the findings of its review? Did the company voluntarily disclose information our staff did not directly request and otherwise might not have uncovered? Did the company ask its employees to cooperate with our staff and make all reasonable efforts to secure such cooperation?

12. What assurances are there that the conduct is unlikely to recur? Did the company adopt and ensure enforcement of new and more effective internal controls and procedures designed to prevent a recurrence of the misconduct? Did the company provide our staff with sufficient information for it to evaluate the company's measures to correct the situation and ensure that the conduct does not recur?

13. Is the company the same company in which the misconduct occurred, or has it changed through a merger or bankruptcy reorganization?

Source: Report of Investigation Pursuant to Section 21(a) of the Securities Exchange Act of 1934 and Commission Statement on the Relationship of Cooperation to Agency Enforcement Decisions, Accounting and Auditing Enforcement, Release No. 1470, October 23, 2001.

personhood, detailed in chapter 2, have less to do with metaphysics or even matters of public policy than with worries over the costs and burdens of corporate criminal liability.

There seems also to be a disconnect between the granting of prosecutorial credit and prevailing conceptions of corporate criminal liability. Corporations that cooperate are perceived to be less culpable, less deserving of liability and sanctions. But why is that so? Certainly, to the extent that corporations are subjected to a form of vicarious criminal liability, cooperation from top management that results in a downward deflection of blame—as is the case with RWB—makes little or no sense, unless, of course, only low-level employees are culpable. Otherwise, the direction of liability is wrong. The fairness of holding subordinates liable for the actions and inaction of management seems wrong as well.

In chapters 2 and 3, I argued that the narrow focus of culpability required at trial is simply not satisfied by inquiries into an organization's proactive and reactive efforts or, as is the case here, its willingness to cooperate. The failure of a corporation to cooperate with authorities on the discovery of defense procurement fraud, for example, may reveal culpability. It is, however, culpability in relation to the failure to cooperate, to show remorse, to assure the government of certain facts. The law must continue to distinguish between fraud as a culpable individual or corporate act and the extent of blame that should be attributed to the entity for its failure to cooperate or, for that matter, to respond reasonably in light of the commission of fraud. It should never be forgotten that the procurement fraud, for example, is the criminal act. The failure of the corporation to cooperate or respond reasonably in light of the circumstances is not, in itself, a crime.

An analogous point was made some years ago by Peter French in his discussion of the principle of responsive adjustment (PRA). The PRA expresses the expectation that a person or organization that contributed in some way to the commission of a crime may be less blameworthy if it engages in a course of conduct that prevents subsequent offending. The reasoning of PRA can easily be extended to the value ascribed to a corporation's decision to cooperate. According to French, "PRA does not assume, however, that a failure to 'mend one's ways' after being confronted with an unhappy outcome of one's actions is strong presumptive evidence that one had originally intended that outcome. The matter of intentions at the time it occurred is closed. If it were not intentional, nothing after the action could make it intentional when it occurred."[99] But for its distinct utility, in other words, corporate cooperation would not serve as a liability rule any more than the reasonableness of a corporation's response to the discovery of illegalities would. But for its distinct utility, cooperation would not relieve an entity of liability any more than efforts to act reasonably in light of the discovery of crimes would. It certainly would not affect the determination of constructive corporate fault.

COOPERATION AND THE SEARCH FOR CULPRITS

The effects of the incentives from the prosecutorial and sentencing guidelines raise a different set of challenges for the regulated and regulators. To be sure, FWB, RWB, and EWB serve important complementary law enforcement functions: EWB effectuates self-policing, while FWB and RWB encourage corporate agents to ensure effective compliance with law. More important, the combination of EWB, FWB, and RWB generously opens an otherwise closed organization to the sights of prosecutors and regulators.

This openness, though, does not come without a price—one that differs from co-option, capture, and unavoidable regulator-regulated confrontations. It is a price paid for the individualistic bias of the corporate criminal law, the strong desire by the government to find and affix blame, the overwhelming dependence of prosecutors on information and evidence difficult to obtain from complex organizations without incentives, and the limited resources of prosecutors' offices. Moreover, it is a price paid for the collaborative pursuit of culprits. And, unfortunately, the literature is not rife with solutions.

Proposals to increase judicial scrutiny of internal investigations, to empower employees to seek redress when subjected to scapegoating, to expand the procedural rights of employees, and to escalate sanctions when evidence of scapegoating appears are either weak or unlikely to be adopted. More important, such proposals leave unaffected the incentives to engage in RWB and the trend toward ever-increasing concessions by corporations under investigation or indictment.

An elementary though inelegant solution is to provide explicit disincentives for nonconsensual RWB. To be effective, recognition of RWB concerns, along with appropriate disincentives, should appear in the guidelines, regulatory policy statements, negotiated plea agreements, and corporate ethics codes.[100] The cautionary statement in the Thompson Memo does no more than admonish.[101] Explicit prohibitions against the practice of RWB are required. Alternatively, incentives to cooperate must be changed.

The obvious solution is the denial of mitigation credit, leniency, or amnesty to corporations that resort to scapegoating. The Corporate Leniency Policy of the Antitrust Division of the U.S. Department of Justice, for example, accomplishes this denial with a requirement that the confession of the corporation truly be a corporate act—not "isolated confessions of individual executives or officials."[102] A less obvious and yet more creative solution allows for employers and agents to share in amnesty. This solution has the effect of aligning interests and, obviously, minimizing the inevitable conflicts between employer and employee. As one commentator noted, "[i]ndividual offenders who either seek amnesty by themselves or who cooperate with their employers' amnesty applications can avoid being treated by their corporate employers as scapegoats for past misconduct."[103] It is notable that the Department of Health and Human Services Office of Inspector General prescribes the nonprosecution of all employees in corporations that qualify for leniency.[104]

Calls for a more "expansive view" of corporate social control, one that harnesses a wide variety of incentives and institutions, could hold the most promise in combating RWB by increasing organizational transparency.[105] Braithwaite's notion of tripartism and Shearing's model of constitutive regulation have inspired more general proposals to leverage the power and place of consumer lobbies, unions, and nongovernmental organizations.[106]

Increasingly, third-party participation in the regulatory process is recognized for opening a window to both compliance and deviance.[107] As shall become clear in chapter 6, the same is true of the ever-expanding role of a vast number of public interest groups and their potential to more formally monitor the regulated and regulators.[108]

Finally, the adoption of any liability rule will affect the value of cooperation and the corporate-government trading of favors. With vicarious fault and constructive fault, the object is to shift liability as far down the hierarchy as possible, from the perspective of corporate counsel. At least in theory, vicarious liability is a form of strict liability. But its strict application devolves in practice where the connection between the offending agent and the entity becomes tenuous or incidental, creating the incentive for RWB. For constructive fault, the same incentive is present but for different reasons. Unlike vicarious fault, constructive liability turns on the nexus between the organization's and the agent's action. Under such a regime, corporations would aggressively seek to distance themselves from agents. Given the time-honored place of cooperation in federal law enforcement, perhaps the most that can be said is that all proposals recognizing and accounting for the incentives to unfairly scapegoat employees must be seriously considered.

CONCLUSION

Even with transparency, and the access that it affords, it is only fair to suspect that corporations will continue to game regulators with the pretense of genuine cooperation.[109] The risk of this gaming and the fear that substantive criminal law will no longer be used in the regulation of corporations lead some public interest advocates and progressive criminologists to balk at the recent evolution of cooperative regulation.[110] Putting aside concerns about the further evisceration of an already inadequate corporate criminal law, the risk of this gaming, it may be argued, will only increase as regulators explore progressive innovations in cooperative regulation and migrate, increasingly, to self-regulatory and "reflexive" regulation.[111]

It is an ironic but very understandable twist. Progressive critics argue that, even though a broad range of regulatory strategies may be implemented across industries, the strict enforcement of criminal law is very much required for all serious violations of the law.[112] In the end, the expressive nature of the criminal law is the best hope to control the immense power of corporations.[113] Implicit in this progressive view is the notion that those most closely associated and aligned with principles of public interest—those who would benefit greatly by an increased role in the regulation of big businesses—lack faith in the sincerity of corporations and corporate compliance. Businesses may elect, at any time, to subvert regulation.[114] Ultimately, maintaining this healthy skepticism may be best way to combat practices like RWB.

And there is much to be skeptical about. Nearly five months after signing a cooperation agreement with the United States Attorney's Office, Prudential Securities initiated a $22 million advertising campaign designed to rehabilitate its postscandal image.[115] Jeff Daggett, an assistant manager in Prudential Securities' branch office in Los Angeles, was chosen to star in a television commercial touting the strong relationships of "the Rock" with the investment community, relationships with clients built on trust. "I tell rookies a good relationship evolves from prospect to client to friend," Daggett explains. "I try to recommend investments that won't jeopardize my clients' last years on this planet."[116] Shocking news about Daggett hit the media within days of the commercial's first airing. This icon of trust in the postscandal period was being sued for $750,000 by one of his "trusted" clients, a Roman Catholic priest. Msgr. Maximos Mardelli charged Daggett with deceptively and fraudulently selling him limited partnerships, giving misleading legal advice, and, to add insult to injury, ultimately abandoning the priest's investment account.[117] With the preeminence of corporate branding and reputation management, skepticism should abound.

CHAPTER SIX

Crafting a Soul

To the people of the Altria family of companies:

I am very proud to be an employee of Altria Group, Inc. During my career I have learned that the people who work for the Altria family of companies are good people. I write now to confirm the expectations that the Board of Directors and I have regarding compliance with this code. There is a simple idea that stands behind everything we do: We pursue our business objectives with integrity and in full compliance with all laws. This is the right thing to do and it makes good business sense. By acting with integrity we earn the trust of our customers, consumers, shareholders, co-workers, regulators, suppliers and the communities where we live and work—those whose trust we must have to be successful. Altria Group, Inc. has a Chief Compliance Officer, responsible for overseeing the implementation of the Compliance and Integrity program at each of the Altria companies. In addition, each company has its own compliance management team.

This new Altria Code of Conduct for Compliance and Integrity is another key resource in our commitment to integrity. The new Code replaces and enhances our long-standing Business Conduct Policy in a practical and easy to understand way. It explains many of the basic rules that apply to our businesses and the personal responsibility each of us has to speak up if we ever see something that doesn't seem right.

Read the Code carefully. This will help you make sure that your actions never fall short of Altria's commitment to do the right thing. Web-based training on the code will confirm our commitment to its principles. Nothing is more important than our commitment to integrity—no financial objective, no marketing target, no effort to outdo the competition. No desire to please the boss outweighs that core commitment. Our commitment to integrity must always come first. This Code is about who we are and who we choose to be. It is about how we do business—everywhere and all the time. Together, by following the letter and spirit of this Code, we can help ensure that working for an Altria Group company is a source of great pride.

Sincerely,

Louis C. Camilleri

Chairman and Chief Executive Officer

Altria Group, Inc. April 2003[1]

*

The words of the chairman and chief executive officer of the parent company of Phillip Morris are seemingly heartfelt. So, too, are the sentiments of Altria's chief compliance officer, David Greenberg, who spoke of the company's vision at the Pennsylvania Press Club in July 2002. Corporate leaders must lead with ethics, he said. They need to talk about an ethical culture and ensure that the necessary procedures and processes are in place to make that culture real. Ethics is not about feeling good about what you are doing. It is smart business. It is about understanding what society expects of a company like Altria. This understanding, according Greenberg, is what drives Altria to address concerns that members of the public have about their products. Altria supports federal tobacco regulation, for example, and the funding of youth smoking-prevention programs. "As I said at the start," Greenberg opines, "we at Philip Morris are learning the painful lesson that if you turn your back on society, society will turn its back on you. Opinion research consistently shows that people expect companies not simply to obey the law, but to act in ways that are consistent with a society's sense of what is right."[2]

It is all too easy to dismiss the efforts of Phillip Morris as disingenuous. After all, how could the country's foremost tobacco company not lead with ethics and integrity? This is the company that proudly manufactures Marlboro, Virginia Slims, Benson & Hedges, Merit, Parliament, Alpine, Basic, Cambridge, Bristol, Bucks, Chesterfield, Collector's Choice, Commander, English Ovals, Lark, L&M, Players, and Saratoga. This is the company that challenged aggressive state-funded antitobacco advertising in Florida and California, while it, along with the other major cigarette manufacturers, spent more than $15 billion on advertising and promotional expenditures in 2003, a 21 percent increase in one year.[3] This is the company that has faced an average of more than two hundred individual suits and class-action cases each year since the $206 billion tobacco industry settlement in 1998. This is the company that vigorously appeals almost every legal judgment against it, no matter how disturbing the facts are, no matter how serious the injuries are. Finally, this is one of six tobacco companies (along with R. J. Reynolds,

Brown & Williamson Tobacco Corp., British American Tobacco PLC, Lorillard Tobacco Co., and Liggett Group Inc.) facing $280 billion of fines in the largest civil racketeering case in the history of the United States. The government alleges that Philip Morris, along with the other named defendants, engaged in "a four-decade long conspiracy, dating from at least 1953, to intentionally and willfully deceive and mislead the American public about, among other things, the harmful nature of tobacco products, the addictive nature of nicotine, and the possibility of manufacturing safer and less addictive tobacco products."[4]

But to focus exclusively on the most apparent questions, as Milton Friedman did with empty claims of corporate responsibility, misses some important lessons about the symbolic meaning and motives behind some ethics initiatives.[5] Dismissing Altria's integrity "makeover" as mere window dressing misses an opportunity to discuss the images and metaphors that companies construct to claim and reclaim moral legitimacy.[6] A significant stream of research considers the adoption of legitimation tactics of firms and accompanying disclosures, all designed to close the "legitimacy gap," as Prakash Sethi once called it.[7] More recent research examines the corporate social responsibility movement in terms of reputation building, public relations, and corporate communications.[8]

That a multinational tobacco company once ranked next to last in corporate reputation surveys can ever lead with integrity raises all of the obvious concerns. Perhaps business ethics, for some firms, is little more than an effort to expiate guilt, purchase a corporate soul, and, in the case of Altria, fight the fight against youth smoking so vigilantly that it tends to increase the company's market share of young smokers. This public relations imagery may be "done on the cheap" by claiming integrity and ethics in washing a tarnished corporate reputation, a reputation drawn through the mud of countless tort actions, class-action suits, decadelong appeals, and multibillion-dollar settlements.

The lengths to which some corporations go to fashion a soul is truly remarkable. It is even more remarkable when these representations come from corporations in which senior executives or the entity are targeted for criminal investigation. It is here that the parallels to assessing both corporate compliance and corporate governance are apparent. From Adaptec ("Adaptec strives to operate its worldwide business in accordance with the highest ethical standards in every business relationship . . ."),[9] Adelphia ("We will develop a reputation as a company with outstanding corporate governance."),[10] Charter Communications ("Charter is committed to operating with integrity and honesty, and in accordance with the law."),[11] and Dynegy ("At Dynegy, we are committed to serving our stakeholders with integrity and initiative.")[12] to HealthSouth ("HealthSouth is fully committed to good corporate governance and the highest standards of business conduct."),[13] Peregrine Systems ("Peregrine Systems, Inc. is committed to conducting its business lawfully and ethically in every area of the world in which it does business."),[14] and Rent-Way ("Ethical conduct is critical to the business and future of the Company."),[15] firms targeted for criminal prosecution tend to seek solace in cleansing their reputations.

Corporations also make social disclosures to "legitimize their organizations' place within society."[16] Such disclosures may be made to educate stakeholders about actual changes; alter perceptions of stakeholders without actually changing firm behavior; change external expectations of stakeholders; manipulate stakeholder perceptions through deception; encourage or discourage new regulations; and establish corporate discipline over social movements.[17] There are literally countless instrumental uses of social disclosures.[18] This chapter considers critical questions about these disclosures and other efforts to craft a corporate soul. How much of what is said about newfound corporate values is real and how much is creative and strategic imagery? Is there a true "value shift" in corporations, as one leading business ethicist argues?[19] Or are firms simply resorting to different styles of advertising and image advocacy now that there is a window of regulatory vigilance and the conventional wisdom requires an appearance of organizational integrity and ethicality?

Answers to these questions are hard to come by for some very simple reasons: It is exceedingly difficult to unpack a genuine commitment to business ethics when matters of responsibility, integrity, and compliance with laws are mixed with the spin of moral imagery. Those firms in the ethical vanguard and those that deceive may have engaged the same consultancy, have retained the same outside counsel, have equally impressive compliance and governance standards with world-class environmental programs, and have equally distinguished ethics officers.

Distinguishing between programs of substance and those of appearance is not only one of the many unmet empirical challenges of corporate crime. It is an obstacle for those charged with determining a corporation's criminal responsibility. It is a challenge for theories of liability that look to an organization's behavior, such as constructive corporate fault. And this challenge is attributable in no small part to the consultant-driven business ethics industry. The notion of assuring corporate accountability to voluntary standards was regularly neglected by consultancies in hard-selling the value and power of business ethics, compliance, and good governance. In some cases, overselling seems to have discouraged the critical need for accountability. It is a small and safe step for clients to use well-crafted moral imagery so effectively that it hides the blemishes of corporate deviance.

In this chapter, the images and metaphors of the corporate soul are unpacked with a brief historical overview. An exaggerated form of image creation and management is detailed next: the washing of a corporation's reputation. This discussion is followed by a review of the *Nike v. Kasky* case, perhaps the most notable example of greenwashing in recent years. The chapter concludes with the all-too-familiar problem of verifying the social representations of corporations, this time for the purposes of socially responsible investing.

IMAGES AND METAPHORS OF THE CORPORATE SOUL

In his fascinating treatise on the rise of public relations and corporate imagery in the United States, Roland Marchand started with a description of an idyllic and then imaginary little town called Lambert Hollow through which the dependable Pennsylvania Railroad mail train runs—the Night Mail train. "To Lambert Hollow the mail has come; from Lambert Hollow the mail has gone. The line of glittering windows that flows on into the night has again played its part in weaving together the cities and towns and villages of the world."[20] This contrived sentimental imagery signaled the railroad's desire to be seen as something different from a large, monolithic, impersonal entity. The Pennsylvania Railroad Corporation carries news and mail to every little town from coast to coast with devotion that is simply incompatible with prevailing images of a heartless, soulless bureaucracy. "This fable of the efficient and benevolent giant ever attentive to the welfare of the tiniest entity," according to Marchand, "was simply one of a myriad stories that pervaded corporate publicity during the first half of the twentieth century."[21]

The history of business in the United States reflects a quest for legitimacy that used publicity, iconography, and artistic suggestion as instrumental corporate public relations. In the late 1800s, the size, scope, and newfound reach of corporations—not to mention their relationship with the political machine—all combined to leave the public with great unease. There was a secretive or stealth nature to big business and, according to some historians, a contemporaneous contempt by those wielding corporate power for both the public and critics. At the very least, businessmen engendered public curiosity and increasing calls for public scrutiny. Corporate public relations, or the planned control and cultivation of corporate news and the media, emerged as a tool to shape and reshape perceptions. It was a tool to ensure that corporations enjoyed both legal and political stability. It was a tool to humanize the rough edges of capitalism or its appearance, to personify the corporation. It was a tool, as Neil Mitchell astutely observed, that often encouraged organizational change consistent with a newly minted corporate image.[22]

Large corporations suffered first from a crisis of moral and social legitimacy related to their scale. As Robert Wiebe wrote, the emergence of large corporations was totally incompatible with the island communities of America.[23] The small towns and neighborhoods were filled with closely held social institutions defined by personal relationships, where the meaning found in these social relationships, the social nexus, left no room for the likes of "national" companies such as Standard Oil and United States Steel. Turn-of-the-century sociologists such as Charles Cooley, William Sumner, and Edward Ross would see the emergence of large-scale corporations as competing with the traditional pillars of social control: the family, church, and neighborhood.[24]

Businesses were perceived by the public as cold, harsh, distant, suspicious, and secretive. This perception was not helped by headstrong comments from leading industrialists such as William H. Vanderbilt: "The public be damned. What does the public care for the railroads except to get as much out of them for as small a consideration as possible!"[25] The growth of legitimacy concerns in the late 1800s were fueled by such sentiments. With the very active goading of muckrakers and regular news reports of corporate hedonism, the public soon questioned whether corporations had a conscience and a soul.

Sir Edward Cooke's famed words about corporations lacking a soul were common parlance in the 1800s, joining the sayings of Bacon ("Knowledge is power."), Beccaria ("The greatest happiness of the greatest number . . ."), and Hobbes ("Words are wise men's counters, but the money of fools.").[26] And consumers had little trouble, it seems, with the obvious fiction. In 1864, for example, a rider of the Harlem River Line wrote to the *New York Times* saying, "I know that corporations have no souls—especially railroad corporations. But they have *hides*, and it is hoped that they are not yet so thick, that the shafts of outraged public justice and decency may not penetrate them."[27]

Following an accident on the Hudson River Railroad line in 1871, another railroad passenger wrote, "If corporations have no souls to appeal to, their pockets may be sometimes reached."[28] "It is fortunate that corporations have no souls if they were to be held eternally responsible for all of the lying done in their names, but the officers of Western Union should ponder their individual accountability," wrote one frustrated New Yorker in 1883.[29] In bemoaning the absence of corporate philanthropy by the railways, banks, insurance companies, and oil, iron, and coal companies, an editorial in 1883 noted that "one is apt to accept this as only so much additional testimony to the truth of the popular saying that corporations have no souls."[30] Finally, in questioning whether a corporation can be libeled in 1885, one commentator noted, "There is a certain aphorism to the effect that a corporation has neither a body that can be kicked nor a soul that can be sent to perdition."[31]

At the turn of the twentieth century, complaints about the soulless nature of corporations were so commonplace as to be clichés. Muckrakers published literally thousands of magazine articles on the practices of American businesses between 1903 and 1912.[32] Citizens' frustrations with gross departures from corporate ethics also remained newsworthy and seemingly important.[33] In 1900, Professor Franklin Russell of New York University School of Law predicted that the public's reaction to corporate illegalities and unethical acts would likely prompt change. Corporations, he reasoned, "will some day have a soul. It cannot be that we will have long to wait before an enlightened public opinion will demand that every corporate act be judged by the same standard of lofty morality by which we measure the conduct of the individual man."[34]

The corporate response to allegations of soullessness, as Marchand detailed, included a series of elaborate public reports of soulfulness—perhaps the first evidence of a sustained corporate public relations effort. These reports included John Kimberly Mumford's *This Land of Opportunity: The Heart of a 'Soulless Corporation,'* (1908), Arundel Cotter's *United States Steel: A Corporation with a Soul* (1921), and *Puts Flesh and Blood into 'Soulless Corporation,'* published in Printers' Ink (1922). These portraits defied stereotypes of large impersonal factories without discernable personalities. Detailed stories of the beneficence of enterprises known as narrowly conceived profit engines for their shareholders attempted to counter prevailing opinion. They were attempts to bridge a gap in the classical economic argument that equated private interests with public good. Such efforts were also self-serving in a less-than-obvious way. As Neil Mitchell observed, corporations "not only needed to prove the legitimacy of their power to others, they also needed to prove it to themselves."[35] "I believe that the United States Steel Corporation," Cotter wrote, "is one enterprise that endeavors always to live up fully to the responsibilities it must perforce assume to its employees and to the public, as well as to its shareholders. I believe that it has earned the title of 'A Corporation With A Soul.'"[36]

Such efforts to augment moral legitimacy represented, in Marchand's thinking, a more "feminine reaction" to the public's growing distrust and dislike of yet fascination with big business. Businesses that worried about the financial ramifications of this trend increasingly catered to public opinion, funded corporate public relations efforts, learned the fine art of fashioning images through advertising, and institutionalized employee welfare programs. They developed strategies that connected, or appeared to connect, their businesses with the local community or neighborhood. The railroads in particular were most adept at these strategies and are often credited with building the field of public relations. The railroads hired press agents, started publicity bureaus, bought newspapers, and aggressively disseminated corporate news.

This image consciousness of businesses was in sharp contrast to the independent, stick-to-business attitude that defined these enterprises before and during the industrial revolution. All of this took place during a time when the challenges of running a business were made ever more complex by changing internal and external expectations. As Marchand explained, "In shaping their corporate images, the great business giants of the early 20th century were not only seeking to legitimize their newly amassed power within the nexus of social institutions, they were also constantly renegotiating their position along a series of increasingly fuzzy boundaries within business itself."[37] Defining these boundaries was made that much more difficult as passengers on the railroads and consumers of public utilities, for example, began to think of these services as entitlements or rights.

This cryptic and very incomplete portrait of the birth of corporate public relations is insufficient groundwork for a discussion of the subtle mix of business ethics and reputation management today. There are countless milestones in public relations history that would inform such an analysis, including the effect of organized labor, business associations, and administrative and political agencies, not to mention World Wars I and II. But a consistent theme underwrites these and other historical milestones that will help explain recent trends in business ethics. All too often, the search for the corporate soul through the instrumental use of public relations is accompanied by a particularly insidious form of corporate deception—reputation washing.

Greenwashing and other comparable forms of reputation washing involve more than a genuine quest for social and moral legitimacy through the increasingly sophisticated science and practice of public relations. Reputation washing is different from the genuine effort by corporations to comply with and perform beyond environmental laws.[38] It is more than the "rain forest chic" marketing of Body Shop International cosmetics and Ben & Jerry's Homemade ice cream or Prakash Sethi's early notion of advocacy advertising.[39] It is something different from promoting "The Soul of Dell," Johnson & Johnson's credo, or other attempts to elevate corporate values statements beyond the paper that they are written on. And it extends beyond corporate social marketing and cause-related marketing.[40] The practice requires a brazen form of reputational deception that extends even beyond the significant legitimation tactics seen with the Johns Manville Corp. and asbestos-related diseases; the A. H. Robbins Company and the Dalkon Shield; and the Dow Corning Company and the silicone-gel breast implant.[41] It is trickery that not only uses publicity to explain the problem away but also portrays the ethical laggard—the greenwasher—as an ethical leader. The environmental polluter who still pollutes wears the guise of environmental steward. The financial trickster continues to deceive and defraud while appearing as a trustee and fiduciary.

A powerful example of this ethical juxtaposition was described in some detail by criminologists who identified a new brand of corporate environmental activism in the 1990s that redefined the notion of what it means to be green; allowed corporations to assert control over the green movement; defused and redirected support for the environmental movement; and facilitated a decline in genuine efforts to ensure environmental sustainability.[42]

WASHING CORPORATE REPUTATIONS

In recent years, civil society activists and, in particular, environmental activists have raised concerns about corporate greenwashing. With a mix of anecdotal evidence, the allegations extend well beyond the instrumental use of public relations, concerted lobbying, political and corporate cronyism, and the manipulation of public opinion.[43] The emergence of the terms *greenwashing* (reputation washing under the cover of environmentalist concerns) and *bluewashing* (reputation washing by using an affiliation with the United Nations) reflects an increasing apprehension that at least some corporations creatively manage their reputations with the public, financial community, and regulators so as to hide deviance, deflect attributions of fault, obscure the nature of the problem or allegation, reattribute blame, ensure an entity's reputation, and, finally, seek to appear in a leadership position.[44] The entire cycle of greenwashing, when unchallenged, frees the organization of the burden (e.g., stigma and adverse publicity) and guilt associated with unethical and illegal acts. But what makes the cycle so dastardly is that it also allows for profit to be made off of the very moral failing that is washed.

With such titles as *Global Spin: The Corporate Assault on Environmentalism; Battling Big Business: Countering Greenwash, Infiltration and Other Forms of Corporate Bullying;* and *Greenwash: The Reality Behind Corporate Environmentalism,* the case is made that corporations such as Royal Dutch/Shell, Mobil Corporation, the Gap, Dow Chemical, and many other familiar Fortune 500 companies engage in complex strategies and counterstrategies that serve to shift the focus and attention away from the firm, create confusion, undermine credibility, criticize viable alternatives, and deceptively posture firm objectives, commitments, and accomplishments. Environmentalists refer to countless examples:

> The World's leading ozone destroyer takes credit for leadership in ozone protection. A mammoth greenhouse gas emitter professes the precautionary approach to global warming. A major agrichemical manufacturer trades in a pesticide so hazardous it has been banned in many countries, while implying it is helping feed the hungry. A petrochemical firm uses the waste from one polluting

process as raw materials for another hazardous process, and boasts of an important recycling initiative. Another giant multinational cuts timber from virgin rainforest, replaces it with monoculture plantations and calls the project "sustainable forest development."[45]

It is alleged that corporate activism, in response to increased regulatory activity and heightened public concern about environmental matters, includes a panoply of evils associated with greenwashing, from manipulating public opinion to launching explicit attacks against environmentalists.[46] Greenwashing generally turns on three elements of deception: confusion, fronting, and posturing. To satisfy these elements, some corporations fund advertising and public relations initiatives to aggressively counter adverse publicity and, in its place, further distinguish themselves as leaders in the very areas where they fail. Greenwashing behaviors range from the deceptive advertising of food as wholesome and healthy when it is genetically engineered to the green advertising of power companies known to be some of the worst polluters.

At first, this deception appears to be far more elaborate than tactics employed defensively by corporations when allegations of deviance surface. After all, what civil society activists allege involves multiple stakeholders, third parties, and the participation of senior management. The extent of these differences, however, may be more significant than their direction. As with greenwashing, the defensive strategies employed by firms to protect against entity liability—those discussed in earlier chapters—are aimed both inside and outside the organization. Internally, *confusion* flows naturally from the complex nature of the corporate form, the reliance on decentralized decision making, and the practices of managerial winking. *Fronting* is accomplished through the representations of retained counsel, compliance officers, ethics officers, and ethics committees. *Posturing* seeks to convince internal customers, as much as external stakeholders, of the organization's collective commitment to ethics. Finally, both sets of strategies, interestingly, rely heavily on the advice of a large cottage industry of public relations and reputation management firms.[47]

The effect in both cases is that ethics codes and programs are perceived internally as if designed to manage a firm's reputation.[48] Externally, the firm achieves *confusion* by careful document control and strict limits on the flow of information made available to regulators and prosecutors. *Fronting* is realized by subordinate scapegoating or reverse whistle-blowing. *Posturing* is accomplished through active use of the corporation's public affairs department and, if necessary, the retention of an outside public relations firm.

If there is one striking similarity, it is the potentially perverse nature of these strategies. Both internal and external strategies have the potential to give an organization the appearance of ethicality and leadership, when no such commitment exists. In cases of deviant organizations, as noted in chapter 4, there are distinct moral hazard concerns. The purchase of the "commodity of compliance" sufficient to shift the risk of liability and loss, in certain firms, may result in decreased levels of care by senior managers. The likelihood is magnified in companies where top management fosters an environment of tacit acceptance of illegalities and winks at deviance. With constant pressure on middle and lower management to produce results, levels of deviance may increase throughout the corporate hierarchy. The purchase of compliance for purposes of liability shifting and cost internalization results in a redefinition of this deviance. Acts that were once held to be those of the firm, running a risk of being attributed to the organization as a whole, now remain those of individual employees. The result is that certain compliance orientations, particularly those that prize the purchase of compliance as insurance or hedges against liability, may have the counterintuitive effect of increasing white-collar deviance.

Civil society activists regularly make the same argument. The very firms that wash their reputations through public relations, complex front coalitions, and sponsored "think tanks," and who publicly lead the fight against global warming, nuclear waste, and water pollution, remain some of the worst corporate offenders. The appearance of environmental leadership, for example, like the appearance of corporate compliance, may actually serve to decrease care levels. Corporations can rely on their reputations for compliance and social responsibility with lesser scrutiny. The emblem of certification to certain standards and the reputational advantage of membership or participation in socially responsible organizations distance the firm from any alleged deviance.[49]

Civil society organizations and activists, to their credit, remain profoundly skeptical of good citizenship claims by corporations. Greer and Bruno concluded: "Now they say they have changed. That they are spending money for the environment. That they will regulate and police themselves. That their technologies are safe. That their products help the poor. We urge you to look critically at their real world behavior."[50] Rhetoric from corporations, members of the white-collar bar, and civil society activists, however, share the same vulnerability. Without rigorous reporting methods and assessment of corporate compliance effectiveness, no less social accountability, it is next to impossible to assess the extent of the moral hazard problem or the extent of greenwashing. It is simply impossible to judge how significant the disconnect is between public statements of compliance or social responsibility and a firm's genuine efforts—particularly without external, independent third-party verification and monitoring. Environmental reports, corporate social reports, and sustainability reports require audits, verification, and validation. Trust, intuition, and speculation seem partisan, unscientific, and unfair.[51]

Assuming opportunism, unavoidable conflicts of interest, and manipulation also fails any test of fairness. Unfortunately, as shall become apparent, conclusive evidence of corporate reforms from third parties is most often unavailable. Even when independent third-party audits are performed, it is sometimes unclear whether their assessments are thorough, objective, truth-seeking, and truly independent.[52] All too often, the truth, whatever that might be, is left obscured somewhere between carefully crafted public relations efforts and the natural and quite reasonable suspicions of those with a keen memory of past misrepresentations.

WASHING REPUTATIONS: JUST DO IT?

From the mid-1990s on, sports shoe companies, not unlike many U.S.-based manufacturers, aggressively outsourced production to contract manufacturing companies operating in countries with low labor and material costs, for example, Indonesia, the Philippines, Thailand, China, and Vietnam.[53] Nike, the world's leading athletic footwear, apparel, and equipment manufacturer, was an early entrant in the "race to the bottom" in wages and skills. The company now relies on more than 900 factories with a total workforce of more than 600,000 employees, all of whom are employed by supply chain partners. Most of these employees are located in Southeast Asia.

For more than a decade, Nike has required a memorandum of understanding with all of its subcontractors retaining responsibility for their compliance with local laws and regulations concerning occupational health and safety, minimum wage, overtime, and environmental protection. At the same time, Nike is governed by its own code of conduct that expressly prohibits child labor, requires that workers be paid a fair wage, imposes caps on the days and hours a worker can be forced to work, prohibits mistreatment or discrimination of workers in any form, obligates factories to implement programs that benefit workers' health and safety, and recognizes and respects the workers' right to freedom of association.

Nike's self proclaimed mission is "to make responsible sourcing a business reality that enhances workers' lives."[54] Its stated goals are to (1) manage a consistent, effective, and comprehensive monitoring system; (2) build capacity to achieve compliance; (3) refine and manage the remediation process; (4) develop, invest, and build capacity to improve the workplace, workers' lives, and the community; (5) integrate compliance into the business model; (6) foster balanced understanding inside and outside Nike of the realities of the factory floor; and (7) use transparency to improve monitoring, promote compliance, increase leverage, and build credibility.[55]

The allegations against Nike began in 1989 with evidence of worker abuse and labor law violations in company subcontractors.[56] Sporadic news reports on sweatshop violations and abuses continued for a number of years with little recognition by Nike of a problem until 1992. Late that year, Nike introduced a code of labor practices, following the lead of Levi Strauss, which responded to exposés of the working conditions in contractor facilities on the island of Saipan.[57] Subsequent reports from Christian Aid in 1995, the Christian Industrial Committee and Asia Monitor Resource Center Ltd. in 1996, and Community Aid Abroad in 1996 added allegations of inhumane work conditions and compromised worker rights at Nike-contracted manufacturers in Asia. In a segment on CBS's *48 Hours* on October 17, 1996, correspondent Roberta Baskin reported on "sweatshops" in Vietnam where she found that workers producing Nike sneakers were paid below minimum wage, faced physical abuse, and worked excessive hours. Baskin also found that the employees in these Nike-contracted sweatshops earned less than 25 cents an hour in working conditions that were at times unbearable. Reports of workers being hit by supervisors, having their mouths taped shut, and being victimized by sexual assault were detailed.[58]

The very same month that CBS aired this segment of *48 Hours,* Ernst & Young performed a company-sponsored environmental and labor practice audit of one of its larger subcontractors, the Tae Kwang Vina Industrial Ltd. Co., Bien Hoa City, South Vietnam, which employed more than 9,500 workers. The results of the audit, leaked to the public ten months after its completion, revealed a host of similar health and safety concerns, including possible worker exposure to carcinogens and a significant reliance on child labor. These revelations were once again confirmed by a six-month audit performed by Vietnam Labor Watch (VLW) investigating the claims made by the *48 Hours* television show. VLW combined invited visits with surprise tours of plants examining labor law compliance, working conditions, health and safety practices, and evidence of sexual harassment. VLW's conclusion: "We are glad that Nike is providing needed jobs in Vietnam, but we are deeply concerned about the company's labor practices. Nike contractors are exploiting the Vietnamese workers in many areas, including wages, working conditions, health and safety practices. Nike has a fine Code of Conduct but this Code of Conduct is being violated consistently by Nike contractors in Vietnam. While Nike claims it is trying to monitor and enforce its Code, its current approach to monitoring and enforcement is simply not working."[59]

Nike commissioned other audits. Initially, the company retained former United Nations Ambassador Andrew Young and his firm GoodWorks International LLC to briefly visit four Nike-contracted factories in Vietnam, Indonesia, and China. GoodWorks' conclusion: Nike was doing a "good job" but could do better. Young reported, however, that there was no evidence of widespread abuse. The GoodWorks audit was followed by a review of wages paid to contract workers in Indonesia and China performed by MBA students at Dartmouth's Tuck School, a report on Nike contract facilities in Southeast Asia by Professor Linda Lim in 2000, and a factory evaluation of Kukdong International Mexico by Verite in 2001. The results generally minimized the concerns of civil society activists and fair-labor groups who took it upon themselves to publicize the less-than-impressive results of earlier audits. According to Nike, these audits indicated significant progress toward compliance with the company's codes.[60]

To counter a maelstrom of adverse publicity from revelations of supply-chain abuses flowing from network television documentaries, newspapers, consumer groups, human-rights groups, labor unions, nongovernmental organizations, and religious organizations, Nike began placing advertisements, writing letters to university presidents and directors of athletic departments, writing letters to newspapers, and issuing press releases. This campaign was designed to advise the public that Nike's foreign contract workers were not in fact subjected to physical and sexual abuse, were paid living wages in accordance with local law that far exceeded minimum wage, received free meals and health care, and worked in conditions that were both safe and sanitary.[61]

Marc Kasky, a self-proclaimed environmentalist from California, sued Nike on behalf of the general public of the State of California (as a "private attorney general"), viewing the Ernst & Young audit and Nike's publicity campaign as an opportunity to test the veracity of the company's publicized supply-chain claims. In April 1998, he filed a complaint alleging that Nike violated state consumer protection statutes. Specifically, Kasky alleged that Nike induced consumers to buy its products and, in response to adverse publicity, made false statements about its labor practices and the working conditions in contract factories. These statements included a letter to a leading California newspaper that boasted: "We'd like consumers to know that Nike has helped create 500,000 good-paying jobs all over the world . . ." and "During the [Christmas] shopping season, we encourage shoppers to remember that Nike is the industry's leader in improving factory conditions."[62]

Other allegedly deceptive advertising noted in the complaint included the contents of a two-page letter with Nike's logo from Nike's director of sports marketing to university presidents and directors of athletics; a thirty-three-page illustrated pamphlet entitled "Nike Production Primer"; a posting of a press release with Nike's logo on Nike's Web site; a three-page document on Nike's letterhead with Nike's logo; a press release with Nike's logo; a five-page letter with Nike's logo from Nike's director of labor practices to the chief executive officer of YWCA of America; a two-page letter with Nike's logo from Nike's PR manager, Europe, to International Restructuring

Education Network Europe; and a letter to the editor of the *New York Times* from Nike's chairman and chief executive officer.[63] These communications, extolling Nike's improved production practices, were false and misleading statements, according to Kasky. Moreover, they were made with negligence and carelessness, and with knowledge or reckless disregard of the laws of California prohibiting false and misleading statements.

Kasky argued that the First Amendment regulates false, deceptive, and misleading commercial speech, and Nike's misrepresentations were just that because they gave consumers information—erroneous factual information—used in deciding whether to buy products from Nike. The misrepresentations were promotional in nature. And Nike realized that consumers are increasingly concerned about products made in working conditions considered inhumane. Consumer purchasing decisions are affected by knowledge of "sweatshop" manufacturing practices. Thus, the company sought to assure customers that such was not the case in Nike's supply chain. This representation satisfies the requirement of commercial speech. In addition, to the extent that customers rely on these assurances, and they are false, the company must be held accountable under state consumer fraud laws.

Nike maintained, in response, that the suit must be dismissed under the First Amendment. "It is settled," argued Nike, "that the full protections of the First Amendment apply except in the limited circumstance that speech—generally in the form of advertising—is intrinsically tied to a commercial transaction within the government's traditional power to regulate." Discussion of "public issues," by contrast, "occupies the 'highest rung of the hierarchy of First Amendment values,' and is entitled to special protection."[64] And this was merely a lively debate.

In a sharply divided opinion, the California Supreme Court ruled that Nike's representations were in fact commercial speech. The court held that "because the messages in question were directed by a commercial speaker to a commercial audience, and because they made representations of fact about the speaker's own business operations for the purpose of promoting sales of its products, . . . [the] messages are commercial speech."[65] The United States Supreme Court granted certiorari. The usual suspects joined the petitioner and respondent as amicus curiae. Lawrence Tribe argued for the company before the high court:

> In the mid-1990s there was, of course, an intense debate on the pros and cons of globalization, and of the impact of companies like Nike on workers in the Third World, where Nike contracted out much of its production to some 900 factories in 51 countries with over 600,000 employees.
>
> Now, the critics, many from pro-labor groups, denounced Nike as the chief exemplar of the evils of globalization, arguing that Nike was simply shifting

production to places where it could exploit the workforce and act in ways that were illegal and immoral, and the critics took much of their documentation from the media.

Of course, Nike disagreed, using the same media venues as the critics had used to document what it thought were the connections between its presence and activities in countries like South Korea and Vietnam and the development of technological expertise in those countries, as well as the expansion of job opportunities there, and also arguing that it had put in place significant safe-guards against abuse.

The products were mentioned only in response to people who said, well, look, this product is made in such-and-such country and it's exploitative, and Nike would have a press release, or it—sometimes it would be an op ed say-ing no, you've got the wrong country, this product is made in such-and-such other place. These were letters to the editor, pamphlets. It was on the Internet, correspondence.

As you might expect, the critics talked back. There was a lively political dialogue about the realities of the Third World and Nike's role in it, a little hard to separate the two, when, as the dissenter below, one of the dissenters below said Nike had become the poster child for the evils, supposedly, of globalization, so not surprisingly the debate was inconclusive.[66]

To the surprise of many, the Court dismissed the case as improvidently granted, allowing the state action brought by Kasky to continue. The cen-tral legal question that the Court would have decided, but did not, was whether a corporation in a public debate should be liable for misstating facts that may affect consumer purchasing decisions and thus constitute commercial speech. In spite of the importance of the commercial speech question—which has everyone justifiably exercised—the issue for the pur-poses of a discussion on greenwashing is not whether corporations should be liable for such public misstatements or exaggerated claims. The issue is also not the challenge, difficulty, or peril of working through supply-chain partners in emerging and transitional economies. It is, indeed, a daunting challenge to ensure supply-chain compliance. The issue is the strategic and deceptive use of public relations by multinational corpora-tions (MNCs) to assume an undeserved leadership position on an issue of significant consumer importance. All MNCs advertise extensively and make claims concerning their products. Many MNCs leverage the low labor costs of subcontracted workers in economies that are far from developed. These very companies are not, however, on the front lines of the movement for workers' rights and fair wages, while seriously and even callously exploiting child labor, requiring seven-day workweeks, physically abusing workers, and engaging in other supply-chain abuses. Moreover, they are not continuing such practices or remaining deliberately indifferent to them, while at the same time selling their ethical leadership on these issues to the consuming public.

Tribe's oral argument, therefore, would be made far more powerful had Nike outsourced its production to subcontractors, identified labor and human-rights violations, corrected them, and put in place effective programs and initiatives to ensure continued and vigilant compliance. If true, then Nike's affiliation with the Global Compact would be commendable. If true, then Nike's cosponsorship (with Gap Inc., Inditex, and the World Bank) of the Global Alliance for Workers and Communities must be lauded. If so, then Nike's publicity campaign, challenged in this litigation, would be a genuine effort to undo an old and now unfair image of a company that leverages the resources of companies in emerging economies only to trade ethics for margins.

There is substantial evidence that certain kinds of collaborative partnerships between MNCs and subcontractors dramatically improve local working conditions and wages. But the contractor must commit to the relationship, according to Frenkel and Scott. In addition, there must be a commitment by senior managers "to high labor standards as a means of improving workplace performance; frequent and open communication between managers and workers to promote mutual understanding and respect; and a competent labor practices team to ensure that there is no gap between practice and policy and that workers' interests are taken into account."[67]

In support of its more recent efforts to ensure minimal working standards in its supply-chain partners, Nike was a founding participant in 1996 of an independent nonprofit monitoring organization called the Fair Labor Association (FLA), which originated with the White House Apparel Industry Partnership during the Clinton administration. The FLA is designed to hold Nike and other participating companies accountable through the enforcement of an industry-wide Workplace Code of Conduct based on the labor standards of the *International Labor Organization (ILO)*. These standards, comparable to Nike's own code of conduct, include prohibitions on forced labor, child labor, harassment and abuse, discrimination, unsafe and unhealthy work environments, restrictions on freedom of association, inadequate pay, and excessive work hours. Nike committed to implement its FLA obligations over the course of a three-year period, beginning in 2001.

The FLA is a coalition of companies, universities, and nongovernmental organizations (NGOs) committed to the implementation of workplace codes of conduct as well as monitoring and remediation to ensure compliance with FLA standards. Adidas-Salomon, Eddie Bauer, GEAR for Sports, Joy Athletic, Liz Claiborne, Nordstrom, Nike, Patagonia, Reebok, Phillips—Van Heusen, Polo Ralph Lauren, and Zephyr Graf-X are members. This membership represents production of more than $30 billion in sales from more than three thousand factories throughout eighty countries. In joining the FLA, all companies commit to a rigorous program of Code of Conduct implementation, internal and external monitoring, and remediation in order to promote compliance with international labor standards in their supply chains.

In the course of the first year in which the FLA provided compliance reports (August 2001 through July 2002), Nike compliance and sourcing staff performed more than one thousand Safety, Health, Attitudes, People, and Environment (SHAPE) audits. Third-party monitoring groups conducted more than four hundred management audits. During this period, more than sixty factories were monitored by FLA-accredited independent external monitors, including Cal Safety, Cotecna, Global Standards, Intertek Testing Services, Kenan Institute Asia-Thailand, Merchandise Testing Laboratory, Phulki, and Verité. Where SHAPE audits, management audits, and FLA-sponsored visits revealed noncompliance, Nike compliance staff enlisted factory management to develop corrective action plans. Remediation of noncompliant practices was required by Nike. The FLA has only started disclosing tracking charts of individual factories or the results of individual audits of subcontractors in China, Bangladesh, India, Pakistan, Indonesia, Malaysia, Thailand, Vietnam, Brazil, Dominican Republic, Honduras, Mexico, and the United States. Those reports that are publicly available reveal, on average, multiple supply-chain violations, including problems associated with child labor. In a light most favorable to Nike, it shares the burdens of production and persuasion in proving compliance.

A leading expert in the role and importance of international codes, Prakash Sethi, is far from convinced that Nike will satisfy its burden. He and others find significant flaws with the FLA. Sethi notes that the monitoring processes mandated by the FLA are perceived to be weak; the governance structure of the FLA is highly bureaucratic, with a singular objective—protecting member companies from NGOs and the media; the FLA code, monitoring procedures, and issuance of reports are all designed to protect its primary stakeholder, corporate members; and the independence of auditing firms is often at issue, and their results are at times less than objective. Without public disclosure or required expulsion, Sethi worries about the consequences to firms with poor records of compliance with FLA standards. "In the end," Sethi concludes, "the entire process is reduced to a house of cards, where each flimsy and unsustainable assertion is used to justify the next level of equally flimsy and unsustainable assertion. We are left with the distressing observation that after all the expense and efforts of a large number of well-intentioned groups and individuals, the current structure and operation of the Fair Labor Association is unlikely to make significant and observable improvement in the working and living conditions of workers."[68]

Sethi is equally dismissive of Nike's efforts to ensure workplace compliance. "By its own admission," he reasons, "Nike's record leaves a great deal to be desired. It has not done enough to prevent worker harassment or curb demands for excessive overtime. Nor has Nike taken sufficient steps to ensure payment of correct wages for regular and overtime work."[69]

To argue against Sethi, one must maintain that what Nike did, or did not do, is no different from the actions or inaction of a host of those firms in search of their own Lambert Hollow. To a certain extent, this is the sad truth. Corporations have learned the language of corporate compliance, corporate governance, and corporate ethics so that those who lead and those who don't both sound the same. This is, indeed, a central challenge in regulating firms, obtaining incriminating evidence of organizational wrongdoing, and building a criminal case against a corporation. It is an old penologist's tale that virtually all prison inmates proclaim their innocence, making the cries of the factually innocent and guilty sound alike. The same is certainly true here. But, like claims of innocence, direct evidence may ultimately undermine attempts at deception. If audit and remediation data, once fully released, fail to uphold Nike's self-portrayal as an industry leader in improving factory conditions, then this will become a classic case—an archetypical case—of reputation washing.

And recent audits of working conditions in Nike-contracted factories outside of the FLA, funded by Press for Change, UNITE! (Union of Needletrades, Industrial & Textile Employees), the National Labor Committee, the People of Faith Network, Global Exchange, Resource Center of the Americas, and United Students Against Sweatshops, suggest that Nike has yet to remediate. Serious labor abuses are noted in surveys of workers in Indonesia and China, as well as in factories in Thailand, Cambodia, and Indonesia. "These reports contradict the powerful messages being sent out by Nike's public relations campaign to portray itself as a company that cares about working conditions," this report concludes. "In fact, some of the specific claims made by Nike to bolster its image are directly contradicted by these new studies."[70] Perhaps the best assessment of Nike and its audits is captured by the title of the most recent survey of sweatshop conditions in Asia performed by Global Exchange: *Still Waiting For Nike to Do It.*[71]

The efforts of activist NGOs to document abuses well illustrate the challenges of both internal and third-party social auditing for corporations. As Thomas Dunfee has noted, social audits also may bring about independence concerns if, for example, other consulting services are offered to the audit client.[72] Fees for social audits are typically a small part of the fees paid to a company's accounting partner. "In a conflict over aspects of an audit," according to one commentator, "resistance to management pressure could engender implicit threats regarding the retention of the financial audit (and indeed other non-audit services)."[73] There are, of course, many other obvious concerns about social auditing, ranging from perceptions that auditors are little more than paid agents of the corporation to the corresponding hesitancy by workers at contracted facilities to reveal inculpatory evidence.

Perhaps no concern is as prominent as the risk that audits will foster underserved perceptions of legitimacy. Michael Power, in his book *The Audit Society: Rituals of Verification,* made this point perfectly clear: "Auditing quality labels or certificates . . . do not invite or provoke public dialogue; they are not designed to support public debate or to connect the audit process to wider representative organs or to further machinery or regulatory escalation. . . . It is a dead-end in the chain of accountability . . . the fact of being audited deters public curiosity and inquiry and the users of audits are often just a mythical reference point within expert discourses. Audit is in this respect a substitute for democracy rather than its aid."[74] Nowhere are concerns over legitimacy and the challenges of performing social audits more apparent than with the practice of corporate social reporting for socially screened investments.

WASHING AND SOCIAL ACCOUNTING

The dramatic rise in the number and assets of socially screened mutual funds and indexes highlights concerns about the auditing of socially responsible investing (SRI). There is a conspicuous absence of literature on the integrity of corporate representations resulting in a screening inclusion or exclusion. In its most favorable light, a "specious gloss" is said to characterize social reporting initiatives in the United States and Europe.[75]

In discussing the future of SRI, a principal with Domini Social Investments observes that "[a]lthough an increasing number of corporations publish environmental and health and safety reports, many are simply token efforts—greenwashing—and few address the full range of social issues necessary to assess adequately a corporation's behaviour."[76] A committee formed by the International Standards Organization (ISO) to examine the prospects of ISO corporate responsibility standards concurred, with an additional caveat. "In the absence of credible, verifiable information," according to the ISO report, "it is difficult for shareholders, investors, and pension fund managers to make meaningful assessments and decisions about the CR [corporate responsibility] practices."[77]

Some scholars have been even less kind.[78] As Rob Gray wrote, "the quality of attestation to social and environmental reports is woefully poor."[79] After reviewing ethical reporting in the United Kingdom, John Stittle concluded that "there are significant distortions and omissions of information concerning ethical issues in current UK reporting systems."[80] Ensuring attestation and mechanisms by which corporate representations are systematically assessed remains an unmet challenge.[81]

Leading proponents of legitimacy theory reason that social and environmental disclosures are generally made for strategic reasons having little or nothing to do with perceived responsibilities or obligations.[82] These institutional and managerial strategies range from those designed to "gain or to extend legitimacy, to maintain its level of current legitimacy, or to repair or to defend its lost or threatened legitimacy."[83] Unsubstantiated and unverified social and environmental disclosures may amount to little more than public relations—issued to manage public perceptions, to respond to public pressure, or to react to perceived public opinion.[84] Efforts to achieve corporate legitimacy, according to Milne and Patten, reflect organizational myths, or words and actions that are decoupled from the operational code. These initiatives may be nothing more than an "elaborate and convincing facade designed or adopted to conceal the "back stage" activities from prying eyes."[85] Distinct threats to an organization's legitimacy prompt deception, as "[f]irms have an incentive to offset or mitigate the negative image portrayed through the required disclosures with information exhibiting other, presumably more positive, aspects of environmental performance."[86]

Social Accounting and the Limits of Voluntary Reporting

At the heart of the practical debate over corporate social accountability are fundamental questions of regulation. Should social and environmental disclosure be voluntary? A growing consensus bemoans the quality and reliability of voluntary disclosure.[87] An almost equal number raise problems with an interventionist stance.[88] While this debate proceeds, however, a host of international standards for social accounting have emerged since the mid-1990s, including AA1000, ACCA (Association of Chartered Certified Accountants), and SA 8000 among those holding out the promise of something more than voluntary corporate disclosures. A comprehensive review by the ILO of all initiatives, from intergovernmental and government-legislated to recognized standards bodies and investor-driven, is less than inspiring. Initiatives are credited for having variable scope, variable levels of inclusivity and engagement of stakeholders, variable levels of transparency in code and standards development, variable content, variable ability to measure and ensure compliance, variable flexibility in addressing differing operating contexts, variable quality of implementation and reporting, and, most important, variable compliance verification approaches. They are, in the words of the ISO committee, much like the efforts of the first generation of corporate responsibility initiatives.[89]

If there is an exception, a second-generation effort, it is the Global Reporting Initiative (GRI). Its mission is to "[e]levate sustainability reporting practises worldwide to a level equivalent to financial reporting; design, disseminate, and promote standardised reporting practises, core measurements, and customised, sector-specific measurements; [and] ensure a permanent and effective institutional host to support such reporting practises worldwide."[90] In the GRI *Sustainability Reporting Guidelines 2002*, impressive lists of performance indicators appear in three categories: economic, environmental, and social.[91]

The 2002 guidelines are a much-improved version of the 2000 GRI, with many thoughtful revisions. For all of the obvious reasons, much is now made of the need for reporting transparency, inclusiveness, completeness, relevance, and auditability. Indeed, independent assurance of corporate reports is repeatedly encouraged in the guidelines. Unfortunately, however, the 2002 GRI fails to require external audits and simply reports that the way in which the GRI may play a "constructive role" in ensuring the validity of sustainability reports is still being considered. To be fair, the GRI provides guidance on how to select an assurance adviser. Firms should consider:

- the assurance provider's degree of independence and freedom from bias, influence, and conflicts of interest.
- the assurance provider's ability to balance consideration of the interests of various stakeholders.
- that the assurance provider has not been involved in the design, development, or implementation of the organization's sustainability monitoring and reporting systems or assisted in compiling the sustainability report.
- that sufficient time is allocated to the assurance provider to enable the assurance process to be carried out effectively, using due professional care.
- that the assurance provider is collectively or individually competent to meet the objectives of the assurance assignment, as demonstrated through an appropriate level of experience and professional judgment.[92]

And the GRI leverages the current focus on corporate governance by suggesting the need for board members to

- recognize explicitly that they are responsible for the content of the sustainability report.
- recognize explicitly that the assurance provider alone is responsible for the content of the independent assurance report and will agree, at the beginning of the engagement, to publish the assurance report in full.
- ensure that adequate resources are made available for the independent assurance provider's work and that the assurance provider will have

access to all individuals, groups, sites, records, and information that it considers necessary to carrying out the assurance engagement.[93]

But companies are not left with anything more than some intuitive advice and a simple caveat: "In designing data collection and information systems, reporting organizations therefore should anticipate that internal auditing and external assurance processes may be used in the future."[94]

How serious a problem is this omission? The emergence of countless reporting initiatives reflects a growing trend of corporations to provide more than annual financial reports. Results from KPMG's International Survey of Corporate Sustainability Reporting (2002), for example, reveal a significant increase over a three-year period ending in 2002 in the number of sustainability, environmental, and social reports from the Global Fortune 250 (GFT250; 35 percent versus 45 percent).[95] Notably, this increase does not include health, safety, and economic reports. Reporting varied by sector, not surprisingly, with higher reporting rates in industries that have the most significant environmental impact, for example, mining, forestry, pulp and paper, chemicals and synthetics, transport, and pharmaceuticals. The United States, Japan, Germany, the United Kingdom, and France led reporting rates.

Assuring the accuracy of corporate reports, as the 2002 GRI suggests, is still a prominent challenge. According to KPMG's 2000 survey, only 29 percent of the GFT250 had their reports independently verified—a modest increase of 10 percent over 1999. Most verified reports, approximately two-thirds, are reviewed by major accountancy firms. Even so, the scope and approach taken by auditors differ widely. This fact and the ad hoc nature of verification more generally led authors of the KPMG 2000 survey to conclude that the approach to verification was too inconsistent to ensure verification. It is far from surprising, therefore, that "NGOs have real concerns about the potential for companies, espousing sustainable rhetoric, to use the GRI to engage in 'greenwash' for the marketing benefit it would give their companies. Which is where the question of verification becomes relevant."[96]

Similar concerns have been raised with the United Nations Global Compact, an initiative credited to the leadership of UN Secretary General Kofi Annan, designed to promote a core set of human rights, environmental, and social principles within the private sector. Not long after its conception, civil society activist groups raised the now familiar charge "that by attaching themselves to the United Nations, corporations may be able to 'greenwash' themselves throughout the developing world."[97] The Global Compact, like the GRI, fails to require more than mere corporate representations of social responsibility.[98]

The growing conventional wisdom is that companies must produce verified accountability reports—verified reports by auditors specializing in social accounting and auditing. Some claim, however, that this does not go far enough to protect the independence of social auditors from management influence. Brendan O'Dwyer posed a critical question, yet to be answered: "Can we expect anything different if financial accountants move into the realm of social auditing, particularly as social accounting consulting services are being promoted alongside social audit services as part of packages aimed at reputation assurance and risk management?"[99]

It remains to be seen whether O'Dwyer's unease would be lessened by court-certified receivers, independent monitors, or Independent Private Sector Inspector Generals (IPSIGs). Ronald Goldstock has long argued that IPSIGs, with their reporting responsibilities to both the board and governmental agencies, escape conflicts and maintain independence. According to Goldstock, "The IPSIG must remain independent, autonomous and self-sufficient, and, although interactive with the organization, unconstrained by organizational biases which might seek to protect the corporate reputation at the expense of exposing illegal or unethical behavior."[100]

Beyond Verified Disclosure

Answers to questions of auditor independence may rest with the engagement of stakeholders outside the firm, such as IPSIGs. This is familiar ground for those who seek independent sources and metrics for "effective" corporate compliance. Peter N. Grabosky long ago called for various forms of nongovernmental social control of corporate behavior, for example, indirect "hybrid" governance with third-party coproduction of compliance.[101] Ayres and Braithwaite argued for tripartism, or the integration of a third party into the regulatory arena occupied by an organization and a regulator.[102] In theory, tripartism insures against regulatory capture, enhances communication, and allows for independent third-party monitoring.

Stakeholder engagements that marry state activity and private interests, approximating Grabosky, Ayres, and Braithwaite's conceptions of third parties, are now codified in social accountability standards, for example, Accountability Standard AA1000. Stakeholders and other elements of civil society, including NGOs, are beginning to serve an increasing role in ensuring the integrity of corporate social and environmental disclosures.[103] In fact, some notable successes have been described in detail.[104] A logical next step for social accounting, one day, is stakeholder governance.[105] Whether or not that day has arrived, Lydenberg makes the incisive observation that the vocabulary of SRI and corporate social responsibility are now an integral part of the "debate about the proper form and role of global capitalism."[106]

In asking whether the potential of corporations to do good can be harnessed, the potential to do bad tamed, and the goals of transnational corporations reconciled with the social objectives of national governments,

Lydenberg calls for corporations to fully disclose "actual" data on social and environmental impacts. This important call must be heard not only by corporations but also by those reporting bodies and initiatives seeking a corporate constituency with integrity. Organizations that promulgate corporate standards assume a distinct responsibility to institutionalize required mechanisms for independent verification. Abdicating this responsibility by deferring mandatory third-party auditing to or foregoing it entirely strongly undermines appearances of legitimacy and invites gaming. There are, of course, countless other reasons for such a mandatory requirement, including the value of ensuring accurate and relevant disclosure to assuage concerns of the investing public following recent accounting debacles. To say that the future of our capital markets is inextricably tied to trustworthy disclosures is far from an overstatement.

CONCLUSION

One cannot imagine a more responsible and caring company. Altria assumes full responsibility for seeing that its products are used responsibly by adults. It cares not only about those issues that touch smoking but also about the broader concerns of the many stakeholders of Philip Morris USA. These stakeholders include the general public, parents, leaders in the community, public health officials, and the government. With a dedicated youth smoking prevention department that has an annual budget of more than $100 million, Philip Morris USA promotes education programs for parents and teachers, funds to support youth smoking prevention, initiatives to help restrict youth access to cigarettes, and research on youth smoking prevention. "Youth smoking prevention is a long-term commitment for Philip Morris USA," according to the company. "We will continue to support initiatives in collaboration with others who share our goal to help prevent youth smoking and contribute to the decline in youth smoking rates while promoting positive youth development."[107]

One cannot imagine a more giving company. The companies comprising Altria have been awarding grants to nonprofit organizations since 1956. Since the mid-1990s, Altria has contributed more than $1 billion in cash and food. In 2002 alone, the company awarded $138.3 million to a host of philanthropic causes, including funds to combat hunger, domestic violence, and AIDS.

One cannot imagine a company more committed to the environment. Altria requires each company to maintain a focused and phased environmental strategy. Moreover, each company must commit to Altria's Environmental Principles:

1. Management Systems: To design and maintain effective management systems consistent with the spirit and intent of these principles.
2. Compliance: To conduct its business in accordance with all applicable environmental laws, regulations, requirements and corporate commitments.
3. Environmental Footprint: To take initiatives to minimize the current and future environmental impact of its activities on the land, air, water and other natural resources.
4. Packaging: To minimize, consistent with its business priorities, the environmental impact of its product packaging while maintaining the integrity of its products.
5. Innovation: To undertake and commission research and development consistent with its business priorities in order to minimize its environmental footprint and to foster solutions to environmental issues.
6. Public Policy: To constructively engage with representatives of industry, government, and civil society to anticipate environmental issues and to promote the development of shared environmental policy goals.
7. Internal Communication: To promote environmental awareness and individual responsibility among its employees through education and training and to recognize and reward achievements and continuous improvement.
8. Stakeholder Engagement: To build trust, credibility, and meaningful relationships with its consumers, business partners, and other stakeholders through its environmental commitment, performance, and expectations.
9. Alignment: To periodically evaluate these principles and ensure that they remain consistent with and supportive of the Environmental Policy.

One cannot imagine a more compliant company, committed to integrity and values. When the time came for testimony before the United States Sentencing Commission on the need for changes in the guidelines to accommodate recent governance scandals, the views of Philip Morris USA were well-conceived, intelligent, and elegant. As David Greenberg wrote, Philip Morris (PM) "believes that organizations should be encouraged to employ an ethics or a values-based approach in formulating their basic business conduct guidelines and compliance policies. PM prefers the term 'values'-based to 'ethics'-based because it is a more neutral term. PM supports the view that in order for a compliance program to become part of a company's culture and embedded in its basic business processes, senior management must define a set of shared values and standards for business conduct with the objective of improving employee decision-making across a broad range of practical business situations."[108]

One can now only imagine how far corporate strategy and corporate public relations have converged, a convergence that defies simple calls for transparency.[109] Altria is transparent. This convergence defies calls for accountability. Atria is accountable. This convergence defies calls for integrity-based compliance. Altria is committed to integrity. This convergence requires all to rethink the metrics and methods by which business ethics are judged. More specifically, it requires reporting and standards bodies offering corporations a haven for reclaimed legitimacy to assume their long-overdue responsibility—to impose mandatory third-party audits. Failure to do so risks complicity with corporate gamesmanship and deception, a risk that casts a shadow on the very need for standards. There was a time, a somewhat simpler time, when all we wondered about was whether Lambert Hollow was real.

CHAPTER SEVEN

Making and Unmaking the Pessimist's Account

The vast majority of American business leaders are responsible, honest men and women. But left unchallenged, corporate cultures that foster criminal behavior have an impact felt far beyond the corporation itself. Investors lose savings. Employees lose jobs. Families lose providers. And American markets lose integrity in the eyes of our citizens and the world.

In the face of such damage, prosecutors, investigators and regulators do not have the luxury of time. We simply cannot afford to wait to challenge corporate corruption until jobs are lost, retirement funds are depleted and confidence is destroyed.

The Department of Justice is working in extraordinary cooperation with the Securities and Exchange Commission to bring about real time enforcement of the nation's corporate fraud statutes. That means that investigations and prosecutions are carefully executed but quickly paced in order to end criminal activity before jobs, investments and assets are squandered.

We must work together. We must work swiftly. We must pursue allegations of corporate fraud regardless of the size or the prominence of the company under scrutiny. And in response, those corporations under investigation have a fateful decision to make.

Companies such as Homestore.com, whose leadership is choosing to cooperate with law enforcement in order to contain the damage to employees and investors, are to be commended. The nature and extent of a company's cooperation is always a significant factor in deciding what charges will be brought.

In contrast, companies such as Arthur Andersen that choose to impede and obstruct the investigation of corporate corruption deny themselves the benefit of cooperation, sometimes inviting their own demise. The Department of Justice has long recognized the principle that an employee's criminal conduct does not mean that the employing company should automatically be charged with a crime.

> *But those corporations that choose to prolong the damage to the public by refusing to cooperate with investigators should be forewarned: if you obstruct, if you impede—you leave your company vulnerable to public indictment, prosecution, and conviction.*

Remarks of former attorney general John Ashcroft, Corporate Fraud/Responsibility Conference Enforcing the Law, Restoring Trust, Defending Freedom, September 27, 2002.

*

Aggressive enforcement of the federal criminal law, unparalleled coordination of regulatory agencies in corporate investigations and prosecutions, and success stories in deterring corporate crime and encouraging compliance with law are the milestones marking progress in the war against corporate fraud. The accounts are credible, convincing, and poignant. And they are made more so with high-priced images and neatly packaged rhetoric about corporate citizenship, compliance, and governance in the wake of a host of governance reforms and the latest iteration of the United States Sentencing Guidelines for Organizations. It is difficult not to be naive and placid consumers of the institutionalization of business ethics, no matter what the flavor: good corporate citizenship, good corporate governance, or good corporate compliance.

A stream of front-page business news feeds the public's appetite for retribution, reconciliation, and restoration. As the attorney general suggests, there are identifiable victims of corporate fraud who deserve recompense. Employees, their families, and our markets must know that a battle is waged in their name: the Securities and Exchange Commission gets tough with settlement in Lucent; Nortel faces more restatements; Strong Funds and regulators agree to settle cases; Spitzer charges that Glaxo concealed Paxil data; firms close in on settlement of an initial public offering inquiry—Goldman Sachs and Morgan Stanley agree to pay $40 million each after accusations of "laddering," PricewaterhouseCoopers agrees to pay $41 million in civil penalties. Our progress in the battle against corporate deviance is marked, it seems, by record-setting judgments and settlements.

Compliance and law abidance under the banner of business ethics are all too often illusory. Media reports of indicted white-collar criminals and white-shoe corporations are scripted morality plays with distinctly good and bad guys, images of corporate souls that are canned, superficial, or simply incredible. They are offered with all the best of intentions, with all the right moral rhetoric, by well-intended and well-informed champions of corporate citizenship. One is left asking: Who dares oppose ethical business practices and governance reforms necessary to ensure fair markets? Who opposes markets that are perceived to be legitimate?

The pitch and plot of this incarnation of ethics, compliance, and governance are so convincing that too few are left to ask how recent reforms may be taken seriously, not in the short term when the ire of the public demands justice, but long after the images of Enron, WorldCom, and Andersen fade. This is not to suggest that recent legislative and regulatory reforms lack meaning and effect. There is a heightened awareness of the harm of corporate fraud that is an important precursor for meaningful reform. There are high-profile cases and, with certain agencies, significantly more staff, larger caseloads, and substantially higher fines.[1] There is a reconception of the critical role of audit committees in supervising corporate-wide compliance with law. But the narrowly drawn, rigid accounting standards at the foundation of legislative and regulatory reforms touch only a portion of corporate deviance and, in doing so, reflect challenges seen throughout this book: our ambivalence with regulating corporations, the absence of a strong constituency favoring resort to corporate criminal liability, the inevitable gaming that accompanies regulation, and, perhaps most important, the failure of substantive law reform. That state and federal authorities are successful in policing only a small fraction of corporate crime, given this ambivalence, is far from surprising.

Admittedly, this skeptical and seemingly pessimistic account, one that pervades *Corporate Bodies and Guilty Minds*, is subject to empirical scrutiny and challenge. To be fair, the same may be said of any argument to the contrary. But our history, in addition to anecdotal evidence and a remarkable lack of empirical evidence, makes the skeptical and pessimistic account most plausible. Moreover, this account deserves at least some recognition, if only to balance a patriotic fervor about government prescriptions of exemplary compliance, best practices in good governance, upstanding corporate citizenship, and the "moralization" of American businesses.[2] The near-consensus view is that this sea change in expectations was "a wake-up call for corporate America" and is a "resounding success."[3] It is most remarkable that despite untold harm and victimization across a wide range of vulnerable stakeholders, dramatic social costs, and vast business expenditures to combat such deviance, systematic social science research offers few clues about corporate compliance with law. And, in the absence of such evidence-based research, there are far too few critics who sound a skeptical and pessimistic tone about the progress made in this "war against corporate waste, fraud and abuse."[4] This chapter explores some of the reasons supporting the skeptic's and pessimist's account. It concludes with recognition of the importance of a new "benign big gun" to start proving would-be skeptics and pessimists wrong.

REASONS FOR SKEPTICISM AND PESSIMISM

Successful or Failed Corporate Citizenship?

In reflecting on the genesis of the corporate sentencing guidelines, one of its original architects noted three factors that contributed to their birth. First, there were some distinct limits to the role that law enforcement could play in preventing corporate crime. Law enforcement was, for some, like "the occasional patrol car along millions of miles of highway."[5] Second, existing law grounded in the doctrine of vicarious liability was perceived to be unfair. Rogue employees could implicate a firm that had done everything possible to institutionalize ethics. And third, a sentencing scheme that rewarded compliance efforts would encourage all corporations to take such efforts seriously.[6] Corporations, as rational actors, would invest in compliance just as they commit the firm's capital to human resources, legal counsel, and insurance. The result would be less deviance.

There is, however, scant evidence that the "good corporate citizenship movement" decreased corporate deviance.[7] The absence of empirical data on the rate of corporate crime; problems with unreported and undetected corporate crime; the absence of rigorous evaluations of compliance program effectiveness; and concerns over the independence of internal audits, no less third-party social and environmental audits, make claims for success ring hollow. Definitive claims are also undercut by first, evidence that some compliance initiatives are more cosmetic than real and that regulators and prosecutors are poorly positioned to evaluate the effectiveness of compliance programs and second, the prospects that compliance expenditures might actually increase deviance in some firms. Without good base rate data on corporate deviance over time, increased law enforcement efforts—resulting in larger caseloads, more convictions, and larger aggregate fine levels—leave a distinct appearance that the rate of corporate crime is increasing when the inverse may or may not be true. Annual global fraud and economic crime surveys by top-tier accounting firms, occupational fraud surveys, and surveys of white-collar crime offer a rare glimpse of the almost inconceivable harm from white-collar crime and occupational fraud. Far less is revealed, however, about crimes committed by corporations.

Research on corporate crime is almost always conducted with limited survey instruments, sampling small numbers of employees across only a few industries, and interpreted with basic descriptive statistics. Much of this research suffers from some familiar definitional and methodological concerns, including little convergence over how to define the nature of the problem or frame the dependent variable, a host of sampling biases, design limitations, and unsupported causal assumptions derived from moderate to weak associations. Corporate compliance research faces other challenges.

Without randomized controlled field experiments, like those prescribed by the Campbell Collaboration in pushing for evidence-based research, it is impossible to know with confidence what works, what doesn't, what is promising, and what is unknown. Courts, legislators, and regulators will be hard-pressed to satisfy at least some articulated penal objectives (particularly one of "mixed goals") and deliver legally prescribed standards consistent with these objectives. Those who design compliance and governance programs will continue to be guided by a mix of intuition and untested hypotheses in attempts to satisfy internally and externally prescribed standards. And there will continue to be "critical knowledge gaps," as Lawrence W. Sherman called them, giving lawmakers and regulators free rein to add program elements driven by available resources or the politics of the moment, often on the periphery or outside of stated objectives.[8]

Evaluation research imposes distinct hurdles that reveal just how little is known about crime prevention, more generally, and how intuitions about what actually works are often so very often wrong. As Lawrence W. Sherman noted, "Even where evaluations attempt to measure crime prevention, they often lack the basic scientific elements needed for inferring cause and effect. . . . Only a random selection of equally eligible program targets can conclusively eliminate alternative theories about the effects of a crime prevention program."[9] In evaluating the strength of program effects, Sherman and his colleagues looked for a combination of (1) reliable and statistically robust measures, in combination with adequate sample sizes and sufficient response rates, (2) consistent temporal ordering of both dependent and independent variables, and (3) valid control and comparison groups. All three together, forming the Maryland Scale of Scientific Methods, provide strong evidence of a program effect, made that much stronger by subsequent replications.[10]

Failing to minimize measurement error by controlling for extraneous variables or failing to rely on statistics capable of detecting meaningful differences are surely not problems specific to corporate crime research.[11] They are, however, that much more apparent given the dearth of controlled experimental research on corporate crime and the words of those who, even with good intentions, make generalized empirical claims that programs promoting good corporate citizenship actually matter.

Appearances to the Contrary

In bemoaning the disappearance of organizational deviance defined as corporate crime, Laureen Snider mocked the value and prowess of the corporate criminal law. "It is expensive, inefficient, a club over the head when a whisper in the ear would suffice."[12] Persuasion and reason must replace command and control, she wrote. Market incentives and tax breaks, Snider chided, work better than lengthy trials and stiff fines. Models of responsive regulation hinge on an ideal game, one that relies on increasingly formal controls. Snider concluded that cooperative models of regulation are politically wise, if nothing else, because they enshrine and legitimize power relations, preserving the status quo where regulatory forces are outgunned by corporate power and corporate elites. "The result of enshrining this disparity in official policy," according to Snider "is to stabilize it, weakening thereby the forces that seek to strengthen regulation."[13]

Snider captured a very subtle effect of the dominance of corporate power in cooperative regulatory systems: that cooperative regulatory systems are designed to be victims of corporate dominance. It is all too easy to dream up regulatory solutions for fundamental governance problems, such as ownership separation, and the heavy-handedness of command and control policies. It is another to craft a regulatory game that avoids the mere appearance of control. Corporations face new and burdensome regulation, but they still have insurmountable information advantages, the currency of compliance expenditures, the power of cooperation, vast resources, and the rich guise of the corporate form. Satisfying guidelines standards a priori diminishes the rationale and incentive to investigate, prosecute, and convict an offending firm. Being "in compliance" with these standards reduces the fine level and, moreover, the justification for corporate liability in the first place.

Realizing such due diligence is a good outcome if firms are law abiding and blameworthy only to the extent that wayward agents disregard compliance policies. Yet there is little to no empirical evidence that this is so, all of which makes assessing the effect of corporate compliance programs and good corporate governance initiatives more of a challenge and, to be skeptical and pessimistic at the same time, that much more unlikely.

Complying after the Fact

Some observers trace the origins of the good corporate citizenship movement of the 1990s to the price-fixing scandal that culminated in *U.S. v. Allegheny Bottling Company*.[14] Critics of *Allegheny* found it strange that a corporation could be imprisoned, fined, and sentenced to community service at once, all within the meaning of the Sherman Act. To personify the defendant corporation was as disturbing, at least for some, as the failure of courts to sanction firms such as Allegheny Bottling consistently and uniformly. The rationale for extending the sentencing guidelines to corporate offenders, however, ultimately hinged on what has been characterized as an "astonishing" fact: courts were not giving adequate credit to corporations for their efforts to comply with laws. According to this rationale, the government must not only consider how it may regulate and punish corporate misconduct. The government must also design incentives so that companies will understand why it is in their interest to fashion strong and effective compliance mechanisms. When criminal offenses occur, it is the firm's reaction that determines fault. "Even the best efforts to prevent crime may not be successful in every case," argued the chairman of the United States Sentencing Commission. "But we have to reward the corporation that was trying to be a good corporate citizen."[15]

While the government's leadership in promoting corporate integrity and good corporate citizenship is laudable, effective regulatory enforcement strategies supplanted the substantive criminal law in the absence of legislative action. Regulators and prosecutors use their vast discretion to circumvent the strictures of the substantive law, leaving regulated corporations in two very different worlds. Postoffense behavior is the cornerstone of the regulated response to the discovery of illegality. But the recognition of corporate postoffense behavior is simply inimical to the extant law.

Why give so much credit to postoffense behavior? Why reconceive the corporate criminal law so that determinations of both liability and blame turn on something other than the underlying offense? It is all too easy to conclude, as was done in a number of earlier chapters, that the ambivalence with organizational liability moved the substantive law away from connecting the corporate person with corporate blame for nearly a century; that cooperative regulation requires the consideration of postoffense behavior for reasons of access to evidence and subsequent remediation; and, to be a bit more critical, that the diversion of cases into plea and integrity agreements contributes to a discretionary morass that the Sentencing Reform Act of 1984 should have fixed. Far less clear, but certainly as important, is its effect on the social construction of corporate deviance and our perceptions of the extent and rate of corporate offending.

There is a subtlety to the recognition of postoffense behavior that is often missed, especially when the firm's compliance program is held out as evidence of corporate due diligence: Corporations are receiving credit for their failures. In theory, rewards are generally far less effective than other regulatory mechanisms, such as the threat of punishment.[16] As a practical matter, crediting failure also seems to miss the mark. "Were we to credit failed compliance programs at this charging phase," remarked one prosecutor, "there would be less incentive for companies to make sure these programs work, to refine the programs, and to make them effective. The ultimate goal, after all, is a compliance program that prevents crimes, not one that excuses the corporation in the event that one occurs."[17]

More to the point, the recognition of postoffense behavior by courts and guidelines abandons the substantive law while it redefines blame. From the aftermath of *Hudson* to the most recent wave of prosecutions, the harm in the underlying offense is all too often considered far less important than the firm's response to the offense and any subsequent governmental investigation. The message: corporations are blameworthy, just as Attorney General Ashcroft opines, when after committing a criminal offense they just do not get the message that corporate crime is wrong. Heeding this message obviates the need for a substantive criminal law, narrowly reserving corporate liability for those firms that are so poorly counseled that they cannot conceive a due diligence defense or, remarkably, are just too proud or defiant to do so.

And finally, our allegiance to postoffense behavior as the tipping point for ascribing liability and blame makes assessing the extent and rate of corporate offending difficult. After all, firms are not criminally liable and thus not conceived of or counted as "corporate criminals" if after committing an offense they engage in such diligence as the Thompson Memo or the sentencing guidelines prescribe. Just how significant is the problem of corporate crime? Insignificant, if one defines corporate criminality as requiring action other than the commission of a criminal offense.

Susan Shapiro's words ring true as she carefully disentangled the status of perpetrators from their misdeeds in refashioning this brand of deviance. "The related concepts of white-collar, corporate, and occupational crime," Shapiro wrote, "have created an imprisoning framework for contemporary scholarship, impoverishing theory, distorting empirical inquiry, oversimplifying policy analysis, inflaming our muckraking instincts, and obscuring fascinating questions about the relationship between social organization and crime."[18]

The Whim of Corporate Criminal Liability

Embracing postoffense behavior offers yet another reason to be skeptical: the whim of ascribing criminal liability to an entity. In spite of very clearly drafted prosecutorial guidelines, there remains an arbitrariness and unpredictability to the construction and processing of "corporate crime" cases, making empirical research on organizational deviance an even more formidable challenge.

The construction of corporate deviance turns on a host of factors, from the response of senior management to the outcome of internal investigations to the reactions of criminal justice functionaries in multiple agencies with very different priorities, agendas, and resources; the extent to which the firm cooperated with authorities; the status of the agent or group of agents largely responsible for the act in question; the implications for the firm of allegations by internal whistle-blowers; the visibility of the firm in the community; and the extent to which the firm should have uncovered what authorities ultimately discovered.

Even with the new legislative initiatives to combat corporate fraud, the framing of behavior amounting to a criminal offense remains subject to the influence of multiple stakeholders, most of whom have every incentive to fashion an agent's deviance as something less than a crime committed in the scope of their authority, in the name of the firm, for the firm, or by the firm. Looking inside the "black box" of prosecutorial discretion, one sees a series of decisions that often turn on nothing short of luck and fortune.[19]

Was the matter first referred to the civil division? If so, it is rare for it to be then referred to the criminal division. How much time and resources have been invested by the prosecutor and investigating agents in preparing the case? The more time and money spent, the more likely an indictment and less likely a settlement.

Kenneth Mann's portrait of white-collar defense counsel may be sharply contrasted with accounts of private and appointed counsel representing those accused of street crime. Comparable differences are found in corporate crime cases. The likelihood that corporate crime cases exacting equally serious harm, equally deserving of criminal prosecution, are treated alike as criminal cases is too often remote. The same case may be trumpeted as a symbolic prosecution to encourage general deterrence or may never be conceived of as a criminal matter; may be cast as a white-collar crime rather than a corporate offense; may result in a local or state prosecution after being dropped by the Department of Justice; or may remain in a civil or administrative division and never referred out. Or threats of an indictment may be used by prosecutors as a lever to prompt disclosures in the making of a civil case.[20] As Sutherland, Clinard, and Yeager quickly realized, research on corporate crime is difficult without a willingness to expand one's sample well beyond limiting legal definitions of the corporate criminal law.[21] The alternative, of course, is to be constrained by the limitations of relying on, for example, conviction or sentence data.

Solved Problems, Created Others

The freedom to define behavior amounting to corporate criminality as something less harmful, serious, and blameworthy is attributable, at least in part, to the driving force behind the sea change in corporate regulation: the sentencing guidelines. This freedom is surely strange if uniformity, consistency, and fairness are the shared values underlying the guidelines. That guidelines designed to structure the discretion of the judiciary magnify the discretion of other criminal justice functionaries is distressing at best. As Marc Miller notes, "The overwhelming and dominant fact of the federal sentencing system, beyond the Commission and the guidelines and mandatory penalties, is the virtually absolute power the system has given prosecutors over federal prosecution and sentencing."[22] The guidelines, even if something less than mandatory, are simply an extravagant gift to prosecutors. Prosecutors set the parameters of the defendant's sentence by their charging decision. At the same time, they hold the key to any downward departures through their decision to grant or deny substantial assistance reductions.[23]

The effects of the guidelines, however, extend well beyond the problem of shifting discretion. A rational sentencing system is inextricably tied to a rational criminal code. Order may not be brought to the substantive law through sentencing reform and piecemeal legislation alone. How can the law achieve the lofty goals of honesty, uniformity, and proportionality in the absence of generally adhered-to principles of corporate culpability and liability? What then does proportionality mean? What good are uniformity and honesty at the time of sentencing when both may be missing in the initial determination of liability?

It may or may not be too late to lament the shift in discretion from judges to prosecutors in the long wake of the sentencing guidelines. The United States Supreme Court has more than chipped away at the Sentencing Commission's impenetrable armor, first in *Blackley* and more recently in *United States v. Booker* and *United States v. Fanfan*.[24] It is neither too late nor unwise, though, to question the exercise of that discretion, as was done in earlier chapters, and the remarkable inversion of the sentencing law. Without the substantive law as a guide, prosecutors regularly adopt the provisions and commentary of the sentencing guidelines as the law's general part. Without the substantive law as a guide, regulators craft liability rules in policies and policy statements that effectively replace the extant law. And finally, as if the substantive law matters not, prosecutors and regulators rather than judges leverage their discretion in an effort to seek justice.

Politicized Prosecutions Risking Legitimacy

In discussing his paradigmatic regulatory pyramid, John Braithwaite said trust first, and the benefits of cooperative regulation will follow. At the same time, check strength with strength; ensure the motivation of the regulated to maintain the trust by clearly signaling willingness to escalate social controls when there is an abuse of trust.[25] "Desire to avoid severe sanctions," Braithwaite argued, "channels more of the regulatory game down to the base of the pyramid."[26] Herein lies the *pyramid paradox*; signaling the availability of progressively more formal social controls that assume an inherent distrust prompts trust and trustworthy regulation.

The regulatory pyramid represents a complex legal and behavioral prescription. And even though there are many necessary ingredients, two stand out among many others: (1) a credible criminal law to check the strength of corporate power with strength and (2) trust in the very institutions that oversee, administer, and enforce corporate regulation. In the zeal to reestablish the legitimacy of markets, to reinforce the ethicality of key financial institutions, politicized and symbolic prosecutions that take a heavy toll earn an honored place in the state's strategy to counter strength with strength.[27] But in exercising this brand of state power, well-coordinated, high-profile prosecutions of large firms must be perceived as both fair and just; otherwise they engender questions of trust, confidence, and motivation.[28]

The regulatory lessons of heavy-handed prosecutions, such as those resulting in the death of large, viable, and otherwise healthy firms, are rarely long-lasting. Corporate crime control strategies calling for occasional severe punishments are, as Sally Simpson notes in her research on corporate crime deterrence, unlikely to work.[29] The lessons are soon lost because they do not appear to be part of a legitimate and sustainable regulatory strategy, especially if prosecutorial zeal is not in proportion to the perceived harm of corporate misdeeds. They are unpredictable "hard shoves," as Dan Kahan writes. Some believe, and quite reasonably so, that the inglorious end of Arthur Andersen, discussed in chapter 2, will one day be another lost regulatory lesson. Certainly the reversal of Andersen's conviction for obstruction of justice by the United States Supreme Court supports this belief.

Diane Markowski from the human resources department at Andersen was in a state of disbelief after the conviction of her firm for obstructing justice. "My first thought was that I wanted to tell the jury they had just destroyed thousands of people's reputations. I wanted to ask them why."[30] And in Andersen's final press release, the firm questioned the government's motives as well: "It is clear that the government failed to uphold its moral responsibility to the public by indicting and prosecuting a firm of 26,000 innocent people that self-reported its findings, fully cooperated with the Department of Justice, the Securities and Exchange Commission (SEC), and Congress, and worked in good faith to find a solution that would have prevented this trial. Given these circumstances, there is no rationale for indicting a cooperating Arthur Andersen and destroying the firm as we knew it."[31] Whether or not one feels sympathy for Andersen and its employees, the firm's prosecution along with a number of other high-profile targets raises almost as many concerns as it addresses. The corporate criminal law must be perceived as strong but at the same time morally legitimate.

Reliving History

In *The Timid Corporation*, Benjamin Hunt makes the case that the rise of self-regulation ushered in a new era of caution, restraint, and timidity by corporations typified by a culture of risk aversion.[32] Fearing loss of reputation and appearances of errant behavior, protective measures rule corporate behavior, including a new role for the board of directors and the inculcation of risk-management principles throughout the firm. There is a new intolerance for risk, argues Hunt, one that invites a strong allergy to innovation and entrepreneurial creativity. Corporations practice a form of *Cowardly Capitalism,* to borrow a portion of a book title from Daniel Ben-Ami.[33]

Hunt's portrait of the risk-averse corporation is fair but seemingly incomplete. Corporations may be increasingly timid and risk-averse, but risk-shifting strategies born from direct and vicarious experience with failed compliance and governance practices are well in place. There is far less in law to fear than corporations suggest. Even with the generous contributions of Sarbanes-Oxley, ambivalence over corporate criminal liability persists, as it always has. With insignificant exceptions, substantive law reform is nowhere to be found. Corporate power, by any and all metrics, remains formidable. The law's status quo demonstrates remarkable capabilities by those regulated to satisfy and, in certain situations, deceive regulators. Regulators, prosecutors, employees, and other agents are also timid and, in different but comparable ways, risk-averse. All stakeholders worthy of mention resist corporate criminal liability in spite of its perceived regulatory importance.

This portrait of corporations and the criminal law is timeless, so timeless that the calls for and grumbles over corporate governance today, as noted in chapter 1, bear remarkable similarity to those in the mid- to late 1800s: "Corporation affairs are carried on upon the confidence principle entirely. Men who would not trust any individual, even the most honest and responsible, without good security and close watchfulness, yet place large interests in the keeping of Directors, to manage as they please."[34] In the late 1800s, the role of corporate lobbyists in influencing legislative reform further compromised the governance of corporations: "They block the wheels of National legislation, and by bribes and bottles are continually tampering with those to whom are intrusted our public interests."[35]

Faith in the integrity of our markets may be placed in jeopardy by a single iconic company, such as Enron in 2002 or Erie Railroad in the 1860s. "Overissues of stock, a reckless perversion of power, corrupt legislation in the interest of common swindlers, and a systematic tampering with the administration of law, are occurrences that would naturally destroy all faith in the conditions or management of the Erie Corporation,"[36] wrote editors of the *New York Times* in 1870.

The likelihood that we will continue to relive history appears strong: Corporate governance in the United States is inherently unstable. Mark Roe astutely attributes this instability and recurring breakdowns to the effects of ownership separation and our decentralized, porous regulatory system. According to Roe, "We'll patch it up, we'll move on, we'll muddle through. That's what will happen this time, and that's what will happen next time."[37]

Thirsting For Corporate Virtue

Following in the tradition of Braithwaite, Shearing, and Grabosky, the work of Fiona Haines points to the importance of organizational culture, character, context, and structure. Haines explored the complementary nature of organizational trust and virtue, flirting with ideas as to how both might be promoted to ensure the integrity of regulatory regimes. She concluded that while the "exercise of nurturing virtue may be fruitful in certain arenas, the undertaking may be more complex than previously suggested."[38] Haines's cautious words reflect the need for regulation to influence and direct organizational culture. Where such influence fails, deviance and liability naturally follow.

Haines's work is notable in calling for corporate virtue from the responsive regulatory process. It is also inspiring, even with the equivocal results of her study. But as much as there is thirst for the common good and public good of corporate virtue, as inspiring as it is to see an owner's benevolence toward his employees in Malden Mills, the social responsibility of Merck in using precious research and development expenses to cure the dreaded disease of river blindness in Africa, and the heroic recall of tampered-with and, most especially, nontampered-with capsules of Tylenol by McNeil Consumer Products, there is a sober and somber reality to intrinsic corporate behavior, no less instrumental corporate behavior, to borrow words from Roger Martin's *The Virtue Matrix: Calculating the Return on Corporate Responsibility.*[39]

This reality, decidedly shaded by skepticism and pessimism, is one of the impressive and stirring examples of unrepresentative goodwill, of the disingenuousness that accompanies business ethics and corporate conscience award winners, of moral exemplars in one or more aspects of social, human, and environmental performance that successfully divert attention from the narrowly conceived notion of value as profit making, from failed compliance and governance, and from leadership that uses prepared scripts to find the right words. If corporate virtue is "a generally shared notion of what business is honestly about and behaving honestly, even when not being watched," as Margit Osterloh and Bruno Frey argue, the virtuous path is claimed to be well worn but seems, alas, rarely tread.[40]

Mixed Goals, Mixed Messages

Advocates of corporate criminal liability and punishment fall into at least three camps: (1) deterrence-based liability regimes offering the optimal allocation of risk of financial loss and liability;[41] (2) desert-based regimes requiring evidence of moral fault in the offending person, whether human or corporate;[42] and (3) a mixed-goals approach such as that found in the sentencing guidelines. Connecting liability regimes with one or more penal objectives is conceptually easy. In spite of ease and convenience, though, most courts and commentators sidestep or ignore the challenges of wrestling with individual or mixed philosophical objectives, focusing instead on the functional purposes of the Sentencing Reform Act of 1984, for example, reducing unwarranted sentencing disparity; achieving greater honesty in sentencing; developing a purpose- and knowledge-driven system; and producing greater severity in federal sanctions.

Prosecutors and regulators, in particular, embrace mixed-goals approaches in ways that add many degrees of freedom to office, department, or division strategies. We read about plea agreements and wonder what connects corporate liability and blame with these creative diversions from the criminal justice system. With mixed goals, liability rules are tied to penal objectives and functions that are so varied, so mutable, as to be incidental and generally unimportant. This makes the connection between the sources of liability and the value of punishment so muddled that the only thing maximized is discretion. The commitment to mixed goals also makes the possibility of law reform that much more unlikely.[43]

CRONY CAPITALISM, POLITICAL OPACITY, AND GENUINE REFORMS

The likelihood of lasting governance reforms is tempered, at least in part, by a history of overlapping and conflicting interests by all of the familiar bedfellows—from auditors, senior management, and boards of directors to underwriters, lenders, lawyers, analysts, and credit rating or bond rating services. These interests are expressed in a complex and often opaque political environment that preserves the status quo, if not special interests.

Before the collapse of Enron, WorldCom, and Adelphia, for example, proposals from the Financial Accounting Standards Board (FASB), a private-sector standard-setting and oversight organization, to ensure that stock options appear on a company's balance sheets pitted the might of the accounting industry lobby and interested legislators against the skeletal leadership of the SEC. Accountancies won. Heavy lobbying of key politicians resulted in other critical victories for corporate gatekeepers, including overturning President Clinton's veto of the Private Securities and Litigation Reform Act of 1995.[44] Accountancies, which faced ever-increasing tort liability, won again. Between 1999 and 2000, SEC Chairman Arthur Levitt pushed hard for principles of auditor independence that prohibited accounting firms from offering their audit clients consulting services. Levitt's position on auditor independence, soon thereafter a pillar of Sarbanes-Oxley, was also compromised by extensive pressure from accounting industry lobbyists.

The most thoughtful critics of corporate governance reform see its evolution in political terms, where crafting well-conceived law is often incidental to a special interest. Roberto Romano writes that the provisions relating to corporate governance found in Sarbanes-Oxley were misconceived and poorly considered by Congress. "[Sarbanes-Oxley] was emergency legislation," according to Romano, "enacted under conditions of limited legislative debate, during a media frenzy involving several high-profile corporate fraud and insolvency cases, in conjunction with an economic downturn and what appeared to be a free-falling stock market, and the prospect of an election campaign in which the corporate scandals would be a looming issue. The healthy ventilation of issues that occurs in the usual give-and-take negotiations over competing policy positions and which works to improve the quality of decisionmaking did not occur in the case of [Sarbanes-Oxley] because the collapse of Enron and its auditor, Arthur Andersen, politically weakened key groups affected by the legislation, the business community and the accounting profession."[45]

Remarkably, Romano and others recognize how Congress, in an effort to respond, missed the opportunity to consider a well-developed body of empirical corporate finance literature. Efficacy, scholars argue, should take precedence over appearance, symbolism, and perceptions of legitimacy.[46]

If critics of recent government mandates agree, it is that debating the success or failure of post-Enron reforms is no more important than considering the human dynamics of any organizational response to good governance. In detailing the myths of governance metrics, Jeffrey Sonnenfeld argues that boards of directors must be seen and evaluated as social systems, systems characterized by a distinct leadership style, ethical values, decision-making processes, strategies, and conflict management.[47] Approaching governance reform with a distinct political agenda and a corresponding legislative laundry list of reforms is unlikely to produce lasting change. "Such a 'check the box' approach to good corporate governance," observes former SEC chairman William Donaldson, "will not inspire a true sense of ethical obligation. It could merely lead to an array of inhibiting, 'politically correct' dictates."[48]

UNMAKING THE SKEPTIC'S AND PESSIMIST'S ACCOUNT

A critical piece of the legacy of Ayres and Braithwaite's responsive regulation is the deceptively simple notion that the success of less-intrusive, less-centralized forms of governmental intervention, such as cooperative regulation, hinges on a demonstrated willingness of the state to regulate more intrusively. The benign big gun, or the capacity of regulatory agencies to enforce formal social controls such as law, pushes enforcement down the base of the pyramid of sanctions to levels where informal social controls are effective. Deterrence or incapacitating strategies sit at the apex of the pyramid as a reminder that regulators are prepared to do more if their trust is abused.

Braithwaite's idea that institutionalizing distrust enculturates trust is a logical extension of the notion that informal regulation works when regulators have the capacity and willingness to escalate formal social control. And the consequences are dramatic. "Both timidity about maximizing interpersonal trust and failure of robust institutionalization of distrust," according to Braithwaite, "are paths to poverty, corruption, and maladministration."[49] As with the previously discussed paradox of compliance, distrust increases trust-based regulation.

At the heart of the skeptic's and pessimist's account is the view, reflected here and in earlier chapters, that the history of the corporate criminal law is defined by only the pretense and rhetoric of a benign big gun. In disregard of substantive law, and in the context of some well-developed games, tough enforcement and regulatory strategy are inconsistent, arbitrary, sometimes symbolic, and inredible. Such pretense and rhetoric are compounded by regulatory institutions that are, at times, insufficiently distrustful; by informal social controls, such as ethics codes and ethics programs, that are uncritically received and evaluated; and by the moral imagery of integrity and social responsibility that make genuine and inauthentic citizenship often indistinguishable. This rhetoric and insufficient distrust combine to pose a challenge for those claiming genuine, lasting compliance and governance reforms. After all, even without them, it is difficult to see how a history marked by ambivalence with the social control of business can be countered with simple governance and compliance prescriptions.[50]

If the pessimist's and skeptic's account is vulnerable, if their case may be unraveled even slightly, it is not with the dismissal of corporate criminal liability by economists seeking efficiency in liability rules and sanctions; it is not with the promotion of punitive "middle-ground" forms of civil justice; and it is not with a libertarian deference to business interests, the market economy, and a respect for state versus federal rights. Reforms that reconceive the substantive corporate criminal law, that refashion the big gun, will begin to undercut the long-standing ambivalence with formal social controls (i.e., principles and rules will have credibility and legitimacy, provide clear notice to those regulated), recognize the rights and concurrent responsibilities of personhood (i.e., principles and rule will recognize features of the corporate form that fairly and genuinely approximate blame), minimize the gaming around compliance and governance (i.e., principles and rules that maximize cooperation and minimize defection), move prosecutors to pursue the substantive offense committed and not postoffense behavior (i.e., principles and rules that prosecutors see as fairly attributing blame), and create liability rules that are in substance and principle well-defined, understood by those regulated, and consistent with sentencing law.

When Ayres and Braithwaite first wrote about the notion of responsive

regulation, there was a need "to transcend the intellectual stalemate between those who favor strong state regulation of business and those who advocate deregulation."[51] This need has been largely addressed in the interven-
ing decade with a definitive shift in regulatory theory and practice toward
a creative mix of enforced persuasion.[52] With this shift, the focus moved
from illustrating the weakness of strict command and control regulation
to understanding the notion of cooperation, capture, empowerment, and
corruption; the benefits of tripartism; the inherent weaknesses of guardian-
ship; the limits of private regulation; and the challenges of standard setting
as well as monitoring. The casualty of this shift was and continues to be a
credible body of law that provides regulatory capacity and power, when and
where corporations are deserving of this most formal social control.

CONCLUSION

"Too many corporate managers, auditors and analysts are participating in a
game of nods and winks," warned former SEC chairman Arthur Levitt on
September 28, 1998, in his famed speech "The Numbers Game." "I fear that
we are witnessing an erosion in the quality of earnings, and therefore, the
quality of financial reporting. Managing may be giving way to manipulation; Integrity may be losing out to illusion. . . . Today, American markets
enjoy the confidence of the world. How many half-truths, and how much
accounting sleight-of-hand, will it take to tarnish that faith?"[53]

Levitt's speech is remarkable for so many reasons. Long before Enron was
Enron, Andersen was Andersen, and WorldCom was WorldCom, Levitt spoke
of the selective disclosure of material nonpublic news; the custom of earnings management; compromised financial reporting; accounting gimmicks;
and the need to improve the transparency and comparability of financial
reporting. The accounting practices that today look so surprising, disturbing, and dastardly were well known and well tolerated in spite of recent
voices to the contrary. Such accounting practices included "big-bath" restructuring charges, creative acquisition accounting, "cookie-jar reserves,"
"immaterial" misapplications of accounting principles, and the premature
recognition of revenue.

"Many in corporate America are just as frustrated and concerned about
this trend as we, at the SEC, are," Levitt said. "They know how difficult it
is to hold the line on good practices when their competitors operate in the
gray area between legitimacy and outright fraud."[54] Levitt knew what most
of Wall Street knew—what was wrong and how to right the wrong. What was
missing then and now is the motivation to do so; the genuine intention to
do so; the consensus to accomplish necessary reforms; a strong constituency
supporting change; and the requisite priority accorded to the most significant and powerful social control of corporations: the criminal law.

After advocating a nine-point plan for structural changes in accounting practices and assumptions, Levitt concluded his speech with a plea for a sea change in corporate culture that failed to take place. "Finally, I'm challenging corporate management and Wall Street to re-examine our current environment," argued Levitt. "I believe we need to embrace nothing less than a cultural change. For corporate managers, remember, the integrity of the numbers in the financial reporting system is directly related to the long-term interests of a corporation. While the temptations are great, and the pressures strong, illusions in numbers are only that—ephemeral, and ultimately self-destructive. . . . To Wall Street, I say, look beyond the latest quarter. Punish those who rely on deception, rather than the practice of openness and transparency."[55]

Former chairman of the SEC Roderick Hills, another champion of regulatory reform, is fond of quoting Will Rodgers when asked about the lasting impact of Sarbanes-Oxley and other reforms on the accounting profession. "Nothing is quite as good or quite as bad as it is said to be," Hills remarks with confidence.[56] If only there were more critics of corporate citizenship and governance reform.

Notes

CHAPTER ONE

1. George W. Bush, President Bush Signs Corporate Corruption Bill, Office of the Press Secretary, The White House, July 30, 2002, available at: http://www.whitehouse.gov/news/releases/2002/07/20020730.html.

2. See generally Lawrence A. Cunningham, The Sarbanes-Oxley Yawn: Heavy Rhetoric, Light Reform (and It Might Just Work), 35 Conn. L. Rev. 915 (2003); Cary Coglianese, Thomas J. Healey, Elizabeth K. Keating, and Michael L. Michael, The Role of Government in Corporate Governance, Regulatory Policy Program Report RPP-08 (2004), Cambridge, MA: Center for Business and Government, John F. Kennedy School of Government, Harvard University.

3. For an incisive interpretation of this period, see Donald C. Langevoort, Resetting the Corporate Thermostat: Lessons from the Recent Financial Scandals about Self-Deception, Deceiving Others and the Design of Internal Controls, 93 Geo. L.J. 285 (2004).

4. Cf. Donald C. Langevoort, Managing the "Expectations Gap" in Investor Protection: The SEC and the Post-Enron Reform Agenda, 48 Vill. L. Rev. 1139 (2003).

5. For a critical take on governance reforms, see Roberto Romano, The Sarbanes-Oxley Act and the Making of Quack Corporate Governance, Yale Law School, Center for Law, Economics and Public Policy, Research Paper No. 297 (discussing reforms as symbolic politics and window dressing). For an excellent review of the role of politics and political economy, see Vikramaditya S. Khanna, Politics and Corporate Crime Legislation, Regulation (Spring 2004) (working paper) (on file with University of Michigan School of Law), at 30; Vikramaditya S. Khanna, Corporate Crime Legislation: A Political Economy Analysis, 82 Wash. U. L.Q. 95 (2004).

6. See Kenneth Mann, White Collar Crime and the Poverty of the Criminal Law, 17 Law & Soc. Inquiry 561 (1992).

7. See Mark J. Roe, The Inevitable Instability of American Corporate Governance, Discussion Paper No. 493, The Harvard John M. Olin Discussion Paper Series, September 2004, p. 1.

8. See John Braithwaite, Convergence in Models of Regulatory Strategy, 2 Current Issues Crim. Just. 59 (1990); see also John Braithwaite, To Punish or Persuade: Enforcement of Coal Mine Safety (Albany: State University of New York Press, 1985) (extending theories of self-regulation to the coal industry); John Braithwaite, Enforced Self-Regulation: A New

Strategy for Corporate Crime Control, 80 Mich. L. Rev. 1466 (1982) (proposing a new concept of regulatory cooperation).

9. Ian Ayres and John Braithwaite, Responsive Regulation: Transcending the Deregulation Debate (New York: Oxford University Press, 1992) (articulating a new paradigm for regulatory cooperation). Cf. Jeffrey S. Parker, Doctrine for Destruction: The Case of Corporate Criminal Liability, 17 Managerial & Decision Econ. 381 (1996).

10. John Braithwaite, Institutionalizing Distrust, Enculturating Trust, in Trust and Governance, ed. Valerie Braithwaite and Margaret Levi (New York: Russell Sage Foundation, 1998), p. 356; Ayres and Braithwaite, *supra* note 9. For a review of *Responsive Regulation*, see John Mendeloff, Overcoming Barriers to Better Regulation, 18 Law & Soc. Inquiry 711 (1993).

11. Cf. John Braithwaite, The Limits of Economism in Controlling Harmful Corporate Conduct, 16 Law & Soc'y Rev. 481 (1982); A. Mitchell Polinsky and Steven Shavell, The Economic Theory of Public Enforcement of Law, 38 J. Econ. Literature 45, 45–47 (2000); John C. Coffee Jr., Does "Unlawful" Mean "Criminal"? Reflections on the Disappearing Tort/Crime Distinction in American Law, 71 B.U.L. Rev. 193, 216 (1991).

12. Cf. Jonathan M. Karpoff and John R. Lott Jr., The Reputational Penalty Firms Bear from Committing Criminal Fraud, 36 J.L. & Econ. 757 (1993).

13. Cicero J. Lindley, Criminal Acts of Corporations and Their Punishment, 7 Am. Law. 564 (1899).

14. For a list of early accounts of the robber barons, see Chester McArthur Destler, Entrepreneurial Leadership among the "Robber Barons": A Trial Balance, 6 J. Econ. Hist. 28 (1946). See also Burton J. Hendrick, The Life of Andrew Carnegie (Garden City, NY: Doubleday, Doran, 1932); Allan Nevins, John D. Rockefeller: The Heroic Age of American Enterprise (New York: Charles Scribner's Sons, 1940); Wheaton J. Lane, Commodore Vanderbilt: An Epic of the Steam Age (New York: Alfred A. Knopf, 1942); Robert Irving Warshow, Jay Gould: The Story of a Fortune (New York: Greenberg, 1928).

15. See, e.g., Kathleen F. Brickey, Corporate Criminal Liability: A Treatise on the Criminal Liability of Corporations, Their Officers and Agents (Wilmette, IL: Callaghan, 1984).

16. See Steven Walt and William S. Laufer, Why Personhood Doesn't Matter: Corporate Criminal Liability and Sanctions, 18 Am. J. Crim. L. 263 (1991); Steven D. Walt and William S. Laufer, Corporate Criminal Liability and the Comparative Mix of Sanctions, in White Collar Crime Reconsidered, ed. Kip Schlegel and David Weisburd (Boston: Northeastern University Press, 1992). See also Donald R. Cressey, The Poverty of Theory in Corporate Crime Research, in Advances in Criminological Theory, vol.1 (New Brunswick, NJ: Transaction Publishers, 1988), p. 31; John Braithwaite and Brent Fisse, On the Plausibility of Corporate Crime Control, in Advances in Criminological Theory, vol. 2 (New Brunswick, NJ: Transaction Publishers, 1990), p. 15; and Gilbert Geis, A Review, Rebuttal, and Reconciliation of Cressey and Braithwaite and Fisse on Criminological Theory and Corporate Crime, in Advances in Criminological Theory, vol. 5 (New Brunswick, NJ: Transaction Publishers, 1994), p. 321.

17. For a discussion of the history of corporate criminal liability, see Celia Wells, Corporations and Criminal Responsibility (Oxford: Clarendon Press, 1993); G. R. Sullivan, Expressing Corporate Guilt, 15 Oxford J. Legal Stud. 281 (1995).

18. The notion of an innocent stakeholder is made much more complex with ownership separation. See Roe, *supra* note 7, at 15.

19. See Craig Haney, Criminal Justice and the Nineteenth-Century Paradigm: The Tri-

umph of Psychological Individualism in the "Formative Era," 6 Law & Hum. Behav. 191 (1982); John M. Clark, Social Control of Business, 2d ed. (New York: McGraw-Hill, 1939).

20. See, e.g., Sally S. Simpson, Cycles of Illegality: Antitrust Violations in Corporate America, 65 Soc. Forces 943 (1987).

21. See David R. Simon and Stanley Swart, The Justice Department Focuses on Corporate Crime, 30 Crime & Delinq. 107 (1984).

22. Cf. Peter C. Yeager, Structural Bias in Regulatory Law Enforcement: The Case of the U.S. Environmental Protection Agency, 34 Soc. Probs. 330 (1987) (finding small firms burdened by regulation in a disproportionate manner).

23. See, e.g., PricewaterhouseCoopers, Economic Crime Survey 2003 (52 percent of those organizations surveyed with more than 1,000 employees reported the commission of fraud).

24. Whether the names are remembered or not, research consistently reveals the long-term effects of a criminal investigation, indictment, and conviction. See, e.g., Jonathan M. Karpoff and John R. Lott Jr., The Reputational Penalty Firms Bear from Committing Criminal Fraud, 36 J.L. & Econ. 757 (1993); Cindy R. Alexander, On the Nature of the Reputational Penalty for Corporate Crime: Evidence, 42 J.L. & Econ. 489 (1999); Melissa S. Baucus and David A. Baucus, Paying the Piper: An Empirical Examination of Longer-Term Financial Consequences of Illegal Corporate Behavior, 40 Acad. Mgmt. J. 129 (1997); Wallace N. Davidson III and Dan L. Worrell, The Impact of Announcements of Corporate Illegalities on Shareholder Returns, 31 Acad. Mgmt. J. 195 (1988). For an interesting extension of this work, see Peter Schwartz and Blair Gibb, When Good Companies Do Bad Things: Responsibility and Risk in an Age of Globalization (New York: John Wiley & Sons, 1999).

25. Recently, deferred-prosecution agreements have been reached with the following corporations: Monsanto Co., Time Warner Inc., American International Group Inc., and Computer Associates International Inc. Approximately twenty corporations have received deferred-prosecution agreements over the past two decades. For a discussion of the theory behind deferred prosecutions, see Benjamin Greenbaum, Comment: What Happens to a Prosecution Deferred? Judicial Oversight of Corporate Deferred Prosecution Agreements, 105 Colum. L. Rev. (forthcoming October 2005). See also Vanessa Blum, DOJ Soups Up Wheels of Justice with "Deferred Prosecution," *Legal Intelligencer,* March 23, 2005, p. 1. Remarkably, recent overseas scandals are nearly forgotten; see, e.g., Nikos Passas, The Genesis of the BCCI Scandal, 23 J.L. & Soc'y 57 (1996).

26. See, e.g., Penelope Patsuris, The Corporate Scandal Sheet, available at: http://www .forbes.com/home/2002/07/25/accountingtracker.html.

27. Louis Galambos, The Agrarian Image of the Large Corporation, 1879–1920: A Study in Social Accommodation, 28 J. Econ. Hist. 341 (1968).

28. See, e.g., Oscar Handlin and Mary F. Handlin, Origins of the American Business Corp., 5 J. Econ. Hist. 1 (1945); William C. Kessler, Incorporation in New England: A Statistical Study, 1800–1875, 8 J. Econ. Hist. 43 (1948); W. C. Kessler, A Statistical Study of the New York General Incorporation Act of 1811, 48 J. Pol. Econ. 877 (1940).

29. See James R. Elkins, Corporations and the Criminal Law: An Uneasy Alliance, 65 Ky. L.J. 73, 89–91 (1976) (describing the rise of corporate criminal liability beginning in colonial times).

30. See Jeremy Atack, Firm Size and Industrial Structure in the United States during the Nineteenth Century, 46 J. Econ. Hist. 463 (1986). This soon changed; see Alfred D. Chandler Jr. and Louis Galambos, The Development of Large-Scale Economic Organizations in Modern

America, 30 J. Econ. Hist. 201 (1970); Harold C. Passer, Development of Large-Scale Organization: Electrical Manufacturing Around 1900, 12 J. Econ. Hist. 378 (1952). See generally Alfred D. Chandler Jr., The Visible Hand: The Managerial Revolution in American Business (Cambridge, MA: Harvard University Press, 1977).

31. See, e.g., Frederick W. Lehmann, National Control of Corporations, 11 The Brief 3, 9 (1911).

32. Consider Baron Manwood's syllogism, "None can create souls but God; but a corporation is created by the king; therefore a corporation can have no soul." Lord Thurlow is credited with asking the ingenuous question: "Did you ever expect a corporation to have a conscience when it has no soul to be damned, and no body to be kicked?" Wilberforce, Life of Thurlow, iii App. Case of Sutton's Hospital (1612), 10 Co. Rep. at 32b, 77 E.R. at 973.

33. Frederick Pollock, Has the Common Law Received the Fiction Theory of Corporations?, 27 Law Q. Rev. 219 (1911) (quoting Lord Selborne).

34. The notion that criminal acts are ultra vires has been revived. See, e.g., Kent Greenfield, Ultra Vires Lives! A Stakeholder Analysis of Corporate Illegality (with Notes on How Corporate Law Could Reinforce International Law Norms), 87 Va. L. Rev. 1279 (2001).

35. See Adelbert Hamilton, Indictment of Corporations, 6 Crim. L. Mag. & Rep. 317 (1885). The heritage of corporate criminal liability in England is instructive. In the 1600s, corporations were first found liable for nonfeasances. Courts convicted corporations for misfeasance in the early 1800s. It was not until the mid-nineteenth century that they became indictable for criminal acts. Offenses requiring mens rea first appear at the turn of the twentieth century. The history of English law is described in detail by Brickey, supra note 15, vol. 1. See also V. S. Khanna, Corporate Criminal Liability: What Purpose Does It Serve?, 109 Harv. L. Rev. 1477 (1996). For a series of comparative reports on corporate criminal liability, see L. H. Leigh, The Criminal Liability of Corporations and Other Groups: A Comparative View, 80 Mich. L. Rev. 1508 (1982); Guy Stessens, Corporate Criminal Liability: A Comparative Perspective, 43 Int'l & Comp. L.Q. 493 (1994).

36. 17 U.S. 520. See, e.g., State v. Great Works Milling & Manufacturing Co., 20 Me. 41, 44 (1841) ("It is a doctrine then, in conformity with the demands of justice, and a proper distinction between the innocent and the guilty, that when a crime or misdemeanor is committed under color of corporate authority, the individuals acting in the businesses, and not the corporation should be indicted.").

37. McKim v. Odom, 3 Bland (Md.) 407 (1841).

38. See, e.g., State v. Morris & Essex R.R., 23 N.J.L. 360 (1852).

39. N. C. Collier, Impolicy of Modern Decision and Statute Making Corporations Indictable and the Confusion in Morals Thus Created, 71 Cent. L.J. 421 (1910).

40. 118 U.S. 394 (1886). Santa Clara expanded the conception of personhood and in doing so ushered in a host of decisions vesting corporations with constitutional rights.

41. See, e.g., United States v. Baltimore & Ohio Railroad Co., 24 F.Cas. 972 (C.C.W.Va. 1868); United States v. John Kelso Co., 86 F. 304 (N.D. Cal. 1898); United States v. Van Schaick, 134 F. 592 (S.D.N.Y. 1904); United States v. MacAndrews & Forbes Co., 149 F. 823 (S.D.N.Y. 1906).

42. Indignation in Brooklyn: Two Shocking Deaths Caused by Trolley Cars in Two Days, New York Times, March 28, 1885, p. 9.

43. Id.

44. Manslaughter Charged: An Indictment against Brooklyn Heights Railroad Company, New York Times, May 4, 1885, p. 8.

45. Explosion Causes Death and Wreck: Six Men Killed by Dynamite in Herkimer Railroad House, *New York Times*, August 20, 1901, p. 1.

46. Railroad Indictments Stand: Companies Will Be Tried for Failure to Protect Grade Crossings, *New York Times*, August, 11, 1889, p. 5.

47. Brooklyn Railway Indicted: Charged That the Brooklyn Heights Company Has Violated the Labor Laws, *New York Times*, October 30, 1898, p. 12.

48. Express Company Indicted, *New York Times*, October 23, 1902, p. 1.

49. Central Indicted for Manslaughter: Grand Jury Holds Company and Two Officials for the Woodlawn Wreck, *New York Times*, March 28, 1907, p. 20; Overspeeding Cause of Central Wreck, *New York Times*, December 11, 1907, p. 8; Felt Motor Lurch at Woodlawn Curve, *New York Times*, December 12, 1907, p. 16.

50. Corporate Responsibility, December 11, 1852, p. 4. Consider, for example, a *New York Daily Times* editorial in 1852 questioning the responsibility of the New Haven Railroad Company for a deadly collision. Who should bear responsibility for the negligence of the conductor—the conductor or the company that employed him? "If the company is considered careless, on account of the carelessness of its agents, why should not the Company also be considered responsible for their willful criminality?" The appropriate legal theory is that a company is simply the amalgam of its employees. This means that the "[c]ompany does what the agents do."

51. Werner Troesken, Exclusive Dealing and the Whiskey Trust, 1890–1895, 58 J. Econ. Hist. 755 (1998); Under the Antitrust Law, *New York Times*, March 23, 1892, p. 5; Whisky Trust: Motion Made to Quash the Boston Indictments, *New York Times*, March 23, 1892.

52. See, e.g., Sugar Trust Indictments, *New York Times*, October 3, 1894, p. 4; The Sugar Trust and the Law, *New York Times*, May 4, 1892, p. 4; Tobacco Trust Rights, *New York Times*, November 18, 1896, p. 13; A Great Legal Battle: The Case Against the American Tobacco Company Being Argued, *New York Times*, December 10, 1896, p. 12; Tobacco Men to Be Tried, *New York Times*, January 23, 1897, p. 4.

53. See, e.g., Northern Sec. Co. v. United States, 193 U.S. 197 (1904); Armour Packing Co. v. United States, 209 U.S. 56 (1908).

54. See, e.g., Meat Trust Head under Indictment, *New York Times*, July 2, 1905, p. 1; Railroads and Trust Indicted for Rebating, *New York Times*, May 5, 1906, p. 1; Elkins Law Violated without Conspiracy, *New York Times*, July 7, 1906, p. 1; Sugar Trust and Roads Indicted for Rebating, *New York Times*, October 10, 1906, p. 1; Sugar Trust Guilty of Receiving Rebates, *New York Times*, November 21, 1906, p. 1; Standard Oil Wins; Taft to Drop Suits, *New York Times*, March 11, 1909, p. 1.

55. See, e.g., H. St. Geo. Tucker, Have the Corporations Been Law-Abiding? 16 Va. L. Reg. 880 (1911).

56. Roosevelt Bitter in Attack on Wilson, *New York Times*, September 22, 1912, p. 2.

57. For a discussion of this crisis, see Lessons of the Financial Crisis, 31 Annals 301–469 (1908).

58. Wealthy Brokers in Chicago Are Indicted: Board of Trade Members Accused of Bucket Shopping, *New York Times*, April 4, 1903, p. 1. Bucket shops were groups or associations of gamblers who wagered on the direction of futures prices. For a more current view of bucket shopping, see Kip Schlegel, Crime in the Pits: The Regulation of Futures Trading, 525 Annals 59 (1993).

59. Two Brokers Suspended, *New York Times*, November 24, 1898, p. 12.

60. Working of Schemes to Steal Insurance: Prosecutors Tells of Millions a Year Obtained on Fire Losses, *New York Times*, December 8, 1903, p. 16.

61. Indictment of Directors, *New York Times*, March 10, 1892, p. 4. In 1896, Henry Wynans Jessup read a paper before the New York State Bar Association entitled *Are Directors of Corporations Held to a Sufficient Accountability?* His answer, as obvious to him then as it is to us now, vents a familiar frustration: "The skill, audacity, experience and talent of the highest order of administrative ability have reduced to a certainty the methods of diverting the profits, capital and even the existence of the corporation itself to the enrichment of the corporate managers and their co-conspirators—corporations become insolvent, and stockholders lose their investment, while individuals become millionaires. Illegitimate gains are secured and enormous fortunes are amassed by the few at the expense of the defrauded, by generally helpless, stockholders." Henry Wynans Jessup, Are Directors of Corporations Held to a Sufficient Accountability?, 53 Alb. L.J. 86 (1896). Civil remedies, Jessup concludes, fail to protect innocent shareholders from the financial fraud and breaches of trust of corporate directors and managers. See also Frederick Dwight, Liability of Corporate Directors, 17 Yale L.J. 33 (1907); The Responsibilities of Directors, *New York Times*, September 6, 1903, p. 6.

62. Walter S. Logan, The Use and Abuse of Corporations, 9 Am. Law. 158 (1901).

63. William W. Cook, Legal Possibilities of Federal Railroad Incorporation, 26 Yale L.J. 207 (1917); Robert W. Harbeson, Railroads and Regulation, 1877–1916: Conspiracy or Public Interest?, 27 J. Econ. Hist. 230 (1967).

64. H. L. Wilgus, Need for a National Incorporation Law, 2 Mich. L. Rev. 358, 367 (1904).

65. Thomas C. Cochran, Railroad Leaders, 1845–1890: The Business Mind in Action (Cambridge, MA: Harvard University Press, 1953).

66. Don E. Mowry, The Abuse of the Corporate Charter, 64 Cent. L.J. 49, 52 (1907).

67. Richard S. Tedlow, Keeping the Corporate Image: Public Relations and Business, 1900–1950 (Greenwich, CT: JAI Press, 1979), p. 5.

68. See J. Newton Baker, Regulation of Industrial Corporations, 22 Yale L.J. 306 (1913). The desirability of a new federal incorporation law was discussed extensively; see, e.g., Frederick H. Cooke, State and Federal Control of Corporations, 23 Harv. L. Rev. 456 (1910) (discussing the relative benefits of state versus federal control); Max Thelen, Federal Incorporation of Railroads, 5 Cal. L. Rev. 273 (1917) (arguing against existing plans and proposals for a federal incorporation law); George W. Wickersham, Government Control of Corporations, 18 Colum. L. Rev. 187 (1918) (noting the importance of both state and federal regulatory efforts). See also Dissolution of Corporation—Illegal Purposes—Restraining Competition—People v. Milk Exchange, 6 Crim. L. Mag. & Rep. 408 (1885). The effects of vertical integration and the separation of ownership and control on the emergence of the modern multidivisional corporation were strongly felt. See George David Smith and Davis Dyer, The Rise and Transformation of the American Corporation, in The American Corporation Today, ed. Carl Kaysen (New York: Oxford University Press, 1996), pp. 40–41; Harold C. Livesay, Andrew Carnegie and the Rise of Big Business (Boston: Little, Brown, 1975). For an extensive treatment of the rise of the diversified firm, see Neil Fligstein, The Transformation of Corporate Control (Cambridge, MA: Harvard University Press, 1990), pp. 258–94. Departments, managerial oversight, and employee functions and roles became increasingly specialized. See, e.g., George David Smith, The Anatomy of a Business Strategy: Bell, Western Electric, and the Origins of the American Telephone Industry (Baltimore: Johns Hopkins University Press, 1985). With decentralization, specialization, and an increasing organizational complexity came concerns over loss

of corporate control across the managerial hierarchy or authority leakage. See Marshall B. Clinard et al., Illegal Corporate Behavior (Washington, DC: U.S. Dept. of Justice, 1979), p. 7 (Decentralization "is almost by definition, accompanied by the establishment of elaborate hierarchies, based on authority position and functional duties. This allows the abdication of personal responsibility for almost every type of decision. Under these conditions almost any type of criminality, from production of faulty or dangerous products to bribery, bid-rigging and even theft is possible."); Gilbert Geis, The Heavy Electrical Equipment Antitrust Cases of 1961, in White-Collar Crime: Offenses in Business, Politics, and the Professions, rev. ed., by Gilbert Geis and Robert F. Meier (New York: Free Press, 1977), p. 117; Diane Vaughan, Toward Understanding Unlawful Organizational Behavior, 80 Mich. L. Rev. 1377 (1982) (discussing authority leakage, as well as the effects of tall hierarchies, organizational specialization, and complexity on control functions and resulting deviance).

69. Walter S. Logan, The Use and Abuse of Corporations, 9 Am. Law. 158 (1901).

70. Mowry, *supra* note 56, at 49.

71. Cf. George F. Canfield, Is a Large Corporation an Illegal Combination or Monopoly under the Sherman Anti-Trust Act?, 9 Colum. L. Rev. 95 (1909). For an early account of the importance of corporate criminal liability with particular attention to trusts as a violation of public policy and public welfare, see Cicero J. Lindley, Criminal Acts of Corporations and Their Punishment, 7 Am. Law. 564, 566 (1899).

72. See Thomas S. Ulen, Cartels and Regulation: Late Nineteenth-Century Railroad Collusion and the Creation of the Interstate Commerce Commission, 40 J. Econ. Hist. 179 (1980). For a review of the origins of corporate criminal law, see Brent Fisse, The Duality of Corporate and Individual Criminal Liability, in Corporations as Criminals, ed. Ellen Hochstedler (Beverly Hills, CA: Sage Publications, 1984), p. 69 (describing the main reasons why both entity and individual liability exists); Kip Schlegel, Just Deserts for Corporate Criminals (Boston: Northeastern University Press, 1990) (discussing Fisse's justifications), pp. 85–86. See also John C. Coffee Jr., "No Soul to Damn: No Body to Kick": An Unscandalized Inquiry into the Problem of Corporate Punishment, 79 Mich. L. Rev. 386, 448 (1981); Richard S. Gruner, Corporate Crime and Sentencing, 2d ed. (Chesterland, OH: Business Laws, 1997).

73. See, e.g., Herbert Hovenkamp, The Classical Corporation in American Legal Thought, 76 Geo. L.J. 1593 (1988) (discussing critical factors and forces responsible for the evolution of the modern corporation at the turn of the twentieth century); Smith and Dyer, *supra* note 68. For a pre-Hudson discussion of the emerging principles of corporate criminal liability, see Charles G. Little, Punishment of a Corporation—The Standard Oil Case, 3 Ill. L. Rev. 446 (1909). Early scholarship questioned the need for a corporate criminal law; see George F. Canfield, Corporate Responsibility for Crime, 14 Colum. L. Rev. 469 (1914) ("Our final conclusion, therefore, is that, notwithstanding this or similar statutory provisions, a corporation, according to sound theory and general principles of the law of corporations, is not indictable for any crimes except those for which if committed on behalf of or under the general direction of an individual or partnership, such individual or a member of such partnership, although innocent, would be indictable."); Ervin Hacker, The Penal Ability and Responsibility of the Corporate Bodies, 14 J. Am. Inst. Crim. L. & Criminology 91 (1923) (debating the virtues of corporate criminal liability); Frederic P. Lee, Corporate Criminal Liability, 28 Colum. L. Rev. 1 (1928) (following Lee with a critical examination of liability rules); Joseph F. Francis, Criminal Responsibility of the Corporation, 18 Ill. L. Rev. 305 (1924) (concluding that "[u]ntil and unless it is demonstrated that the social good demands that

corporations be held responsible for crimes, there is no sound reason for holding them."); Henry W. Edgerton, Corporate Criminal Responsibility, 36 Yale L.J. 827 (1927) (considering the benefits and drawbacks of corporate criminal liability). The history of corporate criminal liability has been discussed at length elsewhere; see Kathleen F. Brickey, Corporate Criminal Accountability: A Brief History and an Observation, 60 Wash. U.L.Q. 393 (1982); Khanna, *supra* note 35.

74. 212 U.S. 481 (1909). For a wonderful historical treatment of Standard Oil, see Paul H. Giddens, Standard Oil Company (of Indiana): Old Pioneer of the Middle West (New York: Appleton-Century-Crofts, 1955). For an important extension of state law upholding a homicide indictment against a railroad, see State v. Lehigh Valley R.R., 103 A. 685 (N.J. 1917).

75. 212 U.S. at 494.

76. Brief for the United States, The New York Central and Hudson River Railroad Company v. The United States, No. 57, pp. 14–15 ("If punishment for such payments when prohibited by law can be administered only on proving authorization from the president or directors no railway corporation can ever be legally punished for such payments. But, on the other hand, if a railroad corporation may be made criminally responsible for the acts of its officers or agents, to whom have been delegated power to control its corporate action within the sphere represented by the transaction then no case can more completely show ground for liability than the case at bar.") Brief on file with author.

77. This argument was made much earlier in state cases; see, e.g., Commonwealth v. Pulaski County Agric. & Mech. Ass'n, 17 S.W. 442 (1891) ("With the growth of corporations came the necessity for this rule [corporate criminal liability], and its adaptability to changed circumstances is an excellence of the common law. . . . The object should be to reach and punish the real power in the matter, and thus prevent a repetition of the offense.")

78. The Court reasoned that the doctrine of respondeat superior in tort law supplied the necessary ingredients for a vicarious criminal liability. See *Hudson*, 212 U.S. at 494 ("Applying the principle governing civil liability, we go only a step farther in holding that the act of the agent, while exercising the authority delegated to him to make rates for transportation, may be controlled, in the interest of public policy, by imputing his act to his employer and imposing penalties upon the corporation for which he is acting in the premises.").

79. 212 U.S. at 496. See also Brent Fisse and John Braithwaite, The Allocation of Responsibility for Corporate Crime: Individualism, Collectivism and Accountability, 11 Sydney L. Rev. 468 (1988).

80. 212 U.S. at 496.

81. See Sanford H. Kadish, Some Observations on the Use of Criminal Sanctions in Enforcing Economic Regulations, 3 U. Chi. L. Rev. 432, 433 (1963) ("The case for corporate criminality rests presumably upon the inadequacy of the threat of personal conviction upon the individual actors."). For a recent case that refers to the importance of incentives in vicarious liability, see United States v. Sun-Diamond Growers of California, 138 F.3d 961, 971 (D.C. Cir. 1998).

82. See Reiner H. Kraakman, Corporate Liability Strategies and the Costs of Legal Controls, 93 Yale L.J. 857, 858 (1984).

83. The discussion of agency issues in relation to criminal liability assumes that both principal and agent are utility maximizers. All other contract assumptions apply as well, such as the importance of the equity contract; limited liability; and diversified investment portfolios as risk-bearing devices for shareholders. See Michael C. Jensen and William H.

Meckling, Theory of the Firm: Managerial Behavior, Agency Costs, and Ownership Structure, 3 J. Fin. Econ. 305 (1976) (discussing the importance of market and contract controls that, at least in theory, are designed to align the divergent interests of owners and managers).

84. See Jennifer H. Arlen and William J. Carney, Vicarious Liability for Fraud on Securities Markets: Theory and Evidence, 1992 U. Ill. L. Rev. 691, 700; Jonathan R. Macey, Agency Theory and the Criminal Liability of Organizations, 71 B.U. L. Rev. 315, 319 (1991).

85. See H. Lowell Brown, Vicarious Criminal Liability of Corporations for the Acts of Their Employees and Agents, 41 Loy. L. Rev. 279 (1995). For a discussion of models of regulation that extend well beyond vicarious liability, see Braithwaite, Enforced Self-Regulation, *supra* note 8; Ayres and Braithwaite, *supra* note 9.

86. See Edgerton, *supra* note 73, at 835. To illustrate the proper use of a vicarious criminal liability, Lee pointed to the case of Overland Cotton Mill Company v. People, 32 Colo. 263, 75 P. 924 (1904).

87. See, e.g., Standard Oil Co. v. United States, 307 F.2d 120 (5th Cir. 1962) (conviction of corporation reversed where evidence that employees' acts did not benefit their employers); cf. Old Monastery Co. v. United States, 147 F.2d 905, 908 (4th Cir. 1945) ("We do not accept benefit as a touchstone of corporate criminal liability; benefit, at best, is an evidential, not operative, fact.").

88. See Jennifer Arlen, The Potentially Perverse Effects of Corporate Criminal Liability, 23 J. Legal Stud. 833 (1994), who comments that "[o]n the one hand, increased enforcement expenditures reduce the number of agents who commit crimes by increasing the probability of detection and thus each agent's expected cost of crime. On the other hand, these expenditures also increase the probability that the government will detect those crimes that are committed, thereby increasing the corporation's expected criminal liability for those crimes. . . . [A] corporation subject to vicarious liability may spend less on enforcement than it would absent vicarious liability.").

89. Arlen, *supra* note 88 at 836; David A. Dana, The Perverse Incentives of Environmental Audit Immunity, 81 Iowa L. Rev. 969, 970 (1996) ("[C]ommentators stress that corporations may forgo internal audits if they fear that they will be held liable for, and hence punished for, any violations that they might uncover.").

90. This appears to be a classic risk trade-off. See John D. Graham and Jonathan Baert Wiener, eds., Risk versus Risk: Tradeoffs in Protecting Health and the Environment (Cambridge, MA: Harvard University Press, 1995).

91. See, e.g., C. Y. Cyrus Chu and Yingyi Qian, Vicarious Liability Under a Negligence Rule, 15 Int'l Rev. L. & Econ. 305, 306 (1995) ("[T]he principal has an incentive to hide the evidence, or to collude with the agent, to avoid their joint and several liability.").

92. See Developments in the Law—Corporate Crime: Regulating Corporate Behavior through Criminal Sanctions, 92 Harv. L. Rev. 1227, 1257 (1979) ("A new system of corporate liability based on the reasonableness of the corporation's practices and procedures to avert illegal conduct would better reflect the blameworthiness of the corporation as an entity.").

93. Liability was restricted to high managerial agents for certain crimes under a regime proposed by the Model Penal Code; see Kathleen F. Brickey, Rethinking Corporate Liability under the Model Penal Code, 19 Rutgers L.J. 593 (1988).

94. See John Gund Brewing Co. v. United States, 204 F. 17 (8th Cir.), modified, 206 F. 386 (8th Cir. 1913). For a discussion of *Gund* and the advent of the due diligence defense, see Brown, *supra* note 85, at 309–12.

95. Brown, supra note 85, at 309–12.

96. See, e.g., United States v. General Motors Corp., 212 F.2d 376 (7th Cir. 1941); United States v. Austin-Bagley Corp., 31 F.2d 229 (2d Cir. 1929); American Med. Ass'n v. United States, 130 F.2d 233 (D.C. Cir. 1942). Courts inconsistently ruled on matters of acting on express instructions or corporate policy; see United States v. Armour & Co., 168 F.2d 342, 343–344 (3d Cir. 1948) ("The employer does not rid himself of that duty because the extent of the business may preclude his personal supervision, and compel reliance on subordinates. He must then stand or fall with those who he selects to act for him."); United States v. American Radiator & Standard Sanitary Corp., 433 F.2d 174 (3d Cir. 1970); United States v. Hilton Hotels Corp., 467 F.2d 1000 (9th Cir. 1973); United States v. Cadillac Overall Supply Co., 568 F.2d 1078 (5th Cir. 1978); Note, Corporate Criminal Liability for Acts in Violation of Company Policy, 50 Geo. L.J. 547 (1962). The drafters of the MPC discussed this issue extensively; see ALI, Model Penal Code, Tentative Draft No. 4, 149 (1955).

97. Nobile v. United States, 284 F.253 (3d Cir. 1922); Holland Furnace Co. v. United States, 158 F.2d 2, 8 (6th Cir. 1946); United States v. Hilton Hotels Corp., 467 F.2d 1000, 1007 (9th Cir. 1972), cert. denied, 409 U.S. 1125 (1972) (policy statements and specific instructions along with appropriate enforcement would give an organization immunity from the criminal law). Questions regarding the strict nature of vicarious liability persist, as do policy concerns more generally with the strict application of the criminal law; see John Shepard Wiley Jr., Not Guilty by Reason of Blamelessness: Culpability in Federal Criminal Interpretation, 85 Va. L. Rev. 1021 (1999).

98. Dan M. Kahan, Gentle Nudges v. Hard Shoves: Solving the Sticky Norms Problem, 67 U. Chi. L. Rev. 607 (2000).

99. 163 F.2d 168, 177 (7th Cir. 1947). It is notable that a due diligence defense was raised in the electrical antitrust cases (United States v. Westinghouse Electrical Corp., 1960 Trade Cas. ¶ 69,699, at 76,759 (E.D. Pa. 1960).

100. Convicted of Rebating: Verdict against Reading, Lehigh Valley, and Bethlehem Steel, New York Times, June 16, 1910, p. 1. See, e.g., Seymour D. Thompson and Joseph W. Thompson, eds., Commentaries on the Law of Corporations, 3d ed. (Indianapolis: Bobbs-Merrill, 1927), vol. 7, § 5645 ("The fact that a corporation's agent exceeds his authority or acts without the knowledge or sanction of his principal is a matter of defense."); Floyd R. Mechem, Outlines of the Law of Agency, 3d ed. (Chicago: Callaghan, 1923), § 562 ("A principal will not ordinarily be held liable for the crimes of his agent unless he in some way directed or participated in, or approved the act.").

101. Henry Wollman, The Court and the Corporations, New York Times, January 8, 1911, p. 10.

102. Wickersham's Talk against the Trusts, New York Times, September 24, 1911, p. 1.

103. Frank Fayant, What Is to Be Done with the Trusts? New York Times, December 5, 1909, p. 2.

104. Wilson Calls for Control of Trusts, New York Times, October 1, 1910, p. 2.

105. Id.

106. Condign Punishment for the Trusts, New York Times, September 19, 1911, p. 12.

107. Urges Business Amnesty, New York Times, December 25, 1914, p. 10.

108. For a critical account, see Ted Nance, Gangs of America: The Rise of Corporate Power and the Disabling of Democracy (San Francisco: Berrett-Koehler, 2003).

109. 303 U.S. 77, 90 (1938). For an account of the corporate person in relation to constitutional rights, see Carl J. Mayer, Personalizing the Impersonal: Corporations and the Bill of Rights, 41 Hastings L.J. 577 (1990).

110. See Donald E. Schwartz, Federalism and Corporate Governance, 45 Ohio St. L.J. 545, 546 (1984).

111. See, e.g., Wants Roads Free to Change Charters: Chamber of Commerce Committee Favors Law for Voluntary Federal Incorporation, *New York Times*, November 23, 1923, p. 13; SEC Asks Congress for Corporate Law: Urges Federal Licensing of Companies as Way to Curb Reorganization Abuses, *New York Times*, May 11, 1938, p. 29.

112. Licensing Opposed for Corporations: O'Mahoney Bill for Federal Control Assailed by Counsel to Manufacturers' Group, *New York Times*, March 26, 1937, p. 32.

113. Id.

114. See, e.g., 17 Rubber Concerns Cited in Charges, *New York Times*, April 7, 1935, p. 31; Paper Conspiracy Denied: 14 Individual and 34 Corporate Defendants Enter Pleas, *New York Times*, December 7, 1939, p. 17.

115. First Bans Issued under Patman Act, *New York Times*, July 19, 1937, p. 29.

116. Letters to the Times, Speaking of Monopoly: Administration Charged with Fostering Those of Which It Complains, *New York Times*, May 3, 1938, p. 22.

117. SEC Report Hits Stock Exchanges: Failure to Check Manipulation and Deception Puts Burden on Commission, *New York Times*, December 31, 1937, p. 19. For the classic treatment of the development of Wall Street and the SEC, see Joel Seligman, The Transformation of Wall Street: A History of the Securities and Exchange Commission and Modern Corporate Finance, 3d ed. (New York: Aspen, 2003). See also Steve Fraser, Every Man a Speculator: A History of Wall Street in American Life (New York: HarperCollins, 2005).

118. Curbs on Trusts Suggested to SEC, *New York Times*, May 29, 1937, p. 23; SEC Seen Aligning with State Bodies, *New York Times*, October 11, 1936, p. F1; SEC to Push for New Controls, *New York Times*, April 14, 1937, p. 37; New Proxy Rules Held Too Drastic, *New York Times*, December 31, 1939, p. 1.

119. Fidelity Enjoined on SEC Complaint: Investment Company Stayed from "Misrepresentation" in Violation of Law, *New York Times*, December 23, 1938, p. 27.

120. Bankers Hear Plea for Free Business, *New York Times*, December 4, 1937, p. 30; see also Business Turns for Aid in Trials to Congress, *New York Times*, May 7, 1939, p. F7.

121. See John M. Clark, Social Control of Business (Chicago: University of Chicago Press, 1926), p. 4.

122. See Mayer, *supra* note 109, at 989.

123. The Constitution of the United States, *Fortune*, July 1936, 57, 60.

124. See Kraakman, *supra* note 82.

125. This is, no doubt, an empirical claim. Evidence of the infrequency of criminal indictments and convictions against large corporations is supportive. See chapter 4.

126. Kraakman, *supra* note 82, at 862; Adolf A. Berle and Gardner C. Means, The Modern Corporation and Private Property (New York: Macmillan, 1933).

127. Edwin H. Sutherland, White Collar Crime: The Uncut Version (New Haven, CT: Yale University Press, 1983); Edwin H. Sutherland, The Sutherland Papers, ed. Albert Cohen, Alfred Lindesmith, and Karl Schuessler (Bloomington: Indiana University Press, 1956); see also William J. Chambliss, White Collar Crime and Criminology, 13 Contemp. Soc. 160, 160–62 (1984) (book review).

128. Sutherland, White Collar Crime, *supra* note 127, at 85.

129. Sutherland, Sutherland Papers, *supra* note 127, at 82.

130. Charge 18 Cheated Boston and Montana, *New York Times*, April 24, 1923, p. 31; D. G.

Dery Indicted on Forgery Charge, *New York Times*, April 30, 1925, p. 3; State Starts War on Stock Frauds, *New York Times*, January 18, 1923, p. 1; P. W. French & Co., Art Firm, Accused of Fraud on Bank, *New York Times*, May 2, 1922, p. 1; Lindsay Russell, Three Classes of "Suckers" in Stock Fraud Schemes, *New York Times*, January 21, 1923, p. 21; Stock Jobbing War Begins with Charge of $80,000 Fraud, *New York Times*, July 6, 1923, p. 1; Seven Found Guilty of Big Mail Frauds, *New York Times*, June 18, 1925, p. 23; Oil Fraud Is Charged, Involves Seven Companies; Six Individuals, Including a Woman, Accused, *New York Times*, April 6, 1922, p. 1; Tick Bid Charged in War Fraud Case, *New York Times* August 8, 1922, p. 36; Stone Firms Guilty, Pay $80,000 Fines, *New York Times*, December 18, 1920, p. 3.

131. Financial Crime Loss Is Three Billions Yearly, *New York Times*, July 6, 1924, p. 25; see also Puts Business Frauds at Billions a Year, *New York Times*, October 20, 1928, p. 29.

132. Financial Crime Loss Is Three Billions Yearly, *supra* note 131; see also Business Bureau Reports on Frauds, *New York Times*, March 9, 1926, p. 32.

133. Richard Whitney's Sentence, *New York Times*, April 12, 1938, p. 22.

134. Starts Pipeline Case, *New York Times*, February 9, 1932, p. 18; Investment Group Accused of Fraud, *New York Times*, May 30, 1933, p. 7; W. J. Moore Indicted in $58,000,000 Fraud, *New York Times*, August 26, 1931, p. 4; Gunder and 3 Aides Indicted for Fraud, *New York Times*, January 17, 1930, p. 25; 3 Bankers on Trial $5,000,000 Deals, *New York Times*, September 8, 1931, p. 15; "Bankers" Indicted in $250,000 Fraud, *New York Times*, May 22, 1931, p. 12; Federal Jury Indicts Carnegie Steel, *New York Times*, June 5, 1943, p. 27; Dried Egg Fraud Charged to Ten, *New York Times*, May 1, 1943, p. 13; Ex-Aide of Moore Is Held in Fraud, *New York Times*, November 7, 1939, p. 25.

135. Cf. Harry V. Ball and Lawrence M. Friedman, The Use of Criminal Sanctions in the Enforcement of Economic Legislation: A Sociological View, 17 Stan. L. Rev. 197 (1965).

136. Brickey, *supra* note 93.

137. Model Penal Code § 2.07(1)(a) (Proposed Official Draft 1962).

138. Model Penal Code § 207(1)(b) (Proposed Official Draft 1962).

139. Model Penal Code § 207(1)(c) (Proposed Official Draft 1962).

140. This difference in approach is in sharp contrast to federal liability rules. Cf. United States v. Basic Constr. Co., 711 F.2d 570 (4th Cir. 1983); Holland Furnace Co. v. United States, 158 F.2d 2 (6th Cir. 1946).

141. For a review of the development of culpability in state law, consider Ronald L. Gainer, The Culpability Provisions of the Model Penal Code, 19 Rutgers L.J. 575, 578–79 (1988) ("The disorder of the American criminal law concerning culpable mental states assured the drafters of the Model Penal Code of a daunting task. It also assured the drafters of at least some degree of success; there was virtually no chance that their product would be worse than that produced over the centuries by a succession of judges and legislators.").

142. These mens rea requirements come from Alabama's pre-MPC criminal laws. See English v. Jacobs, 82 So. 2d 542 (Ala. 1955); Padgett v. State, 56 So. 2d 116 (Ala. App. 1952); Martin v. State, 25 So. 255 (Ala. 1898); Burton v. State, 107 Ala. 108 (1894).

143. See generally Herbert Wechsler, Codification of Criminal Law in the United States: The Model Penal Code, 68 Colum. L. Rev. 1425 (1968).

144. Model Penal Code (Tentative Draft No. 4, 1955). Statutory law in a host of states reflects this view; see, e.g., Ill. Rev. Stat., ch. 38, para. 5-4, § 720 (1997) ("Since, however, the major purpose of subsection (1)(a) is to encourage diligence on the part of managerial personnel to prevent criminal conduct on the part of corporate employees, it seems appro-

priate to permit the corporation to defend by proof that the criminal conduct occurred despite the exercise of due diligence on the part of supervisory personnel.").

145. Model Penal Code § 2.07(5) ("In any prosecution of a corporation or an unincorporated association for the commission of an offense included within the terms of Subsection (1)(a) or Subsection (3)(a) of this Section, other than an offense for which absolute liability has been imposed, it shall be a defense if the defendant proves by a preponderance of evidence that the high managerial agent having supervisory responsibility over the subject matter of the offense employed due diligence to prevent its commission.")

146. See State v. Adboud, Inc., 1995 WL 680920 (Ohio App. 8 Dist.).

147. See Gruner, *supra* note 72.

148. The notion of delegated authority is critical. See, e.g., C.I.T. v. United States, 150 F.2d 85 (9th Cir. 1945) ("It is the function delegated to the corporate officer or agent which determines his power to engage the corporation in a criminal transaction."). See Restatement (Third) of Agency § 1.01 (Preliminary Draft No. 2, 1998) ("Agency is the fiduciary relationship that arises when one person [the "principal"] consents that another person [the "agent"] shall act on the principal's behalf and subject to the principal's control, and the agent consents so to act.").

149. See Recent Cases, 95 U. Pa. L. Rev. 557 (1947) (arguing this point but conceding that "[i]t is not, however, clearly settled whether a corporation may be indicted for a crime committed by its agents within the scope of his authority but without the knowledge of the corporation or against its instructions.").

150. This is the position taken by the Antitrust Division of the United States Department of Justice. See, e.g., Robert E. Bloch, Corporate Compliance Programs, Antitrust Enforcement and the New Organizational Sentencing Guidelines: A Prosecutor's Perspective (remarks from the annual meeting of the American Bar Association, San Francisco, CA, August 10, 1992).

151. Gary R. Spratling, The Experience and Views of the Enforcement Community, in Proceedings of the Second Symposium on Crime and Punishment in the United States, Corporate Crime in America: Strengthening the "Good Citizen" Corporation, September 7–8, 1995 (Washington, DC: United States Sentencing Commission, 1995) [hereinafter "Proceedings"], 319. It is unclear how the Antitrust Division's Amnesty Program is consistent with Mr. Spratling's position. According to the most recent Division policy, amnesty from federal prosecution for antitrust violations is automatic "if corporation comes forward before our investigation begins." Spratling, Proceedings, 321. See "Front-End" Benefits of Antitrust Compliance Program, Self-Reporting Offer Best Hope of Avoiding Fine Floor, 4 Prevention Corp. Liability: Current Rep. 10 (1996).

152. For a discussion of this point in relation to vicarious liability, see Brickey, *supra* note 15 at 628–29 ("Under the respondeat superior rule, if the corporation has entrusted the miscreant agent with responsibility for the function he is performing, he is deemed to act and speak for the corporation when he unlawfully transacts its business.").

153. See Spratling, Proceedings, *supra* note 151, at 120.

154. See Coffee, *supra* note 11 at 229 ("In fact, if corporate penalties were greatly reduced to reflect the adoption of corporate compliance plans or other monitoring systems, corporations would rationally develop an interest in cosmetic monitoring—so they could both benefit from illegal behavior and also incur only modest penalties, if apprehended.").

155. See, e.g., the revelations regarding corporate culture at Con Edison in Neil S.

Cartusciello, The Con Edison Case and Emerging Principles of Corporate Prosecution, Bus. Crimes Bull.: Compliance & Litig., May 1995, at 1.

156. See, e.g., Richard S. Gruner, Compliance Programs and Corporate Liability: A Look into the Future in Corporate Compliance: Caremark and the Globalization of Good Corporate Conduct, ed. Carole L. Basri, Joseph E. Murphy, and Gregory J. Wallance (New York: Practising Law Institute, 1998), pp. 201, 205 ("Compliance programs that are treated by management as a sham tend to encourage cynicism by employees. Such cynicism, in turn, tends to cause employees to pay less attention to legal requirements and to be more willing to commit offenses. Hence, a poor compliance program may actually increase levels of offenses, making things work.").

157. See Mark Pastin, A Study of Organizational Factors and Their Effect on Compliance, in Proceedings, *supra* note 151, at 177–78 ("Codes of conduct viewed by employees as legalistic and one-sided, i.e., in favor of the company, increased the likelihood that employees would exhibit behavior that they identified as unethical or illegal. . . . Our summary reading of the results of this study is that many compliance measures being taken by companies have no effect or a negative effect on the compliance environment of the company.").

158. See F. Joseph Warin and Jason C. Schwartz, Deferred Prosecution: The Need for Specialized Guidelines for Corporate Defendants, 23 J. Corp. L. 121 (1997).

159. Lynn Sharp Paine, Managing for Organizational Integrity, Harv. Bus. Rev., March–April 1994, at 106 ("Prompted by the prospect of leniency, many companies are rushing to implement compliance-based ethics programs. Designed by corporate counsel, the goal of these programs is to prevent, detect, and punish legal violations. But organizational ethics means more than avoiding illegal practice, and providing employees with a rule book will do little to address the problems underlying unlawful conduct.").

160. See Model Penal Code § 2.07(1)(c) ("A corporation may be convicted of the commission of an offense if: The commission of the offense was authorized, requested, commanded, performed or recklessly tolerated by the board of directors or by a high managerial agent acting in behalf of the corporation within the scope of his office or employment.").

161. Id. at 151 ("The general respondeat superior approach of paragraph a is rejected for these cases, and corporate liability is confined to situations in which the criminal conduct is performed or participated in by the board of directors or by corporate officers and agents sufficiently high in the hierarchy to make it reasonable to assume that their acts are in some substantial sense reflective of the policy of the corporate body.").

162. The best illustration of this is where courts have found corporate criminal liability for a breach of a nondelegable duty. In such cases, corporations have been estopped from attributing a breach of statutory duty to subordinate employees or, for that matter, from claiming organizational diligence, because the duty cannot be delegated.

163. See United States v. E. Brooke Matlack, Inc., 149 F. Supp. 814 (D. Md. 1957) (holding that corporations cannot avoid liability by claiming that a subordinate neglected his duty); United States v. Armour & Co., 168 F.2d 342 (3d Cir. 1948) (deciding that good-faith precautions did not overcome nondelegable duty).

164. See Developments in the Law, *supra* note 92, at 1254 ("Consequently, liability can be evaded whenever illegal activity occurs without the authorization or reckless toleration of top officials. Since an executive cannot authorize or recklessly tolerate an offense unless he knows about it, a corporation can escape liability under this system as long as high officials remain ignorant of illegal activity.").

165. Id., borrowing language from United States v. Van Riper, 154 U.S. 492, 493 (3d Cir. 1946).

166. The Honorable Edmund G. Brown, chairperson of the National Commission on Reform of Federal Criminal Laws, submitted a final report to the president and Congress on January 7, 1971. In this report, the Brown Commission described the many features of the proposed criminal code: Unlike existing Title 18, the proposed Code is comprehensive. It brings together all federal felonies, many of which are presently found outside Title 18; it codifies common defenses, which presently are left to conflicting common-law decisions by the courts; it establishes standard principles of criminal liability and standard meanings for terms employed in the definitions of offenses and defenses. National Comm'n on Reform of Fed. Criminal Laws, Final Report of the National Commission of Reform of Federal Criminal Laws at xii (1971).

167. Working Papers of the National Commission on Reform of Federal Criminal Laws 168 (1970)..

168. See, e.g., Louis B. Schwartz, Reform of the Federal Criminal Laws: Issues, Tactics, and Prospects, 41 Law & Contemp. Probs. 1 (1977).

169. S. 1630, 97th Cong., 2d Sess., 402 (1982). This section superseded the liability rules found in S. 1722, 96th Cong., 1st Sess. (1979). Congress never passed S. 1722, due in part to insufficient time.

170. Barbara Ann Stolz, Interest Groups and Criminal Law: The Case of Federal Criminal Law Revision, 30 Crime & Delinq. 91 (1984).

171. See, e.g., Mark W. Schneider, Criminal Enforcement of Federal Water Pollution Laws in an Era of Deregulation, 73 J. Crim. L. & Criminology 642 (1982); Peter Cleary Yeager, Industrial Water Pollution, 18 Crime & Just. 97 (1993); Joseph F. DiMento, Criminal Enforcement of Environmental Law, 525 Annals 134 (1993); Ira M. Millstein and Salem M. Katsh, The Limits of Corporate Power: Existing Constraints on the Exercise of Corporate Discretion (New York: Macmillan, 1981), pp. 126–37 ("[A] virtual explosion of federal regulation took place beginning in the mid-1960's.").

172. See, e.g., Gilbert Geis, White Collar Crime: The Heavy Equipment Antitrust Cases of 1961, in Criminal Behavior Systems: A Typology, ed. Marshall B. Clinard and Richard Quinney (New York: Holt, Rinehart and Winston, 1967); Wayne E. Baker and Robert R. Faulkner, The Social Organization of Conspiracy: Illegal Networks in the Heavy Electrical Equipment Industry, 58 Am. Soc. Rev. 837 (1993); Richard A. Whiting, Antitrust and the Corporate Executive, 47 Va. L. Rev. 929 (1961). See also Leo Davids, Penology and Corporate Crime, 58 J. Crim. L. & Police Sci. 524 (1967).

173. Harry First, Business Crimes: Case and Materials (Westbury, NY: Foundation Press, 1990), p. 4. For a parallel development outside of the criminal law, see Craig Calhoun and Henryk Hiller, Coping with Insidious Injuries: The Case of Johns-Manville Corp. and Asbestos Exposure, 35 Soc. Probs. 162 (1988).

174. Robert L. Rabin, Federal Regulation in Historical Perspective, 38 Stan. L. Rev. 1189, 1259 (1986).

175. Peter Cleary Yeager, The Limits of Law: The Public Regulation of Private Pollution (Cambridge: Cambridge University Press, 1991), p. 26.

176. New Justice Unit Sought to Combat Corporate Crime: 4 in Congress and Nader Ask Levi to Back Plan to Curb "Wave" of Illegal Actions, *New York Times,* August 25, 1975, p. 55.

177. For an overview of these cases and the most incisive thinking about corporate

criminal liability and sanctions, see John C. Coffee Jr., Beyond the Shut-Eyed Sentry: Toward a Theoretical View of Corporate Misconduct and an Effective Legal Response, 63 Va. L. Rev. 1099 (1977); John W. Egan, The Internal Revenue Service and Corporate Slush Funds: Some Fifth Amendment Problems, 69 J. Crim. L. & Criminology 59 (1978); Michael C. Jensen, Corporate Corruption Is Big Business, *New York Times*, September 14, 1975, p. 173.

178. Francis T. Cullen, William J. Maakestad, and Gray Cavender, Corporate Crime under Attack: The Ford Pinto Case and Beyond (Cincinnati: Anderson, 1987). For interesting critiques of the rhetoric surrounding the Pinto case, see Matthew T. Lee and M. David Ermann, Pinto "Madness" as a Flawed Landmark Narrative: An Organizational and Network Analysis, 46 Soc. Probs. 30 (1999); Victoria Lynn Swigert and Ronald A. Farrell, Corporate Homicide: Definitional Processes in the Creation of Deviance, 15 Law & Soc'y Rev. 161 (1980).

179. New Justice Unit Sought to Combat "Corporate Crime," *New York Times*, August 25, 1975, p. 1.

180. Id.

181. See Ralph Nader and Mark J. Green, eds., Corporate Power in America (New York: Grossman Publishers, 1973); Ralph Nader, Mark Green, and Joel Seligman, Taming the Giant Corporation (New York: W. W. Norton, 1976). See also The Case for Federal Corporate Charters, *New York Times*, May 9, 1976, p. 112; Robert M. Smith, Nader Group Urges the Federal Chartering of Big Corporations, *New York Times*, January 25, 1976, p. 28.

182. S. Prakash Sethi, One Way to Punish a Corporation: Jail the Boss, *New York Times*, February 12, 1978, p. F3.

183. Alfonso A. Narvaez, White Collar Crime Deterrents Urged, *New York Times*, December 2, 1978, p. 26.

184. Leonard Orland, Jail for Corporate Price Fixers? *New York Times*, December 12, 1976, p. F16.

185. See, e.g., S.E.C. v. Corporate Crime, *New York Times*, March 13, 1977, p. 125.

186. Narvaez, *supra* note 183, at 26.

187. Orland, *supra* note 184, at F16.

188. Philip Taubman, U.S. Attack on Corporate Crime Yields Handful of Cases in 2 Years, *New York Times*, July 15, 1979, p. 1.

189. Ralph Nader, The Ralph Nader Reader (New York: Seven Stories Press, 2000), p. 137.

190. Id. at 142–43, see also Ralph Nader, Reforming Corporate Governance, Cal. Mgmt. Rev., Summer 1984, at 126.

191. For a discussion of Ralph Nader's "Crime in the Suites," see Judith Miller, Nader-Led Drive Aims at Business, *New York Times*, April 10, 1980, p. D1.

192. Id.

193. Clinard et al., *supra* note 68. Additional research on the perceptions of business-people added to the perception that corporate deviance was widespread. See, e.g., Raymond C. Baumhart, How Ethical Are Businessmen?, Harv. Bus. Rev., July–August 1961, at 6. This work was replicated by Steven N. Brenner and Earl A. Molander, Is the Ethics of Business Changing?, Harv. Bus. Rev., January–February 1977, at 57.

194. Clinard et al., *supra* note 68, at xvii. In a minority of cases that were criminal, the factors that contributed to a decision to prosecute rather than proceed with civil or administrative actions include: (1) the degree of loss to the public; (2) the level of complicity by high-level corporate managers; (3) the duration of the violation; (4) the frequency of the violation by the corporation; (5) the evidence of intent to violate; (6) the evidence of

extortion, as in bribery cases, (7) the degree of notoriety engendered by the media; (8) the precedent in law; (9) the history of previous serious violations by the corporation; (10) the deterrence potential; and (11) the degree of cooperation evinced by the corporation. For additional empirical research on white-collar and corporate offending, see Stanton Wheeler and Mitchell Lewis Rothman, The Organization as Weapon in White-Collar Crime, 80 Mich. L. Rev. 1403 (1982).

195. Notably, there is an insignificant literature on the external initiatives of firms through the lobbying of legislative bodies and law reform commissions to avoid the criminal law, whether individually, by public interest organizations, or through representative trade associations. See, e.g., Peter M. Gillon and Steven L. Humphreys, Corporate Officer Liability under Clean Air Act May Create Disincentives, Inside Litig., May 1992, at 6 (discussing the lobbying by labor groups that contributed to the shifting of liability onto corporate managers for criminal violations of the Clean Air Act. According to the authors, "The shifting of liability to corporate managers reflects a victory for labor groups who lobbied hard to exempt hourly laborers and other union members from penalties for non-compliance under the Act, even if they are responsible for a violation. . . . [T]he amendments deliberately shift liability for criminal violations of the statute away from employees at the operational level or those merely 'following orders.' "). See generally Note, Decisionmaking Models and the Control of Corporate Crime, 85 Yale L.J. 1091 (1976) for an extensive consideration of the role of the political process in shaping liability rules. The focus on corporate criminal liability in relation to the aborted recodification of the Federal Criminal Code is instructive. For a discussion of changing regulatory enforcement policies, see Jed S. Rakoff, Four Postulates of White-Collar Practice, *New York Law Journal*, November 12, 1993, p. 3 (discussing the growing reliance on civil remedies for white-collar and corporate crimes).

196. Nancy Frank and Michael Lombness, Controlling Corporate Illegality: The Regulatory Justice System (Cincinnati: Anderson, 1988), p. 3.

197. Ralph Nader and Mark Green, Corporate Democracy, *New York Times*, December 28, 1979, p. F17.

198. Mutual Funds Told Social Issues Should Guide Their Investments, *New York Times*, April 21, 1971, p. 62.

199. Elineen Shanahan, Good Guys and Bad Guys: Institutions Asked to Consider Morality, *New York Times*, April 11, 1971, p. F7.

200. Ernest Holsendoph, Spreading the Word about Good Works: Companies Report on New Social Approach, *New York Times*, April 8, 1973, p. 212; Milton Moskowitz, Emergence of the Corporate Conscience, *New York Times*, January 6, 1974, p. 205. Early conceptions of corporate social responsibility may be traced to a famous exchange between A. A. Berle Jr., Corporate Powers as Powers in Trust, 44 Harv. L. Rev. 1049 (1931), and E. Merrick Dodd Jr., For Whom Are Corporate Managers Trustees?, 45 Harv. L. Rev. 1145 (1932). For critiques, see C. A. Harwell Wells, The Cycles of Corporate Social Responsibility: An Historical Retrospective for the Twenty-First Century, 51 U. Kan. L. Rev. 77 (2002); A. A. Sommer Jr., Whom Should the Corporation Serve? The Berle-Dodd Debate Revisited Sixty Years Later, 16 Del. J. Corp. L. 33 (1991).

201. Richard Halloran, Ralph Nader to Press for G.M. Reform, *New York Times*, February 8, 1970, p. 44.

202. Herbert Mitgang, G. M. Challenged on "Responsibility," *New York Times*, May 17, 1970, p. SM31.

203. James M. Roche, Defending Big Business, *New York Times*, April 21, 1971, p. 47.

204. Vik Khanna notes, however, that corporate persons enjoy lesser protections than human persons do. See Vikramaditya S. Khanna, Corporate Defendants and the Protections of Criminal Procedure: An Economic Approach (2004) (unpublished manuscript, on file with University of Michigan School of Law).

205. Mayer, *supra* note 109, at 620.

206. Yeager, *supra* note 175, at 11.

207. Foreign Corrupt Practices Act of 1977, Pub. L. No. 95-23, 91 Stat. 1494 (codified as amended at 15 U.S.C. §§ 78m(b), (d)(1), (g)–(h), 78dd-2, 78ff (1994)), amended by Foreign Corrupt Practices Act Amendments of 1988, Pub. L. No. 100-418, at 924 (1988), and the International Anti-Bribery and Fair Competition Act of 1998, 15 U.S.C. §§ 78dd-1 to 78dd-3, 78ff (West Supp. 1999).

208. E.g., *Protection of Shareholders Rights Act of 1980: Hearings on S. 2567 Before the Subcomm. on Securities of the S. Comm. on Banking, Housing and Urban Affairs*, 96th Cong. (1980); *Corporate Rights and Responsibilities: Hearings Before S. Comm. on Commerce*, 94th Cong. (1976). For a history and critique of corporate governance in the United States, see Mark J. Roe, The Inevitable Instability of American Corporate Governance, Discussion Paper No. 493, The Harvard John M. Olin Discussion Paper Series, September 2004.

209. Tamar Lewin, The Corporate-Reform Furor, *New York Times*, June 10, 1982, p. D1.

210. Nathaniel C. Nash, E. F. Hutton Guilty in Bank Fraud; Penalties Could Top $10 Million, *New York Times*, May 3, 1985, p. A1.

211. Ralph Nader, White Collar Fraud: America's Crime Without Criminals, *New York Times*, May 19, 1985, p. F3.

212. These calls were joined by questions regarding the handling of E. F. Hutton and, in particular, defense contractor fraud; see, e.g., Philip Shenon, Senate to Study Handling by U.S. of Prosecutions of Corporations, *New York Times*, September 13, 1985, p. A1.

213. Winston Williams, White-Collar Crime: Booming Again, *New York Times*, June 9, 1985, p. F1.

214. Henry N. Pontell and Kitty Calavita, White-Collar Crime in the Savings and Loan Scandal, 525 Annals 31 (1993).

215. See, e.g., Michael Masuch, Book Review, 32 Admin. Sci. Q. 303 (1987) (reviewing Robert P. Gandossy, Bad Business: The OPM Scandal and the Seduction of the Establishment (New York: Basic Books, 1985)).

216. Morton Mintz, At Any Cost: Corporate Greed, Women, and the Dalkon Shield (New York: Pantheon Books, 1985).

217. See, e.g., Jay A. Sigler and Joseph E. Murphy, Interactive Corporate Compliance: An Alternative to Regulatory Compulsion (New York: Quorum Books, 1988); Jay A. Sigler and Joseph E. Murphy, eds., Corporate Lawbreaking and Interactive Compliance: Resolving the Regulation-Deregulation Dichotomy (New York: Quorum Books, 1991).

218. President's Blue Ribbon Commission on Defense Management. A Quest for Excellence: Final Report to the President, 1986. (Washington, DC: The Commission).

219. The Defense Industry Initiative on Business Ethics and Conduct, 2002 Annual Report to the Public and the Defense Industry, available at: http://www.dii.org/. For a more recent examination of defense procurement fraud, see Jonathan M. Karpoff et al., Defense Procurement Fraud, Penalties, and Contractor Influence, 107 J. Pol. Econ. 809 (1999).

220. Cf. Martin F. McDermott, Occupational Disqualification of Corporate Executives:

An Innovative Condition of Probation, 73 J. Crim. L. & Criminology 604, 604–41 (1982); Charles B. Renfew, The Paper Label Sentences: An Evaluation, 86 Yale L.J. 590 (1977). For a brief review of the first decade of the guidelines, see Jeffrey M. Kaplan, The Sentencing Guidelines: The First Ten Years, Ethikos, November–December 2001, at 1.

221. Gary S. Becker, Crime and Punishment: An Economic Approach, 76 J. Pol. Econ. 169 (1968); M. K. Block and J. M. Heineke, A Labor Theoretic Analysis of the Criminal Choice, 65 Am. Econ. Rev. 314 (1975); Richard A. Posner, An Economic Theory of the Criminal Law, 85 Colum. L. Rev. 1193 (1985); Cindy Alexander, On the Nature of the Reputational Penalty for Corporate Crime: Evidence, 42 J.L. & Econ. 489 (1999); Mark A. Cohen, Theories of Punishment and Empirical Trends in Corporate Criminal Sanctions, 17 Managerial & Decision Econ. 399 (1996); Mark A. Cohen, Environmental Crime and Punishment: Legal/Economic Theory and Empirical Evidence on Enforcement of Federal Environmental Statutes, 82 J. Crim. L. & Criminology 1054 (1992); John R. Lott Jr., Corporate Criminal Penalties, 17 Managerial & Decision Econ. 349 (1996); Thomas S. Ulen, The Economics of Corporate Criminal Liability, 17 Managerial & Decision Econ. 351 (1996). For a summary of the philosophical bases for imposing sanctions, as specified by Congress, see 28 U.S.C. § 991(b)(1)(A) (1991).

222. U.S. Sentencing Guidelines Manual § 8C2.1(d) (Tentative Draft 1990).

223. Id. § 8C2.2.

224. Michael K. Block and John R. Lott Jr., Is Curbing Crime Worth the Cost?, *New York Times*, May 5, 1991, p. F13.

225. See, e.g., Neil A. Lewis, Bush Aide Intervened on Stiff Fines for Businesses, *New York Times*, April 29, 1990, p. 23.

226. Amitai Etzioni, A Vote for Peer Pressure, *New York Times*, May 5, 1991, p. F13; see also Amitai Etzioni, The U.S. Sentencing Commission on Corporate Crime: A Critique, 525 Annals 147 (1993). For a review of the progress of postguidelines cases, see Cindy R. Alexander et al., Regulating Corporate Criminal Sanctions: Federal Guidelines and the Sentencing of Public Firms, 42 J.L. & Econ. 393 (1999).

227. See U.S. Sentencing Guidelines Manual 3 (1991). For a critical review of the 1990 Draft, see John C. Coffee Jr., "Carrot and Stick" Sentencing: Structuring Incentives for Organizational Defendants, 3 Fed. Sent'g Rep. 126 (1990).

228. 18 U.S.C. app. 8C2.5 (b)–(g) (1992).

229. 18 U.S.C. app. 8C2.5(b)(1)(A)(i) (1992).

230. 18 U.S.C. app. 8C2.5 (b)(1)(A)(ii) (1992).

231. U.S. Sentencing Guidelines Manual 71 (1991).

232. Cf. Leonard Orland, Corporate Punishment by the U.S. Sentencing Commission, 4 Fed. Sent'g Rep. 50 (1991) (Orland criticizes the Sentencing Commission's conception of corporate culpability, finding it to be based upon assumptions that run counter to organizational theory.).

233. See William S. Laufer and Diana C. Robertson, Corporate Ethics Initiatives as Social Control, 16 J. Bus. Ethics 1029 (1997).

234. Cf. Lynn Sharp Paine, Managing for Organizational Integrity, Harv. Bus. Rev., March–April 1994, at 106; Jay A. Sigler and Joseph E. Murphy, Interactive Corporate Compliance: An Alternative to Regulatory Compulsion (New York: Quorum Books, 1988); Note, Growing the Carrot: Encouraging Effective Corporate Compliance, 109 Harv. L. Rev. 1783 (1996).

235. See Proceedings, *supra* note 151; Joseph E. Murphy and Gregory J. Wallance, eds., Corporate Compliance: How to be a Good Citizen Corporation through Self-Policing (New

York: Practising Law Institute,1996). The notion of the "good corporate citizen" may be distinguished from organizational citizenship behavior; see, e.g., Linn Van Dyne et al., Organizational Citizenship Behavior: Construct Redefinition, Measurement, and Validation, 37 Acad. Mgmt. J. 765 (1994).

236. See U.S. Sentencing Guidelines Manual § 8A1.2 cmt. 3(k)(1)–(7) (1991).

237. See, e.g., Peter A. French, Integrity, Intentions, and Corporations, 34 Am. Bus. L.J. 114, 119 (1996), who noted that "the person of integrity is required to have a set of intentions . . . intentions to pursue the proper moral principles and the truth of one's convictions." See also Richard T. De George, Competing with Integrity in International Business (New York: Oxford University Press, 1993), p. 39.

238. See French, *supra* note 237, at 114 ("What that means, as I understand it, is that corporations can adopt policies that require them to continually pursue the truth of their corporate commitments and that regularly expose their convictions and corporate policies to moral scrutiny.").

239. Accordingly, corporate integrity is more than mere desires or beliefs. As French has argued, integrity, as due diligence, is corporate planning and action, consistent with corporate policies. In law, due diligence is conceived of by degree and extent.

240. See Paine, *supra* note 234, at 106, 106–7 ("An integrity-based approach to ethics management combines a concern for the law with an emphasis on managerial responsibility for ethical behavior. Though integrity strategies may vary in design and scope, all strive to define companies' guiding values, aspirations, and patterns of thought and conduct."); Are Compliance and Ethics Related?, Benchmarks, March 1994, at 3; Alan R. Yuspeh and Rebecca E. Goodell, Terms Such as "Compliance Program," "Ethics Program" Aren't Synonymous, 3 Prevention of Corp. Liability: Current Rep. 1 (1995). See generally Winthrop M. Swenson, An Effective Program to Prevent and Detect Violations of Law, in Compliance Programs and the Corporate Sentencing Guidelines: Preventing Criminal and Civil Liability, ed. Jeffrey M. Kaplan, Joseph E. Murphy, and Winthrop M. Swenson (Deerfield, IL: Clark Boardman Callaghan, 1993), § 4:07.75.

241. Paine, *supra* note 234, at 111.

242. Paine's conception of integrity and compliance is analogous to French's formalistic and nonformalistic account of integrity.

243. See Gary R. Weaver et al., Corporate Ethics Programs as Control Systems: Influences of Executive Commitment and Environmental Factors, 42 Acad. Mgmt. J. 41 (1999).

244. See Note, Growing the Carrot, *supra* note 234.

245. See generally William E. Knepper and Dan A. Bailey, Liability of Corporate Officers and Directors, 5th ed. (Charlottesville, VA: Michie, 1993), pp. 11–51.

246. For a wonderful discussion of the genesis of compliance as self-regulation, see Braithwaite, Enforced Self-Regulation, *supra* note 8. See also Brent Fisse, Reconstructing Corporate Criminal Law: Deterrence, Retribution, Fault, and Sanctions, 56 S. Cal. L. Rev. 1141 (1983).

247. French comments that integrity may be demonstrated with policies that require a continual pursuit of corporate commitments, along with a regular exposure of corporate commitments and policies to moral scrutiny. French suggests that this might be possible with a "compliance system, and an active ethics officer plugged into the CID Structure in a significant way." See French, *supra* note 237, at 11. See also Swenson, *supra* note 240, § 4:07.50.

248. See Robert C. Solomon, Ethics and Excellence: Cooperation and Integrity in Business (New York: Oxford University Press, 1992), pp. 168–74; Richard De George wrote: "Acting with integrity extends beyond satisfying the bare moral minimum; it involves acting in accordance with moral norms willingly, knowingly, purposely, and because one is in command of one's actions." De George, *supra* note 237, at 6–7.

249. According to Robert S. Litt, deputy assistant attorney general, Criminal Division, U.S. Department of Justice, "A good corporate citizen, one that is devoted to an effective compliance program, is much less likely to be prosecuted itself for the acts of its wayward employees than a rogue corporation with a culture that encourages or condones misbehavior. . . . But it is true that in deciding whether or not to prosecute a corporation, most prosecutors will take a look at the compliance policies, take a look at the preventive and reporting procedures that the company has adopted, judge whether they were effective and appropriate given the company's size and type of business, and give a company credit for that in determining whether or not to prosecute." Litt, The Experience and Views of the Enforcement Community, in Proceedings, *supra* note 151, at 305.

250. Litt gives the following example: "[O]ne United States Attorney's Office declined to prosecute a major corporation in a fraud case. The company, when it learned of the wrongdoing, promptly fired the responsible employees, made an agreement to settle by paying restitution, and agreed to adopt a compliance program in writing that required it to report to the government any allegations about which it learns concerning potential criminal conduct involving government contracts. In other words, this company got credit in the prosecutive decision for, among other things, agreeing to set up an effective compliance program." Id. at 305.

251. Litt notes: "In addition, it is also common for prosecutors, in making an agreement not to prosecute a company, to require that the company promise, in writing, to establish a compliance policy if it does not already have one, or to strengthen its existing policy and to report periodically to the government on how it is working. In other words, even if you don't have a compliance program at the time you come into the prosecutor's office, you ought to think about setting up an effective one and offering this up as part of a plea bargain or an agreement not to prosecute the corporation." Id. at 305.

252. 698 A.2d 959 (Del. Ch. 1996). See H. Lowell Brown, The Corporate Director's Compliance Oversight Responsibility in the Post Caremark Era, 26 Del J. Corp. L. 1 (2001); Charles M. Elson and Christopher J. Gyves, In re Caremark: Good Intentions, Unintended Consequences, 39 Wake Forest L. Rev. 691 (2004).

253. See Kirk S. Jordon, Board of Directors' Liability for Inadequate Compliance Programs: In Re Caremark International Inc. Derivative Litigation, Del. Chancery, C.A. 13670 (Chancellor Allen, September 15, 1996), 5 Corp. Conduct Q. 31 (1996); Richard S. Gruner, Director and Officer Liability for Defective Compliance Systems: *Caremark* and Beyond, in Corporate Compliance: After *Caremark*, ed. Carole L. Basri, Joseph E. Murphy, and Gregory J. Wallance (New York: Practising Law Institute, 1997).

254. Charles Hanson, The Duty of Care, the Business Judgment Rule, and the American Law Institute Corporate Governance Project, 48 Bus. Law. 1355 (1993); Joseph F. Savage Jr., *Caremark*: Director's Fiduciary Duty in a Sentencing Guidelines World, Bus. Crimes Bull.: Compliance & Litig., January 1997, at 4. For an interesting pre–*Caremark International* discussion of director liability, see James L. Griffith Jr., Director Oversight Liability: Twenty-First Century Standards and Legislative Controls on Liability, 20 Del. J. Corp. L. 653 (1995);

Melvin A. Eisenberg, The Board of Directors and Internal Control, 19 Cardozo L. Rev. 237 (1997). See Principles of Corporate Governance § 4.01 cmt. (c) (1994) ("One aspect of the board's general duty of care obligation in the oversight and inquiry areas is an affirmative obligation of directors to be reasonably concerned with the existence and effectiveness of procedures, programs and other techniques . . . to assist the board in overseeing the corporation's business.").

255. Notably, the *Caremark* decision fails to specify the boundaries of a director's duties, the meaning of "good faith" efforts by directors, or the extent of a director's duty to supervise and monitor compliance efforts.

256. 698 A.2d at 970.

257. See, e.g., *supra* note 156; *supra* note 253. According to Pitt and his colleagues, directors must ensure that managers demonstrate a respect and allegiance to the law; update codes; ensure that the corporation provides sufficient compliance-related training and education; provide an anonymous means of communicating unethical or illegal acts when observed by employees; maintain an awareness of relevant legal issues; and maintain the supervisory oversight of corporate internal controls. See Harvey L. Pitt, Karl A. Groskaufmanis, and Vasiliki B. Tsaganos, Director Duties to Uncover and Respond to Management Misconduct, Insights: Corp. & Sec. L. Advisor, June 1997, at 5, 8

258. Report of Investigation Pursuant to Section 21(A) of the Securities Exchange Act of 1934 Concerning the Conduct of Certain Former Officers and Directors of W. R. Grace & Co., 65 S.E.C. Docket 1240 (1997).

259. Corporate Governance: SEC "Should Be More Outspoken" On Directors' Duty to Monitor Management, 30 Sec. Reg. & L. Rep. (BNA) 398 (1998). See also Corporations Discuss Ethics Challenges and Opportunities, Fed. Ethics Rep., June 1998, at 1.

260. Guidance on Prosecutions of Corporations, U.S. Department of Justice, June 16, 1999, reprinted in BNA Compliance Manual, 41 Prevention of Corp. Liability 1200 (1999).

261. Notably, these guidelines require prosecutors to take into account "the very special nature of the corporate person" as well as to ensure that the general purposes of the criminal law are fulfilled. This fulfillment includes the "assurance of warranted punishment." Id. at 3.

262. Prosecutorial guidelines consider organizational factors that reveal organizational fault. These factors, it will be argued, have become the default liability rules under federal law.

263. The Department of Justice and a host of regulatory agencies settled many cases with organizations where compliance measures were part of the settlement agreement, including fifteen civil antitrust offenses, nine environmental offenses, four health-care fraud cases, and two defense contracting fraud cases.

264. Data from the United States Sentencing Commission reveal a disturbing artifact about completed federal prosecutions. An overwhelming number of the between two hundred and four hundred corporations convicted in federal courts each year are small, privately held businesses with fifty or fewer employees. Virtually all are without an established compliance program. Fortune 1000 companies that have invested in compliance programs are simply diverted from the criminal process, whether by plea agreements, through civil or administrative law sanctions, or by individual prosecutions of white-collar offenders. Of course, there remain corporate prosecutions under substantive law. In the 1990s, for example, the top one hundred corporate criminals violated environmental (38), antitrust (20), mail and wire fraud (13), campaign finance (7), food and drug (6), financial (4), false

statements (3), illegal exports (3), illegal boycott (1), worker death (1), bribery (1), obstruction of justice (1), public corruption (1), and tax evasion (1) laws, amassing fines in excess of $121 billion. For a revealing look at the prevalence and scale of corporate crime, in the absence of more reliable sources, see the Corporate Crime Reporter, available at: http://www.corporatecrimereporter.com/top100.html.

265. A host of reasons are associated with earnings restatements, including CEO compensation, debt covenant constraints, ability to raise additional capital, ability to make acquisitions, and effective monitoring by the board. For a review and empirical test of these factors, see Jap Efendi, Anup Srivastava, and Edward P. Swanson, Why Do Corporate Managers Misstate Financial Statements? The Role of Option Compensation, Corporate Governance, and Other Facts, Working Paper, Texas A&M University, May 17, 2004.

266. See Patricia M. Dechow and Douglas J. Skinner, Earnings Management: Reconciling the Views of Accounting Academics, Practitioners, and Regulators, 14 Acct. Horizons 235 (2000); Roger Lowenstein, Origins of the Crash: The Great Bubble and Its Undoing (New York: Penguin Press, 2004).

267. See United States General Accounting Office, Financial Statements Restatement: Trends, Market Impacts, Regulatory Responses and Remaining Challenges. Report 03–138 (Washington, DC: Government Printing Office), p. 26.

268. Arthur Levitt, The "Numbers Game," Remarks by Chairman Arthur Levitt of the Securities and Exchange Commission Delivered at the NYU Center for Law and Business, New York, NY, September 28, 1998 (available at: http://www.sec.gov/news/speech/speecharchive /1998/spch 220.txt).

269. John C. Coffee Jr., Understanding Enron: "It's About the Gatekeepers, Stupid," 57 Bus. Law. 1403 (2002); see also Assaf Hamdani, Gatekeeper Liability, 77 S. Cal. L. Rev. 53 (2003) (arguing that there is an inherent trade-off between giving third parties adequate incentives to stop corporate deviance and minimizing the perverse impact of imputing liability to law-abiding clients); Jeffrey N. Gordon, What Enron Means for the Management and Control of the Modern Business Corporation: Some Initial Reflections, 69 U. Chi. L. Rev. 1233 (2002).

270. Coffee, *supra* note 269; see also Peter J. Henning, Sarbanes-Oxley Act § 307 and Corporate Counsel: Who Better to Prevent Corporate Crime?, 8 Buff. Crim. L. Rev. 323 (2004).

271. For an intriguing explanation of "Enronitis," see, e.g., Daniel J. H. Greenwood, Enronitis: Why Good Corporations Go Bad, 2004 Colum. Bus. L. Rev. 773 ("*Enronitis* (n. neologism derived from Enron, a large company that went bankrupt amid allegations of market manipulation, phony accounting, looting, and other corporate misbehavior)").

272. Richard Posner, The Economics of Business Scandals and Financial Regulation (October 2002) (unpublished manuscript, on file with author).

273. George Benston et al., Following the Money: The Enron Failure and the State of Corporate Disclosure (Washington, DC: AIE-Brookings Joint Center for Regulator Studies, 2003), p. 66.

274. See, e.g., William J. Carney, The Costs of Being Public after Sarbanes-Oxley: The Irony of "Going Private," Emory School of Law: Law and Economics Research Paper Series, Working Paper No. 05–4 (2004).

275. Deborah Solomon and Ian McDonald, Spitzer Decries Lax Regulation over Insurance, *Wall Street Journal*, November 17, 2004, p. C1.

276. For a discussion of transnational economic crime, see John Braithwaite, Transnational Regulation of the Pharmaceutical Industry, 525 Annals 12 (1993); Jurg Gerber and

Eric L. Jensen, Controlling Transnational Corporations: The Role of Governmental Entities and Grassroots Organizations in Combating White-Collar Crime, 44 Int'l J. Offender Therapy & Comp. Criminology 692 (2000); Kip Schlegel, Transnational Crime: Implications for Local Law Enforcement, 16 J. Contemp. Crim. Just. 365 (2000).

277. In bringing fraud charges against McAfee, Inc., (formerly known as Network Associates, Inc.) and Applix, Inc., in Jaunary, 2006, the SEC announced guidelines for determining whether and how much to civilly fine companies. These guidelines consider two principal factors: the presence or absence of a direct benefit to the corporation as a result of the violation, and the degree to which the penalty will recompense or further harm the injured shareholders. Eight additional factors were also identified: the need to deter the particular type of offense; the extent of the injury to innocent parties; whether complicity in the violation is widespread throughout the corporation; the level of intent on the part of the perpetrators; the degree of difficulty in detecting the particular type of offense; presence or lack of remedial steps by the corporation; remedial steps is a factor supporting the imposition of a corporate penalty; and extent of cooperation with Commission and other law enforcement. Securities and Exchange Commission, Statement of the Securities and Exchange Commission Concerning Financial Penalties, 2006-4, January 4, 2006.

278. Christopher Bowe and Joshua Chaffin, Convictions for US Healthcare Fraud Up by 22%, *Financial Times,* August 11, 2003, p. 1.

279. Cf. Jonathan M. Karpoff, D. Scott Lee, and Gerald S. Martin, The Costs to Firms of Cooking the Books, (July 25, 2005), available at http://ssrm.com/abstract=652121 (arguing that penalties for cooking the books are far from de minimis).

280. President Roosevelt Speaks on Trusts, *New York Times,* April 4, 1903, p. 1.

281. Charles G. Dawes, The Problem of the Trusts, *New York Times,* November 7, 1911, p. 8.

282. Frank Partnoy, Infectious Greed: How Deceit and Risk Corrupted the Financial Markets (New York: Times Books, 2003), p. 5.

283. For a discussion of the development and progression of white-collar crime, see David Weisburd and Elin Waring, White-Collar Crime and Criminal Careers, with Ellen F. Chayet (Cambridge: Cambridge University Press, 2001).

284. Brient T. O'Connor and Peter L. Welsh, Vicarious Corporate Criminal Liability: How to Manage the Risks, Bus. Crimes Bull.: Compliance & Litig., June 2002, at 3.

CHAPTER TWO

1. Hundreds of Andersen Employees Protest Indictment, *Houston Chronicle,* March 20, 2002, p. 1.

2. Deputy Attorney General Transcript, News Conference: Arthur Andersen Indictment, March 14, 2002, available at: http://www.usdoj.gov/dag/speech/2002/031402newsconference arthurandersen.htm.

3. United States v. Arthur Andersen, LLP, Criminal Number H-01-121, United States District Court, Southern District of Texas, March 7, 2002, available at: http://news.findlaw.com /hdocs/docs/enron/usandersen030702ind.pdf.

4. Deputy Attorney General Transcript, *supra* note 2.

5. Cf. Ross D. Fuerman, Differentiating between Arthur Andersen and the Surviving Big Four on the Basis of Auditor Quality (January 1, 2005) (working paper, on file with author), concluding the auditor quality at Andersen was inferior relative to the surviving Big Four CPA firms.

6. Jenalia Moreno, Andersen Settles Charges after Audits, *Houston Chronicle*, June 20, 2001, p. 1.

7. Arthur Andersen & Co, A Vision of Grandeur (Chicago: A. Andersen, 1988).

8. The First Sixty Years, 1913–1973 (Chicago: A. Andersen, 1974).

9. Susan E. Squires et al., Inside Arthur Andersen: Shifting Values, Unexpected Consequences (Upper Saddle River, NJ: FT Prentice Hall, 2003), p. 137.

10. Cf. V. S. Khanna, Corporate Criminal Liability: What Purpose Does It Serve?, 109 Harv. L. Rev. 1477 (1996). For a general treatment of corporate criminal liability, see James Gobert and Maurice Punch, Rethinking Corporate Crime (London: Butterworths/LexisNexis, 2003); Richard S. Gruner, Corporate Crime and Sentencing (Charlottesville, VA: Michie, 1994); Kathleen Brickey, Corporate Criminal Liability: A Treatise on the Criminal Liability of Corporations, Their Officers and Agents, 3 vols., (Wilmette, IL: Callaghan, 1984). The general public has a strong grasp on corporate wrongdoing; see Valerie P. Hans and M. David Ermann, Responses to Corporate versus Individual Wrongdoing, 13 Law & Hum. Behav. 151 (1989); Marvin E. Wolfgang and Robert M. Figlio, Weighing Social Responsibility: How Receptions Differ for Individual and Corporate Crimes, 9 Wharton Ann. 32 (1985).

11. Kent Greenfield, From Metaphor to Reality in Corporate Law (Boston College Law Sch. Pub. Law & Legal Theory Research Paper Series, Paper No. 2001–10, 2001).

12. See Vikramaditya S. Khanna, Double Jeopardy's Asymmetric Appeal Rights: What Purpose Do They Serve?, 82 B.U. L. Rev. 341 (2002). See also Steven Walt and William S. Laufer, Why Personhood Doesn't Matter: Corporate Criminal Liability and Sanctions, 18 Am. J. Crim. L. 263 (1991) (arguing that human and corporate persons are indistinguishable in law and may be so in fact); John J. Flynn, The Jurisprudence of Corporate Personhood: The Misuse of a Legal Concept, in Corporations and Society: Power and Responsibility, ed. Warren J. Samuels and Arthur S. Miller (New York: Greenwood Press, 1987), p. 131.

13. Gregory A. Mark, The Personification of the Business Corporation in American Law, 54 U. Chi. L. Rev. 1441 (1987).

14. The debate over the purpose and objective of business enterprises is an old one, wonderfully captured by the debate between A. A. Berle Jr., Corporate Powers as Powers in Trust, 44 Harv. L. Rev. 1049 (1931); and E. Merrick Dodd Jr., For Whom Are Corporate Managers Trustees?, 45 Harv. L. Rev. 1145 (1932).

15. What We Talk About When We Talk about Persons: The Language of a Legal Fiction, 114 Harv. L. Rev. 1745 n (2001); see also Valerie P. Hans, Business on Trial: The Civil Jury and Corporate Responsibility (New Haven, CT: Yale University Press, 2000), pp. 79–111.

16. See Greenfield, *supra* note 11.

17. See Vikramaditya S. Khanna, Corporate Liability Standards: When Should Corporations Be Held Criminally Liable?, 37 Am. Crim. L. Rev. 1239 (2000).

18. See, e.g., Mark A. Seabright and Lance B. Kurke, Organizational Ontology and the Moral Status of the Corporation, 7 Bus. Ethics Q. 91 (1997).

19. For a wonderful treatment of the role of individualism in law more generally, see Craig Haney, Criminal Justice and the Nineteenth-Century Paradigm, 6 Law & Hum. Behav. 191 (1982).

20. W. Ullman, The Delictual Responsibility of Medieval Corporations, 64 Law Q. 77 (1948).

21. See generally Harold J. Laski, The Early History of the Corporation in England, 30 Harv. L. Rev. 561 (1917); Samuel Williston, History of the Law of Business Corporations before

1800, 2 Harv. L. Rev. 105 (1888) (part 1); Samuel Williston, History of the Law of Business Corporations before 1800, 2 Harv. L. Rev. 149 (1888) (part 2).

22. W. S. Holdsworth, English Corporation Law in the 16th and 17th Centuries, 31 Yale L.J. 382 (1922).

23. William S. Holdsworth, A History of English Law (London: Methuen, 1903), p. 482.

24. See, e.g., Otto Gierke, Associations and Law: The Classical and Early Christian Stages (Toronto: University of Toronto Press, 1977).

25. For an excellent review of the theories of corporate personality, see L. H. Leigh, The Criminal Liability of Corporations in English Law (London: Weidenfeld & Nicolson, 1969).

26. See, e.g., Sanford A. Schane, The Corporation Is a Person: The Language of a Legal Fiction, 61 Tul. L. Rev. 563 (1987).

27. Mark M. Hager, Bodies Politic: The Progressive History of Organizational "Real Entity" Theory, 50 U. Pitt. L. Rev. 575, 583–84 (1989).

28. 17 S.W. 442 (Ky. 1891).

29. Simeon E. Baldwin, A Legal Fiction with Its Wings Clipped, 41 Am. L. Rev. 38, 43 (1907).

30. Id.

31. Id.

32. In United States v. Milwaukee Refrigerator Transit Co., where prosecutors secured an injunction against a company for Elkins Act violations, Judge Sanborn observed that "[a] corporation, as expressive of legal rights and powers, is no more fictitious or intangible than a man's right to his own home or his own liberty. 142 Fed. 247 (1905). Similar observations were made in the Standard Oil, New York Sugar, and Whiskey Trust cases. George F. Canfield, The Scope and Limits of the Corporate Entity Theory, 17 Colum. L. Rev. 128 (1917); Ralph W. Hidy, Development of Large-Scale Organization: The Standard Oil Co. (New Jersey), 12 J. Econ. Hist. 411 (1952).

33. W. J. Lampton, The Offender, *New York Times,* January 27, 1910, p. 8.

34. Frederick Hallis, Corporate Personality: A Study in Jurisprudence (London: Oxford University Press, 1930), p. xxi ("What the extreme individualist and the extreme collectivist do is to deny one half of the facts in order to retain without logical contradiction the other half."). In wrestling with the fiction and realist theories, Frederick Hallis concluded that "philosophers have lost themselves in a maze of their own abstractions, and losing sight of the real problem as presented by the facts, they have constructed a one-sided metaphysic which simply puts aside the logical difficulty. . . . Others have maintained an extreme collectivism which denies the concrete independence of the individual life and affirms the sole reality of society as a unitary organism. Both have avoided the real problem, which is to explain individuality and sociality as aspects of a single reality, the complete life of personality."

35. Cf. Joachim Vogel, "How to Determine Individual Criminal Responsibility in Systemic Contexts: Twelve Models" (paper presented at 14th International Congress on Social Defence: Social Defence and Criminal Law for the Protection of Coming Generations, Lisbon, May 17–19, 2002); Ellen S. Podgor, Corporate and White Collar Crime: Simplifying the Ambiguous, 31 Am. Crim. L. Rev. 391 (1994).

36. John J. Flynn, The Jurisprudence of Corporate Personhood: The Misuse of a Legal Concept, in Corporations and Society: Power and Responsibility, ed. Warren J. Samuels and Arthur S. Miller (New York: Greenwood Press, 1987), p. 133 ("There can be little doubt from

a jurisprudential view that the Court's method for recognizing corporate personhood in *Santa Clara* constituted a serious misuse of concepts for legal purposes. . . . It resembles a dictatorial edict issued without reason, explanation, or argument.").

37. These variables are often associated with corporate deviance. According to Clinard and Yeager, "These factors—size, delegation, and specialization—combine to produce an organizational climate that allows the abdication of a degree of personal responsibility for almost every type of decision, from the most inconsequential to one that may have a great impact on the lives of thousands. At all levels of the corporation, there may be an institutionalization of irresponsibility that permits the corporation to function as if encumbered by blinders and may allow individuals in the corporation to remain largely unaccountable, often legally so as well as morally." Marshall B. Clinard and Peter C. Yeager, Corporate Crime (New York: Free Press, 1980), p. 44.

38. For a discussion of the global context of corporate power, see Caroline Bradley, Corporate Power and Control in the 1990s: The Transnational Dimension, 15 Oxford J. Legal Stud. 269 (1995); J. E. Parkinson, Corporate Power and Responsibility: Issues in the Theory of Company Law (Oxford: Clarendon Press, 1993).

39. Ralph Nader, Mark Green, and Joel Seligman, Taming the Giant Corporation (New York: Norton, 1976).

40. Resolution on Corporate Personhood in the City of Point Arena, April 25, 2000, available at: http://www.reclaimdemocracy.org/personhood/arcata_pointarena_resolutions .html.

41. PA Township Bans Corporate Involvement in Governing, December 9, 2002, available at: http://www.reclaimdemocracy.org/corporate_accountability/porter_township_ordi nance.html.

42. Wayne Township Environmental Protection Ordinance,1997, available at: http://www .celdf.org/scm/ord/ord2.asp.

43. Ralph Nader and Mark J. Green, eds., Corporate Power in America: The Ralph Nader Reader (New York: Grossman Publishers, 1973).

44. Richard L. Grossman, Wresting Governing Authority from the Corporate Class: Driving People into the Constitution, 1 Seattle J. Soc. Just. 147, 147–48 (2002).

45. Marjorie Kelly, The Divine Right of Capital: Dethroning the Corporate Aristocracy, new ed. (San Francisco: Berrett-Koehler Publishers, 2003), p. 159.

46. Nader and Green, *supra* note 43, at 100.

47. Ralph Nader, introduction to Corporate Predators: The Hunt for Mega-Profits and the Attack on Democracy, by Russell Mokhiber and Robert Weissman (Monroe, ME: Common Courage Press, 1999), p. ii.

48. It is interesting to note that when Clinard and Yeager wrote their wonderful 1980 treatise on corporate crime, the five largest corporations had a combined annual revenue of approximately $240 billion. As of 2004, the largest corporation in the world, Wal-Mart Stores, exceeded this aggregate revenue figure—with the next four corporations not so far behind. See Clinard and Yeager, *supra* note 37, at ix.

49. See, e.g., Sarah Anderson and John Cavanagh, Top 200: The Rise of Corporate Global Power (Washington, DC: Institute for Policy Studies, 2000); Richard J. Barnet and John Cavanagh, Global Dreams: Imperial Corporations and the New World Order (New York: Simon & Schuster, 1994).

50. Anderson and Cavanagh, *supra* note 49.

51. Id.

52. Arthur T. Hadley, The Constitutional Provision of Property in America, 64 Indep. 834, 836 (1908).

53. See, e.g., Bank of United States v. Deveaux, 9 U.S. (5 Cranch) 61 (1809).

54. Santa Clara County v. Southern Pac. R. Co., 118 U.S. 394 (1886); Minneapolis and St. L. Ry. Co. v. Beckwith, 129 U.S. 26 (1889); Noble v. Union River Logging R. Co., 147 U.S. 165 (1893).

55. See, e.g., First National Bank of Boston v. Bellotti, 435 U.S. 765 (1978); Central Hudson Gas & Electric Corp. v. Public Utilities Comm'n, 447 U.S. 557 (1980); Pacific Gas & Electric Co. v. Public Utilities Commission, 475 U.S. 1 (1986); Hale v. Henkel, 201 U.S. 43 (1906); United States v. Morton Salt Co., 338 U.S. 632 (1950); United States v. Martin Linen Supply Co., 430 U.S. 564 (1977); Pennsylvania Coal Co. v. Mahon, 260 U.S. 393 (1922); 147 U.S. at 165; United States v. R. L. Polk and Co., 438 F.2d 377 (6th Cir. 1971); Ross v. Bernhard, 396 U.S. 531 (1970). For a summary of corporate constitutional rights, see David Graver, Comment, Personal Bodies: A Corporeal Theory of Corporate Personhood, 6 U. Chi. L. Sch. Roundtable 235 (1999); Peter J. Henning, The Conundrum of Corporate Criminal Liability: Seeking a Consistent Approach to the Constitutional Rights of Corporations in Criminal Prosecutions, 63 Tenn. L. Rev. 793 (1996). The recently dismissed case of *Nike v. Kaskey*, 539 U.S. 654 (2003), represented an opportunity to restrict corporate personhood. Protecting corporate speech and personhood by seeing a distinction between commercial and political speech further erodes the power of citizenry and the meaning of democracy.

56. For a discussion of the role of the media, see, e.g., Philip Schlesinger et al., The Media Politics of Crime and Criminal Justice, 42 Brit. J. Soc. 397 (1991).

57. Id. at 23.

58. Kelly, *supra* note 45, at 160.

59. Dirty Money, Corporate Criminal: Donations to the Two Major Parties, *Corporate Crime Reporter*, July 3, 2003.

60. Mark Green, Selling Out: How Big Corporate Money Buys Elections, Rams through Legislation, and Betrays Our Democracy (New York: Regan Books, 2002), p. 3.

61. Carl J. Mayer, Personalizing the Impersonal: Corporations and the Bill of Rights, 41 Hastings L.J. 577, 661 (1990).

62. Gerhard O. W. Mueller, Mens Rea and the Corporation, 19 U. Pitt. L. Rev. 21, 22 (1957).

63. The notion of vicarious liability is tied to the idea of loyalty. Firms inherit liability from agents who act for the company, in the name of the company. This sense of loyalty is captured by William H. Whyte in his famed work *The Organizational Man* (New York: Doubleday, 1957). See, e.g., Donna M. Randall, Commitment and the Organization: The Organizational Man Revisited, 12 Acad. Mgmt. Rev. 460 (1987).

64. PCF was first proposed in Developments in the Law, Corporate Crime: Regulating Corporate Behavior through Criminal Sanctions, 92 Harv. L. Rev. 1227 (1979) [hereinafter Regulating Corporate Behavior]. Later it was discussed in relation to reactive corporate fault (RCF) or reactive corporate mens rea in Brent Fisse, Reconstructing Corporate Criminal Law: Deterrence, Retribution, Fault, and Sanctions, 56 S. Cal. L. Rev. 1141, 1200 (1983) ("Reactive and proactive corporate mens rea provide alternative bases of corporate blameworthiness, with proactive fault being relevant until the commission of the actus reus of an offense, and reactive fault being relevant thereafter.") Most recently, PCF was incorporated into the federal sentencing guidelines for organizations.

65. See, e.g., Anthony J. Daboub et al., Top Management Team Characteristics and Corporate Illegal Activity, 20 Acad. Mgmt. Rev. 138 (1995); Donald C. Hambrick and Phyllis A. Mason, Upper Echelons: The Organization as a Reflection of Its Top Managers, 9 Acad. Mgmt. Rev. 193 (1984).

66. The rationale for a due diligence defense in corporate criminal law was noted by Elkins: "The principal argument in favor of a defense of due diligence is that the purpose for imposing liability is to encourage the corporation's efforts to secure statutory compliance by its employees. That purpose is not served, this argument concludes, where the corporation has in fact diligently supervised its employees and they violate the statute contrary to express instructions." James R. Elkins, Corporations and the Criminal Law: An Uneasy Alliance, 65 Ky. L.J. 73 (1976).

67. Department of Justice, Banco Popular de Puerto Rico Enters Into Deferred Prosecution Agreement with U. S. Department of Justice, January 16, 2003, available at: http://www.fin cen.gov/bancofinalpr1.pdf#search='banco%20popular%20and%20press%20release%20and %20Chertoff'.

68. A variation of RCF was proposed earlier in Regulating Corporate Behavior, *supra* note 54, at 71. It was proposed for inclusion, along with PCF and corporate policy, in drafts of the Australian Model Crimes Code. See Brent Fisse, Corporate Criminal Responsibility, 15 Crim. L.J. 166, 173–74 (1991). Fisse (173–74) suggested that Australia adopt a two-condition test of corporate criminal responsibility: "(1) the external elements of the offence have been committed by a person for whose conduct the corporate defendant is vicariously responsible; and (2) the corporation has been at fault in one or other of the following ways: (a) by having a policy that expressly or impliedly authorizes or permits the commission of the offence or an offence of the same type; (b) by failing to take reasonable precautions or to exercise due precautions to prevent the commission of the offence or an offence of the same type; (c) by having a policy of failing to comply with a reactive duty to take preventive measures in response to having committed the external elements of the offence; or (d) by failing to take reasonable precautions or to exercise due diligence to comply with a reactive duty to take preventive measures in response to having committed the external elements of the offence." See also Brent Fisse, The Attribution of Criminal Liability to Corporations: A Statutory Model, 13 Sydney L. Rev. 277 (1991); Alfred A. Marcus and Robert S. Goodman, Victims and Shareholders: The Dilemmas of Presenting Corporate Policy During a Crisis, 34 Acad. Mgmt. J. 281 (1991).

69. A number of commentators have joined in calling for a consideration of corporate culture, personality, and ethos as culpability. See Pamela H. Bucy, Corporate Ethos: A Standard for Imposing Corporate Criminal Liability, 75 Minn. L. Rev. 1095 (1991); Ann Foerschler, Comment, Corporate Criminal Intent: Toward a Better Understanding of Corporate Misconduct, 78 Cal. L. Rev. 1287 (1990). Cf. Susan Key, Organizational Ethical Culture: Real or Imagined?, 20 J. Bus. Ethics 217 (1999); Linda K. Trevino, A Cultural Perspective on Changing and Developing Organizational Ethics, 4 Res. Organizational Change & Dev. 195 (1990).

70. See Bucy, *supra* note 69, at 1099, in which she argued that corporate ethos "results from the dynamic of many individuals working together toward corporate goals." Corporations should only be liable, Bucy further argued, where the entity acted purposely in relation to the criminal act. Accordingly, there is criminal liability "only if the corporation encouraged the criminal conduct at issue."

71. For an excellent treatment of policy in relation to culpability, see Peter A. French, Collective and Corporate Responsibility (New York: Columbia University Press, 1984).

72. There is a complexity to the attribution of blame that is often overlooked. See, e.g., Calvin Morrill et al., It's Not What You Do, but Who You Are: Informal Social Control, Social Status, and Normative Seriousness in Organizations, 12 Soc. F. 519 (1997).

73. The one notable exception to this is found in the Discussion Draft of the proposed Model Criminal Code of Australia, which used CE or corporate culture to convey the notion of "tacit authorization" or the "expectation of non-compliance." Both notions, according to the drafters, suggest corporate knowledge. See Australian Model Criminal Code § 501.3 (Discussion Draft 1992) at § 501.3.1. As noted in commentary, the code allows for evidence that the company's unwritten rules tacitly authorized noncompliance or failed to create a culture of compliance. It would catch situations where, despite formal documents appearing to require compliance, the reality was that noncompliance was expected, as with, for example, employees who know that if they do not break the law to meet production schedules, they will be dismissed.

74. See Ronald L. Gainer, The Culpability Provisions of the Model Penal Code, 19 Rutgers L.J. 575 (1988); Paul H. Robinson and Jane A. Grall, Element Analysis in Defining Criminal Liability: The Model Penal Code and Beyond, 35 Stan. L. Rev. 681 (1983).

75. Paul H. Robinson, A Brief History of Distinctions in Criminal Culpability, 31 Hastings L.J. 815 (1980).

76. See, Arthur Andersen L.L.P. v. United States, No. 04–368 (April 27, 2005).

77. Jennifer Moore, Corporate Culpability under the Federal Sentencing Guidelines, 34 Ariz. L. Rev. 743, 768 (1992).

78. For a discussion of these policies, see F. Joseph Warin and Jason C. Schwartz, Deferred Prosecution: The Need for Specialized Guidelines for Corporate Defendants, 23 J. Corp. L. 121 (1997).

79. Guidance on Prosecutions of Corporations, U.S. Department of Justice, June 16, 1999, reprinted in BNA Compliance Manual, 41 Prevention Corp. Liability 1200 (1999).

80. Id. at 4.

81. Id.

82. "In gauging the extent of the corporation's cooperation, the prosecutor may consider the corporation's willingness to identify the culprits within the corporation, including senior executive." Id. at 5.

83. "Although neither a corporation nor an individual target may avoid prosecution merely by paying a sum of money, a prosecutor may consider the corporation's willingness to make restitution and steps already taken to do so, as well as other remedial actions such as implementation [of] an effective corporate compliance program, improving an existing one, and disciplining wrongdoers, in determining whether to charge a corporation." Id. at 7.

84. "In evaluating a corporation's response to wrongdoing, prosecutors may evaluate the willingness of the corporation to discipline culpable employees of all ranks and the adequacy of the discipline imposed. The prosecutor should satisfy himself or herself that the corporation's focus is on the integrity and credibility of its remedial and disciplinary measures rather than on the protection of the wrongdoers." Id. at 8.

85. "For instance, the balance may tip in favor of prosecuting corporations in situations where the scope of the misconduct in a case is widespread and sustained within a corporate

division (or spread throughout pockets of the corporate organization). In such cases, the possible unfairness of visiting punishment for the corporation's crime upon shareholders may be of much less concern where those shareholders have substantially profited, even unknowingly, from widespread or pervasive criminal activity." Id.

86. Id.

87. Principles of Federal Prosecution of Business Organizations, United States Department of Justice, January 20, 2003, available at www.usdoj.gov/dag/cftf/corporate_guidelines .htm.

88. Id.

89. U.S. Sentencing Guidelines Manual § 8 (introductory commentary) (1998).

90. For a review of the sentencing guidelines in relation to the federal substantive criminal law, see William S. Laufer, Culpability and the Sentencing of Corporations, 71 Neb. L. Rev. 1049 (1992).

91. United States Sentencing Commission, Amendments to Chapter 8, 11. Effective Compliance and Ethics Programs in chapter 8 available at: http://www.ussc.gov/2004guid/RFMay 04_Corp.pdf. See Steven A. Lauer, Corporate Ethics Fine-tuned: New Sentencing Guidelines Expect Companies to Polish Their Compliance Programs, 27 LegalTimes 1 (2004); Keeping Compliance Training Programs Up To Date, Metropolitan Corp. Couns., June 2004, at 38.

92. More than eighty years later, the U.S. Sentencing Guidelines recognized the same equivalence. In provision after provision, the sentencing guidelines speak of organizational culpability as if the substantive criminal law somehow and somewhere took it seriously.

93. For a critical analysis of the notion of corporate intentionality, see Michael Keeley, Organizations as Non-Persons, 15 J. Value Inquiry 149, 152 (1981) ("It seems fairly clear that organizations have some collective properties of their own. It is not clear, however, that intentionality is among them.").

94. Stephanie Kirchgaessner, The Confessions of a Corporate Crime Fighter, *Financial Times*, September 6, 2005, p. 10.

95. Id.

96. Kristen Hays, Andersen Judge Rules on Impasse, Associated Press, June 14, 2002. See also Kristen Hays, Judge Rules Andersen Jurors Need Not Agree on Wrongdoer, *Detroit News*, June 15, 2002, available at www.detnews.com/2002/business/0206/15/business-515598.htm.

97. Hays, Andersen Judge Rules on Impasse, *supra* note 96.

98. Id.

99. Fortunately, the United States Supreme Court found the jury instructions on culpable mental states to be defective in Arthur Andersen L.L.P. v. United States, No. 04-368 (April 27, 2005). Unfortunately, the Court did little to fill the necessary gaps in the substantive corporate criminal law.

CHAPTER THREE

1. WorldCom, Inc., Form 8-K, United States Securities and Exchange Commission, June 9, 2003, p. 18.

2. See, e.g., Roosevelt Severe on the Equitable: Crooked Methods, He Says—Wants Federal Supervision, *New York Times*, June 22, 1905, p. 1.

3. William R. Givens, The Financial Situation, *New York Times*, July 19, 1903, p. 25.

4. Moral outrage over corporate abuse and corporate concentration was outdone only

by the debate over corporate punishment. Standard Oil Found Guilty, *New York Times*, April 14, 1907, p. 1; cf. Oil Trust Fine Denounced, *New York Times*, September 23, 1907, p. 2.

5. See Meir Dan-Cohen, Rights, Persons, and Organizations: A Legal Theory for Bureaucratic Society (Berkeley and Los Angeles: University of California Press, 1986).

6. Larry May, The Morality of Groups: Collective Responsibility, Group-Based Harm, and Corporate Rights (Notre Dame, IN: University of Notre Dame Press, 1987).

7. See also Diane Vaughan, Toward Understanding Unlawful Organizational Behavior, 80 Mich. L. Rev. 1377 (1982); Peter C. Yeager, Analyzing Corporate Offenses: Progress and Prospects, 8 Res. Corp. Soc. Performance & Pol'y 93, 104–12 (1986); Richard B. Stewart, Organizational Jurisprudence, 101 Harv. L. Rev. 371 (1987) (book review).

8. Cf. John Shepard Wiley Jr., Not Guilty by Reason of Blamelessness: Culpability in Federal Criminal Interpretation, 85 Va. L. Rev. 1021 (1999); Kenneth W. Simons, When Is Strict Criminal Liability Just?, 87 J. Crim. L. & Criminology 1075 (1997).

9. 464 F.2d 1000 (9th Cir. 1972).

10. Model Penal Code, § 2.07 (Proposed Official Draft 1962).

11. See Kathleen F. Brickey, Rethinking Corporate Liability Under the Model Penal Code, 19 Rutgers L.J. 593 (1988).

12. 275 N.E.2d 33 (Mass. 1971), cert. denied, 407 U.S. 914 (1972). See, e.g., United States v. NYNEX Corp., 788 F. Supp. 16 (D.D.C. 1992); United States v. Johns-Manville Corp., 231 F. Supp. 690 (E.D. Pa. 1963); State v. Garette, 699 S.W.2d 468 (Mo. Ct. App. 1985).

13. Howard M. Friedman, Some Reflections on the Corporation as Criminal Defendant, 55 Notre Dame L. Rev. 173, 179–80 (1979).

14. John Ladd, Morality and the Ideal of Rationality in Formal Organizations, 54 Monist 488, 493 (1970).

15. See James R. Elkins, Corporations and the Criminal Law: An Uneasy Alliance, 65 Ky. L.J. (1976). United States v. Empire Packing Co., 174 F.2d 16 (7th Cir.), cert. denied, 337 U.S. 959 (1949).

16. First Year Report to the President, Corporate Fraud Task Force, iii (2003).

17. See, e.g., Joel Prentiss Bishop, New Commentaries on the Criminal Law upon a New System of Legal Exposition, 8th ed., 2 vols. (Chicago: T. H. Flood, 1892), pp. 255–56.

18. See, e.g., United States v. Hayes Int'l Corp., 786 F.2d 1499 (11th Cir. 1986); United States v. Dye Constr. Co., 510 F.2d 78 (10th Cir. 1975); United States v. American Radiator & Standard Sanitary Corp., 433 F.2d 174 (3d Cir. 1970), cert. denied, 401 U.S. 948 (1971).

19. See, e.g., Apex Oil Co. v. United States, 530 F.2d 1291 (8th Cir.), cert. denied, 429 U.S. 827 (1976); United States v. Little Rock Sewer Comm., 460 F. Supp. 6, 9 (E.D. Ark. 1978).

20. *Working Papers of the National Commission on Reform of Federal Criminal Laws* (No. 168, 1970) [hereinafter *Working Papers*].

21. Report of the Federal Courts Study Committee 106 (1990) [hereinafter Federal Courts Study Committee]; see Gregory E. Maggs, Reducing the Costs of Statutory Ambiguity: Alternative Approaches and the Federal Courts Study Committee, 29 Harv. J. on Legis. 123 (1992).

22. See William S. Laufer, Culpability and the Sentencing of Corporations, 71 Nev. L. Rev. 1049, 1065–66 (1992).

23. Chief Justice Rehnquist acknowledged this in United States v. Bailey, 444 U.S. 394 (1980).

24. John Austin, Lectures on Jurisprudence; or, The Philosophy of Positive Law, 5th ed., 2

vols., ed. Robert Campbell (London: J. Murray, 1911), pp. xix–xx; Courtney Stanhope Kenny, Outlines of Criminal Law, 19th ed. (Cambridge: Cambridge University Press, 1966); John William Salmond, Salmond on Jurisprudence, 11th ed., ed. Glanville Williams (London: Sweet & Maxwell, 1957).

25. Drafters of the MPC were concerned that the breadth of the term intentionality in common language results in ambiguity. See Model Penal Code, *supra* note 10, § 2.02.

26. According to Williams, "Intention is, by definition, the desire that prevails and issues in action." Glanville Williams, Criminal Law: The General Part (London: Stevens, 1961), p. 48.

27. White argues that foreseeability plays a multiple role in intention. Alan R. White, Grounds of Liability: An Introduction to the Philosophy of Law (New York: Oxford University Press), p. 75.

28. See, e.g., *Working Papers, supra* note 20, at 123–24.

29. Other examples of small to medium-size firms include American Banknote Corp., a publicly traded company with more than $300 million in revenues, where the CEO and coconspirators perpetrated frauds and sham transactions that defrauded investors of more than $100 million.

30. Dan Morse, U.S. Closes Firm Accused of Fraud, *Wall Street Journal*, May 6, 2004, p. C3.

31. The Brown Commission consultant made reference to a man, rather than a corporation or entity. See *Working Papers, supra* note 20, at 124.

32. For a fascinating take on the notion of corporate knowledge, see Donald C. Langevoort, Agency Law Inside the Corporation: Problems of Candor and Knowledge, 71 U. Cin. L. Rev. 1187 (2003). The role of top management is considered by Vikramaditya S. Khanna, Should the Behavior of Top Management Matter?, 91 Geo. L.J. 1215 (2003).

33. Ultimately the trial court's instruction regarding the firm's "knowledge" led to a reversal by the United States Supreme Court; see Arthur Andersen, L.L.P., No. 4–368 (April 27, 2005).

34. 135 F.3d 484 (1998).

35. 135 F.3d at 492–93.

36. In England, the House of Lords decision in Regina v. Caldwell, [1982] A.C. 341 (H.L.), established an objective test of recklessness that has since been the source of much controversy. See R. A. Duff, et al., The Retreat from Subjectivism, 3 Oxford J. Legal Stud. 77 (1983).

37. For a theory of corporate recklessness and gross negligence, see Celia Wells, Corporations and Criminal Responsibility (Oxford: Clarendon Press, 1993). See also G. R. Sullivan, Expressing Corporate Guilt, 15 Oxford J. Legal Stud. 281 (1995).

38. Christopher D. Stone, Where the Law Ends: The Social Control of Corporate Behavior (New York: Harper & Row, 1975), p. 53.

39. Model Penal Code, *supra* note 10, § 2.02.

40. See, e.g., Vaughan, *supra* note 7.

41. See L. H. Leigh, The Criminal Liability of Corporations and Other Groups: A Comparative View, 80 Mich. L. Rev. 1508, 1514 (1982).

42. Culpability provisions are contained in Model Penal Code § 2.02(2)(a)–(d).

43. See United States v. Investment Enter., Inc., 10 F.3d 263, 269 n.9 (5th Cir. 1993) ("The defendant's purposeful contrivance to avoid learning of the illegal conduct may be established by either direct or circumstantial evidence.").

44. Morissette v. United States, 342 U.S. 246, 250 (1951).

45. See Gerald H. Gordon, Subjective and Objective Mens Rea, 17 Crim. L.Q. 355 (1975); Warren A. Seavey, Negligence—Subjective or Objective?, 41 Harv. L. Rev. 1 (1927); John E. Stannard, Subjectivism, Objectivism, and the Draft Criminal Code, 101 Law Q. Rev. 540 (1985).

46. Williams, *supra* note 26, at 100.

47. H. L. Pohlman, Justice Oliver Wendell Holmes and Utilitarian Jurisprudence (Cambridge, MA: Harvard University Press, 1984), pp. 26–29.

48. Oliver W. Holmes, The Common Law, ed. Mark DeWolfe Howe (Boston: Little, Brown, 1963), pp. 42–43.

49. Id. at 50–51.

50. Id. at 61–62.

51. See Dolores A. Donovan and Stephanie M. Wildman, Is the Reasonable Man Obsolete? A Critical Perspective on Self-Defense and Provocation, 14 Loy. L.A. L. Rev. 435, 451 (1981).

52. Holmes wrote: "Acts should be judged by their tendency under the known circumstances, not by the actual intent which accompanies them." Holmes, *supra* note 48, at 66.

53. According to Holmes, "in most cases, the question of knowledge is a question of the actual condition of the defendant's consciousness; the question of what he might have foreseen is determined by the standard of prudent man, that is, by general experience." Id. at 47; see Abrams v. United States, 250 U.S. 616, 621 (1919).

54. Herbert L. Packer, The Limits of the Criminal Sanction (Stanford, CA: Stanford University Press, 1968), pp. 128–29.

55. George P. Fletcher, The Theory of Criminal Negligence: A Comparative Analysis, 119 U. Pa. L. Rev. 401, 510 (1971).

56. Id. at 510.

57. Id. at 509.

58. Id. at 414.

59. Mental states have a permanent place in the criminal law. See, e.g., Stephen L. Golding, The Adjudication of Criminal Responsibility: A Review of Theory and Research, in Handbook of Psychology and Law, ed. Dorothy K. Kagehiro and William S. Laufer (New York: Springer-Verlag, 1992), 230.

60. Stephen J. Morse, The Guilty Mind: Mens Rea, in Handbook of Psychology and Law, *supra* note 59, at 207–10.

61. Kent Greenawalt, Law and Objectivity (New York: Oxford University Press, 1992), p. 112.

62. See, e.g., John C. Coffee Jr., "No Soul to Damn, No Body to Kick": An Unscandalized Inquiry into the Problem of Corporate Punishment, 79 Mich. L. Rev. 386, 397 (1981).

63. See Stephen A. Saltzburg, The Control of Criminal Conduct in Organizations, 71 B.U. L. Rev. 421, 422–29 (1991).

64. Empirical evidence of crime in large organizations was first reported in Edwin H. Sutherland, White Collar Crime (New York: Dryden Press, 1949). For recent evidence, see Cindy R. Alexander and Mark A. Cohen, New Evidence on the Origins of Corporate Crime, 17 Managerial & Decision Econ. 421 (1996) (finding larger firms more likely to have engaged in crime than smaller firms).

65. For an excellent discussion of models of organizational decision making in relation to law, see Michael B. Metzger, Organizations and the Law, 25 Am. Bus. L.J. 407, 420–36 (1987).

66. See V. Lee Hamilton and Joseph Sanders, Responsibility and Risk in Organizational Crimes of Obedience, 14 Res. Organizational Behav. 49 (1992) 246 n.

67. See John C. Coffee Jr., Beyond the Shut-Eyed Sentry: Toward a Theoretical View of Corporate Misconduct and an Effective Legal Response, 63 Va. L. Rev. 1099 (1977).

68. See Daniel R. Denison, Corporate Culture and Organizational Effectiveness (New York: Wiley, 1990).

69. See Daniel Katz and Robert L. Kahn, The Social Psychology of Organizations, 2d ed. (New York: Wiley, 1978); Lawrence B. Mohr, Explaining Organizational Behavior (San Francisco: Jossey-Bass, 1982); Diane Vaughan, Controlling Unlawful Organizational Behavior: Social Structure and Corporate Misconduct (Chicago: University of Chicago Press, 1983); Frederick Bird and James A. Waters, The Nature of Managerial Moral Standards, 6 J. Bus. Ethics 1 (1987); J. Longenecker, Management Priorities and Management Ethics, 4 J. Bus. Ethics 65 (1985); Joanne Martin and Caren Siehl, Organizational Culture and Counterculture: An Uneasy Symbiosis, 12 Organizational Dynamics 52 (1983); Barry M. Staw and Eugene Szwajkowski, The Scarcity-Munificence Component of Organizational Environments and the Commission of Illegal Acts, 20 Admin. Sci. Q. 345 (1975); Linda Trevino, A Cultural Perspective on Changing and Developing Organizational Ethics, 4 Res. Organizational Change & Dev. 195 (1990); Linda Trevino, Ethical Decision Making in Organizations: A Person-Situation Interactionist Model, 11 Acad. Mgmt. Rev. 601 (1986); Bart Victor and John B. Cullen, The Organizational Bases of Ethical Work Climates, 33 Admin. Sci. Q. 101 (1988).

70. Clinard and Yeager noted that "decentralization of decisionmaking is almost by definition, accompanied by the establishment of elaborate hierarchies, based on authority position and functional duties. Marshall B. Clinard and Peter Yeager, Corporate Crime (New York: Free Press, 1980), p. 7.

71. Cf. Michael B. Metzger, Organizations and the Law, 25 Am. Bus. L.J. 407, 416–17 (1987).

72. According to the United States Sentencing Commission, "for all practical purposes, most closely-held organizations are the alter egos of their owner-managers." U.S. Sentencing Guidelines Manual, 8C3.4 commentary; see Table 3.

73. See Michael L. Benson et al., Community Context and the Prosecution of Corporate Crime, in White-Collar Crime Reconsidered, ed. Kip Schlegel and David Weisburd (Boston: Northeastern University Press, 1992), p. 280.

74. H. L. A. Hart, Punishment and Responsibility: Essays in the Philosophy of Law (Oxford: Clarendon Press, 1968), pp. 38–39.

75. See, e.g., Henry M. Hart Jr., The Aims of the Criminal Law, 23 Law & Contemp. Probs. 401, 410 (1958).

76. Liparota v. United States, 471 U.S. 419, 423 (1985).

77. Cf. Kenneth Mann, Punitive Civil Sanctions: The Middle-ground between Criminal and Civil Law, 101 Yale L. Rev. 1795 (1992).

78. United States v. Nearing, 252 F. 223, 231 (S.D.N.Y. 1918).

79. See Arave v. Creech, 113 S. Ct. 1534, 1541 (1993) ("The law has long recognized that a defendant's state of mind is not a 'subjective' matter, but a fact to be inferred from the surrounding circumstances.").

80. Model Penal Code, § 2.02; see also James Marshall, Intention in Law and Society (New York: Funk & Wagnalls, 1968), pp. 137–66.

81. United States Postal Serv. Bd. of Governors v. Aikens, 460 U.S. 711, 716–17 (1983) (quoting Edgington v. Fitzmaurice, 29 Ch. D. 459, 483 (Ch. 1885)).

82. Jerome Hall wrote that since most defendants are reasonable men, both the objective method of fact-finding and the objective standard of liability function accurately and justly in most cases. In other words, although the defendant is directly and verbally held to the objective standard of liability, that standard in most cases also fits the defendant's actual (subjective) state of mind. Jerome Hall, General Principles of Criminal Law (Indianapolis: Bobbs-Merrill, 1960), p. 97.

83. Hall noted the same convergence with the "reasonable man" method, or the objective appraisal of evidence used in constructive liability. Id. at 155.

84. Letter from William P. Barr, U.S. attorney general, to commissioner of SEC (March 19, 2003) (on file with author), p. 1, available at: http://www.corporatecrimereporter.com/sec-letter-final.pdf.

85. Id. p. 4.

CHAPTER FOUR

1. Enron, Code of Ethics, July 2000.

2. Robert W. Lear and Boris Yavitz, Boards on Trial, Chief Executive, Oct. 2000, at 40 (ranked as third-best board in the United States).

3. Russ Banham, Andrew S. Fastow—Enron Corporation, Category: Capital Structure Management, How Enron Financed Its Amazing Transformation from Pipelines to Piping Hot, CFO Magazine, October 1, 1999 (lauded for "ground-breaking strategy" in creating an innovative capital structure).

4. Kevin B. Huff, The Role of Corporate Compliance Programs in Determining Corporate Criminal Liability: A Suggested Approach, 96 Colum. L. Rev. 1252 (1996); William S. Laufer, Corporate Culpability and the Limits of Law, 6 Bus. Ethics Q. 311 (1996); Note, Growing the Carrot: Encouraging Effective Corporate Compliance, 109 Harv. L. Rev. 1783 (1996).

5. See generally ALI-ABA, Organizing for Corporate Compliance: Avoid Corporate Lawbreaking through Preventive Lawyering (Philadelphia, PA: ALI-ABA, 1992); William S. Laufer and Diana C. Robertson, Corporate Ethics Initiatives as Social Control, 16 J. Bus. Ethics 1029 (1997). For a discussion of the discovery of compliance as a growth industry, see Stuart Auerbach, Company Lawyers in Shadows at Seminar on Crime, Washington Post, October 16, 1977, p. A4; George P. Stamas and Joanne F. Catanese, Compliance Programs Create a Shield from Corporate Wrongs, 37 Legal Times (February 24, 1997). See also William S. Laufer, Integrity, Diligence, and the Limits of Good Corporate Citizenship, 34 Am. Bus. L.J. 157 (1996) (arguing that the sentencing guidelines have shifted discretion from the judiciary to prosecutors and regulators); William S. Laufer, Corporate Bodies and Guilty Minds, 43 Emory L.J. 647 (1994) (suggesting how corporate culpability and liability may be reconceptualized as constructive fault); Steven D. Walt and William S. Laufer, Corporate Criminal Liability and the Comparative Mix of Sanctions, in White-Collar Crime Reconsidered, ed. Kip Schlegel and David Weisburd (Boston: Northeastern University Press, 1992) (discussing the relation between liability rules and corporate sanctions). For a discussion of Chapter Eight prescriptions, see Jeffrey M. Kaplan and George F. Meierhofer Jr., Compliance Programs on Trial, Preventive L. Rep., Spring 1997, at 27 (discussing compliance initiatives in the securities industry).

6. See, e.g., John H. Baker, Who Wants to Buy Preventive Law?, Preventive L. Rep., Fall 1995, at 21 (noting how compliance may be marketed as a product).

7. Neil S. Cartusciello, The Con Edison Case & Emerging Principles of Corporate Prosecution, Bus. Crimes Bull., May 1995, at 1, 3.

8. Susan P. Shapiro, The Road Not Taken: The Elusive Path to Criminal Prosecution for White-Collar Offenders, 19 Law & Soc'y Rev. 179 (1985); John Hagen, I. Nagel, and Celesta A. Albonetti, The Social Organization of White-Collar Sanctions: A Study of Prosecution and Punishment in the Federal Courts, in White-Collar and Economic Crime: Multidisciplinary and Cross-National Perspectives, ed. Peter Wickman and Timothy Dailey (Lexington, MA: Lexington Books, 1982).

9. Robert S. Litt, The Experience and Views of the Enforcement Community, in Proceedings of the Second Symposium on Crime and Punishment in the United States, Corporate Crime in America: Strengthening the "Good Citizen" Corporation, September 7–8, 1995 (Washington, D.C.: United States Sentencing Commission), p. 306. The following companies entered into non-prosecution agreements between 1993 and 2006: American Electric Power; Adelphia Communications; Aetna; Aurora Foods; Bank of New York; Coopers and Lybrand; Hilfiger; John Hancock Mutual Life; Lazard Freres; MCI; Merrill Lynch; Micrus Corporation; Salomon Brothers; Sequa; Shell Oil; and Symbol Technologies. Deferred prosecution agreements were executed with: AIG; America On-Line; Arthur Andersen; BDO Seidman; Banco Popular; Bristol Myers Squibb; Canadian Imperial Bank of Commerce; Computer Associates; InVision Technologies; KPMG; MCI; Monsanto; New York Racing Association; PNC Financial; Prudential Securities, and Sears. See Crime without Conviction: The Rise of Degerred Prosecution Agreements, Corporate Crime Reporter, Special Report, December 28, 2005, available at http://www.corporatecrimereporter.com/deferredreport.htm. For an insightful review of these agreements, see Benjamin M. Greenblum, What Happens to a Prosecution Deferred? Judicial Oversight of Corporate Deferred Prosecution Agreements, 105 Colum. K. Rev. 1863 (2005).

10. See, e.g., Gary R. Weaver et al., Corporate Ethics Programs as Control Systems: Influences of Executive Commitment and Environmental Factors, 42 Acad. Mgmt. J. 41 (1999); Toni Makkai and Valerie Braithwaite, Professionalism, Organizations, and Compliance, 18 Law & Soc. Inquiry 33 (1993).

11. See, e.g., David Weil, If OSHA Is So Bad, Why Is Compliance So Good?, 27 Rand J. Econ. 618 (1996); Ana-Maria Wahl and Steven E. Gunkel, Due Process, Resource Mobilization, and the Occupational Safety and Health Administration, 1971–1996: The Politics of Social Regulation in Historical Perspective, 46 Soc. Probs. 591 (1999).

12. These games vary across industries and regulatory environments. They extend beyond the traditional two-player prisoner's dilemma (cooperating or defecting regulatory agency and firm) described in some detail by Ian Ayres and John Braithwaite in Tripartism: Regulatory Capture and Empowerment, 16 Law & Soc. Inquiry 435 (1991) and subsequent collaborations. See, e.g., John Braithwaite, To Punish or Persuade: Enforcement of Coal Mine Safety (Albany, NY: State University of New York Press, 1985); John Braithwaite, Corporate Crime in the Pharmaceutical Industry (London: Routledge & Kegan Paul, 1984); Peter Grabosky and John Braithwaite, eds., Of Manners Gentle: Enforcement Strategies of Australian Business Regulatory Agencies (Melbourne: Oxford University Press, 1986); John Braithwaite, The Nursing Home Industry, 18 Crime & Just. 11 (1993).

13. John Braithwaite's work on corporate regulation, liability, and sanction is noteworthy and quite accessible; see e.g., Brent Fisse and John Braithwaite, Impact of Publicity of Corporate Offenders (New York: State University of New York Press, 1983); Braithwaite, Corporate Crime and the Pharmaceutical Industry, *supra* note 12; Braithwaite, To Punish or Persuade, *supra* note 12; Grabosky and Braithwaite, Of Manners Gentle, *supra* note 12; Ian

Ayres and John Braithwaite, Responsive Regulation: Transcending the Deregulation Debate (New York: Oxford University Press, 1992); Brent Fisse and John Braithwaite, Corporations, Crime and Accountability (Cambridge: Cambridge University Press, 1993); John Braithwaite, Restorative Justice and Responsive Regulation (Oxford: Oxford University Press, 2002). For an interesting compilation of Braithwaite's work, see John Braithwaite, Regulation, Crime, and Freedom (Aldershot: Dartmouth, 2000).

14. Christine Parker, Is There a Reliable Way to Evaluate Organizational Compliance Programs? (September 2002) (unpublished manuscript, on file with the Australian Institute of Criminology), p. 2, available at: http://www.aic.gov.au/conferences/regulation/parker.pdf #search='christine%20parker%20permeable%20and%20self%20regulation'.

15. Organisation for Economic Cooperation and Development (OECD), Reducing the Risk of Policy Failure: Challenges for Regulatory Compliance (2000), p. 10, available at: http://www.oecd.org/dataoecd/48/54/1910833.pdf. See Philip A. Wellner, Effective Compliance Programs and Corporate Criminal Prosecutions, 27 Cardozo L. Rev. 497 (2005).

16. Consider research on diversion, e.g., Shapiro, *supra* note 8.

17. William B. Lytton and Winthrop M. Swenson, The Effective Answer to Corporate Misconduct: Public Sector Encouragement of Private Sector Compliance Programs, ACCA Docket 20, no. 10 (2002).

18. Research on the rationality of corporate offending reveals the complexity of any successful compliance regime. See, e.g., Raymond Paternoster and Sally Simpson, Sanction Threats and Appeals to Morality: Testing a Rational Choice Model of Corporate Crime, 30 Law & Soc'y Rev. 549 (1996). See also Sally S. Simpson, The Decomposition of Antitrust: Testing a Multi-Level, Longitudinal Model of Profit-Squeeze, 51 Am. Soc. Rev. 859 (1986). Add to this complexity the very ways in which corporate crime is both defined and conceived; see, e.g., V. Lee Hamilton and Joseph Sanders, Corporate Crime through Citizens' Eyes: Stratification and Responsibility in the United States, Russia, and Japan, 30 Law & Soc'y Rev. 513 (1996); Eugene Szwajkowski, Organizational Illegality: Theoretical Integration and Illustrative Application, 10 Acad. Mgmt. Rev. 558 (1985).

19. The following three policies are representative of the concessions now available to cooperative companies. First, the Environmental Protection Agency (EPA) will generally elect not to recommend criminal prosecution for any company that satisfies at least conditions 2 through 9 below, so long as its self-policing, discovery, and disclosures were conducted in good faith and the entity adopts a systematic approach to preventing recurrence of the violation.

1. *Systematic discovery of the violation through an environmental audit or a compliance management system.* The violation must have been discovered through either (a) an environmental audit, or (b) a compliance management system that reflects due diligence in preventing, detecting, and correcting violations.

2. *Voluntary discovery.* The violation must have been identified voluntarily, and not through a monitoring, sampling, or auditing procedure that is required by statute, regulation, permit, judicial or administrative order, or consent agreement.

3. *Prompt disclosure.* The entity must disclose the violation in writing to the EPA within 21 calendar days after discovery.

4. *Discovery and disclosure independent of government or third-party plaintiff.* The entity must discover the violation independently. That is, the violation must be discovered and

identified before EPA or another government agency likely would have identified the problem either through its own investigative work or from information received through a third party.

5. *Correction and remediation.* The entity must remedy any harm caused by the violation and expeditiously certify in writing to appropriate federal, state, and local authorities that it has corrected the violation.

6. *Prevent recurrence.* The regulated entity must agree to take steps to prevent a recurrence of the violation after it has been disclosed. Preventive steps may include, but are not limited to, improvements to the entity's environmental auditing efforts or compliance management system.

7. *No repeat violations.* Repeat offenders do not receive audit policy credit.

8. *Other violations excluded.* The policy excludes violations that result in serious actual harm to the environment or which may have presented an imminent and substantial endangerment to public health or the environment.

9. *Cooperation.* The entity must cooperate as required by the EPA and provide the agency with the information it needs. The entity must not hide, destroy, or tamper with possible evidence following discovery of potential environmental violations.

Available at:

http://www.epa.gov/compliance/resources/policies/incentives/auditing/finalpolstate.pdf.

Second, the Antitrust Division of the Department of Justice will grant leniency to a corporation reporting illegal activity before an investigation has begun, if the following six conditions are met:

1. At the time the corporation comes forward to report the illegal activity, the division has not received information about the illegal activity being reported from any other source.

2. The corporation, upon its discovery of the illegal activity being reported, took prompt and effective action to terminate its part in the activity.

3. The corporation reports the wrongdoing with candor and completeness and provides full, continuing, and complete cooperation to the division throughout the investigation.

4. The confession of wrongdoing is truly a corporate act, as opposed to isolated confessions of individual executives or officials.

5. Where possible, the corporation makes restitution to injured parties.

6. The corporation did not coerce another party to participate in the illegal activity and clearly was not the leader in, or originator of, the activity.

Available at: http://www.usdoj.gov/atr/public/speeches/2247.pdf.

And finally, according to OSHA, where a voluntary self-audit identifies a hazardous condition and the employer has corrected the condition prior to the initiation of an inspection and taken appropriate steps to prevent a recurrence of the violative condition, OSHA will not issue a citation, even if the condition existed within the six-month limitations period during which OSHA is authorized to issue citations. Where a self-audit identifies a hazardous condition and the employer promptly takes measures to correct the condition and provides interim employee protection, but has not completely corrected the condition when an OSHA inspection occurs, OSHA will treat the audit report as evidence of good faith, which may lead to a substantial reduction in a civil penalty. This policy does not require the disclosure of violations discovered during an audit to qualify for forbearance or mitigation of penalties. OSHA, Final Policy Concerning Voluntary Safety and Health Self-Audits (July 28, 2000), available at: http://www.osha.gov/pls/oshaweb/owadisp .showdocument?p_table=FEDERAL_REGISTER&p_id=16434.

20. Richard F. Duffy, Measuring the Success of Compliance and Enforcement Programs (proceedings from Fourth International Conference on Environmental Compliance and Enforcement, Chaing Mai, Thailand, April 22–26, 1996), available at: http://www.inece.org/ 4thvol1/duffy2.pdf.

21. Christine Parker and Natalie Stepanenko, Compliance and Enforcement Project: Preliminary Research Report (August 2003) (on file with Centre for Competition and Consumer Policy, Australian National University), available at: http://www.cccp.anu.edu.au/ Preliminary Research Report.pdf.

22. See, Donald C. Langevoort, Monitoring: The Behavioral Economics of Corporate Compliance with Law, 2002 Colum. Bus. L. Rev. 71.

23. Harvey S. James Jr., Estimating OSHA Compliance Costs, 31 Pol'y Stud. 321 (1998).

24. See Marie McKendall et al., Ethical Compliance Programs and Corporate Illegality: Testing the Assumptions of the Corporate Sentencing Guidelines, 37 J. Bus. Ethics 367 (2002); M. Mathews, Codes of Ethics: Organizational Behavior and Misbehavior, Res. Corp. Soc. Performance & Pol'y (1987); Marie A. McKendall and John A. Wagner III, Motive, Opportunity, Choice, and Corporate Illegality, 8 Org. Sci. 624 (1997); E. Molander, A Paradigm for Design, Promulgation and Enforcement of Ethical Codes, 6 J. Bus. Ethics 619 (1987).

25. For a discussion of the effects of privatizing the law enforcement function, see Pamela H. Bucy, Privatizing Law Enforcement, 543 Annals 144 (1996).

26. Bayer Pleads Guilty in Medicaid Fraud Case, to Pay 5.5 Million Dollar Criminal Fine, $251 Million to Settle Civil Case, Glaxo to Pay $87 Million, 17 Corporate Crime Reporter 1 (2003).

27. Program for Legal Compliance and Corporate Responsibility at Bayer, available at: http://www.bayer.com/medien/pages/1878/corporate_compliance_en.pdf.

28. Cf. Constance E. Bagley and Karen L. Page, The Devil Made Me Do It: Replacing Corporate Directors' Veil of Secrecy with the Mantle of Stewardship, 36 San Diego L. Rev. 897 (1999).

29. For a discussion of Enron in relation to gatekeeper risk, managerial incentives, and herding/persistence bias, see John C. Coffee Jr., *What Caused Enron?: A Capsule Social and Economic History of the 1990s* (Columbia Law Sch., Working Paper No. 214, January 20, 2003); John C. Coffee Jr., *Understanding Enron: It's About the Gatekeepers, Stupid* (Columbia Law Sch., Working Paper No. 207, July 30, 2002). See also Jeffrey N. Gordon, *Governance Failures of the Enron Board and the New Information Order of Sarbanes-Oxley* (Columbia Law Sch., Working Paper No. 216, March 2003). For a review of shareholder incentives to monitor officers, see Richard Posner, The Economics of Business Scandals and Financial Regulation (October 2002) (unpublished manuscript, on file with author).

30. References to corporate governance seemed to be added to compliance-related standards as an afterthought. See, e.g., the consideration of corporate governance in the Thompson Memo ("In evaluating compliance programs, prosecutors may consider whether the corporation has established corporate governance mechanisms that can effectively detect

and prevent misconduct. For example, do the corporation's directors exercise independent review over proposed corporate actions rather than unquestioningly ratifying officers' recommendations; are the directors provided with information sufficient to enable the exercise of independent judgment; are internal audit functions conducted at a level sufficient to ensure their independence and accuracy; and have the directors established an information and reporting system in the organization reasonably designed to provide management and the board of directors with timely and accurate information sufficient to allow them to reach an informed decision regarding the organization's compliance with the law? *In re: Caremark,* 698 A.2d 959 (Del. Ct. Chan. 1996)).

31. Jeffrey M. Kaplan, The Sentencing Guidelines: The First Ten Years, Ethikos, November–December 2001, at 1.

32. Russell Mokhiber and Robert Weissman, Cracking Down on Corporate Crime, Really, available only online at: http://corpwatch.radicaldesigns.org/article.php?id=2949.

33. Coffee notes that that the facts of Enron are "maddeningly unique," making lessons about corporate governance difficult to learn. Coffee, *Understanding Enron, supra* note 29, at 3.

34. Ronald E. Berenbeim and Jeffrey M. Kaplan, Ethics Programs: The Role of the Board: A Global Study (New York: Conference Board, 2004).

35. John B. Radzin, Are You the Next Enron? Why You Might Be . . . and What to Do about It, Conference Board Executive Action, August 2002, at 2.

36. David Vogel, The Split Personality of Corporate America, Responsive Community, Winter 2002/2003, at 7, 8–9.

37. ERC, Insights 2000: A Report of the ERC Fellows Program 14 (2001).

38. See, e.g., Lawrence A. Cunningham, The Sarbanes-Oxley Yawn: Heavy Rhetoric, Light Reform (and It Just Might Work), 35 Conn. L. Rev. 915 (2003).

39. Robert A. G. Monks and Nell Minow, Corporate Governance, 2d ed. (Oxford: Blackwell, 2001), p. 192.

40. Working Directors, *New York Times,* March 11, 1939, p. 10.

41. Decoy Directors, *New York Times,* January 21, 1871, p. 4.

42. Congressional Study Accuses Penn Central Directors of "Mismanagement," *New York Times,* January 2, 1972, p. 33.

43. Suing Director Accused, *New York Times,* September 12, 1903, p. 5.

44. The Failure to Police Empire, *New York Times,* July 2, 1993, p. A14.

45. Arthur J. Goldberg, Debate on Outside Directors, *New York Times,* October 29, 1972, p. F1.

46. Stephen M. Bainbridge, Why a Board? Group Decisionmaking in Corporate Governance, 55 Vand. L. Rev. 1 (2002).

47. Id.

48. Ira M. Millstein and Paul W. MacAvoy, The Active Board of Directors and Performance of the Large Publicly Traded Corp., 98 Colum. L. Rev. 1283, 1289 (1998).

49. Grant Thorton, Corporate Governance in Practice or " . . . Don't Forget about Turnbull," p. 3, available at: www.scottishdirector.com/uploaded_docs/cgu_reports/grantthornton.pdf.

50. 698 A.2d at 970.

51. See, e.g., Carole L. Basri, Joseph E. Murphy, and Gregory J. Wallance, eds., Corporate Compliance: Caremark and the Globalization of Good Corporate Conduct (New York:

Practising Law Institute, 1998); Carole L. Basri, Joseph E. Murphy, and Gregory J. Wallance, eds., Corporate Compliance: After Caremark (New York: Practising Law Institute, 1997). According to Pitt and his colleagues, directors must ensure that managers demonstrate a respect and allegiance to the law; update codes; ensure that the corporation provides sufficient compliance-related training and education; provide an anonymous means of communicating unethical or illegal acts when observed by employees; maintain an awareness of relevant legal issues; and conduct the supervisory oversight of corporate internal controls. See Harvey L. Pitt et al., Director Duties to Uncover and Respond to Management Misconduct, Insights, June 1997, at 5, 8.

52. 325 F.3d 795 (7th Cir. 2003).

53. 242 F.3d 191 (4th Cir. 2001).

54. 239 F.3d 808 (6th Cir. 2001).

55. Robert J. Haft, Business Decisions by the New Board: Behavioral Science and Corporate Law, 80 Mich. L. Rev. 1 (1981).

56. Deborah Solomon and Cassell Bryan-Low, Companies Complain about Cost of Corporate-Governance Rules, Wall Street Journal, February 10, 2004, p. 4.

57. Ivy Xiying Zhang, Economic Consequences of the Sarbanes-Oxley Act of 2002 (January 10, 2005) (unpublished Ph.D. dissertation, William E. Simon Graduate School of Business Administration) (on file with author).

58. Id.

59. Jonathan Weil, Behind Wave of Corporate Fraud: A Change in How Auditors Work, Wall Street Journal, March 25, 2004, p. 1.

60. See, e.g., Catherine M. Daily et al., Corporate Governance: Decades of Dialogue and Data, 28 Acad. Mgmt. Rev. 371 (2003).

61. Unfortunately, this is far from a new issue. See Elliott J. Weiss and Donald E. Schwartz, Using Disclosure to Activate the Board of Directors, Law & Contemp. Probs., Summer 1977, at 63; Timothy F. Malloy, Disclosure Stories, 32 Fla. St. U. L. Rev. 617 (2005).

62. Robert W. Lear and Boris Yavitz, Boards on Trial, Chief Executive, October 2000, at 40.

63. Id.

64. Rhonda L. Rundle, Tenet Ex-Director Sees No Progress, Wall Street Journal, April 12, 2004, p. A12.

65. United States Sentencing Commission, Public Hearing of the Ad Hoc Advisory Group on Organizational Guidelines, Washington, DC, November 14, 2002, available at: http://www.ussc .gov/corp/ph11_02/agd1102.htm. See Paul Fiorelli, Will U.S. Sentencing Commission Amendments Encourage a New Ethical Culture Within Organizations?, 39 Wake Forest L. Rev. 565 (2004).

66. Id. Statement of James W. Conrad Jr., November 14, 2002.

67. If the recent case of In re the Walt Disney Co. Derivative Litigation is an indication of a trend, corporate reforms are moving courts further in the direction of individual liability. Individual directors who breach their duty of care by making decisions without adequate information were determined by the Delaware Chancery Court to be acting in bad faith. Memorandum Opinion, case no. 15452, May 28, 2003.

68. See, e.g., Michael M. Baylson, Getting the Demons into Heaven: A Good Corporate Compliance Program, Corp. Conduct Q., Winter 1992, at 33, 34.

69. For data from 1995 through 2002, see United States Sentencing Commission, Or-

ganizations Sentenced under Chapter Eight: Culpability Factors, available only online at: http://www.ussc.gov/corp/organizsp.htm.

70. See John Scalia Jr., An Update on Cases, in Proceedings, *supra* note 9, at 247.

71. See Baylson, *supra* note 68, at 35.

72. Litt, *supra* note 9, at 289.

73. Id. at 304.

74. Langevoort, *supra* note 22.

75. See Kirk S. Jordan and Joseph E. Murphy, Compliance Programs: What the Government Really Wants, in Corporate Compliance: How to Be a Good Citizen Corporation through Self-Policing, ed. Joseph E. Murphy and Gregory J. Wallance (New York: Practising Law Institute, 1996), p. 127 (discussing common elements of compliance programs in civil antitrust cases; civil and criminal settlements in environmental cases; health-care fraud cases; defense contracting fraud cases; and an assortment of other settled civil allegations).

76. Gary R. Weaver and Linda Klebe Trevino, Compliance and Values-Oriented Ethics Programs: Influences on Employees' Attitudes and Behavior, 9 Bus. Ethics Q. 315 (1999); Gary R. Weaver et al., Corporate Ethics Programs as Control Systems: Influences of Executive Commitment and Environmental Factors, 42 Acad. Mgmt. J. 41 (1999).

77. Professors Trevino and Weaver, along with their colleagues, are responsible for the most significant and important line of research revealing the effects of compliance strategies. Much of this work consists of employee surveys and thus reports on *perceptions* of compliance effectiveness. See, e.g., Linda Klebe Trevino et al., Managing Ethics and Legal Compliance: What Works and What Hurts, Cal. Mgmt. Rev., Winter 1999, at 131.

78. National Center for Preventative Law, Corporate Compliance Principles (Denver, CO: National Center for Preventative Law, 1997), p. iii. Regulators are generally unhelpful in their efforts to explain effectiveness; see Michael L. Shaw, How to Assess the Effectiveness of a Compliance Program, J. Health Care Compliance, 1999, at 44.

79. See also Jeffrey N. Gordon, *Governance Failures of the Enron Board and the New Information Order of Sarbanes-Oxley* (Columbia Law School, Working Paper No. 216, March 2003).

80. Edwin Unsworth, "Rogue Trader" Risks Covered by New Policy: First Buyer from U.S., *Business Insurance*, February 16, 1998, p. 55; Edwin Unsworth, Lloyd's Offers Cover for Rogue Trading, *Business Insurance*, October 13, 1997, p. 25. See generally Paul K. Freeman and Howard Kunreuther, Managing Environmental Risk through Insurance (Boston: Kluwer Academic Publishers, 1997).

81. See, e.g., R. Mark Keenan and Pablo Quiones, Unraveling the Mystery of Insurance Coverage for Criminal Losses, Managing Risk, May 1998, at 10; Thomas K. Bourke, Their Own Worst Enemies: What Companies Can Do to Guard Against Fidelity Losses, 56 Bus. Ins. (June 1992). For an old but interesting account, see Note, Liability Insurance for Corporate Executives, 80 Harv. L. Rev. 648 (1967).

82. For an outline of the common motivations for self-insurance, see Herbert S. Denenberg et al., Risk and Insurance, 2d ed. (Englewood Cliffs, NJ: Prentice-Hall, 1974), pp. 126–27.

83. Jon D. Hanson and Kyle D. Logue, The First-Party Insurance Externality: An Economic Justification for Enterprise Liability, 76 Cornell L. Rev. 129, 147 (1990) ("Fire extinguishers constitute a form of self-insurance; they are 'consumed' to reduce the expected cost of an accident.").

84. See Dana Freyer and Joseph E. Murphy, Obvious Legal Risks—Hidden Business Rewards, 3 Corp. Conduct Q. 8 (1994).

85. See Helvering v. Le Gierse, 312 U.S. 531 (1941) (insurance transactions require a transaction that involves both risk shifting and risk distribution).

86. See, e.g., James M. Fischer, The Presence of Insurance and the Legal Allocation of Risk, 2 Conn. Ins. L.J. 1 (1996).

87. See, e.g., Jill B. Berkely, Recent Developments in Self-Insurance Law, 33 Tort & Ins. L.J. 693 (1998) ("Self-insurance is a broad and relatively amorphous term that has been inconsistently used to describe any entity that lacks commercial insurance, either altogether or that otherwise retains ascertainable portions of its own risk.").

88. Denenberg, *supra* note 82, at 125.

89. Id.

90. This consideration raises, more generally, the problem of moral hazard. See Thomas S. Ulen, The Coasean Firm in Law and Economics, 18 J. Corp. L. 301 (1993) ("Moral hazard is an adverse consequence of having insurance. It is defined as the increased probability of an insurable loss that arises solely because a person has insurance.").

91. Ralph A. Winter, Moral Hazard and Insurance Contracts, in Contributions to Insurance Economics, ed. Georges Dionne (Boston: Kluwer Academic Publishers, 1991), p. 61.

92. For a discussion of the origins of moral hazard, generally, see Tom Baker, On the Genealogy of Moral Hazard, 75 Tex. L. Rev. 237 (1996).

93. An individual's care and activity level have distinct meanings. See Steven Shavell, On Moral Hazard and Insurance, 93 Q.J. Econ. 541 (1979).

94. See Baker, *supra* note 92, at 241.

95. Arrow's article sparked an invaluable debate over the incentives and disincentives created by government-sponsored health insurance; see Kenneth J. Arrow, Uncertainty and the Welfare Economics of Medical Care, 53 Am. Econ. Rev. 941 (1963); Mark V. Pauly, The Economics of Moral Hazard: Comment, 58 Am. Econ. Rev. 531 (1968); Kenneth J. Arrow, The Economics of Moral Hazard: Further Comment, 58 Am. Econ. Rev. 537 (1968).

96. See, e.g., Hanson and Logue, *supra* note 83; George L. Priest, A Theory of the Consumer Product Warranty, 90 Yale L.J. 1297 (1981); Howell E. Jackson, The Expanding Obligations of Financial Holding Companies, 107 Harv. L. Rev. 507 (1994); Mancur Olson, A Less Ideological Way of Deciding How Much Should Be Given to the Poor, Daedalus, Fall 1983, at 217.

97. See Winter *supra* note 91, at 63 ("The importance of moral hazard extends beyond the context of insurance to the entire paradigm of agency theory.").

98. Tom Baker did a wonderful job in undermining the logic of this "conventional lesson." He maintained that key assumptions supporting the economics of moral hazard are violated. See Baker, *supra* note 92, at 276.

99. After paying that minimum expenditure toward compliance necessary to shift liability downward, firms have reduced incentives to ensure against deviance. Organizations at the lower operating range of compliance are, for obvious reasons, most at risk. Here the cost is minimal, a primary objective of compliance is achieved, and, with an often less-than-genuine commitment of top management, deviance or pressures leading to deviance may be encouraged with little to no risk to the firm.

100. For a review of corporate crime causation theory, see Sally S. Simpson, Strategy, Structure, and Corporate Crime: The Historical Context of Anticompetitive Behavior, in New Directions in Criminological Theory: Advances in Criminological Theory, vol. 4, ed. Freda

Adler and William S. Laufer (New Brunswick, NJ: Transaction,1993), p. 71. See also Melissa S. Baucus and Janet P. Near, Can Illegal Corporate Behavior Be Predicted? An Event History Analysis, 34 Acad. Mgmt. J. 9 (1991); Charles W. L. Hill et al., An Empirical Examination of the Causes of Corporate Wrongdoing in the United States, 45 Hum. Rel. 1055 (1992); Jon M. Joyce, Effect of Firm Organizational Structure on Incentives to Engage in Price Fixing, Contemp. Pol'y Issues, October 1989, at 19; Szwajkowski, *supra* note 16.

101. See, e.g., Diane Vaughan, Toward Understanding Unlawful Organizational Behavior, 80 Mich. L. Rev. 1377 (1982) (discussing the crime in relation to the role of top management in establishing the norms and reward systems that shape the ethical conduct of subordinates); Note, Decisionmaking Models and Control of Corporate Crime, 85 Yale L.J. 1091 (1976) (noting the situations in which top management may direct, enable, or acquiesce to illegal activity). For an extensive discussion of the role of top management in corporate crime, see Marshall B. Clinard, Corporate Ethics and Crime: The Role of Middle Management (Beverly Hills, CA: Sage Publications, 1983), p. 71 ("In our survey, middle management was clearly of the opinion that the very nature of top management's position and its actual behavior is largely responsible for unethical or illegal corporate behavior.").

102. Anthony J. Daboub et al., Top Management Team Characteristics and Corporate Illegal Activity, 20 Acad. Mgmt. Rev. 138 (1995) (describing the consensus view that corporate crime is most often the result of the inactions of top management).

103. See Vaughn, *supra* note 101; M. David Ermann and Richard J. Lundman, Corporate and Governmental Deviance: Problems of Organizational Behavior in Contemporary Society, 3d ed. (New York: Oxford University Press, 1987), p. 8. Courts recognize the problem of control in their consideration of corporate liability; see Commonwealth v. Beneficial Fin. Co., 360 Mass. 188, 275, 275 N.E.2d 33, 83 (1971), cert. denied, 407 U.S. 914 (1972) ("In a large corporation, with many numerous and distinct departments, a high ranking corporate officer or agent may have no authority or involvement in a particular sphere of corporate activity, whereas a lower ranking corporate executive might have much broader power in dealing with a matter peculiarly within the scope of her authority.").

104. Videotape: Vision and Values (n.d.) (on file with author). This corporate videotape was distributed to new employees.

105. See, e.g., Christopher D. Stone, Where the Law Ends: The Social Control of Corporate Behavior (New York: Harper & Row, 1975) (discussing how top managers report in ways that make it difficult, if not impossible, to prove involvement in or complicity with illegal acts).

106. See John E. Conklin, "Illegal but Not Criminal": Business Crime in America (Englewood Cliffs, NJ: Prentice-Hall, 1977), p. 65 ("The delegation of responsibility and unwritten orders keep those at the top of the corporate structure remote from the consequences of their decisions and orders, much as the heads of organized crime families remain "untouchable" by the law."); John C. Coffee Jr., "No Soul to Damn: No Body to Kick": An Unscandalized Inquiry into the Problem of Corporate Punishment, 79 Mich. L. Rev. 386 (1981) (According to Coffee, decentralization "permits the central headquarters to insulate itself from responsibility for operational decisions while simultaneously pressuring for quick solutions to often intractable problems.").

107. Quoted in Comment, Increasing Community Control Over Corporate Crime—A Problem in the Law of Sanctions, 71 Yale L.J. 280, 303–4 (1961). See also Sanford H. Kadish, Some Observations on the Use of Criminal Sanctions in Enforcing Economic Regulations, 30 U. Chi. L. Rev. 423, 431–32 (1963).

108. ALI, Model Penal Code, Tentative Draft No. 4, § 149 (1955).

109. According to one of Clinard's respondents, "You get the pressure so strong from top management that you will make judgmental efforts to make things come out right even if you use unethical practices such as lying about production or marketing progress. Pressures can result in cutting corners, e.g., on quality; a corporation has got to be a going concern." Id. at 142.

110. Clinard, *supra* note 101, at 140 ("Middle management executives tended to feel that corporate pressures at their level were extensive and serious. Undue pressures from top management, they maintained, may result in unethical or illegal behavior.") The concept of winking may be traced back to Standard Oil Co. of Texas v. United States, 307 F.2d 120 (5th Cir. 1962); see also Steere Tank Lines, Inc., v. United States, 330 F. 719 (5th Cir. 1962).

111. See John M. Darcey, How Organizations Socialize into Evil Doing, in Codes of Conduct: Behavioral Research into Business Ethics, ed. David M. Messick and Ann E. Tenbrunsel (New York: Russell Sage Foundation, 1996) (for a discussion of the costs of disobeying orders from superiors to engage in unethical or illegal actions).

112. The effects of both winking and scapegoating are seen most clearly in organizations where there is significant diffusion and fragmentation of information and responsibility. Id. at 132.

113. See, e.g., James W. Coleman, The Theory of White Collar Crime: From Sutherland to the 1990s, in White-Collar Crime Reconsidered, ed. Kip Schlegel and David Weisburd (Boston: Northeastern University Press, 1992), p. 69 ("Numerous social scientists have commented on the way large corporations encourage a narrow pragmatic approach to organizational responsibilities among their employees, which discourages independent ethical judgment.").

114. Robert Jackall, Moral Mazes: The World of Corporate Managers (New York: Oxford University Press, 1988), p. 87.

115. Peter Cleary Yeager, Management, Morality, and Law: Organizational Forms and Ethical Deliberations, in Corporate Crime: Contemporary Debates, ed. Frank Pearce and Laureen Snider (Toronto: University of Toronto Press, 1995), p. 147.

116. Id. at 154.

117. Professor Yeager observed that, "these guiding values, policies, and goals appear to be both internally consistent and rationally related to the companies' legitimate purposes. But under the complex requirements of management in large organizations, managers often experience them as dictating contradictory choices, and ones often ethically (if not always legally) suspect." Id.

118. Yeager noted that "business hierarchies impart a characteristic moral stance to their managers, which typically minimizes many private moral concerns in the service of organizational ends." Id.

119. 360 Mass. 188 at 275.

120. It is far from oversimplification to say that the choice for a strained and burdened middle management is an attribution of incompetence—with the possibility of demotion or dismissal—or the taking of shortcuts that risk violations of law. For an extensive consideration of the problems and pressures of middle management, see Coffee, *supra* note 106, 396–400.

121. Baker, *supra* note 92, at 269.

122. See Sentencing Commissioner Predicts Compliance Efforts Will Only Become More Crucial to Success in Business, 4 Prevention Corp. Liability 8 (1996) (discussing the results

of research that found that common compliance practices actually "may contribute to a poor compliance environment.").

123. See David Yellen, Compliance Programs and Coordination of Corporate Sanctions, Bus. Crimes Bull., October 1995, at 6.

124. See Amitai Etzioni, The Moral Dimension: Toward a New Economics (New York: Free Press, 1990), p. 69 (Etzioni noted that "the stronger the moral underwriting of implicit contracts, the lower the transaction costs, resulting in less of a need to buy hedge protection.").

125. See Stephen J. Schulhofer, Criminal Justice Discretion as a Regulatory System, 17 J. Legal Stud. 43 (1988); Ann P. Bartel and Lacy Glenn Thomas, Direct and Indirect Effects of Regulation: A New Look at OSHA's Impact, 28 J.L. & Econ. 1 (1985); Frank H. Easterbrook, Criminal Procedure as a Market System, 12 J. Legal Stud. 289 (1983); James Vorenberg, Decent Restraint of Prosecutorial Power, 94 Harv. L. Rev. 1521 (1981); Eugene Bardach and Robert A. Kagan, Going by the Book: The Problem of Regulatory Unreasonableness (Philadelphia: Temple University Press, 1982).

126. See, e.g., Michael L. Benson and Francis T. Cullen, Combating Corporate Crime: Local Prosecutors at Work (Boston: Northeastern University Press, 1998); Ian Ayres and John Braithwaite, Responsive Regulation: Transcending the Deregulation Debate (New York: Oxford University Press, 1992); Braithwaite, Corporate Crime in the Pharmaceutical Industry, *supra* note 12; Braithwaite, To Punish or Persuade, *supra* note 12; R. Kagan and J. T. Scholz, The Criminology of the Corporation and Regulatory Enforcement Strategies, in Enforcing Regulation, ed. Keith Hawkins and John M. Thomas (Boston: Kluwer-Nijhoff, 1984); John T. Scholz, Voluntary Compliance and Regulatory Enforcement, 6 Law & Pol'y 385 (1984).

127. John Braithwaite, Enforced Self-Regulation: A New Strategy for Corporate Crime Control, 80 Mich. L. Rev. 1466 (1982); Fisse and Braithwaite, *supra* note 13, at 159.

128. For a discussion of the analogous issue in tort law, see John E. Calfee and Richard Craswell, Some Effects of Uncertainty on Compliance with Legal Standards, 70 Va. L. Rev. 965 (1984) (discussing the common problem of uncertainty about legal standards and the resulting problem of overcompliance or undercompliance).

129. See Mark Pastin, A Study of Organizational Factors and Their Effect on Compliance, in Proceedings, *supra* note 9.

130. See Lynn S. Paine, Managing for Organizational Integrity, 72 Harv. Bus. Rev. 106 (1994).

131. Jeffrey Sonnenfeld, Good Governance and the Misleading Myths of Bad Metrics, Acad. Mgmt. Executive, February 2004, at 108.

CHAPTER FIVE

1. See Sue Reisinger, Corporate Privilege in Fraud Cases Is at Stake, *National Law Journal*, April 22, 2003, p. 2. Legal briefs, complaints, press releases, and regulatory actions regarding McKesson are available at: www.sec.gov.cgi_bin/text-srch-sec?text=mckesson.

2. Legal briefs, complaints, press releases, and regulatory actions regarding Seaboard Inc. are available at: www.sec.gov.cgi_bin/text-srch-sec?text=seaboard.

3. Report of Investigation Pursuant to Section 21(a) of the Securities Exchange Act of 1934 and Commission Statement on the Relationship of Cooperation to Agency Enforcement Decisions, available at: www.sec.gov/litigation/investreport/34-44969.htm.

4. Id. at 1. See also Dale A. Oesterle, Early Observations on the Prosecutions of the Business

Scandals of 2002–2003: On Sideshow Prosecutions, Spitzer's Clash with Donaldson Over the Choice of Civil or Criminal Actions, and the Tough Tactic of Coerced Cooperation, 1 Ohio St. J. Crim. L. 443 (2004); Ashok M. Pinto, Cooperation and Self-Interest Are Strange Bedfellows: Limited Waiver of the Attorney-Client Privilege Through Production of Privileged Document in a Goverment Investigation, 106 W. Va. L. Rev. 359 (2004); Michael A. Simons, Vicarious Snitching: Criime, Cooperation, and "Good Corporate Citizenship", 76 St. John's L. Rev. 979 (2002).

5. Letter from Scott W. Muller and Carey R. Dunne, lawyers with Davis Polk & Wardell, (October 12, 1994) (on file with author).

6. Letter from Mary Jo White, United States attorney, Southern District of New York (October 27, 1994), p. 2 (on file with author).

7. Kurt Eichenwald, Serpent on the Rock (New York: HarperBusiness, 1995); Kathleen Sharp, In Good Faith (New York: St. Martin's Press, 1995).

8. See Principles of Federal Prosecution of Business Organizations, U.S. Dept. of Justice, January 20, 2003, available at: www.usdoj.gov/dag/cftf/corporate_guidelines.htm.

9. Securities and Exchange Commission (SEC) v. Worldcom, Inc., No. 02 Civ. 4963, opinion and order (S.D.N.Y. Jul. 7, 2003), p. 5. See also, Richard C. Breeden, Restoring Trust, Report to The Hon. Jed S. Rakoff, The United States District Court for the Southern District of New York on Corporate Governance for the Future of MCI, Inc., Corporate Monitor v. WorldCom, 2003 WL 21523992 (S.D.N.Y.).

10. SEC v. Worldcom Inc., *supra* note 9, at 15.

11. According to the chairman of the board of directors, Nicholas Katzenbach,

Since joining MCI's Board of Directors in July, 2002, I've had the opportunity to witness firsthand the company's absolute commitment to the highest standards of corporate governance and ethics.

That commitment is evident at every level of the company, beginning with its leadership. When Michael Capellas and the Board of Directors approved the separation of the roles of Chairman and CEO last year, it was another cornerstone in building a corporate governance model that is unsurpassed in American business.

Such leadership through example is mirrored throughout the MCI organization and embodied in its employees. It is a community marked by integrity, transparency and accountability. It is an organization with a committed Board of Directors and management team, including a revitalized finance and internal controls organization. In addition, as a leader in this era of enhanced corporate governance, MCI has established codes of ethics and business conduct, and governance and guiding principles that are truly corporate touchstones.

As MCI continues to deliver new solutions to the markets and customers it serves, it is the company's unwavering commitment to those touchstones—across the board, and at every level—that will define the company's value and success in the future.

I am proud to serve as Chairman of MCI's Board of Directors—and proud to serve a company so profoundly dedicated to serving its shareholders, customers, employees and the public-at-large with both innovation and integrity.

Nicholas Katzenbach, A Note from the Chairman of the Board of Directors, September 1, 2004, available at: http://global.mci.com/about/governance/.

12. See generally Diane Vaughan, Controlling Unlawful Organizational Behavior: Social Structure and Corporate Misconduct (Chicago: University of Chicago Press, 1983) (discussing corporate crime in relation to the complexity of the corporate form); M. David Ermann and Gary A. Rabe, Organizational Processes (Not Rational Choices) Produce Most Corporate Crimes, in Debating Corporate Crime, ed. William S. Lofquist, Mark A. Cohen, and Gary A. Rabe (Highland Heights, KY: Academy of Criminal Justice Sciences, 1997), p. 53 (arguing strongly for the consideration of organizational factors in accounting for corporate crime).

13. Mary Zey, The Subsidiarization of the Securities Industry and the Organization of Securities Fraud Networks to Return Profits in the 1980s, 26 Work & Occupations 50 (1999).

14. Ilene H. Nagel and Winthrop M. Swenson, The Federal Sentencing Guidelines for Corporations: Their Development, Theoretical Underpinnings, and Some Thoughts about Their Future, 71 Wash. U. L.Q. 205, 227 (1993).

15. Ian Ayres and John Braithwaite, Responsive Regulation: Transcending the Deregulation Debate (New York: Oxford University Press, 1992), p. 19. For an extension of Braithwaite's tripartite vision of corporate regulation, see Peter Grabosky, The System of Corporate Crime Control, in Contemporary Issues in Crime and Criminal Justice: Essays in Honor of Gilbert Geis, ed. Henry N. Pontell and David Shichor (Upper Saddle River, NJ: Prentice Hall, 2001), p. 137 (arguing in favor of an expanded view of corporate social control that relies significantly on complementary institutions and instruments).

16. For analogous reasoning with plea bargains, see generally Robert E. Scott and William J. Stuntz, Plea Bargaining as Contract, 101 Yale L.J. 1909 (1992) (discussing a plea bargain as a promissory exchange).

17. See generally Joseph F. Savage Jr. and Stephanie A. Martz, How Corporations Spell Relief: Substituting Civil Sanctions for Criminal Prosecution, Crim. Just., Spring 1996, at 10.

18. See Eugene Spector, Corporate Amnesty in Antitrust Suits: For Some Companies, an Offer Too Good to Refuse, *Legal Intelligencer*, March 22, 2000, at 9; see also Gary R. Spratling, Making Companies an Offer They Shouldn't Refuse: The Antitrust Division's Corporate Leniency Policy—An Update, in Corporate Compliance 2000, by Practicing Law Institute (New York: Practicing Law Institute, 2000), pp. 645–51 (arguing that companies should report antitrust violations and seek leniency instead of remaining silent).

19. F. Joseph Warin and Jason C. Schwartz, Deferred Prosecution: The Need for Specialized Guidelines for Corporate Defendants, 23 J. Corp. L. 121, 125 (1997) (discussing the nature of the trade for cooperation prior to the adoption of the Federal Prosecutorial Guidelines).

20. See Nancy Frank and Michael Lombness, Controlling Corporate Illegality: The Regulatory Justice System (Cincinnati, OH: Anderson, 1988), pp. 53–55 (discussing paradigms of regulatory oversight of corporations).

21. See, e.g., John T. Scholz, Cooperative Regulatory Enforcement and the Politics of Administrative Effectiveness, 85 Am. Pol. Sci. Rev. 115, 116 (1991) (raising concerns with the limitations of a deterrent style of regulation).

22. See generally Peter Grabosky and John Braithwaite, Of Manners Gentle: Enforcement Strategies of Australian Business Regulatory Agencies (Melbourne: Oxford University Press, 1986) (illustrating the limits of a deterrence style of regulation); John T. Scholz, Cooperation, Deterrence, and the Ecology of Regulatory Enforcement, 18 Law & Soc'y Rev. 179 (1984) (analyzing the role of egoistic cooperation in regulatory enforcement); John T. Scholz, Voluntary Compliance and Regulatory Enforcement, 6 Law & Pol'y 385 (1984) (analyzing enforcement strategies that require "voluntary compliance").

23. See generally Linda D. Maxfield and John H. Kramer, Substantial Assistance: An Empirical Yardstick Gauging Equity in Current Federal Policy and Practice (Washington, DC: U.S. Sentencing Commission, 1998) (reviewing the uneven application of substantial assistance in federal courts); Frank O. Bowman III, Departing Is Such Sweet Sorrow: A Year of Judicial Revolt on "Substantial Assistance" Departures Follows a Decade of Prosecutorial Indiscipline, 29 Stetson L. Rev. 7 (1999).

24. 212 U.S. 481 (1909), aff'd, 212 U.S. 500 (1909); see also William S. Laufer, Corporate Bodies and Guilty Minds, 43 Emory L.J. 647, 651-58 (1994) (discussing origins of corporate criminal liability).

25. For a discussion of the concept of negotiated compliance, see Neil Shover, Donald A. Clelland, and John Lynxwiler, Enforcement or Negotiation: Constructing a Regulatory Bureaucracy (Albany, NY: State University of New York Press, 1986), pp. 11-15.

26. For a discussion of corporate and white-collar cooperators, see Ellen S. Podgor, White-Collar Cooperators: The Government in Employer-Employee Relationships, 23 Cardozo L. Rev. 795 (2002).

27. Press Release, White House, A New Ethic of Corporate Responsibility (July 9, 2002), available at http://www.whitehouse.gov/news/releases/2002/07/20020709.html.

28. Principles of Federal Prosecution of Business Organizations, *supra* note 8, at 1.

29. See, e.g., Alan F. Westin, ed., Whistle Blowing: Loyalty and Dissent in the Corporation (New York: McGraw-Hill, 1981); Marcia P. Miceli and Janet P. Near, Blowing the Whistle: The Organizational and Legal Implications for Companies and Employees (New York: Lexington Books, 1992); Janelle Brinker Dozier and Marcia P. Miceli, Potential Predictors of Whistle-Blowing: A Prosocial Behavior Perspective, 10 Acad. Mgmt. Rev. 823 (1985); D. B. Greenberger et al., Oppositionists and Group Norms: The Reciprocal Influence of Whistle-Blowers and Co-Workers, 7 J. Bus. Ethics 527 (1987); Janet P. Near and Marcia P. Miceli, Effective Whistle Blowing, 20 Acad. Mgmt. Rev. 679 (1995). For the effect of Sarbanes-Oxley on forward whistle-blowing, i.e., prohibiting employers from retaliating against employees, see Robert G. Vaughn, America's First Comprehensive Statute Protecting Corporate Whistleblowers, 57 Admin. L. Rev. 1 (2005).

30. For a review of these and other cases, see First Year Report to the President: Corporate Fraud Task Force (Washington, DC: Dept. of Justice, 2003); Second Year Report to the President: Corporate Fraud Task Force (Washington, DC: Dept. of Justice, 2004).

31. Press Release, White House Press Briefing by SEC Chairman William Donaldson and Deputy Attorney General Larry Thompson, July 22, 2003, available at: www.whitehouse.gov/news/releases/2003/07/20030722-2.html.

32. See, e.g., T. R. Goldman, United States v. Potomac Electric Power Co., Legal Times, July 24, 1995, at 25.

33. For a discussion of scapegoating, the mechanism underlying RWB, see C. Allen Carter, Kenneth Burke and the Scapegoat Process (Norman: University of Oklahoma Press, 1996), pp. 54-136 (discussing a language-based analysis of the scapegoat tendency); and Sylvia Brinton Perera, The Scapegoat Complex: Toward a Mythology of Shadow and Guilt (Toronto: Inner City Books, 1986), pp. 34-72 (offering a Jungian analysis of the scapegoat phenomenon). For scapegoating in relation to corporations, see generally P. Eddy Wilson, The Fiction of Corporate Scapegoating, 12 J. Bus. Ethics 779 (1993) (providing evidence of this practice in complex organizations); and Jeffrey J. Bailey, Individual Scapetribing and Responsibility Ascriptions, 16 J. Bus. Ethics 47 (1997) (discussing parallel responsibility ascriptions).

34. See, e.g., Joyce Rothschild and Terrance D. Miethe, Whistleblower Disclosures and Management Retaliation: The Battle to Control Information about Organization Corruption, 26 Work & Occupations 107 (1999).

35. See, e.g., John C. Coffee Jr., Corporate Criminal Responsibility, in Encyclopedia of Crime and Justice, ed. Sanford H. Kadish (New York: Free Press, 1983), pp. 253, 260 ("Moreover, an insistence on finding a responsible individual decision-maker might produce a scapegoat system of criminal justice, in which lower-echelon operating officials would probably bear the primary responsibility and risk of exposure.").

36. Brent Fisse and John Braithwaite, Corporations, Crime and Accountability (Cambridge: Cambridge University Press, 1983), p. 185.

37. Id.

38. Bridget M. Hutter, Structure Model: Reforming Regulation, in Debating Corporate Crime, ed. W. S. Lofquist, Mark A. Cohen, and Gary A. Rabe (Cincinnati: Anderson, 1997), p. 208.

39. For a discussion of the role of scapegoating in assuring the long-term viability of an offender, see Tom Douglas, Scapegoats: Transferring Blame (London: Routledge, 1995), pp. 13–50.

40. Principles of Federal Prosecution of Business Organizations, *supra* note 8.

41. Laurie P. Cohen, Prosecutors' New Tactics Turn Companies against Employees, *Wall Street Journal*, June 4, 2004, p. 1 (quoting Jan Handzik, former counsel to the chief operating officer of Homestore.com in a technical fraud prosecution).

42. Id.

43. Refusing to talk, Dynegy's Olis Goes to Prison, *Wall Street Journal*, May 20, 2004, B1. Qwest Ex-Executives' Lawyers Claim Clients Were Sacrificed, *Wall Street Journal*, April 6, 2004, p. C5.

44. See, e.g., Diana E. Murphy, The Federal Sentencing Guidelines for Organizations: A Decade of Promoting Compliance and Ethics, 87 Iowa L. Rev. 697 (2002).

45. Interestingly, concerns over protecting employee rights were raised by early advocates of a regulatory partnership with business. See Joseph E. Murphy, Corporate Counsel's Role in Interactive Compliance, in Corporate Lawbreaking and Interactive Compliance: Resolving the Regulation-Deregulation Dichotomy, ed. Jay A. Sigler and Joseph E. Murphy (New York: Quorum Books, 1991), p. 91, 102.

46. See David A. Dana, The Perverse Incentives of Environmental Audit Immunity, 81 Iowa L. Rev. 969, 970 (1996).

47. David N. Zornow and Keith D. Krakaur, On the Brink of a Brave New World: The Death of Privilege in Corporate Criminal Investigations, 37 Am. Crim. L. Rev. 147, 147 (2000) (considering the role of corporate counsel in organizations that have identified criminal acts); see also Jed S. Rakoff, The Corporation as Policeman: At What Price?, N.Y. L.J., January 9, 1992, at 3 (discussing the conflict in incentives from the sentencing guidelines).

48. See *infra* note 54 (discussing the role of cooperation in criminal prosecution).

49. See, e.g., Zornow & Krakaur, *supra* note 47, at 148; id.

50. Peter Bowal, Expensive Day at the Office: Can Corporations Indemnify Their Agents Who Suffer Personal Liability for Regulatory Offenses?, 45 U. Toronto L.J. 247 (1995); Pamela H. Bucy, Indemnification of Corporate Executives Who Have Been Convicted of Crimes: An Assessment and Proposal, 24 Ind. L. Rev. 279 (1991); Bennett L. Ross, Special Project, Protecting Corporate Directors and Officers: Insurance and Other Alternatives, 40 Vand.

L. Rev. 775 (1987); William S. Laufer, Corporate Liability, Risk Shifting, and the Paradox of Compliance, 52 Vand. L. Rev. 1343, 1358 (1999).

51. Jonny J. Frank, How to Cooperate with the Prosecutors, N.J. L.J., February 6, 1995, at 24 (discussing the escalating expectations of prosecutors and detailing collaborative initiatives).

52. For a discussion of flipping, see Laufer, *supra* note 50, at 1385.

53. Mark Hansen, Balancing a Client and the Corporation, 33 A.B.A. J. E-Report 5 (2004).

54. See, e.g., Ellen S. Podgor, White-Collar Cooperators: The Government in Employer-Employee Relationships, 23 Cardozo L. Rev. 795 (2002); Proposed Legislation Hammered Out by ERC Fellows Group Would Protect Whistleblowers, Results of Compliance Efforts, 41 BNA/ACCA Compliance Manual: Prevention of Corp. Liability 128 (1999); Richard Gruner, Avoiding Fines through Offense Monitoring, Detection, and Disclosure: The Race for Amnesty, in Corporate Compliance 2001, by Practising Law Institute (New York: Practising Law Institute, 2001), pp. 275, 282; Frank, *supra* note 51, at 26 ("A cooperating corporation acts, in effect, as a government informant.").

55. KPMG, 2000 Organizational Integrity Survey: A Summary 3 (2001).

56. Id. at 120.

57. Id. at 98.

58. Id. at 119, 114, 123, 125.

59. See Joshua Joseph, Ethics Resource Center's 2000 National Business Ethics Survey, vol. 1, How Employees Perceive Ethics at Work (Washington, DC: Ethics Resource Center, 2000), p. 19.

60. Howard W. Goldstein, Pavlov's Dogs and the Duty to Report a Client's Wrongdoing, N.Y. L.J., January 4, 2001, at 5.

61. See Warin and Schwartz, *supra* note 19, at 122 (describing prosecutorial guidelines and their relation to cooperation).

62. See Dominic Bencivenga, Prudential's Novel Deal: Plea Satisfies Business and Law Enforcement, N.Y. L.J., November 10, 1994, at 5; id.

63. Press releases from some of the more notable cases prosecuted by the United States attorney, Southern District of New York, highlight the expanding role of cooperation in corporate criminal prosecution. See, e.g., Sequa Corporation, 93–122, June 24, 1993; Prudential Securities, 94–151, October 27, 1994.

64. See E. Scott Gilbert, Keeping Your Nose Clean: Compliance Has to Be Thorough and Immediate, Corp. Legal Times, September 1995, at 5 ("Criminal prosecutions have been the death knell of many securities firms. E. F. Hutton is no longer in business because of criminal prosecutions on its cash management schemes. Drexel Burnham Lambert is out of business as well."). Jed S. Rakoff, Four Postulates of White-Collar Practice, N.Y. L.J., November 12, 1993, at 3.

65. See, e.g., Graham Hughes, Agreements for Cooperation in Criminal Cases, 45 Vand. L. Rev. 1, 15 (1992) (reviewing the nature of cooperation agreements); Daniel C. Richman, Cooperating Clients, 56 Ohio St. L.J. 69, 73 (1995) (discussing the history and current practice of exchanging leniency for cooperation).

66. Richman, *supra* note 65, at 73.

67. See William J. Bauer, Reflections on the Role of Statutory Immunity in the Criminal Justice System, 67 J. Crim. L. & Criminology 143, 150 (1976) (discussing issues of betrayal);

Stanley S. Arkin, Moral Issues and the Cooperating Witness, N.Y. L.J., June 9, 1994, at 3, 7 (discussing issues of shame).

68. For a discussion of inverted sentencing, see United States v. Brigham, 977 F.2d 317, 318 (7th Cir. 1992) ("The more serious the defendant's crimes, the lower the sentence—because the greater his wrongs, the more information and assistance he has to offer to a prosecutor.").

69. Vikramaditya S. Khanna, Should the Behavior of Top Management Matter?, 91 Geo. L.J. (2003).

70. Brent Fisse, The Duality of Corporate and Individual Criminal Liability, in Corporations as Criminals, ed. Ellen Hochstedler (Beverly Hills, CA: Sage Publications, 1984), pp. 69, 74.

71. For a review of this research, see Ann L. McGill, Responsibility Judgments and the Causal Background, in Codes of Conduct: Behavioral Research into Business Ethics, ed. David M. Messick and Ann E. Tenbrunsel (New York: Russell Sage Foundation, 1996), pp. 228, 235.

72. Id. at 235.

73. Gilbert, *supra* note 64, at 13.

74. Dean Starkman, Pollution Case Highlights Trend to Let Employees Take the Rap, *Wall Street Journal*, October 9, 1997, p. B10. See also Gregory J. Wallance and Jay W. Waks, Internal Investigation of Suspected Wrongdoing by Corporate Employees, 11 Corp. Couns. Q. 77, 78 (1995).

75. See Richard Cooper, Bold Move Becoming a Trend: Is It Always Smart to Let Employees Take the Rap?, Corp. Couns., November 1997, at 1 ("Prompt disciplinary action against wrongdoers may send a clear message that the company does not condone wrongdoing and does not need to be taught a lesson.").

76. The first large-scale study of corporate crime reported that "approximately two-thirds of large corporations violated the law, some of them many times." Marshall B. Clinard et al., National Institute of Law Enforcement and Criminal Justice, Illegal Corporate Behavior (Washington, DC: U.S. Dept. of Justice, 1979), p. xxv. Rates of offenses have been estimated in employee survey research, e.g., the percentage of employees who personally observed misconduct either often or occasionally has remained at 31 percent in both the 1994 and 2000 National Business Ethics Survey. See Joseph, *supra* note 59, at 12. For a discussion of the organizational aspects of corporate crime, see John M. Darley, How Organizations Socialize Individuals into Evildoing, in Codes of Conduct,, *supra* note 71, at 13, 13–14 ("[M]any evil actions are not the volitional products of individual evildoers but rather essentially organizational products that result when complex social forces interact to cause individuals to commit multiple acts of terrible harm."). Some of the better research on corporate crime details the organizational variables associated with deviance. See, e.g., Marshall B. Clinard, Corporate Ethics and Crime: The Role of Middle Management (Beverly Hills, CA: Sage Publications, 1983), p. 71 ("In our survey, middle management was clearly of the opinion that the very nature of top management's position and its actual behavior is largely responsible for unethical or illegal corporate behavior."); Anthony J. Daboub et al., Top Management Team Characteristics and Corporate Illegal Activity, 20 Acad. Mgmt. Rev. 138 (1995) (describing the consensus view that corporate crime is most often the result of the inactions of top management); Diane Vaughan, Toward Understanding Unlawful Organizational Behavior, 80 Mich. L. Rev. 1377, 1389–93 (1982) (discussing crime in relation to the role of top management

in establishing norms and reward systems that shape the ethical conduct of subordinates); Note, Decisionmaking Models and the Control of Corporate Crime, 85 Yale L.J. 1091, 1098 (1976) (noting situations in which top management may direct, enable, or acquiesce to illegal activity).

77. Clinard et al., *supra* note 76, at 17; see Gary Slapper and Steve Tombs, Corporate Crime (Harlow: Longman, 1999), p. 126.

78. John C. Coffee Jr., "No Soul to Damn: No Body to Kick": An Unscandalized Inquiry into the Problem of Corporate Punishment, 79 Mich. L. Rev. 386, 410 (1981).

79. The notion of winking may be traced to remarks by Senator Estes Kefauver on the Electrical Equipment Antitrust cases (July 13, 1961):

> [I]t has been found many times, top corporation executives "wink" at criminal antitrust violations going on right under their noses. Rather than assure that the antitrust laws were being obeyed by their subordinates, such executives take great pains to make certain that they have no "knowledge" of any illegal activities.

Comment, Increasing Community Control Over Corporate Crime—A Problem in the Law of Sanctions, 71 Yale L.J. 280, 303 n.71 (1961) (quoting Press Release from Senator Kefauver's Office, (July 13, 1961)).

80. Fisse and Braithwaite, *supra* note 36, at 182–83.

81. See, e.g., Marshall B. Clinard and Peter C. Yeager, Corporate Crime (New York: Free Press, 1980), p. 44 (noting that organizational size, delegation, and specialization "combine to produce an organizational climate that allows the abdication of a degree of personal responsibility. . . . Under these conditions, almost any type of corporate criminality is possible. Executives at higher levels can absolve themselves of responsibility.").

82. See Serge Moscovici and Miles Hewstone, Social Representations and Social Explanations: From the "Nave" to the "Amateur" Scientist, in Attribution Theory: Social and Functional Extensions, ed. Miles Hewstone (Oxford: B. Blackwell, 1983), pp. 98, 124 ("When society undergoes suffering for its sickness, it feels the need to find someone whom it can hold responsible, on whom it can avenge its misfortunes.") (quoting Durkheim). Carter, *supra* note 33, at 18, has appropriately called this phenomenon "vicarious atonement."

83. Douglas, *supra* note 39, at 5.

84. Carl Keane, Loosely Coupled Systems and Unlawful Behaviour: Organization Theory and Corporate Crime, in Corporate Crime: Contemporary Debates, ed. Frank Pearce and Laureen Snider (Toronto: University of Toronto Press, 1995), pp. 168–69.

85. William S. Laufer, Corporate Bodies and Guilty Minds, 43 Emory L.J. 647, 683–89 (1994) (discussing the challenges of determining corporate authorship of action).

86. Fisse and Braithwaite, *supra* note 36, at 184–85.

87. See Douglas, *supra* note 39, at 14.

88. See Laufer, *supra* note 50, at 1383; Lynn Sharp Paine, Managing for Organizational Integrity, Harv. Bus. Rev., March–April 1994, at 106, 106–7 ("An integrity-based approach to ethics management combines a concern for the law with an emphasis on managerial responsibility for ethical behavior. Though integrity strategies may vary in design and scope, all strive to define companies' guiding values, aspirations, and patterns of thought and conduct."); see generally Winthrop M. Swenson and Nolan E. Clark, The New Federal Sentencing Guidelines: Three Keys to Understanding Credit for Compliance Programs, 1 Corp.

Conduct Q. 1 (1991) (discussing the need for organizations to implement effective compliance strategies).

89. See Neil M. Browne et al., The Seductive Danger of Craft Ethics for Business Organizations, 17 Rev. Bus. 23, 27 (1996) ("Citicorp's principles make it clear they are concerned about protecting themselves from the behavior of their own employees."); Betsy Stevens, An Analysis of Corporate Ethical Code Studies: "Where Do We Go From Here?" 13 J. Bus. Ethics 63, 69 (1994).

90. 33 U.S.C. § 1251 (2001).

91. United States v. Darling Int'l, Inc., No. CR 4–96-162 (D. Minn. July 10, 1997) (factual basis statement, plea agreement, and sentencing stipulations on file with author).

92. See Starkman, *supra* note 74, at B10.

93. United States v. Darling Int'l, Inc., No. CR 4–96-162 (D. Minn. Dec. 16, 1996).

94. Defendant's Factual Statement, pp. 5–6.

95. Starkman, *supra* note 74, at C2.

96. Defendant's Plea Agreement and Sentencing Stipulations.

97. Defendant's Sentencing Memorandum, at 8–9.

98. United States v. Darling Int'l, Inc., No. C.V. 97–1611 (D. Minn., order entered Sept. 12, 1997).

99. Peter A. French, Principles of Responsibility, Shame, and the Corporation, in Corrigible Corporations and Unruly Law, ed. Brent Fisse and Peter A. French (San Antonio, TX: Trinity University Press, 1985), p. 31.

100. Explicit recognition of RWB is limited to the prosecutorial guidelines. Incentives to cooperate, on the other hand, are modified by regulatory policy statements, such as the Corporate Leniency Policy of the Antitrust Division.

101. Principles of Federal Prosecution of Business Organizations, *supra* note 8 (outlining eight factors influencing discretionary prosecutorial decision making).

102. Corporate Leniency Policy, Antitrust Division, U.S. Department of Justice, available at: http://www.usdoj.gov/atr/public/guidelines/lencorp.htm (last visited Nov. 27, 2001) (on file with the *Iowa Law Review*).

103. Gruner, *supra* note 54, at 38.

104. With respect to individuals, the principal purpose of the Corporate Leniency Policy is to encourage as many employees as possible to come forward with the company and cooperate fully with the Antitrust Division and give complete and truthful accounts. The intent also is to assure all such employees that they will be granted some form of nonprosecution protection. Gary R. Spratling, The Corporate Leniency Policy: Answers to Recurring Questions, available at: http://www.usdoj.gov/atr/public/speeches/1626.htm (unpublished paper) (last visited Nov. 27, 2001) (on file with the *Iowa Law Review*).

105. See Grabosky, *supra* note 15, at 138 (discussing the transformation of corporate social control).

106. See Ayres and Braithwaite, *supra* note 15, at 54 ("[T]ripartism might prevent harmful capture, identify and encourage efficient capture, enhance the attainment of regulatory goals, and strengthen democracy.").

107. Examples include financial auditing and quality certification. See id. at 138–39 (suggesting the "Fringe-Firm Intervention" to regulate industry).

108. See id. at 57–60 (discussing the role of public interest groups in monitoring the regulator and the regulated).

109. See Laufer, *supra* note 50, at 1416.

110. David O. Friedrichs, Trusted Criminals: White Collar Crime in Contemporary Society (Belmont: Wadsworth, 1996), pp. 340–41.

111. See Eric W. Orts and Kurt Deketelaere, eds., Environmental Contracts: Comparative Approaches to Regulatory Innovation in the United States and Europe (London: Kluwer Law International, 2001). For a discussion of the role of regulators in inspiring corporate virtue, see Fiona Haines, Corporate Regulation: Beyond "Punish or Persuade" (Oxford: Clarendon Press, 1997), pp. 61–80.

112. See, e.g., Laureen Snider, The Politics of Corporate Crime Control, in Global Crime Connections: Dynamics and Control, ed. Frank Pearce and Michael Woodiwiss (Toronto: University of Toronto Press, 1993), pp. 199–203 (discussing the limitations of a cooperative regulatory strategy).

113. For a discussion of this view in relation to the expressive function of the criminal law, see William S. Laufer and Alan Strudler, Corporate Intentionality, Desert, and Variants of Vicarious Liability, 37 Am. Crim. L. Rev. 1285, 1286 (2000).

114. See Friedrichs, *supra* note 110, at 341 ("In the progressive criminologists' view, the capitalist mode of production inevitably promotes violations of law, and as a result regulation violations are widespread for all types of corporations.").

115. See Eichenwald, *supra* note 7, at 431–32.

116. Kurt Eichenwald, Prudential Image Mending Stumbles, *New York Times*, February 17, 1994, p. D5.

117. Id.

CHAPTER SIX

1. Altria Code of Conduct for Compliance and Integrity, p. 5. Available at: http://www.altria.com/download/pdf/responsibility_Altria_Code_of_Conduct.pdf.

2. David Greenberg, A Crossroads for Corporate America (address, Pennsylvania Press Club, Harrisburg, Pennsylvania, July 22, 2002), available at: http://www.altria.com/download/pdf/media_crossroads_corp_america.pdf.

3. Federal Trade Commission Cigarette Report for 2003, available at: http://www.ftc.gov/opa/2005/08/cigreport.htm.

4. U.S. v. Philip Morris et al., Civil Action, 99–2496 (GK) (D.C. D.C., 2005) (complaint). Available at: http://www.dcd.uscourts.gov/99-2496ab.pdf#search='philip%20morris%20and%20complaint%20and%20rico'.

5. See Milton Friedman, The Social Responsibility of Business Is to Increase Its Profits, *New York Times Magazine*, September 13, 1970. In commenting on corporate social responsibility, Professor Friedman noted, "In the present climate of opinion, with its widespread aversion to 'capitalism,' 'profits,' and 'soulless corporation' and so on, this is one way for a corporation to generate goodwill as a by-product of expenditures that are entirely justified in its own self-interest."

6. Claims of legitimacy are often far more complex than appearances suggest; see, e.g., Kimberly D. Elsbach and Robert I. Sutton, Acquiring Organizational Legitimacy through Illegitimate Actions: A Marriage of Institutional and Impression Management Theories, 35 Acad. Mgmt. J. 699 (1992). For an outstanding discussion of legitimacy in relation to corporate governance more generally, see J. Van Oosterhout, The Quest for Legitimacy: On Authority and Responsibility in Governance (February 5, 2002) (unpublished

Ph.D. dissertation, Erasmus Research Institute of Management, Rotterdam) (on file with author).

7. See, e.g., S. Prakash Sethi, Advocacy Advertising—the American Experience, Cal. Mgmt. Rev., Fall 1978, at 55; Gary O'Donovan, Environmental Disclosures in the Annual Report: Extending the Applicability and Predictive Power of Legitimacy Theory, 15 Acct. Auditing & Accountability J. 344 (2002).

8. See John M. Conley and Cynthia A. Williams, Engage, Embed, and Embellish: Theory versus Practice in the Corporate Social Responsibility Movement, J. Corp. L. (forthcoming).

9. Adaptec Conduct Code, available at: http://www.adaptec.com/worldwide/company /compeditorial.html?sess = no&language = English+US&prodkey = conduct_code&cat = %2f Company%2fAbout+Adaptec.

10. Adelphia's Mission and Values Statement, available at: http://www.adelphia.com /about/mission_and_values.cfm.

11. Charter Communications, Governance Highlights, available at: http://phx.corporate-ir.net/phoenix.zhtml?c=112298&p=irol-govhighlights.

12. Dynegy's Corporate Governance Statement, available at: http://www.dynegy.com /Corporate_Governance.shtml.

13. HealthSouth's Corporate Governance and Ethics, available at: http://www.health south.com / medinfo / home / app / frame?cntx = 01abouths&1 = leftnav.jsp,abouths_nav&2 = article.jsp,section_banner,abouths_corpgov.

14. Peregrine's Code of Conduct, available at: http://www.peregrine.com/about-us /investors/pdfs/CodeOfConduct.pdf.

15. Rent-Way's Corporate Code of Conduct, available at: http://media.corporate-ir.net /media_files/irol/98/98799/pdf/CodeofConductPRINTING2_2_04.pdf.

16. Craig Deegan et al., An Examination of the Corporate Social and Environmental Disclosures of BHP from 1983–1997: A Test of Legitimacy Theory, 15 Acct. Auditing & Accountability J. 312 (2002). Cf. Council on Economic Priorities, The Corporate Report Card: Rating 250 of America's Corporations for the Socially Responsible Investor (New York: Penguin Group, 1998).

17. See Craig Deegan, The Legitimizing Effect of Social and Environmental Disclosures—a Theoretical Foundation, 15 Acct. Auditing & Accountability J. 282 (2002); Michael J. Lynch and Paul B. Stretsky, The Meaning of Green: Contrasting Criminological Perspectives, 7 Theoretical Criminology 216 (2003).

18. See, e.g., Thomas P. Lyon and John W. Maxwell, Corporate Environmentalism and Public Policy (New York: Cambridge University Press, 2004); Thomas P. Lyon, "Green" Firms Bearing Gifts, Regulation, Fall 2003, at 36.

19. Lynn S. Paine, Value Shift: Why Companies Must Merge Social and Financial Imperatives to Achieve Superior Performance (New York: McGraw-Hill, 2003).

20. *Saturday Evening Post*, June 18, 1927, quoted in Roland Marchand, Creating the Corporate Soul: The Rise of Public Relations and Corporate Imagery in American Big Business (Berkeley and Los Angeles: University of California Press, 1998), p. 20.

21. Marchand, *supra* note 20, at 1. For a more recent treatment of the soul of a corporation, see William Greider, The Soul of Capitalism: Opening Paths to a Moral Economy (New York: Simon and Schuster, 2003).

22. Neil J. Mitchell, The Generous Corporation: A Political Analysis of Economic Power (New Haven, CT: Yale University Press, 1989).

23. Robert H. Wiebe, The Search for Order: 1877–1920 (New York: Hill and Wang, 1967).

24. Charles H. Cooley, Human Nature and the Social Order (New York: C. Scribner's Sons, 1902); William G. Sumner, Folkways: A Study of the Sociological Importance of Usages, Manners, Customs, Mores, and Morals (Boston: Ginn, 1907); Edward A. Ross, Social Control: A Survey of the Foundations of Order (New York: Macmillan, 1901).

25. Quoted in Mitchell, *supra* note 22, p. 5.

26. Familiar Quotations, *New York Times*, August 28, 1881, p. 4.

27. Letter to the Editor, Complaints of the Management of the Harlem Railroad, *New York Times*, January 31, 1864, p. 5.

28. Notes from the People, *New York Times*, February 13, 1871, p. 2.

29. Op-Ed., *New York Times*, July 28, 1883, p. 4.

30. Editorial, Corporate Charity, *New York Times*, December 21, 1883.

31. Op-Ed., Can a Corporation be Libeled? *New York Times*, June, 24, 1885, p. 4.

32. Mitchell, *supra* note 22, at 14–15.

33. "They say that 'corporations have no souls,' but they ought to have some sense of honor, and it is only by airing our grievances in the newspapers that we can hope to shame them into doing their duty to the public." Letter to the Editor, Complaint Against a Railroad, *New York Times*, January 24, 1901, p. 8.

34. Women Graduate in Law, *New York Times*, March 30, 1900, p. 2.

35. Mitchell, *supra* note 22, at 6–7.

36. Arundel Cotter, United States Steel: A Corporation with a Soul (Garden City, NY: Doubleday, Page and Co., 1921).

37. Marchand, *supra* note 20, at 3.

38. See Michael V. Russo and Paul A. Fouts, A Resource-Based Perspective on Corporate Environmental Performance and Profitability, 40 Acad. Mgmt. J. 534 (1997).

39. See Cathy L. Hartman and Caryn L. Beck-Dudley, Marketing Strategies and the Search for Virtue: A Case Analysis of the Body Shop International, 20 J. Bus. Ethics 249 (1999); Marianne M. Jennings and Jon Entine, Business with a Soul: A Reexamination of What Counts in Business Ethics, 20 Hamline J. Pub. L. & Pol'y 1 (1998); Rain-forest Chic: A Look at the Underside of Ethical Marketing, Reporter on Business, *Toronto Globe & Mail*, October 1995, at 39.

40. See, e.g., Philip Kotler and Nancy Lee, Best of Breed: When It Comes to Gaining a Market Edge while Supporting a Social Cause, "Corporate Social Marketing" Leads the Pack, Stanford Soc. Innovation Rev., Spring 2004, at 14.

41. Cornelius B. Pratt, The 40-Year Tobacco Wars: Giving Public Relations a Black-Eye? Pub. Rel. Q., Winter 1997, at 5.

42. See Lynch and Stretsky, *supra* note 17.

43. David Vogel, Fluctuating Fortunes: The Political Power of Business in America (New York: Basic Books, 1989).

44. Dania Quirola and Michael Schlup, WS19-Sustainability Reporting—Beyond Greenwash (minutes of workshops of the 7th ERCP, Lund, Sweden, May 2001).

45. Kenny Bruno, The World of Greenwash, CorpWatch, January 1, 1997, available at: www.corpwatch.org/campaigns/PCD.jsp?articleid=244.

46. Sharon Beder, Manipulating Public Knowledge, 7 Metascience 132 (1998).

47. Sharon Beder, Global Spin: The Corporate Assault on Environmentalism (White River Junction, VT: Chelsea Green, 1998).

48. Robert Lordi, Corporate Conduct and Professional Integrity: Summary of a PricewaterhouseCoopers Survey, 2 Perspectives, 58–61 (2000).

49. Craig Deegan and G. Carrol, An Analysis of the Incentives for Australian Firms to Apply for Reporting Excellence Awards, 23 Acct. & Bus. Res. 219 (1993).

50. Jed Greer and Kenny Bruno, Greenwash: The Reality Behind Corporate Environmentalism (Penang, Malaysia: Third World Network, 1996), p. 41; Eveline Lubbers, Battling Big Business: Countering Greenwash, Infiltration, and Other Forms of Corporate Bullying (Monroe, ME: Common Courage Press, 2002).

51. Tracey Swift, Trust, Reputation and Corporate Accountability to Stakeholders, 10 Bus. Ethics: Eur. Rev. 16 (2001).

52. Thomas W. Dunfee, Social Investing: Mainstream or Backwater?, 43 J. Bus. Ethics 247 (2003).

53. See, e.g., Pietra Rivoli, Labor Standards in the Global Economy: Issues for Investors, 43 J. Bus. Ethics 223 (2003).

54. Nike, Corporate Responsibility Report, p. 25, available online only at: http://www.nike.com/nikebiz/nikebiz.jhtml?page=25.

55. Id. at 29.

56. See S. Prakash Sethi, Setting Global Standards: Guidelines for Creating Codes of Conduct in Multinational Corporations (Hoboken, NJ: J. Wiley, 2003), p. 160.

57. Stephen J. Frenkel and Duncan Scott, Compliance, Collaboration, and Codes of Labor Practice: The Adidas Connection, Cal. Mgmt. Rev., Fall 2002, at 29.

58. See Boycott Nike, transcript of CBS News *48 Hours*, October 17, 1996, available at: www.saigon.com/ nike/48hrfmt.htm.

59. Vietnam Labor Watch, Nike Labor Practices in Vietnam, March 20, 1997, p. 1.

60. For a critical discussion of the Nike audits, see Dara O'Rourke, Smoke from a Hired Gun: A Critique of Nike's Labor and Environmental Auditing in Vietnam as Performed by Ernst & Young (San Francisco: TRAC, 2001). For a balanced discussion of the audits, see Sethi, *supra* note 56.

61. For a comparable effort on the part of grassroots NGOs to strike back at Nike, see Case Study: The Online Campaign Against Nike, 12 Reputation Impact 9–10 (2002).

62. Br. for the Resp't, Nike, Inc. v. Mark Kasky, U.S. S. Ct., No. 02–575 (2002).

63. Id.

64. 27 Cal. 4th 939, 946, 119 Cal. Rptr. 2d 296, 45 P. 3d 243, 247 (2002).

65. Id.

66. Transcript, oral argument, Nike, Inc. et al. v. Mark Kasky, U.S. S. Ct., April 23, 2003, available at: www.supremecourtus.gov/oral_argument_trnascripts/02–575.pdf.

67. Frenkel and Scott, *supra* note 57, at 44–45.

68. Sethi, *supra* note 56, at 146.

69. Id. at 172.

70. Tim Connor, Still Waiting for Nike to Do It: Nike's Labor Practices in the Three Years Since CEO Phil Knight's Speech to the National Press Club (San Francisco, CA: Global Exchange, 2001).

71. Id.

72. Dunfee, *supra* note 52; see also Sean M. O'Connor, Be Careful What You Wish For: How Accountants and Congress Created the Problem of Auditor Independence, 45 B.C. L. Rev. 741 (2004).

73. Brendan O'Dwyer, The Legitimacy of Accountants' Participation in Social and Ethical Accounting, Auditing and Reporting, 10 Bus. Ethics: Eur. Rev. 27, 33 (2001).

74. Michael Power, The Audit Society: Rituals of Verification (Oxford: Oxford University Press, 1997), p. 127.

75. David Owen and Tracey Swift, Introduction: Social Accounting, Reporting and Auditing; Beyond the Rhetoric?, 10 Bus. Ethics: Eur. Rev. 4 (2001).

76. Steven D. Lydenberg, Envisioning Socially Responsible Investing: A Model for 2006, J. Corp. Citizenship, Autumn 2002, 57.

77. International Standards Organization (ISO), ISO Consumer Policy Committee, Final Report, The Desirability and Feasibility of ISO Corporate Social Responsibility Standards (unpublished report, on file with author), p. iv; available at: www.iso.ch.

78. Dave Owen, Green Reporting: Accountancy and the Challenge of the Nineties (London: Chapman and Hall, 1992); Austin Mitchell et al., Ethical Statements as Smokescreens for Sectional Interests: The Case of the UK Accountancy Profession, 13 J. Bus. Ethics 39 (1994).

79. Rob Gray, Thirty Years of Social Accounting, Reporting and Auditing: What (If Anything) Have We Learnt?, 10 Bus. Ethics: Eur. Rev. 9, 13 (2001).

80. John Stittle, UK Corporate Ethical Reporting—A Failure to Inform: Some Evidence from Company Annual Reports, 107 Bus. & Soc'y Rev. 349 (2002).

81. Sandra Waddock and Neil Smith, Corporate Responsibility Audits: Doing Well by Doing Good, Sloan Mgmt. Rev., Winter 2000, at 75; Rob Gray et al., Struggling with the Praxis of Social Accounting: Stakeholders, Accountability, Audits and Procedures, 10 Acct. Auditing & Accountability J. 325 (1997).

82. Craig Deegan, The Legitimising Effect of Social and Environmental Disclosures—A Theoretical Foundation, 15 Acct. Auditing & Accountability J. 282 (2002); Craig Deegan et al., An Examination of the Corporate Social and Environmental Disclosures of BHP from 1983–1997: A Test of Legitimacy Theory, 15 Acct. Auditing & Accountability J. 312 (2002); Gary O'Donovan, Environmental Disclosures in the Annual Report: Extending the Applicability and Predictive Power of Legitimacy Theory, 15 Acct. Auditing & Accountability J. 344 (2002).

83. O'Dwyer, supra note 73, at 27.

84. Jill Hooks et al., The Information Gap in Annual Reports, 15 Acct. Auditing & Accountability J. 501 (2002); Carol A. Adams, Internal Organisational Factors Influencing Corporate Social and Ethical Reporting: Beyond Current Theorising, 15 Acct. Auditing & Accountability J. 223 (2002).

85. Markus J. Milne and Dennis M. Patten, Securing Organizational Legitimacy: An Experimental Decision Case Examining the Impact of Environmental Disclosures, 15 Acct. Auditing & Accountability J. 372, 375 (2002).

86. Id. at 381.

87. See Gray et al., supra note 81.

88. Sonja Gallhofer and Jim Haslam, The Direction of Green Accounting Policy: Critical Reflections, 10 Acct. Auditing & Accountability J. 148 (1997).

89. ISO, supra note 77.

90. Introducing: The 2002 Sustainability Reporting Guidelines (Boston: GRI, 2002), p. 1.

91. Global Reporting Initiative, Sustainability Reporting Guidelines 2002 (Boston, MA: GRI, 2002), p. 77, available at: http://www.globalreporting.org/GRIGuidelines/2002/gri_2002_guidelines.pdf.

92. Id. at 77–78.

93. Id. at 78.

94. Id. at 25.

95. KPMG, International Survey of Corporate Sustainability Reporting (Amsterdam: KPMG, 2002).

96. Julie Macken, Standard Time for Global Workplace, Australian Financial Review, July 30, 2002, p. 52.

97. Joshua Karliner, UN Plan Fosters "Greenwash," Journal of Commerce, April 19, 1999, p. 8.

98. See Deegan and Carrol, *supra* note 49, at 220.

99. O'Dwyer, *supra* note 73, at 27.

100. Ronald Goldstock, IPSIG: The Independent Private Inspector General Program, 4 Corp. Conduct Q. 38 (1996).

101. See, e.g., Peter N. Grabosky, Using Non-Governmental Resources to Foster Regulatory Compliance, 8 Governance 527 (1995).

102. Ian Ayres and John Braithwaite, Responsive Regulation: Transcending the Deregulation Debate (New York: Oxford University Press, 1992); Ian Ayres and John Braithwaite, Tripartism: Regulatory Capture and Empowerment, 16 Law & Soc. Inquiry 435 (1991). See also Sherry Cable and Michael Benson, Acting Locally: Environmental Injustice and the Emergence of Grass-Roots Environmental Organizations, 40 Soc. Probs. 464 (1993).

103. Jane Cummings, Engaging Stakeholders in Corporate Accountability Programmes: A Cross-Sectoral Analysis of UK and Transnational Experience, 10 Bus. Ethics: Eur. Rev. 45 (2001); Carol A. Tilt, The Influence of External Pressure Groups on Corporate Social Disclosure: Some Empirical Evidence, 7 Acct. Auditing & Accountability J. 47(1994).

104. See Gray et al., *supra* note 81.

105. Adrian Henriques, Civil Society and Social Auditing, 10 Bus. Ethics: Eur. Rev. 40 (2001).

106. Lydenberg *supra* note 76, at 58.

107. Philip Morris USA Policies and Practices, available at: http://www.philipmorrisusa.com/policies_practices/ysp.asp?source=instant_access.

108. David Greenberg, Public Hearing of the Ad Hoc Advisory Group on Organizational Guidelines, November 14, 2002, available at: http://www.ussc.gov/corp/ph11_02/t_greenberg.pdf.

109. See, e.g., M. L. Myers, Philip Morris Changes Its Name, but Not Its Harmful Practices, 11 Tobacco Control 169 (2002).

CHAPTER SEVEN

1. For a discussion of the rise of antitrust penalties, see Stephen Calkins, Corporate Compliance and the Antitrust Agencies' Bi-Modal Penalties, Law & Contemp. Probs., Summer 1997, at 127.

2. Lynn Sharp Paine, Value Shift: Why Companies Must Merge Social and Financial Imperatives to Achieve Superior Performance (New York: McGraw-Hill, 2003), p. 228 (discussing the moralization of corporations). This is not to say that there are no other critics. There is, in fact, a growing consensus that too much is asked of the federal criminal law. Critics point to its unrelenting growth; the political and institutional incentives that drive the persistent passage of new crime legislation; the increasing severity

of associated sanctions; and the fact that the federal criminal law encroaches on the province of state criminal law in indefensible ways. To highlight the importance of corporate criminal law, as I have done throughout this book, counters this emerging wisdom.

3. William B. Lytton and Winthrop M. Swenson, The Effective Answer to Corporate Misconduct: Public Sector Encouragement of Private Sector Compliance Programs, ACCA Docket, November–December 2002, at 42, 47; Dan R. Dalton et al., The "New" U.S. Sentencing Commission Guidelines: A Wake-Up Call for Corporate America, Acad. Mgmt. Executive, February 1994, at 7.

4. 148 Cong. Rec. H4431 (daily ed. July 10, 2002) (members rallying together). See Darryl K. Brown, The Problematic and Faintly Promising Dynamics of Corporate Crime Enforcement, 1 Ohio St. J. Crim. L. 521 (2004); Cristie L. Ford, Toward a New Model for Securities Law Enforcement, 57 Admin. L. Rev. 757 (2005).

5. Id. at 46.

6. Id.

7. See, e.g., Marie McKendall et al., Ethical Compliance Programs and Corporate Illegality: Testing the Assumptions of the Corporate Sentencing Guidelines, 37 J. Bus. Ethics 367 (2002). Explanations of deviance turn on other structural and organizational variables, e.g., Ray Paternoster and Sally Simpson, Sanction Threats and Appeals to Morality: Testing a Rational Choice Model of Corporate Crime, 30 Law & Soc. Rev. 549 (1996); Cindy R. Alexander and Mark A. Cohen, New Evidence on the Origins of Corporate Crime, 17 Managerial and Decision Econ. 421 (1996).

8. Lawrence W. Sherman et al., eds., Preventing Crime: What Works, What Doesn't, What's Promising (Washington, DC: U.S. Department of Justice, 1997).

9. Lawrence W. Sherman, Thinking about Crime Prevention, in Sherman et al., *supra* note 8, at 9.

10. Id.

11. Lawrence Sherman et al., Evidence-Based Crime Prevention (London: Routledge, 2002).

12. Laureen Snider, The Sociology of Corporate Crime: An Obituary, 4 Theoretical Criminology 169, 170 (2000).

13. Laureen Snider, Cooperative Models and Corporate Crime: Panacea or Cop-Out?, 36 Crime & Delinq. 373 (1990).

14. 695 F. Supp. 856 (E.D. Virginia, 1988).

15. William W. Wilkins, in Proceedings of the Second Symposium on Crime and Punishment in the United States, Corporate Crime in America: Strengthening the "Good Citizen" Corporation, September 7–8, 1995 (Washington, DC: United States Sentencing Commission, 1995).

16. John Braithwaite, Rewards and Regulation, 29 J. Law & Soc'y 12 (2002).

17. Gary R. Spratling, The Experience and Views of the Enforcement Community, in Proceedings, *supra* note 15, at 319. It is unclear how the Antitrust Division's Amnesty Program is consistent with Spratling's position. According to the most recent division policy, amnesty from federal prosecution for antitrust violations is automatic "if a corporation comes forward before our investigation begins." Spratling, in Proceedings, *supra* note 15, at 321. See "Front-End" Benefits of Antitrust Compliance Program, Self-Reporting Offer Best Hope of Avoiding Fine Floor, 4 Prevention of Corp. Liability 10 (1996).

18. Susan P. Shapiro, Collaring the Crime, not the Criminal: Reconsidering the Concept of White-Collar Crime, 55 Am. Soc. Rev. 346 (1990).

19. See William S. Laufer, Corporate Liability, Risk Shifting, and the Paradox of Compliance, 52 Vand. L. Rev. 1343 (1999).

20. Michael L. Benson and Francis T. Cullen, Combating Corporate Crime: Local Prosecutors at Work (Boston: Northeastern University Press, 1998), p. 234. Decisions as to which cases are zealously prosecuted, according to Benson and Cullen, should turn on a "common legal culture of prosecution." At least this is true at the level of local prosecutors. But such is not always the case with federal prosecutors.

21. See, e.g., Edwin H. Sutherland, White Collar Crime: The Uncut Version (New Haven, CT: Yale University Press, 1983); Marshall B. Clinard et al., Illegal Corporate Behavior (Washington, DC: U.S. Department of Justice, 1979); Peter C. Yeager, Analyzing Corporate Offenses: Progress and Prospects, in Research in Corporate Social Performance and Policy, vol. 8, ed. J. Post and L. Preston (Greenwich, CT: JAI Press, 1986), p. 93.

22. Marc L. Miller, Domination and Dissatisfaction: Prosecutors as Sentencers, 56 Stan. L. Rev. 1211 (2004).

23. Irvin C. Nathan, Congressional Reforms Needed for Improved Exercise of Prosecutorial Discretion, 8 Bus. Crimes Bull. 1 (2000); Ellen S. Podgor, Department of Justice Guidelines: Balancing "Discretionary Justice," 13 Cornell J. L. & Pub. Pol. 167 (2004).

24. Blackley v. Washington, 124 S. Ct. 2531 (2004); United States v. Booker, United States v. Fanfan, 125 S. Ct. 738; 160 L. Ed. 2d 621; 2005 U.S. LEXIS 628; 73 U.S.L.W. 4056; 18 Fla. L. Weekly Fed. S 70.

25. John Braithwaite, Institutionalizing Distrust, Enculturating Trust, in Trust and Governance, ed. Valerie Braithwaite and Margaret Levi (New York: Russell Sage, 1998), p. 352.

26. Id.

27. Sometimes this strength is displayed carelessly. President George W. Bush, for example, was quoted in a closed-door White House meeting on corporate crime as saying, "the best ethics course is to handcuff the b—." See John R. Wilke, President Praises Work of Task Force on Business Crime, *Wall Street Journal*, September 27, 2002, p. A4.

28. See, e.g., David Garland, The Culture of Control: Crime and Social Order in Contemporary Society (Chicago: University of Chicago Press, 2001), pp. 135–36. The rhetorical imagery surrounding these rare but notable prosecutions mirrors that found with the dramatic exploitation of street crime by both politicians and the media. "The risks they are perceived as posing," argues Garland, "the anxieties they call forth, the sense of powerlessness that they engender, all work to reinforce the felt need for the imposition of order and the importance of a strong state response."

29. Sally S. Simpson, Corporate Crime, Law, and Social Control (Cambridge: Cambridge University Press, 2002), p. 154.

30. Eric Berger, Firm's Employees Find Verdict Unfair, *Houston Chronicle*, June 15, 2002, p. 1.

31. Response from Arthur Andersen LLP on Verdict, *Houston Chronicle*, June 15, 2002, p. 1.

32. Benjamin Hunt, The Timid Corporation: Why Business Is Terrified of Taking Risk (Chichester, UK: John Wiley & Sons, 2003).

33. Daniel Ben-Ami, Cowardly Capitalism: The Myth of the Global Financial Casino (New York: John Wiley & Sons, 2001).

34. Management of Corporations, *New York Times*, March 23, 1859, p. 4.

35. The Lobby at Washington, D.C., *New York Times*, December 31, 1904, p. 4.

36. Want of Confidence in American Railroad Securities, *New York Times*, November 12, 1870, p. 4.

37. Mark J. Roe, *The Inevitable Instability of American Corporate Governance* (Harvard Law Sch. Law and Econ. Discussion Paper Series, Paper No. 493, September 2004), p. 1.

38. Fiona Haines, Corporate Regulation: Beyond "Punish or Persuade" (Oxford: Oxford University Press, 1997), p. 201.

39. Roger L. Martin, The Virtue Matrix: Calculating the Return on Corporate Responsibility, 80 Harv. Bus. Rev. 68 (2002).

40. Margit Osterloh and Bruno Frey, Corporate Governance for Crooks? The Case for Corporate Virtue (July 2003) (working paper) (on file with Institute for Empirical Research in Economics, University of Zurich).

41. See, e.g., Reinier H. Kraakman, Corporate Liability Strategies and the Costs of Legal Controls, 93 Yale L.J. 857 (1984); Jennifer Arlen and Reinier Kraakman, Controlling Corporate Misconduct: An Analysis of Corporate Liability Regimes, 72 N.Y.U. L. Rev. 687 (1997); Jennifer H. Arlen and William J. Carney, Vicarious Liability for Fraud on Securities Markets: Theory and Evidence, 1992 U. Ill. L. Rev. 691.

42. Showing evidence requires an identification of fault. See, e.g., Michael S. Moore, The Moral and Metaphysical Sources of the Criminal Law, in Criminal Justice, ed. J. Roland Pennock and John W. Chapman, Nomos 27 (New York: New York University Press, 1985), p. 12 ("The moral basis of the criminal law is to be found in those moral principles under which fault is properly ascribed to persons for their behavior."). Notably, Moore dismisses corporate criminal liability for reasons of personhood; id. at 12–13.

43. The problem of a mixed goals approach is at times made worse by elaborate settlements that combine civil and criminal sanctions. The blend of sanctions is often designed to satisfy the interests and expectations of multiple stakeholders. Following the disastrous oil spill from the Exxon Valdez in Prince William Sound, Alaska, for example, Exxon, the State of Alaska, and the United States Government settled with a criminal plea agreement, criminal restitution, and a civil settlement that successfully obscured the line between an inadvertent action, or accident, and a gross departure from a standard of care expected, or an act of criminal negligence. See, e.g., Michael M. O'Hear, Sentencing the Green-Collar Offender: Punishment, Culpability, and Environmental Crime, 95 J. Crim. L. & Criminology 133 (2004); John C. Coffee Jr., Does "Unlawful" Mean Criminal? Reflections on the Disappearing Tort/Crime Distinction in American Law, 71 B.U.L. Rev. 193 (1991).

44. Private Securities Litigation Reform Act of 1995, Pub. L. No. 104–67, 109 Stat. 737, 758, codified as amended at 15 U.S.C.A. 78u-4 (West 1997 and Supp. 2000).

45. Roberto Romano, *The Sarbanes-Oxley Act and the Making of Quack Corporate Governance* (Yale Law Sch., Yale International Center for Finance, European Corporate Governance Institute, Finance Working Paper No. 52/2004, 2004), pp.8–9. For additional critiques, see Assaf Hamdani, Gatekeeper Liability, 77 S. Cal. L. Rev. 53 (2003); Jeffrey N. Gordon, What Enron Means for the Management and Control of the Modern Business Corporation: Some Initial Reflections, 69 U. Chi. L. Rev. 1233 (2002); Erica Beecher-Monas, Corporate Governance in the Wake of Enron: An Examination of the Audit Committee Solution to Corporate Fraud, 55 Adm. L. Rev. 357 (2003).

46. Romano, *supra* note 44.

47. Jeffrey Sonnenfeld, Good Governance and the Misleading Myths of Bad Metrics, 18 Acad. Mgmt. Executive 108, 112 (2004).

48. William H. Donaldson, Corporate Governance: What Has Happened and Where We Need to Go, 38 Bus. Econ. 4 (2003).

49. See Braithwaite, *supra* note 25, at 344.

50. Erica Beecher-Monas, Enron, Epistemology, and Accountability: Regulating in a Global Economy, 37 Ind. L. Rev. 141 (2003).

51. See Ian Ayres and John Braithwaite, Responsive Regulation: Transcending the Deregulation Debate (New York: Oxford University Press, 1994), p. 3.

52. See Haines, *supra* note 38.

53. Arthur Levitt, The "Numbers Game" (address, New York University Center for Law and Business, New York, NY, September 28, 1998), available at: www.sec.gov/news/speech/speech archive/1998/spch220.txt.

54. Id. at 1; see also Arthur Levitt with Paula Dwyer, Take on the Street: What Wall Street and Corporate America Don't Want You to Know; What You Can Do to Fight Back (New York: Pantheon Books, 2002), pp. 105–43.

55. Levitt, *supra* note 53.

56. Roderick Hills, personal communication with author, Washington, D.C., January 2004.

Subject Index

due process rights under the Fourteenth
and Fifth Amendments, 54; debates
over, 49–56; fosters an aggressive lobby
that corrupts the political process, 56;
gives corporations the means to weaken
governmental restraints on both their
behavior and their growth, 53; and the
law's convenience, 48–49; obsession
over meaning of from the mid-1800s
to the turn of the twentieth century,
9–15; reflects a legal status that grants
constitutional rights and privileges, 47;
requisite for corporate criminal liability,
xii; rights earned from the status of, 18
corporate policy (CP), 59
corporate power, 54; use and abuse of,
13–14
corporate prosecutions: completed,
222n264; deferred prosecution agreements, 8, 203n25; dependence on
information and evidence difficult
to obtain without incentives, 153;
discretion in determining the type and
extent of liability, 48, 127, 128, 143;
guidelines, 139, 149; politicized and
symbolic, 193; rarity of, 8, 91; selectivity,
40–41; sentencing guidelines, 186; for
substantive law violations, 12
corporate reports, assuring the accuracy of,
178
corporate soul, images and metaphors of,
160–64
corporate virtue, 195
corporations: charters in colonial period,
9; competition with the traditional
pillars of social control, 161; cooperation
with government, 139–40; lobbyists, xi,
194; often distance themselves from
the decision making of management,
92; public relations, x, 160–64;
self-regulation, 5, 32, 35, 128, 193;
separation between ownership and
control, 20; social marketing, 163; social
responsibility movement, 158; strategies
to avoid the attribution of blame, xiv,
18–19; systems and structures, 92;
washing of reputations, 164–80
cost internalization, 166

creative acquisition accounting, 199
credit fraud, 22
Criminal Code Reform Act of 1981, 26
criminal negligence, 87–88
crony capitalism, 9, 196
cross-selling consulting services, 38
culpability score, 34–35
"cultural assessments," 112

D. G. Dery Corp., 22
Dalkon Shield, 32, 163
Darling International Inc., criminal
investigation and prosecution of, 146–49
Dartmouth College v. Woodward, 11
defense contractor fraud, 32
Defense Industry Initiative (DII), 32–33
deferred prosecution agreements, 8,
203n25
delegated authority, 213n148
Dellastatious v. Williams, 115
Deloitte & Touche, 110
democracy, perversion of, 54
Den of Thieves, 70
Department of Justice: Antitrust Division,
238n19; Antitrust Division, Corporate
Leniency Policy, 153, 255n104; Corporate
Leniency Policy of the Antitrust Division,
153, 255n104; definition of corporate
fraud, 74; Division on Corporate Crime,
27
derivative actions, 21
desert-based liability, 195
desire, 78
deterrence-based liability, 195
director and officer insurance (D&O
insurance), 115
Doeren Mayhew & Co. P.C., 41
Domini Social Investments, 175
double standard of justice, 31
Dow Corning Company, 163
Downey, Thomas J., 27
Drexel Burnham Lambert Inc., 142
due diligence, 23, 229n66; allows organizations with ineffective compliance
initiatives to shift blame to their agents,
24; corporate cooperation as proxy for,
133; and Enron, 100; evidence of affects
charging decisions, 35, 37; expenditures

Names Index